Gateways to Trade

Gateways to Trade

Global Value Chains and Governance in Canadian Cities

DORVAL BRUNELLE,
CLAUDIA DE FUENTES, PETER V. HALL,
and JEAN MICHEL MONTSION

UBCPress · Vancouver

Originally printed in Canada
Printed and bound by CPI Group (UK) Ltd, Croydon, CR0 4YY

UBC Press is a Benetech Global Certified Accessible™ publisher. The epub version of this book meets stringent accessibility standards, ensuring it is available to people with diverse needs.

Library and Archives Canada Cataloguing in Publication

Title: Gateways to trade global value chains and governance in Canadian cities / Dorval Brunelle, Claudia de Fuentes, Peter V. Hall, and Jean Michel Montsion.

Names: Brunelle, Dorval, author | Fuentes, Claudia de, author | Hall, P. V. (Peter V.), author | Montsion, Jean Michel, author.

Description: Includes bibliographical references and index.

Identifiers: Canadiana (print) 20250278723 | Canadiana (ebook) 2025027874X | ISBN 9780774872034 (hardcover) | ISBN 9780774872041 (softcover) | ISBN 9780774872058 (PDF) | ISBN 9780774872065 (EPUB)

Subjects: LCSH: Infrastructure (Economics)—British Columbia—Vancouver. | LCSH: Infrastructure (Economics)—Ontario—Toronto. | LCSH: Infrastructure (Economics)—Québec (Province)—Montréal. | LCSH: Infrastructure (Economics)—Nova Scotia—Halifax. | LCSH: Canada—Commerce. | LCSH: Canada—Commercial policy.

Classification: LCC HC120.C3 B78 2026 | DDC 388.0971—dc23

Canada Council for the Arts | Conseil des arts du Canada

Canada

British Columbia Arts Council | British Columbia

UBC Press gratefully acknowledges the financial support for our publishing program of the Government of Canada, the Canada Council for the Arts, and the British Columbia Arts Council.

UBC Press is situated on the traditional, ancestral, and unceded territory of the xʷməθkʷəy̓əm (Musqueam) people. This land has always been a place of learning for the xʷməθkʷəy̓əm, who have passed on their culture, history, and traditions for millennia, from one generation to the next.

UBC Press
The University of British Columbia
www.ubcpress.ca

Contents

Tables and Figures

TABLES

FIGURES

Acknowledgments

The collaborative efforts between the four coauthors and their research could not have led to this publication had it not been, first and foremost, for the financial assistance provided by the Social Sciences and Humanities Research Council of Canada (SSHRC grant #435-2017-0861) and the assistance of our universities and colleagues at Université du Québec à Montréal, York University (including Robarts Centre for Canadian Studies), Saint Mary's University, and Simon Fraser University.

We also wish to acknowledge the precious and indispensable help provided by our research assistants: in Vancouver, Camila Souza; in Toronto (in alphabetical order), Benoit Gibeau, Devin Hotterman, Erin Rose, and Charlotte Sullivan, as well as the additional assistance of Lauren Castelino, Ana Kraljevic, and Max Maccarone; in Montreal, Mélissa Caron, Pierrick Pugeaud, Veronika Riedl, Charles Saliba-Couture, and Alexis Tétreault; and in Halifax, Graham Brown, Holly Foxall, Aisha Leon, Chidi Nwachukwu, and Fariba Seyedjafarrangraz.

Particular assistance was also provided by Camila Souza for data, Arthi Amlipur and Will Flanagan for social network maps, Steve Tornes for maps (who used von J. Bergmann, Aaron Jacobs, and Dmitry Shkolnik's [2022] cancensus: R package to access, retrieve, and work with Canadian Census data and geography, v0.5.7), Viktoria Cseh for copyediting and indexing, and Candida Hadley for copyediting.

Finally, the coauthors wish to thank the two anonymous reviewers for their constructive comments on an earlier version.

Abbreviations

AC	Agglomeration Council
ACOA	Atlantic Canada Opportunities Agency
AGAC	Atlantic Gateway Advisory Council
AGS	Atlantic Growth Strategy
AGTC	Atlantic Gateway and Trade Corridor
APGCI	Asia-Pacific Gateway and Corridor Initiative
APGCTIF	Asia-Pacific Gateway and Corridor Transportation Infrastructure Fund
APGST	Asia-Pacific Gateway Skills Table
BOT	Board of Trade
CAQ	Coalition avenir Québec
CCMM	Chamber of Commerce of Metropolitan Montreal (Chambre de commerce de Montréal métropolitain)
CITM	Interregional Committee on the Transport of Goods (Comité interrégional pour le transport des marchandises)
CIWP	Canada Infrastructure Works Program
CMA	census metropolitan area
CN	Canadian National Railway
CP	Canadian Pacific Railway
CPA	Canada Port Authorities
CTC	Canadian Transport Commission
DOB	Department of Business
FCM	Federation of Canadian Municipalities
FDI	Foreign Direct Investment
FTA	Free Trade Agreement
GBCF	Gateway and Border Crossing Fund

GDP	gross domestic product
GIF	Gateway Infrastructure Fee
GPN	global production network
GTAA	Greater Toronto Airport Authority
GTCF	Gateway Transportation Collaboration Forum
GTHA	Greater Toronto and Hamilton Area
GVC	Global Value Chains
GVGC	Greater Vancouver Gateway Council
GVRD	Greater Vancouver Regional District
HGC	Halifax Gateway Council
HIAA	Halifax International Airport Authority
HP	Halifax Partnership
HPA	Halifax Port Authority
HRM	Halifax Regional Municipality
ICT	Information and communication technologies
ILWU	International Longshore and Warehouse Union Canada
LRC	Livable Region Coalition
LUPDP	Land Use Planning and Development Plan (Schéma d'aménagement et de développement de l'agglomération de Montréal, SAD)
MEDP	Metropolitan Economic Development Plans (Plan métropolitain de développement économique, PMDE)
MLUDP	Metropolitan Land Use and Development Plan (Plan métropolitain d'aménagement et de développement, PMAD)
MMC	Montreal Metropolitan Community (Communauté métropolitaine de Montréal, CMM)
MoU	Memorandum of Understanding
MP	Master Plan
MS	Maritime Strategy
MSIC	Ministry of State for Infrastructure and Communities
MSUA	Ministry of State for Urban Affairs
MTQ	Ministère des Transports du Québec
MVRD	Metro Vancouver Regional District
NTCF	National Trade Corridors Fund
OCPM	Office de consultation publique de Montréal
OECD	Organisation for Economic Co-operation and Development
OQCGTC	Ontario-Quebec Continental Gateway and Trade Corridor

PLQ	Parti libéral du Québec
RCM	Regional County Municipality
RDA	Regional Development Agency
RTA	Regional Trade Agreement
SPP	Special Planning Programs
TFN	Tsawwassen First Nation
TIR	Transportation and Infrastructure Renewal
TNS	Trade Centre Limited
TPP	Trans-Pacific Partnership Agreement
TTC	Toronto Transit Commission
TTR	Toronto Terminal Railways
VIA	Via Rail Canada
WTO	World Trade Organization

Gateways to Trade

Introduction

We inhabit countries, but most of us live in cities and all of us exist on goods that pass through them. In 2021, over 81 percent of Canada's population lived in urban areas. According to the United Nations (2018), over half of the world's population lives in cities or densely populated areas usually with their own governing institutions, and this figure is projected to reach 70 percent by 2050. Today, city life, both physical and mental, governs our being and outlook. In the extended sense, cities and urban lifestyles dominate human existence. The World Bank (2022) estimates that more than 80 percent of global gross domestic product (GDP) is generated in cities.

One of the main drivers of economic growth is connectivity between urban areas in the global economy. As we discuss in this book, cities contribute to national economic well-being as gateways, or multimodal entry points for distribution in a region, and as part of trade corridors for commercial transport. Our focus here is on the physical movement of goods, but of course cities are also vital nodes for the trade in services and international mobility of people. Given their role in trade, cities are necessarily both benefactors and beneficiaries of globalization; however, the participation in globalization via gateways and trade corridors requires the planning and implementation of transportation infrastructure. The planning of this infrastructure goes beyond operational concerns and requires the formation of a common view with respect to the participation and future of a city in the global economy.

In this book, we pursue a primarily institutional approach to urban gateway policies in Canada. We show how the planning for transportation infrastructure for international trade purposes is pursued by urban coalitions and gateway regimes that include private sector actors and senior governments. To the mix we add the importance of municipalities, which are first and foremost governments of proximity. They are the governments closest to their citizens, created to answer local needs. But municipal governments, especially in the Canadian context, and, by extension, the city-regional polities they represent – including their urban area and their hinterland – are frequently seen as powerless bystanders when it comes to questions of trade and trade-supporting transportation infrastructure.

How is it that local governments can be called upon to host trade nodes and corridors and, in so doing, engage in globalization? What are the forces behind these commitments and how are these positioned vis-à-vis the citizens? What does it mean for a city to commit itself to participate in such an operation, notably through gateway initiatives and strategies? How can this involvement benefit the city? How can the harms associated with the physical movement of goods be reduced or mitigated?

These questions and a host of others are the subject of this book on four Canadian gateway cities. The cities – Halifax, Montreal, Toronto, and Vancouver – are designated by the Canadian government as key locations and nodes in its trade gateway and corridor strategy. Our objective is to compare the impact that this strategic positioning has on the four city-regions' urban politics and development, given that as trade gateways they facilitate the implementation of global value chains, or the integration of distribution and production networks in specific locales to create and add value to products. We explore four questions:

1 How do the four cities manage the major impacts and fallouts of global value chains?
2 How do public and private agents pursue trade-enabling transportation-infrastructure investment projects?
3 What network governance schemes, or configurations of stakeholders, are set up to accommodate value chains and to increase or mitigate their fallout at the urban-region level?
4 How are these schemes with their stakeholders and deliverables connected to the different democratic processes or to citizen organizations at the urban level?

Our study is based on the premise that a given city's planning is influenced, if not determined, to a degree that remains to be established, by the prevailing commercial policy adopted by higher tiers of governments.

Tied to this premise, we seek to validate the hypothesis, accredited by many in the field of political economy, that integrative trade, or integrative commerce,[1] represents a paradigm shift that displaced the export promotion and the open economy strategy, which in turn had supplanted the post–Second World War import substitution and economic nationalism strategy. In sociopolitical terms and in chronological order, the first paradigm brought us the Keynesian city, the second, the post-Keynesian city, and the third, the global city.

Many authors before us have argued that the relationship between cities and the global economy shifted fundamentally in the years leading up to the turn of the century (see Brunelle et al. 2021). Often, the global city is said to be connected to and driven by exterior forces, a one-sided interpretation complemented by the approach proposed by Pierre Veltz (2000), who brings to the fore the territorial dispersion now underway within the global economy and the central role played by cities in this new context. For the past three decades, and spurred on by a surge in foreign direct investment (FDI) and the extension of both intrabranch and intrafirm trade, two major phenomena have occurred in parallel: market globalization and an accelerating transnationalization of production networks. These factors lead to what he calls the "metropolitization" of the world economy, referring to the fact that larger cities draw in "an enormous share of economic growth, wealth, and power. Today's economy is just as much inter-metropolitan as it is international ... Modern metropolises aren't any more auto centered systems, but rather powerful cross-currents of innumerable networks" (Veltz 2000, 60–61).

There is an important downside to this because metropolitan economies could end up more disconnected in relation to their own zones of influence or their countryside, generating a decline in the "vertical" proximity of networks that tied them to their traditional hinterland while strengthening "horizontal" networks between megacities. This evolution ushers in what Veltz (2000, 61) calls an "archipelago economy," which creates a normative dissociation and a "disarticulation" between local and inter-metropolitan supply networks. The former notion refers to a separation between two spaces, that of the firm and that of political regulation, and the latter refers to the fact that, by extending their networks, firms distance themselves from their "traditional" territories, while cities act as "gigantic switches" (*gigantesque commutateur*) on the global scale (62–64).[2] These distinctions are important, and our study comes back to this political and spatial dissociation and to the competition between vertical and horizontal supply networks.

The idea of a disconnection between cities and their hinterland reminds us of Jane Jacobs's (1984, 35) argument that "distinctions between city economies and the potpourris we call national economies are important not only for getting a grip on realities; they are of the essence where practical attempts to reshape economic life are concerned." Jacobs contends that although cities should concentrate on "the all-important function of import-replacing or import-substitution [which] is in real life specifically a city function," they must be active rather than passive economies, the latter "meaning economies that do not create economic change themselves but instead respond to forces unloosed in distant cities." For Jacobs, export-promotion – or "supply-regions" in her vocabulary – was a path to underdevelopment typically imposed by empires and by the World Bank (46). In this context, two of her ideas are worth restating. The first is her definition of a city-region as an economy that creates "economic change on its own." "For a city-region something more than exporting or administration is required. That something more is the capacity of the city to replace wide ranges of its imports exuberantly and repeatedly" (47). The second is her approach to the successful city as an engine for an entire region's growth, an objective that proves quite challenging to manage in the context of a globalized economy, as Pierre Veltz (2000) has shown. What is interesting here is the idea that a successful city-region should be proactive and dispose of a margin of economic and political autonomy, a status that many larger city-regions have requested but few have obtained – and none in Canada. But the objectives that city authorities pursue in this context remain to be seen, which prompts the question: How are compromises negotiated between the exigencies tied to the strengthening of a city's position within value chains of the global economy, on one hand, and the maintenance of a city's role in economic and social development at a regional level, on the other?

This emergent (or perhaps more accurately emerged but not yet fully embraced) economic and social role for city-regions is especially challenging in Canada's system of government, where both federal and provincial governments stand between local governments and the levers of power. One way that Canadian scholars have grappled with the implications of the global and metropolitan changes documented by Veltz (2000) and others is through the concept of multilevel governance (Horak and Young 2012). Scholars have documented the rise of intergovernmental arrangements, in a variety of policy arenas (Leuprecht and Young 2006), that seek and find space for more agency by municipalities in these policy arenas (Graham and Andrew 2014). However, the multilevel governance literature understandably tends to focus on what happens within and between levels of big-G government, tracing how the formal arrangement of powers and responsibilities is changing in a modern federal democracy. We attach to that literature but consciously look more broadly and inductively at actual governance practices of those who would promote the gateway functions of city-regions. We show how actually existing urban coalitions, or gateway regimes, govern through a blend of private sector stakeholders and a partial set of multilevel governance arrangements that privilege federally mandated agencies and provincial governments while, more often than not, bypassing both municipal governments and social and community organizations.

Granted, such sidestepping seems justifiable when expertise and efficiency are called for given the delays and costs tied to electoral democracy and public consultation. On the other hand, efficiency should not disallow electoral democracy and citizen participation simply because the stakes are higher and the stakeholders more distant, especially when a decision or project stands to negatively impact a community. When a city or city-region is tied to global economic systems, its citizens are tied as well. Involving its elected representatives ensures that the legality of a decision is complemented by legitimacy, otherwise the process itself is lopsided and its validity can be questioned, if not condemned. Although more exacting, citizen consultation does extend legitimacy.

Unfortunately, as things now stand across Canada, notwithstanding efforts on provincial governments' part to set up democratic governance systems, local governments' delegation of responsibilities to regional governments or bodies turns deliberation and decision making into a closed-door process that has little to do with either direct or participatory democracy. Some refer to this set up as an indirect democracy, but the term is ill-chosen. Indirect democracy is a synonym for representative or electoral democracy. Calling it an executive democracy, a form of government (or governance) in which the executive branch's powers dominate over the elected assembly's in response to meeting global economic requirements, would be more precise (Deblock and Brunelle 1998). Specifically, executive democracy in the present instance refers to the appointment of elected officials at municipal levels, usually the mayor or vice-mayor, to regional councils (metropolitan community, city-region, etc.) that have neither constituents nor elected officials of their own. The net result of this mode of functioning is that there can be no accountability to either elected officials or constituents, on the one hand, while on the other, the elected officials are deemed to possess a communitarian or regional perspective in dealing with their responsibilities while their subjects are deprived of any such perspective. This state of affair does indeed instill a democratic deficit at the regional levels.

Urban regions are implicated and affected by globalization; they suffer the negative externalities of trade while being called upon to make supportive investments. If we want to move beyond the two solitudes of trade promotion and urban livability, the collective-action holdups and often confrontational relationships, we need to give the municipalities and communities within them a stake in the success of economic globalization. This is not possible if we only have technocratic, tokenistic, formulaic consultation with municipal government and civic actors. Instead, cities in the federation need to be trusted as equal players in the nation's economic success.

OVERVIEW OF THE BOOK

We show that these contingent processes have produced differentiated governance models and uneven urban-development outcomes across four Canadian gateway city-regions. We develop a framework for understanding the urban governance of gateways based on the concepts of urban coalitions, gateway regimes, and urban democracy. Our goal is to understand the role of cities and city-regions as they engage global value chains (GVCs) and global production networks (GPNs), terms we use interchangeably.

Chapter 1 places Canadian cities in their provincial, national, and global contexts. We introduce four takes (or characterizations) on the place of cities in Canada to highlight cities' and municipal governments' ambiguous role in terms of political jurisdiction and public governance. In so doing, we situate Vancouver, Toronto, Montreal, and Halifax in the context of Canada's economic development and trade policy. We also provide a note on the methodology used in this study and the comparative analytical framework we develop.

Chapter 2 presents local urban governance in relation to the existing literature on global value chains, global production networks, and international trade integration. In particular, we focus on the notion of urban regimes as a way of understanding the multi-actor and multiscalar coalitions that have formed in and through Canadian metropolitan regions. We identify gateway regimes as both proactive – shaping trade-enabling infrastructure investments in support of existing economic relations – and reactive, or as attaching to provincial, national, and international agendas that offer resources, investment, and connections. This dialectical dynamic plays out unevenly across the urban system with one common feature: a move away from deliberative democratic practices at the local levels and toward executive democracy.

Chapter 3 traces the evolution of the Canadian national gateway strategy, including the various federal initiatives and policies leading to its development and implementation. Within the broader political economy context of trade agreements and liberalization, we examine more specifically how the transition toward trade corridors induced a shift in the federal government's integrative commerce priorities. Focusing on the period from the mid-2000s to 2020, the chapter traces both the consistencies and important changes in approach toward a global and continental orientation. We end the chapter with the creation of the Canada Infrastructure Bank as a new manifestation of federal funding, supposedly aimed at attracting private finance but through a project- and asset-based approach rather than a strategic corridor-based approach.

Each of Chapters 4 through 7 centres on one case study metropolitan region. Given the foundational role of Vancouver's gateway coalition, we start in the west and move east. This ordering is conscious; it inverts the received wisdom that Canadian urbanism's history is one of westward expansion. Implicitly, we show that policy innovation can proceed differently. These chapters also introduce the variety of city-region governance models visible across Canada to complexify and layer our understanding of the relationship between urban and trade corridor development.

In Chapter 8, we conclude with a comparison between the four cases to reflect on the role of trade connections and positioning in global value chains in Canadian city-region governance. Highlighting key similarities and differences across the cases, notably the types of stakeholders involved in local gateway coalitions, allows us to identify distinctive governance models and to focus on the central dilemma between municipal/urban democracy concerns and the insertion of cities in global value chains. In this regard, gateway regimes tend to promote an executive form of democracy instead of a deliberative or a participatory democracy, thereby constraining citizen engagement in ways that do not interfere with the requirements of global value chains and reducing them to community buy-in and social license.

1

Canadian Cities in the Global Context

> The current period of human history can plausibly be identified not only as a global but also as an urban era.
>
> – M. STORPER AND A.J. SCOTT (2016, 3)

> Two important drivers of growth, productivity and jobs today (are) competitive cities and global value chains (GVCs).
>
> – WORLD ECONOMIC FORUM (2016, 4)

In this book, we discuss how four of Canada's major gateway city-regions – namely Halifax, Montreal, Toronto, and Vancouver – have been positioned in global commodity and value chains through infrastructure investment strategies pursued by public and private agents. We have organized our inquiry around the evolution of federal and provincial funding strategies related to Transport Canada's Gateways and Trade Corridors initiatives and the ways that, through distinct urban regimes, local, private, and public sector stakeholders have been involved in the governance of the four city-regions. We consider the direct and indirect roles of various levels of government, private industry, and civic organizations in these strategies, as well as the interactions between them. As questions of urban democracy are frequently set aside in the pursuit of global connections, we pay particular attention to the role of Canadian municipalities and citizens in shaping infrastructure and economic development projects for international trade and investment purposes. We trace and compare the evolution of pro-trade gateway regimes in each city-region – regimes that comprise federally mandated agencies, provincial government bodies, and business proxies. And while we note similarities in membership in these regimes, some important differences across Canada lead us to assume that there are distinctive governance models across our case study sites.

The Canadian economy has long been open to world trade; however, the past three decades saw a substantial increase in exports and imports. Between 1992, when the North American Free Trade Agreement (NAFTA) was signed, and 2019, before the global COVID-19 pandemic, the share of Canadian gross domestic product (GDP) accounted for by trade rose from just over one-half to about two-thirds.[1] NAFTA concentrated the attention of policy makers on north-south and continental trade connections, while subsequent developments such as China's accession to the World Trade Organization in December 2001 focused their attention on east-west and transoceanic connections. But the 9/11 attacks and the financial crisis of 2007–8 led to a reduction in cross-border trade. In response, Canadian governments resorted to integrative commerce (Government of Canada 2008; see also Chapter 3) and the negotiation of trade agreements with countries in Europe, Asia, Africa (Morocco), as well as Central and South America to increase global exports and diversify trade. As noted by the Canada Transportation Act Review (Government of Canada 2016b), since 2006, Canada has increased the number of international trade agreements from five to forty-three. Growing trade volumes, whatever their origins, bring a greater pressure on the infrastructure required to ship goods, including airports, ports, rails, roads, border crossing, logistics, and communications.

As such, trade flows have a geography. They are sourced in places of supply and destined for places of demand. They follow particular air, land, and sea corridors and are processed at distributive nodes. Many of the most important distributive functions are in large metropolitan regions (O'Connor 2010; Hall and Jacobs 2012) commonly called "gateway cities." In this book, "gateway" is taken to refer to the system of trade-enabling infrastructures organized in nodes and corridors that include marine, air, rail, and inland terminals; freight transfer and storage facilities; landside transportation networks; and related human, organizational, and informational systems. Jean-Paul Rodrigue (2020) differentiates gateways from hubs: hubs can be unimodal and are exclusively points of distribution, while gateways combine multiple modes and are points of origin/destination as well as distribution.

During the past two decades, the Government of Canada has supported initiatives that aim to develop infrastructure to ensure trade competitiveness via four major gateways and corridors. Since 2006, they include the Asia-Pacific Gateway and Corridor Initiative (APGCI), the Atlantic Gateway and Trade Corridor, the Ontario-Quebec Continental Gateway and Trade Corridor, and, more recently, the Canadian Northern Corridor. The cases in this book relate to the first three of these gateways and trade corridors initiatives. It should also be noted that federal funds spent in the four major metropolitan areas studied here comprise about a fifth of the total federal funding for gateways and corridors between 2006 and 2019.

Gateway transportation infrastructure plays a key role not only in the physical transportation of goods but also in the development of a gateway city. Andersson and Andersson (2000) differentiate the source (origins), sink (destination), and saddle (redistribution and transshipment) functions of nodes in networks, which can be used to differentiate the characteristics of trade gateways. The combination of saddle, sink, and source gateway functions in the four city-regions studied here reflects the location of each relative to the markets they serve locally, nationally, continentally, and internationally. The gateways of Halifax and Vancouver, while serving modest local markets, occupy a dominant saddle function between the Canadian interior, the United States, Asia, and Europe. Their infrastructures are multimodal, integrating oceanic transport and seaports with corridors to the rest of North America. Montreal and Toronto have significant source and sink functions as they produce and consume international goods. Source and sink functions complement the saddle component at sites such as the Port of Montreal and at Pearson and Hamilton airports in greater Toronto. These functional differences translate in distinctive patterns of infrastructure investment and distinctive political economies of gateway regime-building and governance.

The case studies of the four gateway city-regions show how each comprises a distinctive set of activities that are integrated, in varying degrees, virtually, contractually, organizationally, and physically. These gateway activities are more or less compatible with each other and with other urban activities. Hence, the proponents of these activities – importers, exporters, and the firms providing them with transportation services – are potentially in competition or collaboration, or both, with each other and with other urban stakeholders, as to which activities should receive priority. And because trade-supporting activities rely heavily on transportation-infrastructure investment, this competition and collaboration often centres on government attention and resources. In other words, those seeking government infrastructure funding for road improvements to a port terminal are in competition with those seeking transit system investments, much as those who seek land zoned for warehousing compete with those who seek land for condos or parks.

Another way to think about the governance dilemmas of gateway cities is in how to navigate the relationship between trade corridor development in support of global value chains (GVCs) and municipal democracy in support of urban livability (Hall and Hesse 2013). There are manifest tensions between these two imperatives and the forms of democratic engagement they tolerate; where the former implies the top-down imperatives of integration and control, the latter implies the bottom-up imperatives of localist responsiveness and particularism (Borja and Castells 1997). These tensions shape and limit the space for public engagement and democratic decision making through a division of labour in which senior governments pay attention to trade, while local governments pay attention to amenity.

Hence, and in addition to being infrastructure systems, gateways are also about modes of urban governance in the sense that governance concerns itself with determining how the decisions about allocating these scarce investments get made. To achieve gateway development, disparate trade-enabling activities need to be governed, which is to say that a series of resource, coordination, and collective action challenges must be resolved (Henderson et al. 2002). Ultimately these urban "resolutions" are contingent upon a set of differential coalition-building, regime-formation, and bargaining processes (Wachsmuth 2017). Likewise, writing about the outer suburbs of Paris, Nicolas Raimbault (2022, 1481) argues that "the domination of integrated global firms in logistics real estate depends on their capacity to form local coalitions."

To provide a basis to contrast the urban governance models relating to international trade and investment in the Canadian context, we draw on three sources: original data collected through interviews with key stakeholders, national data for gateway infrastructure projects and involved stakeholders, and documentary analysis of numerous reports from organizations involved in each selected urban context. Throughout the four cases, we show that while federal- and provincial-level stakeholders along with private sector interests are engaged in connecting each locale to global networks through port, airport, road, rail, and border-crossing infrastructure projects, urban-based stakeholders are invested in augmenting the attractiveness and competitiveness of their city-region through multiple, complex arrangements across a variety of economic sectors. Unsurprisingly, urban-based stakeholders typically favour infrastructure investments, plans, and policies that benefit existing residents while resisting trade infrastructures that impose negative externalities on the area.

The tension between these competing sets of interests has profound implications for city-regional governance. Local business interests form part of a range of urban development coalitions. The transportation industry is especially active in the coalitions that form around trade and transportation infrastructure; we term these "gateway regimes." The leading actors in the gateway regimes in the Canadian cities studied here include the federal government, federal agencies such as the port and airport authorities and regional development agencies, provincial ministries of transportation, business associations, and large transportation companies. However, the gateway regimes leave space for only marginal involvement from elected municipal governments – typically involving project implementation. Civil society groups and individual residents are almost entirely left out of discussions about gateway development. This raises important questions about urban democratic praxis, which we turn to in our final chapter.

FOUR TAKES ON THE PLACE OF CITIES IN CANADA

In the Canadian constitutional context, local governments have limited abilities to engage in economic activity, and especially in trade and infrastructure-related realms. Canadian cities are perceived as being acted upon rather than taking action. In this section, we present four such characterizations of the cities' place within the Canadian urban system. These characterizations are presented in highly stylized and general terms, summarizing received facts that circulate in policy, academic, and popular discourses. We do not dispute these characterizations outright; there is an element of truth to each of them, and as heuristic devices, they are consequential. Indeed, this book is motivated in part by a sense that Canadian cities are thought about in a way that entrenches a democratic deficit at the municipal level. At the same time, we also seek to nuance and update these characterizations.

In what follows, we summarize the four takes on these cities' place in Canada as points of contrast with the perspective we have developed through this examination of Canadian cities and their relation to GVCs. Updating the way Canadian cities are perceived is timely, considering Canada's shifting place in contemporary globalization and the rise in recognition of cities' agentive role in various policy processes.

Take One: Canadian Cities Are Creatures of Their Province

Article 92.8 of the 1867 British North America Act gives provincial government exclusive power over the creation of municipal governments – their size/boundaries, their sources of revenue, and their regulatory powers. If intracity road maintenance and transit fall under municipal jurisdiction, provincial governments are responsible for all intraprovincial road transportation, while the federal government has constitutional authority over interprovincial and international transportation. In this context, Canadian cities have been viewed as less agentive than their American counterparts; they have limited fiscal powers related to debt and taxation, and provincial legislation sets limits on what they can do and regulate. They are also unlike the cities and city-states with constitutional status found in many parts of Europe, as well as parts of East Asia, including China, where major coastal cities have been able to combine province/state-level powers with city development strategies since the Open Door Policy was approved (Wang 2016). Canadian cities instead seem to take more of the postcolonial character of the centralized nation-states found in large parts of Africa, South America, and South Asia.

Kirstin Good (2019, 29) argues, "It is time to abandon the constitutional doctrine of 'creatures of the provinces' since it distorts Canada's constitutional reality. By fetishizing a single element of Canada's constitution, it fails to acknowledge municipalities as an essential element of Canada's democratic system and thwarts citizens' ability to realize true local self-government." We strongly agree with this sentiment but, for now, this foundational fact provides important framing for the way Canadian cities are viewed.

Lacking the full range of tools and the legal autonomy to pursue conventional entrepreneurial (business attraction, expansion, retention) and globally oriented strategies, Canadian municipal governments have focused on local services, amenities, and livability (recognizing that these have been reframed as part of urban entrepreneurialism, especially in light of creative class strategies). This perspective on Canadian cities would suggest that urban regimes, if they exist here at all (see Cobban 2003a, 2003b; Leo 2003), are thought to be confined to these localist arenas. Every time municipal government is involuntarily restructured – its boundaries redrawn (most notably in Quebec during the early 2000s and in Ontario during the 1990s and again recently) or funding denied – this understanding of Canadian cities is confirmed.

The provincial-ness of Canadian cities is an important point to bear in mind when understanding the different institutional configurations of local government across Canada, in the sense that each takes on the character of the province it serves. We return repeatedly to this idea in the empirical chapters that document the importance of provincial government priorities and the membership in the gateway regimes of the various provincial ministries of transportation. The ways provinces intervene in their cities, and the way cities relate to their provinces, are some of the most important factors in shaping the gateway regime in each city-region. All four of our case study cities are powerhouses within their provincial economies, but key urban actors seek to position their gateway functions in different ways. For example, actors in Toronto position theirs as the metropolis of Canada, while Montreal has been set up as the metropolis of Quebec following the adoption of Bill 121 in September 2017 (Gouvernement du Québec 2017). While Montreal does serve as a gateway to the continent, in today's Québécois imaginary, the distinction between Canada and the American continent is played down.

At the same time, the provincial picture of Canadian cities ignores the increasing importance of local amenities in global real estate and creative class strategies – and the increasing attention at the local level to a variety of social policy issues (e.g., immigration, housing) attendant to changes in the welfare state. It also ignores the fact that the major Canadian cities exert a disproportionate – and often conflictual – influence within their provincial context. A more nuanced view of Canadian cities is that urban-based interests are engaged in shaping, and are shaped by, provincial and federal agendas including those related to value chains. While the financial dependency of Canadian city-regions on provincial and federal government is exacerbated by their increasing role in regional economic development and GVCs, institutional recommendations to address the situation, either by conferring provincial status on larger city-regions (notably the proposal to establish Toronto as the eleventh province) or involving them in three-level constitutional conferences (as recommended by the Macdonald Commission), remain unaddressed. Unfortunately, the present situation only deepens the divide between responsibilities and fiscal capacities in the governance of Canadian city-regions.

Take Two: Canadian Cities Are Internally Undifferentiated

Perhaps because Canadian cities are viewed by many as creatures of their province, they have been regarded in rather "flat" or internally undifferentiated terms, reinforced by the sense that they are mere jurisdictions of local administration, addressing local concerns. In contrast with the United States, more centralized provision of public school, health, and transport systems has historically reduced the disparities between neighbourhoods and communities, some evidence of increasing income differentiation in Canadian metropolitan regions notwithstanding (Hulchanski 2010).

There assuredly is increasing public awareness of Canada's largest cities' regional dimension, but it is unclear whether that always comes with awareness of the horizontal competition and collaboration within. In Vancouver, for example, there is no end to the images and reports eliding the distinction between the city (2021 population: 662,000) and the region (2021 population: 2.6 million). When Vancouver is portrayed as green and dense, both the autocentric suburbs and the very tangible sustainability achievements of the Greater Vancouver Regional District (cf. Harcourt, Cameron, and Rossiter 2007) are ignored. Toronto is no longer recognized as the old city of York plus its annexures but rather as a metropolitan region of continental significance, comprising an urban core and suburbs that extend beyond the conventional construct of inner and outer rings.

If an understanding of internal differentiation in Canadian city-regions is emerging, it is perhaps because of attempts in the 1990s and 2000s to create ever-larger metropolitan governments in some provinces and the inevitable backlash by some (see Sancton 2000). For example, the municipal merger in 2002 and demerger in 2006 reminded Montrealers of the language and class divisions between the cities on their island. There are still profound gaps and erasures in the characterization of Canadian cites as relatively undifferentiated, especially when it comes to First Nations whose reserves and unceded territories are situated in metropolitan areas.

A more nuanced view of Canadian cities also needs to incorporate the more complex array of vertical connections that differentially shape the city. Scholarly work on Canadian cities' multilevel governance has begun to unpack the vertical connections between municipal, provincial, and federal governments in arenas such as housing, immigrant settlement, and emergency management (cf. Graham and Andrew 2014), and there are celebrated multigovernment agreements, such as the Vancouver and Winnipeg accords. These kinds of governance arrangements are also found in the city-shaping trade infrastructure and value chain arena we explore in this book.

However, a key characteristic of many of these multilevel governance actions is that they are spatially selective within city-regions, so they belie the characterization of Canadian cities as internally undifferentiated. The Vancouver and Winnipeg accords were about the downtown core areas of those cities rather than about poverty everywhere, just as the gateway infrastructure funding is about specific trade-enabling nodes and routes. Likewise, the federally mandated agencies located and acting independently in cities (i.e., the port and airport authorities and Canada's Regional Development Agencies, or RDAs) are present only at certain sites or sectors. The same can be said of the provincial government bodies with mandates to act regionally, such as the transportation bodies Metrolinx (Toronto) and TransLink (Vancouver). When federal and provincial governments act within cities, they necessarily do so in a highly selective and differentiated way, precisely because they are not the general government of these jurisdictions.

Take Three: Canadian Cities Organized the Expansion of the National Staples Economy

We can think of this characterization of Canadian cities as occupying a particular role in organizing and servicing the staples-export economy (Innis 2017) and in tying the development of Canada's urban system to the nation's settler-colonial history and westward settlement pattern. This view of Canadian cities also references the hinterland-heartland distinction (McCann 1987), which places the industrial, managerial, and control cities of Montreal and Toronto firmly in the heartland. Cities such as Halifax, Vancouver, and others are viewed as urban nodes within the hinterland, although an updated perspective might admit them to an "emergent heartland" (Ray et al. 2012). Barry Prentice (2006) has advanced the intriguing idea that cities in Canada are linked in pairs that reflect particular modal connections serving particular commodity export systems; Montreal and Winnipeg are connected by rail and decline together, whereas Toronto and Calgary are connected by trucking and rise together.

This perspective on Canadian cities brings them into direct relation with the federal government's role in supporting international trade and interprovincial transportation. Article 91 of the 1867 British North America Act grants the federal government, among other things, exclusive power on the regulation of trade and commerce as well as on navigation and shipping. As such, it is understandable that the federal government mandates authorities (e.g., port authorities) to act on its behalf and intervenes directly at the subnational level when its heads of power are threatened. A recent example of this is the federal government's purchase and retrofit of the Trans Mountain Pipeline, which carries bitumen to the Port of Vancouver for export – over the objections of the governments of British Columbia, First Nations, and Vancouver-area municipalities.

The idea that the fortunes of Canadian cities are tied to the resource economy is not wrong; they remain important locations for mining, energy, forestry and agricultural services, and finance, and the port/airport/gateway function of cities remains tied to these exporting interests. At the same time, Tom Hutton (2007) and others have asserted that post-industrial activities – education, real estate, health, advanced services, information technology, and so on – are now more important in shaping the economic entanglements of Canadian cities.

We think characterizing Canadian cities as either staples-based or not needs to be more nuanced. Indeed, many of the processes we trace are the result of tensions between these dimensions of the Canadian economy and how they play out in cities. The idea that Canadian gateway cities are focused on the unidirectional flow of resource exports (and of imported manufactured goods) elides the more complex and integrated nature of contemporary supply chains. For example, automobile and plane parts cross the Ontario-US border multiple times before final assembly and resource exports are filling ocean shipping containers that had arrived in Canada carrying manufactured imports. Cities are important sites for organizing these activities but often in more extensive regional (even continental) and networked configurations – all of which support but complicate the idea that Canadian cities are characterized by their relationship to the staples economy.

Take Four: Canadian Cities Are Continental or Global Actors

In opposition to take three (Canadian cities organized the expansion of the national staples economy), there is an increasing appreciation of the continental and global connections and forces shaping the largest Canadian cities. This take asserts that the fortunes of Canadian cities, by becoming less embedded in their respective provincial staples economies, are becoming more tied to developments in the United States and beyond (Norcliffe 2001).

This characterization found substantial public sympathy in discourses on the Canadian branch-plant economy and in anxieties about jobs and activity leaving Canada for the US in the wake of NAFTA and the Canada-United States-Mexico Agreement. And, with the economic base turning to services and finance, this view finds substantial public sympathy in concerns about unaffordable housing markets in the largest cities. Indeed, since Canadian cities are perceived as less tied to other parts of Canada, concerns have been raised about the implications for national unity. Thomas Courchene (2001, 161) argues that "Canada is less and less a single national (east-west) economy and more and more a series of north-south, cross-border economies. Hence, this economic diversity across Canada's provincial/regional economies will lead rather naturally to policy diversity and asymmetry. The Canadian government is contributing to this trend toward decentralization and asymmetry at the provincial level."

Unlike the previous three characterizations of Canadian cities, this take is more open to recognizing the agentive role of local (urban-based) actors in pursuing economic development opportunities. For example, Courchene (2001, 187–88) points out that "Ontario as 'North American region-state' is providing the governance architecture and the needed restructuring and incentives for Toronto to make its likewise inevitable transition from Canada's economic, financial, and cultural capital to a global city-region in the North American context and beyond." We question whether Ontario has really afforded Toronto the powers it seeks in the intervening two decades since Courchene's prediction, but he was right to highlight the interests moving in that direction.

So, as with the other characterizations of the place of cities in the Canadian urban system, we seek to supplement rather than dismiss our fourth and final take. Canadian cities are inevitably attached to both continental (US) and global (Asian, European, and Latin American) trading systems. As we shall see, the federal priorities for trade-enabling infrastructure have favoured both global and continental connections. The gateway in Halifax, for example, promoted by a federal development agency and a federally mandated port authority, has paid considerable attention to exports from the regional hinterland. We show that powerful institutional forces and actors continue to tie Canadian gateway cities to their provincial governments and to local economic interests.

FRAMING GATEWAY CITIES IN A TRADING FEDERATION

Recognizing that there is some degree of truth to each of the four characterizations, or takes, on the place of Canadian cities in the federation helps to illuminate a core dilemma for urban governance and planning. Canadian city polities have to deal not only with the contrasting and contested internal dynamics – the mundane yet deeply felt dynamics around local services, livability, and sustainability, including social service provision, making space for cars, cyclists, and pedestrians, and so on. But they also deal with on-the-ground urban consequences of fitting into the larger – but no less contested and contingent – development projects and schemes of actors whose primary interests transect the regional hinterland, provincial, national, continental, and global economies of which they are a part. Viewed from such an urban perspective, gateway and corridor initiatives are another instance in which the fortunes of Canadian cities are shaped by larger, external forces.

These varying perspectives (or takes) on what Canadian cities "are" prove useful for understanding not only their roles in the economic, social, and political life of the nation and its provinces; they also help us understand what they represent to the citizenry, to investors, to public officials, and to other decision makers. In particular, they are part of the frame that informs how policy makers in other levels of government approach cities to support their own agendas. In their edited volume on multilevel governance in the Canadian federation that features case studies from a much larger collaborative research project on public policy and municipal government, Katherine Graham and Caroline Andrew (2014) note that federal governments retain considerable influence over municipalities when they enter into ostensibly collaborative policy and program development with municipal governments. One way they achieve this is through the power of frames:

> The framing of the program may still sound sensitive to local needs, but in fact it leads to a very different system of the distribution of program funds and can be seen as a realpolitik reaction to provincial concerns. So the federal government can frame and reframe policies to either suggest continuity or radical change, and this gives it an important resource. It need not actually change the program, but it can reframe it in a way that links it to the government's politics. (4–5)

Embedded in this quote are three key observations for thinking about the role of municipal governance and democracy in the creation (construction) of trade-enabling infrastructures in cities. First, the power of the federal government to shape infrastructure priorities in cities comes from both its control over funding (the power of the purse) and its ability to shape the social, economic, and political meaning that is attached to these investments. Indeed, we will see again and again how the gateway frame, which references the derivative status of Canadian cities as places that organize trade, has been used to justify top-down initiatives. Second, Graham and Andrew (2014) remind us that even (and perhaps especially) while federal governments may be working directly with municipal governments, they have to be attentive to provincial concerns because, in the Canadian system, if federal-provincial relations are explicit, constitutionally defined, and politically consequential, municipal politics are far less so. And third, shifting frames do not necessarily imply shifting policy and investment priorities; indeed, reframing can be a way of achieving continuity. For example, the corporatization of major ports and airports as federal authorities following the divisive (and decisive) debate about free trade has reinforced their continued role as ardent promoters of trade while giving them an arms-length and apparently apolitical relationship to the government of the day.

Continuity is especially visible in the second device by which the federal government can assert its will in federal-municipal relations as identified by Graham and Andrew (2014); namely, with respect to policy instruments. Once a policy instrument – such as the gas tax or infrastructure program, which directly benefits municipal government – becomes established in the sense that it attracts and retains local partners, "the federal government gets to be very visible in its policy implementation through choices of policy instruments" (7). Here the old adage that politicians like to be invited to attend ribbon-cutting ceremonies comes to mind; federal governments also like being able to count on the support of local and regional officials as they seek to advance agendas that might otherwise be interpreted as intruding on provincial jurisdictions.

ON SITES AND METHODS: VANCOUVER, TORONTO, MONTREAL, AND HALIFAX

Our study combines key insights from transportation geography, critical infrastructure studies, and actor-network theory to contribute to governance and institutional debates about urban gateway cities. First, we recognize that the global movement of people and goods is experienced locally through specific nodes such as gateway cities; therefore, questions of access, usage, and design are highly contextual based on the mode of transportation and institutional arrangements, for instance (Keeling 2009). Second, we are committed to putting discussions and debates about transportation infrastructure and the built environment front and centre rather than taking infrastructure as a neutral asset (Graham 2009; Wakefield 2018). While often perceived as a "black box" in public affairs, studying commodity chains and other mobility processes enabled by transportation infrastructure helps reveal the political decisions that have shaped and are shaping the built environment. Third, lessons from actor-network theory are fundamental to our approach – namely the importance of networks emerging from interactions, the need to integrate the material world as a constitutive part of the study, and the development of an inductive and process-based inquiry (Müller 2015). We embrace the malleability of actor-network theory as framework, as seen in the attention given to the unique context of each case study (i.e., a multisited analysis rather than a conventional comparative study) and the use of network analysis (e.g., through Gephi) to corroborate and triangulate information revealed in interviews and in analysis of publicly available reports.

Concretely, to understand the distinct ways that major Canadian cities are governed in relation to GVCs, we have structured this study around four different sites that are connected to a similar set of federal infrastructure development and funding initiatives. Vancouver and Prince Rupert, the latter located on the northern coast of British Columbia, along with Calgary, Edmonton, Winnipeg, and other western cities, comprise the APGCI. Halifax anchors the Atlantic Gateway, with funding provided to port, airport, and infrastructure projects across the Maritime provinces. And in the Continental Gateway, Toronto and Montreal are two key urban agglomerations within the Quebec-Windsor corridor.

We chose these case study sites because they represent major trade gateway cities in Canada (see Table 1.1). It is true that other Canadian cities host major seaports and freight airports, railyards, and freight distribution and warehousing activities and some other cities are adjacent to major border crossings. We hope there are lessons in this study for stakeholders in such places as Prince Rupert, Kamloops, Calgary, Edmonton, Winnipeg, Windsor, Cornwall, Quebec City, Saint John, and St. John's, as well as gateway cities in other countries.

Comparisons lend themselves to innumerable possibilities. They can be made between global cities, as Saskia Sassen (2001) does in comparing New York, London, and Tokyo, or between parts of cities, as Geoffrey DeVerteuil (2015) does in comparing inner-city voluntary sectors in London, Los Angeles, and Sydney. Similarly, interesting lessons can be drawn in comparing asymmetrical cities, as John Rennie Short et al. (2000) do with Barcelona, Beijing, Havana, Prague, Seattle, Sioux Falls, and Sydney. For our part, we chose to contrast four cities within the same country that are quite different from one another in terms of size, extension, population, geographical position, and so forth but that each occupy a central role as gateways and trade corridors as defined by successive federal policies and programs.

One distinct methodological advantage of choosing four city-regions within the same country is that we can better understand how the same broad set of federal government policies and programs played out in particular local contexts. This shared policy context allows us to engage in a form of multisited analysis. Multisited analysis has emerged in the

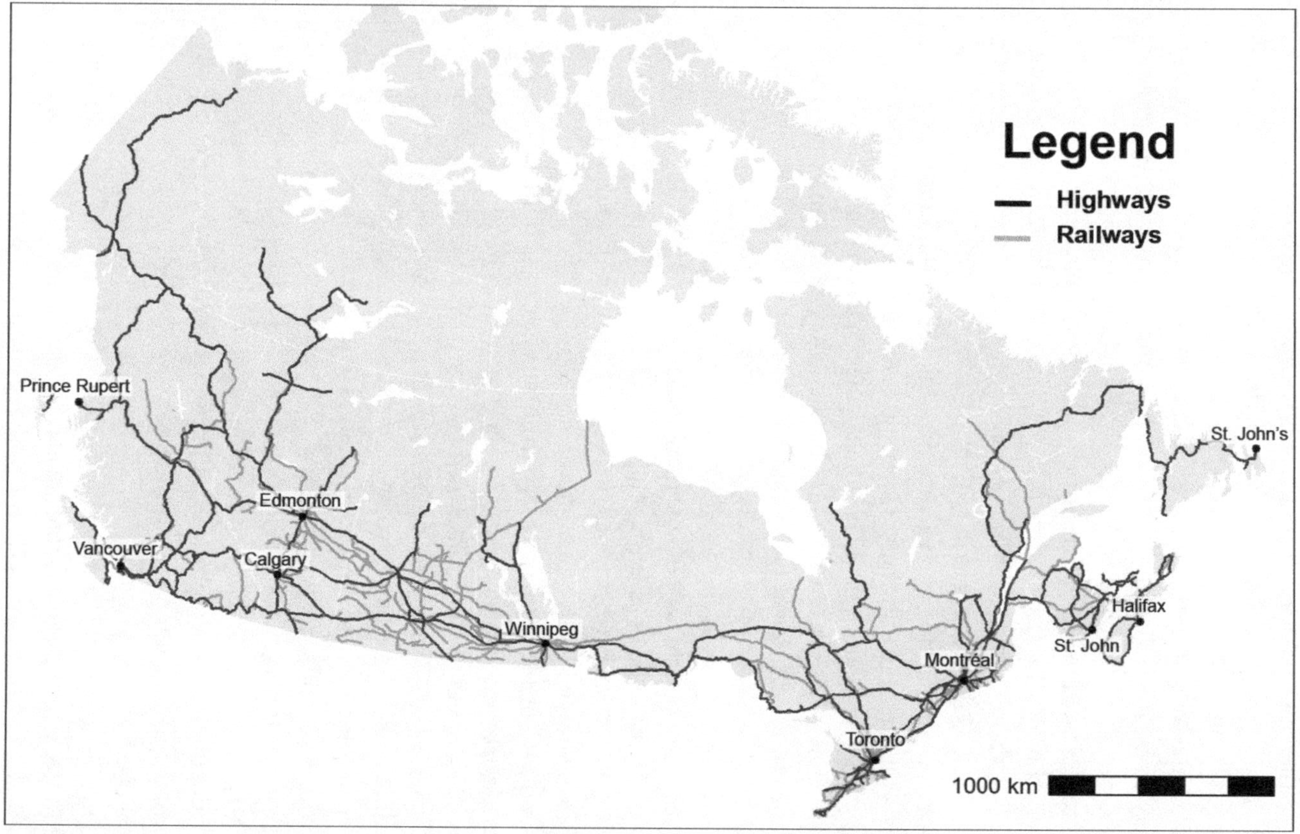

FIGURE 1.1 Canada cities and major transport infrastructure | *Cartography:* Steve Tornes. *Sources:* Government of Canada (2021b), Statistics Canada (2021a, 2021b).

TABLE 1.1

Portrait of four gateway city-regions (CMA), mid-2010s to early-2020s

	Vancouver CMA	*Greater Toronto and Hamilton Area*	*Montreal CMA*	*Halifax CMA*
Province	British Columbia	Ontario	Quebec	Nova Scotia
Province population – 2021	5,000,879	14,223,942	8,501,833	969,383
CMA area (sq. km.)	2,882.68	8,244	4,604.26	7276.22*
CMA population – 2021	2,642,825	7,281,694	4,291,732	465,703
CMA population growth 2006–21 %	24.9	20.2	18.0	24.9
CMA employment – 2021	1,341,570	3,390,640	2,117,370	227,125
CMA employment growth 2006–21 %	21.4	9.0	15.3	13.8
Largest municipality	City of Vancouver	City of Toronto	City of Montreal	Halifax Regional Municipality
Population largest municipality – 2021	662,248	2,794,356	1,762,949	439,819
Port tonnage – 2018 (metric tonnes)	147,093,000	14,128,318	38,925,026	4,769,550
Port containers – 2018 (TEU)	3,396,000	–	1,679,352	547,445
Airport passengers – 2018	25,267,409	48,269,345	18,749,586	4,236,898
Airport cargo – 2018 (tonnes)	321,318	586,847 **	208,054 ***	28,118

Sources: Port of Halifax (2018), Port of Hamilton Oshawa (2018), Port of Montreal (2018), Port of Toronto (2018), Port of Vancouver (2018), Statistics Canada (2017, 2020a, 2020b, 2023).

Note: This table contains demographic information from 2021, the most recent population census year, and throughput data from before the COVID-19 pandemic. CMA stands for census metropolitan area.

* Census 2021 added East Hants on Halifax CMA, changing area from 5,496.31 sq. km to 7,276.22 sq. km.

** Toronto cargo includes John C. Munro Hamilton and Lester B. Pearson Airports.

*** Montreal cargo includes Pierre Elliott Trudeau and Mirabel Airports.

social sciences out of the popularity of George Marcus's (1986) multisited ethnography. Although contested within the field of social anthropology, Marcus's framework has been used in many fields as an alternative methodology to traditional approaches to emphasize a qualitative study of a process or phenomenon appearing in many sites at once (see Cohn 2006; Johnson 2014). While the importance of comparability across sites is not paramount in this study, multisited research does utilize a specific understanding of the world, a lens of sorts, to interpret how local realities are incorporated in a broader, intersite process. It also allows us to adapt the methodological approach used to best study the process or phenomenon based on key features of the site being studied. As Marcus (1995, 101–2) mentions, a multisited approach to qualitative research "takes shape around chains, paths, threads, conjunctions, or juxtapositions of locations" that are useful for the researchers to ground a "logic of association or connection among sites."

In the context of this study, we use the Canadian government's integrative commerce strategy and supporting gateway and corridor strategies to study four different sites. Federal interest in Canada's gateways provides a point of departure or a "prior view of a system" from which we embark on a qualitative examination of four sites where "the gateway" is deployed. Our examinations are based on the methods and research techniques necessary to follow and best account for how these practices and discussions evolved locally (Marcus 1986, 171–72). Building up our understanding of local practices against a common background, we acknowledge some differences in the data collection methods across the four sites: document-based in some, interview-based in others. In line with the precepts mentioned previously, our approach is not to impose a rigid comparative approach but instead to trace how gateway discussions and debates occurred differently across the four sites.

Readers will note differences in the styles and approaches to the four case study chapters (4 to 7) that form the empirical core of this research. Although all the chapters were duly read, discussed, and commented upon, each lead author drew on their own approach and methodology to deal with the subject at hand, a protocol deemed fit to reconcile both the author's own research agenda and the particularities of the case study. Peter Hall took the lead on Vancouver (Chapter 4), Jean Michel Montsion took the lead on Toronto (Chapter 5), Dorval Brunelle took the lead on Montreal (Chapter 6), and Claudia De Fuentes took the lead on Halifax (Chapter 7).

However, we ensure consistency in several respects. In each case, we take a metropolitan or functional urban agglomeration scale as our unit of focus – but we look within these geographies at the precise municipal government configurations they contain to understand where and why municipal government does or does not play a role in trade-related development. In addition to holding the federal initiatives as a constant background to each case, we also pay particular attention to the relationship between the city-region and its province. Finally, we give attention to other actors and their network relationships across the sites; if certain major economic actors, such as industry associations and federal authorities (i.e., port, airport), emerged as important in one site, we would ask whether or not they were important in the other sites and why.

While examining the evolution of the four gateway regimes and their intersections with other urban coalitions, we devoted considerable effort to identifying the relevant actors and their networks of relationships. These relationships were further confirmed through a network analysis using Gephi software. We built a database of connections between stakeholders involved in successful federal gateway-funding proposals between 2007 and 2020 (i.e., the APGCI, the Gateway and Border Crossing Fund, and the National Trade Corridors Fund rounds). This was done using government proactive disclosure, an access-to-information request, as well as official announcements, government reports and project descriptions, and print and online media sources.[2] Then, network analysis allowed us to corroborate and triangulate qualitative information collected on each gateway regime by providing the contours of the gateway coalition, showing the centrality of some stakeholders in leading gateway projects, and highlighting the connections among stakeholders in cooperating on these projects.

The stakeholders included industry associations, civil society groups, private sector firms, including land, port, marine, air, or rail transportation firms, as well as nontransportation firms (importers and exporters), governments (First Nations, municipal, provincial, and federal), government departments and public authorities, and others.[3] We sought to identify any network relationships between these actors (e.g., by linking departments or agencies to their parent government and by tracing links between private sector firms through their memberships in industry associations, to name a few). We further treated the federally funded projects as nodes that created further network linkages between different stakeholders (e.g., a municipal government might be linked to a port authority, a provincial highway ministry, and a railroad through a rail/road grade-separation project). Additional variables collected for each project included the monetary amount of federal government support, matching funds provided by stakeholders, project type, and start and end date.

We do not claim to have comprehensively included all the actors in these networks, but this research strategy did provide one consistent basis for network analysis and visualization using Gephi software across the four study sites. Social network analysis reveals the hierarchy of the actors according to their centrality in the network, how many projects they are involved in, and the number of actors with whom they interact. In each configuration, stakeholders located at the network centre are more involved and connected to others, while stakeholders at the periphery are less engaged and influential. Network visualizations showing which stakeholders are engaged in the federally funded infrastructure projects are included in all the empirical chapters (4 through 7); in each case, standard measures of network centrality are used to identify the dominant actors (for a summary, see Table 8.1). This analysis is used to corroborate and triangulate other primary data collection methods used to identify and discuss the political and spatial configurations of the four city-regions' gateway regimes. Such insights shed light on the interscalar, multilevel, and cross-sectoral tensions or connections between stakeholders involved in the development and the implementation of specific projects and their implications for urban democratic practices and city-region governance.

By painting a more complete picture of how four Canadian gateway city-regions are governed, the lack of attention paid to participatory democratic practices in general, and to citizens' concerns and organizations in particular, comes out clearly.

2

Value Chains, Urban Regimes, and City-Regional Governance

VALUE CHAINS AND GOVERNANCE

Worldwide trade volumes grew by 2.5 to 3 percent per year until 2019. Subsequent trade tensions between the United States and the People's Republic of China, as well as disruptions to the world economy caused by the COVID-19 pandemic (UNCTAD 2020) and several other shocks resulted in a trade collapse in 2020 followed by strong growth in 2021 (OECD 2022). Such tensions and disruptions threaten the world economy and specific regional nodes and gateways that serve as the territorial anchors of international trade and distribution networks (Amador and Cabral 2016; Johnson 2017; Cerina et al. 2015; Zhu et al. 2015; Fagiolo et al. 2010).

In his studies on global value chains (GVCs), Gary Gereffi (1995) brings out the interconnectedness between firms and the governance schemes specific to each industry. Such an approach has been instrumental in tracing interactions at the firm level and also the roles of stakeholders, including governments, in supporting local and national industries' competitiveness (Benito et al. 2019; Kano 2018; Strange and Humphrey 2019). The involvement of firms in GVCs is complex, due to advances in technology and infrastructures both soft and hard that have lowered transportation costs – until recently at least – and due as well to trade policy and agreements that facilitate economic exchanges across national borders (Molle 2002; Sturgeon 2006). Scholars in economic geography have also emphasized the importance of territorial context in examining the involvement of firms in GVCs, including physical infrastructure and intangibles related to local cultural traits and institutions (Martin 2013; Schindler and Kanai 2019).

Jeffrey Henderson et al. (2002) mounted a critique of the verticality and linearity implicit in the notion of "chain" that would be controlled by a single dominant or lead actor (i.e., a multinational firm). Following Dieter Ernst (2002), they defend a more open approach that can foreground the ways companies organize and control their global operations and the ways they are (or can be) influenced by states, trade unions, NGOs, and other institutions – most notably locations and the implications that the resulting combinations of agents and processes might have for industrial upgrading, higher value added, and so on (Henderson et al. 2002, 57–58). The latter part of their global production network (GPN) formulation is of particular interest to us since it highlights the possible ways municipalities and other urban actors may influence value-seeking activities. For this reason, we use the double abbreviation GVCs/GPNs to refer to the organization of economic activities that rely inter alia on the trade-enabling infrastructures provided in such places as gateway city-regions.

Hence the study of firms and GVCs/GPNs cannot be limited to, or exclude, local realities but should be understood as a complex interplay between many local and global dynamics (Bathelt et al. 2004). Coe et al. (2004) describe this relationship through the concept of "strategic coupling." Trond Nilsen (2019) emphasizes the need to anchor the discussion of strategic coupling in how regions provide infrastructure to support global production networks.

The aim of this chapter is to conceptualize the interrelations between municipal governments, local governance schemes, GVCs, and citizen participation in Canada's gateway cities. GVCs require local anchors and government support to successfully connect and benefit from a city-region's physical assets and business activity. We look at urban governance schemes that support this type of international integration of various Canadian regional economies, before evaluating the openness of these schemes to citizen participation. We consider what scholars have had to say about GVCs, production networks and international trade, physical infrastructure assets, institutional arrangements, and local social concerns in framing the governance and development of projects related to GVCs. By putting such gateway regimes front and centre, we focus on governing coalitions composed of private and public actors, with consequential decision-making and resource-allocation powers. We conclude that executive democracy, rather than deliberative or participatory urban democracy, is the privileged mode of engagement with local citizenry on trade transportation-infrastructure matters in Canadian city-regions today.

Gateway cities are physical locations that benefit from the business of moving goods, services, and people. Geographers such as Andrew Burghardt (1971), James Bird (1983), and Peter Taylor (2004) have, since the 1970s, consistently made the argument that gateway cities are connection nodes linking societies to international markets. Burghardt (1971, 282) argues that "gateway cities develop in positions which possess the potentiality of controlling the flows of goods and people" across set production and distribution sectors. Works, such as one by P.J. Taylor (2004) and the edited book by Åke Andersson and David Andersson (2000), develop in-depth analyses of gateway cities and regions as connection points in globalization processes. In this view, the logistical importance of physical locations serving as communication, transportation, and distribution nodes is stressed. Kathy Pain (2008) also emphasizes different ways cities act as conduits of globalization.

The involvement of actors in GVCs/GPNs is structured through specific governance and related institutional arrangements that define their role in relation to others. Bob Jessop (1997, 18–19) defines governance as "the complex art of steering multiple agencies, institutions, and systems which are both operationally autonomous from one another and structurally coupled through various forms of reciprocal interdependence." Governance can serve to either complement or replace the limited formal power, or capacity, of state agencies, especially in support of economic projects involving international networks. As Jan Kooiman (2000, 145) explains, "Governance becomes an interactive process because no single actor has the knowledge or resource capacity to tackle problems unilaterally." Governments count on networks and partnerships to maintain flexible arrangements of governance. For Paul Hirst (2000, 18–19), "governance relates to the new practices of coordinating activities through networks, partnerships and deliberative forums." Focusing on these networks, partnerships, and forums is essential in a study of regional governance schemes. At the centre of many governance schemes are urban regimes and coalitions in which decisions occur between a plethora of public, private, and community stakeholders from different scales (Hirst 2000).

In this chapter, we look to the notion of urban regime as a helpful tool to grasp how constellations of actors seek connections with global economic flows via physical transportation hubs and trade networks. Viewed through the lens of urban regimes, the similarities and differences between various Canadian gateway cities in their adaptation to global requirements, strategic couplings, and local buy-ins can be understood.

Urban regimes are notably active in linking specific city-regions to GVCs/GPNs through their role in shaping local infrastructure projects and physical assets while managing gateways and trade corridors. As Stephen Blank (2008, 323) explains, trade corridors are "streams of products, services, and information moving within and through communities in geographic pattern." They are not just physical structures, as they include the "strategies to attract the increased flow of materials to particular areas." Trade corridors not only rely on complex decision-making processes but also involve myriad stakeholders at different levels, which explains the usefulness of the notion of urban regimes to fully understand the local governance scheme. As trade corridors necessitate a constant exchange between firms seeking to build greater efficiencies into production systems and between groups of local business and metropolitan government leaders offering solutions to help capture these efficiencies, urban regimes become a useful tool to understand and explain these interactions. They also provide a framework for understanding whether and how the input from community organizations is considered – hence the impact of local social concerns and issues on the formation of gateway economies. A focus on urban regimes in managing trade corridors allows us to bring out what is specific in each local economic and social context, thus adding to our understanding of policy changes, new institutional arrangements, and physical improvements to infrastructure and technology (Priemus and Zonneveld 2003; Rodrigue 2021; Fellows and Tombe 2018).

The framework we devised should provide a comprehensive conceptualization of gateway regimes specific to the "city model," or the configuration of stakeholders involved in a local coalition (including the centrality and leadership of some actors) and the norms they follow. More specifically, our framework should bring into view how this configuration uses city-regional governance arrangements (i.e., formal relationships between municipalities, regional bodies, and their province on specific topics like urban freight) to align local GVCs/GPNs plans with national goals and global economic requirements of trade promoters. This framework should prove useful for studies of urban regimes and coalitions. It enables us, as suggested by Alan Harding (1996, 647), to examine "how power is wielded within communities" and "to talk of the power of communities within wider spheres of influence." Such a contribution is all the more important since a comprehensive framework that situates decisions on projects supporting and expanding gateway and trade corridor infrastructure – that recognizes the local specificities (in terms of actors and their interactions) and the strategic coupling (as discussed by Nilsen 2019) – is still lacking in studies of gateway cities in the Canadian context.

City-Regions: Global Value Chains and Global Production Networks

The relationships between GVCs/GPNs and local economic growth have been well documented, with many studies highlighting the question of how to sustain local economies faced with increased fragmentation of production and extra-local interconnectivity between businesses (Amador and Cabral 2016; Molle 2002; Pietrobelli and Rabellotti 2006; Mudambi et al. 2018). Local knowledge and its connection to external sources of knowledge also impact the ways governance arrangements between firms are organized (Bathelt et al. 2004; Los et al. 2015; Gereffi et al. 2005; Iammarino 2011; Pietrobelli and Rabellotti 2006). In this section we discuss the contributions and debates at the intersection of city-regions and GVCs/GPNs, with a key focus on the interplay between regional governance and global networks, to situate the role of various urban stakeholders in decision-making processes pertaining to large infrastructure projects necessary to connect gateways cities and GVCs/GPNs.

Particular institutional arrangements shape the decision-making processes resulting in the selection, development, and implementation of infrastructure projects. In a study of multimodal transportation nodes across central and northern Canada, Rodrigue (2021) identifies opposition and governance issues to related infrastructure projects. Rodrigue's study brings to light the importance of city-regional features in understanding the links between local governance and global networks. A focus on urban regimes enables us to put into perspective the strategic decisions made by local and regional decision makers. As Ivan Turok (2009, 857) suggests, "The conceptualization of city-regions identifies potential divergences between local and regional interests, and a risk that the needs of individual localities may get overlooked with the shift to a larger spatial scale of planning, or larger strategies for globalization." The city-region level brings attention to the requirements for GVCs/GPNs and the needs of local communities.

As locales in which we find increasingly interconnected production systems, city-regions are built on transactional networks that include GVCs/GPNs. Johannes Glückler (2007) combines the notions of city-region, world-city, and global-city with discussions about agglomeration economies. By focusing on agglomeration economies, one can see how the knowledge and competencies generated in specific industries are linked to the physical infrastructure that supports such industries. This is notably seen through studies on global commodity chains, which enable peripheral places to develop economically and to profit from the economic activity elsewhere (Scholvin 2017).

GVCs/GPNs

GVCs have been theorized in the context of an increasing globalization of trade and a national fragmentation of economic activity (Gereffi 1999). Focusing on GVCs allows one to better understand the added value generated by different firms dispersed globally (Baldwin and Lopez-Gonzalez 2015; Benito et al. 2019; Kano 2018). Among the initial concerns are the role of firms in establishing GVC membership, the location and allocation of activities within the GVC, and the distribution of generated value added (Strange and Humphrey 2019). Firms coordinate economic activities through market and nonmarket relationships – including transfer and diffusion of knowledge leading to innovation and performance improvements (Humphrey and Schmitz 2002). However, such an understanding of governance underplays the interactions of many local stakeholders and coalitions of actors specific to the regional context.

As already mentioned, Henderson et al. (2002) critiqued the firm-centric implications of the GVC notion, hence our preference for the abbreviation GVCs/GPNs. Other authors have also sought to address these shortcomings. Marcelo Cano-Kollmann et al. (2016) draw attention to the current reality of GVCs/GPNs, where mobile (capital, labour) and immobile (locations, fixed assets) factors interact – hence the specific nature of the locations in which the activities of firms and people affect the processes of knowledge creation. This perspective echoes Mitchell Koza and Arie Lewin's (1998) study of the co-evolutionary nature of firm-environment relationships, shaping the development of strategic alliances for industries to navigate the constraints of the local environment.

Even though focusing on GVCs puts the attention on significant interactions and activities in determining the decision-making process, Henderson et al. (2002) note that it downplays the role of government, transportation infrastructure, and the involvement of stakeholders such as government officials and local community associations. Rafael Corredoira and Gerald McDermott (2014) have also noted this drawback, considering the importance of strong ties between the private sector and local public organizations in GVCs/GPNs.

Traditionally recognized factors such as distance, geographical barriers, and transport infrastructure are crucial for the economic interaction within GVCs/GPNs (Scholvin 2017, 128). Rodrigue (2021, 8–9) defines transportation infrastructure as "the fixed element of the transportation system that supports the mobility of vehicles and conveyances. This element also includes superstructures that are moveable assets required for the infrastructure to function." Specific to Hong Kong, James Wang and Michael Cheng (2010) report on a three-level hierarchical supply-chain framework – business, gateway, and institutional levels. They indicate that government plays an essential role for regions to participate in GVCs/GPNs through funding and operational or advisory support. In Canada's case, we see that different levels of government play a key role in the conceptualization, development, and implementation of future infrastructure arrangements.

This being said, two caveats are in order here: First, the "restricted ability of states" does extend beyond tariffs and local content rules since integrative trade calls for the involvement of urban and local governments, which in turn may lead to the implementation of innovative forms of collaboration between the three levels of government (Sturgeon 2008, 6). One reason for this is that integrative trade and its GVCs/GPNs call for massive public investments in, for example, port and airport facilities, transportation, technology and logistics services, and artificial intelligence (AI) – investments that are directed at cities or city-regions as nodes or hubs in value chains.

Second, if the idea of a "shift in focus from the state to the actors" (see, for example, Hamel and Keil 2017; Rodrik 2007) applies to higher tiers of governments at both federal and provincial levels, this does not imply that private actors in a GVC/GPN do not call upon and rely on some form of refocusing on the part of governments at the urban and municipal levels. In other words, private actors' governance schemes do not and cannot operate in a watertight environment. Just as they rely on public-private governance schemes established upstream to liberalize the national economy and provide investments in transport infrastructure, they must also rely on governance schemes downstream to put into practice or to apply the ongoing liberalizing process at regional and city levels. But there are important differences between these two processes: while the former involves federal and provincial authorities called upon to redraw rules and regulations in collaboration with private actors and other experts, the latter process involves urban and municipal authorities called upon to produce deliverables and come up with practical decisions and solutions facilitating GVC/GPN operations at the city level.

Then, even if the integrative commerce strategy involves firm-to-firm cooperation or, better still, firm-to-firm coopetition as well as urban policy involvement, this should not lead to the conclusion that governments are dominant. If policy makers in national and provincial governments are incapable or unwilling to make trade-offs, policy makers at other levels – notably in urban or regional governments – are actively involved in such activities. In the absence of explicit federal or even state government leadership, David Wachsmuth (2017, 44) identifies how "new multi-city growth coalitions are currently emerging across the United States, united by a shared interest in supply-chain expansion – the extension of effective supply chains and the intensification of circulatory possibilities in regional transportation networks."

To understand how this has come to be, but also to differentiate the Canadian experience from that of the United States and other countries, we underline that governance is but one of the four key structures that shape GVCs/GPNs, the other three being input-output of goods and services, geography, and institutions (Gereffi 1995; Eckhardt and Poletti 2018). This last concept is key as it is the only structure that connects value chains to external actors, demands, and factors. This is the reason we are concerned with the initiatives that local and urban governments have resorted to, to address GVCs/GPNs and mitigate their impact on the region – initiatives that call for the setting up of an altogether distinct and different governance scheme. This framework has little to do with the one set up among firms in value chains precisely because it incorporates objectives and concerns that are external to value chains. Moreover, this "other" framework must contend with two sets of externalities: economic fallout on the one side and political and social acceptance on the other. What remains to be seen in this context is how the intrafirm and interfirm governance schemes within value chains manage their reliance on external factors – those coming out of higher governments with their norms and rules, as well as those coming out of governance frameworks set up at the urban or local levels.

Urban-Regional Government and Governance

The rise of GVCs/GPNs brought a shift of power from states to multinational firms that was accompanied by a rise in the importance of various levels of governments in governance schemes that entail a diffusion of power from governments to nonstate actors. Roderick Rhodes (1996, 652–53) defines governance as "a change in the meaning of government, referring to a new process of governing; or a changed condition of ordered rule; or the new method by which society is governed." Margit Mayer (2017, 170) underlines that the focus of urban policy making has moved away from citizens' well-being and preoccupations and toward the concerns and interests of private sector actors and that "four dimensions in particular can be distilled as characteristic features of contemporary neoliberal urbanism: growth first; entrepreneurial forms of governance; privatization; tools to deal with intensified polarization."

One explanation for this alignment was provided by Dani Rodrik (2007) with his idea of the "inescapable trilemma of the world economy." The trilemma in question poses that national sovereignty, global economic integration, and democracy cannot be pursued concurrently by state authorities. Consequently, one must choose to either relinquish global integration to shelter democracy or to do away with the latter to pursue the former. But the trilemma in question poses alternatives in a manner much too stark. In reality, what we end up with at the urban or municipal levels is not a shelving of democracy pure and simple but the resort to a minimal variant of democracy and democratic practices known as the executive democracy or a democratic regime less attuned to citizen perspectives on major economic projects and more in line with global economic requirements (Deblock and Brunelle 1998). In other words, a policy based on the development of GVCs/GPNs requires a downplaying of indirect or electoral or representative democracy in favour of a more selective, executive form of democracy. In this regard, seen from the eyes of both elected officials and citizens' organizations, a policy based on the development of GVCs/GPNs does indeed bring about what is known as a democratic deficit.[1]

Governance schemes are embraced by some actors because they are flexible, adaptable, and equipped to tackle changing circumstances quickly and efficiently. Global economic integration, notably through the extension of a GVC/GPN framework, therefore tends to bypass if not shun the electoral process and extend civil society participation in favour of selective social stakeholders' participation. According to Pierre Hamel and Roger Keil (2017), when social and private as well as public stakeholders are involved, a governance scheme provides for a form of deliberative democracy that either complements or replaces the guidelines and instructions coming out of an electoral democracy. Regardless, the questions concerning the respective merits and demerits of each is left in abeyance.

Governance schemes are well-fitted to an approach in which urban policy agendas are shaped by dominant urban regimes, or coalitions, that emerge from institutional, formal, and informal arrangements where actors with complementary strengths and resources work to achieve specific policy goals (Mossberger and Stoker 2001, 829). Focusing on urban regimes enhances the study of urban governance schemes as they place their negotiating capabilities and deliverables at the forefront.

This approach is all the more interesting for our own research agenda since, in Montreal, Toronto, Vancouver, and Halifax, issues concerning the impact of value chains on city-regional development are not dealt with publicly in a municipal council, nor are they debated in electoral platforms; instead, they are entrusted to committees or governance schemes that bring together a wide array of stakeholders involved in different sectors of activities far removed from the concerns of local populations.

What does this mean in practical terms? In the four gateway cities, pro-GVC/GPN coalitions have sought to influence and make alliance with independent government agencies and the private sector rather than with representatives of urban governments. At the local level, cities and city-regions might not be particularly proactive in this regard and may wait for governments to come forward before making any substantial normative adjustment or investments in infrastructure. However, other actors are prone to step up to the challenge and take action. This is precisely what actors in the transportation and logistics sectors do, most notably port and airport authorities and terminal operators, shipping and railroad companies, and trucking associations, as well as experts in these fields. In conjunction with other actors such as chambers of commerce and boards of trade, these transportation and logistics stakeholders also engage with other economic and social stakeholders at all levels, including the international – all of it well outside the purview of city halls. And when they reach out to forge alliances with, and secure resources from, governments, they turn to their provincial government, who is responsible for highway development, and to the federal government, who is responsible for both interprovincial infrastructure and external trade.

In Chapters 4 to 7, we examine what governance schemes are set up in each Canadian city under study and which set of actors and stakeholders are called upon to participate in these schemes.

INSTITUTIONAL ARRANGEMENTS

Francesco Duina's (2006) study on the social dimension of free trade agreements (FTAs) and market building offers a most stimulating contribution to an analysis of institutional arrangements of GVCs/GPNs at the local level. The following quote presents his starting premise:

> The pursuit of free trade in any given region is a *social* endeavor. Much like national market building, it occurs in the midst of rich institutional and political contexts ... The evidence presented in the next chapters has direct implications for three topics of much current debate: globalization, the nature of markets, and the spread of neoliberalism. First, contrary to the fashionable claims of globalization theorists, the local still matters. Enduring differences across geographies still shape social life. Second, despite the belief that most economists hold about the spontaneous rise and functioning of markets, we see that social actors make markets in specific contexts. Third, the spread of neoliberalism at the end of the twentieth century was not, as most observers have assumed, a homogenous affair across the globe. (3–4)

Applied to our study, the local that "matters" is neither the regional nor the national but the urban, and market building at the city level will rely on a different set of social actors with different cultures in each case. Duina (2006) concludes by rejecting two broad interpretations. First, contrary to what many global studies proclaim, neoliberalism "does not lead to greater uniformity in terms of policies and outcomes ... only in some cases... does the pursuit of free trade lead to the harmonization of environmental regulations." Second, scholars who maintain that neoliberalism has not been uniformly implemented "present evidence from *nation states*" (201).

There are at least three ideas worth picking up here. The first is a mere extension of Duina's (2006, 197) approach: "The world is experiencing the pull of three competing forces: the global, the regional, and the national. Any thorough analysis of current events requires that we investigate closely each of these forces and how they relate to each other." In fact, we are out to demonstrate that a fourth competing force operates at the urban level that could very well play a determining role in the new order of affairs. We could even go further and add that the force in question is probably made up of a different mix of private, private-public, and public interests (urban authorities, investors, land speculators, transport associations, port, airport, etc.) rather than both public and private interests in the classic sense of the expression. The second statement is about market building as a social process that is developed in four stages:

> The book shows that regional market building is – much like national market building, if not more – a *social* project. This is so for a number of reasons. First, RTAs [regional trade agreements] constitute planned

> and explicit efforts to create a market space. In that regard, they are imagined and willed by a collective set of actors, often with a model of an ideal RTA in mind. Second, officials actively engage in the crafting of RTAs: regional markets do not "just happen"; on the contrary, thousands of concrete steps such as the making of laws are taken to create those markets. Third, institutional, political, and many other forces guide and influence the process of crafting markets. Fourth, markets stimulate and depend upon the participation of various societal players (economic, political, administrative) to function. Importantly, not everyone is "invited to play." (Duina 2006, 198–99)

And further:

> Market building is a remarkably different endeavor in different geographies ... There exists no single blueprint for market building: markets require supporting structures and the participation of actors, but those needs can clearly be met in a variety of ways [which underlines] the importance of institutional and political factors – and ultimately *continuity* with local conditions – in shaping regional markets efforts. (Duina 2006, 199)

That is, if FTAs or RTAs play an important role in market building, and if the intervention of social actors with their institutions contributes to the social construction of these markets, then this is even more true at the gateway-city level. In this regard, we could further explore the socio-political dimensions of market building in a larger context and incorporate the theses proposed by authors Mark Granovetter (1985) and Henri Lefebvre (1974).

In his numerous contributions to the field of economic sociology, Granovetter (1985) took to task the reductionist approach to markets and the solipsistic definition of *homo economicus* propounded by mainstream economics. Timothy Sturgeon (2008, 12) underlines that "his view is that economic activity is embedded in social relationships, not the other way around, and that trust and even goodwill can and often does build up in the inter-personal relationships that inevitably underlie inter-firm relations." This insight allows us to research how governance schemes are embedded in social relations at the local or urban levels.

Lefebvre's (1974) idea of the emergence of a capitalist system and an "urban society" in which industrialization and urbanization are tightly interwoven in a dialectical process that establishes the crisis of the city as a specifically "political" problem is helpful here.[2] Exchanges of equivalents and contract negotiations in a market economy based on the profit motive stimulate the "implosion-explosion" of the city, with its multiple segregations and its constant creative destruction, instead of contributing to the establishment of an "urban society." In Lefebvre's (1974, 18, 89, 109–22) view, both state and firms work in tandem to absorb and suppress the urban – the former from above, the latter from below – and only the claim of a "right to the city" as a right to an urban life can counter the forces of division and segregation.

Urban Regimes

Oren Yiftachel (2015, 733–34) defines "regime" as "a set of long-term rules, institutions, identities, power relations, practices and discourses that shapes the structures of a particular society, such as the city" and urban regime to "frame, contain and regulate the merging and clashes of power emanating from a wide spectrum of economic and identity players."

Urban regimes are considered political coalitions (Dowding 2001) that cross jurisdictional boundaries. Urban regimes include stakeholders at different scales (i.e., local, regional, national, and global), pushing for projects that affect a specific locale but in ways that insert it in broader regional, national, and global networks. Clarence Stone (2001, 21) briefly defines them as "the set of arrangements through which a community is governed." Such urban regimes in Canada involve all levels of governments, which have their own goals, agencies, and assets with which to structure city-regions.

According to Keith Dowding et al. (1999), Dowding (2001), Stone (2001), and Oren Levin-Waldman (2005, 75), the key elements of an urban regime include:

- An identifying agenda – arrangements adhere to some set of recognized purpose.
  - Arrangements that are relatively stable and survive personnel and leadership changes or political successions, reflecting agreement over fundamental values for members of the coalition.
  - Arrangements that have a cross-sector foundation, a foundation that is embodied in a governing coalition.
  - Arrangements that are informal and tend to bridge institutions and community interests by creating "partnership" forms, spanning the public-private-sector divide.[3]

- Arrangements that have a productive character and are associated with strong or exceptional leadership capable of entrepreneurially assembling an unusual coalition and linking it with a distinctive political vision.

- The ability to provide "incentive" or payoffs to coalition members to keep them engaged.

The fact that urban regimes in urban decision making constitute a form of governance that exists outside democratically elected government, are able to survive electoral changes in power, and seldom include civil society concerns raises questions about the role of local state actors. From these definitions, it is clear that a diverse set of stakeholders, including business leaders, government officials, and other organizations and individuals, is central to the formation and maintenance of urban regimes (de Socio 2010). According to Stone (1993, 2), urban regimes are shaped by three factors: the composition of a community's governing coalition, the nature of the members governing the coalition, and the resources the members bring to the governing coalition. This contribution is of particular importance to our study since conceptualizing urban regimes as social and interorganizational networks places regimes within a wider context of economic and social relations. Business leaders tend to occupy privileged positions in regime coalitions due to the scope of resources and expertise they command for economic development (Dowding 2001; Stone and Sanders 1987).

Ismael Blanco (2015, 123) emphasizes the significance of collaboration between governmental and nongovernmental actors in the making of urban public policies. He also emphasizes that local policy making "increasingly involves multi-agency working, partnership, and policy networks that cut across organizational boundaries." According to Blanco (2015, 24), metagovernance is "a response to the problematic relationship between governance networks and democracy, placing the responsibility of the 'democratic anchorage' of governance networks on state institutions." As such, Blanco (2015, 125) builds on Gerry Stoker (2004) to argue that network community governance allows for greater effectiveness in tackling the complex problems of cities through cross-sectoral and multilevel networks. However, he emphasizes the persistence and intensity of power asymmetries and contends that hierarchy remains dominant.

Blanco (2015) provides examples of urban governance to tackle challenges related to education that city officials could not have solved alone.

He mentions the case of Barcelona as an example, where several public policies in different districts and in different policy areas are currently articulated through different types of network governance arrangements that bring together different coalitions of actors. Patterns of (formal and informal) relationships between government and nongovernmental actors significantly vary across cases. Networks, as recognized by Keith Provan and Patrick Kenis (2008, 128), can "adopt very different forms, respond to very different purposes, and encompass very different types of actors, mobilizing different configurations of resources."

TOWARD AN ANALYTICAL FRAMEWORK ON GATEWAY REGIMES

Drawing on Duina (2006), Granovetter (1985), Lefebvre (1974), Blanco (2015), and others, we arrive at the perspective that urban regime members seeking to build durable (trade-enabling) markets and governance schemes rely on, and are embedded in, local relationships that work out and deliver what is demanded of them by GVCs/GPNs. They do so while seeking to set some distance between their schemes and urban democracy. This general proposition seems especially appropriate when we consider the delivery of trade-enabling transportation infrastructure in gateway cities, since such investments by their nature look to serve users outside the local body politic.

Some scholars who have studied gateway cities integrate local policy interventions and the democratic process in the development of gateway cities and trade corridors (e.g., Evans and Hutchins 2002). The internationalization of economics and politics has forced local governments to develop new context-appropriate strategies (Yáñez et al. 2008; Kennedy et al. 2005). These strategies are characterized by a greater degree of interaction with nongovernmental key actors and, with the business world in particular, constitute local or urban governance. Martin Dijst and Walter Schenkel (2002) suggest that urban governance might become more effective through such policy networks, whereby hierarchical authority is replaced with a constellation of loosely connected political, economic, and social actors. They argue that urban policies often cannot influence urban performance directly but become effective only through an understanding of the relations between processes in urban society, the behaviour of actors, and the development of urban form. "Networking and negotiation between a variety of actors in urban development are now recognized as an important complement of, or even as a substitute for, regulatory measures by local or regional governments" (299).

Our framework presents urban regimes and their coalitions in order to differentiate "city models." We do so by building on the work of Andersson and Andersson (2000, 4) regarding the main functions of gateways, which might serve as specific hubs, source nodes, sink nodes, and saddle nodes within a regional hierarchical network of actors – who benefit from, and are directly impacted by, an increase in transit and mobility activity. As well, we build on the different forms of urban governance and coalitions and briefly signal their intersections with urban democracy practices. Whereas source nodes reflect production diffused outward and sink nodes speak to production consumed within a city-region, saddle nodes refer to the movement of goods through the region. In this way, the combination of these functions within a city-region will necessarily impact the urban coalitions and governance schemes put in place.

Positioning a city-region in GVCs requires the implementation of several actions. They aim to build the city's attractiveness in terms of the accumulation of knowledge so as to engage in the development of technologies and industry sectors necessary to enact productivity processes from business and to contribute to the growth and relevance of the city-region in the global context. In addition, physical and communications infrastructures play a crucial role, since trade between countries has increased and intermediary trade drives a major part of this growth. Therefore, city-regions require the design, implementation, and regulation of large infrastructure projects that contribute to their engagement in GVCs/GPNs.

Governments contribute to the implementation of many of the large infrastructure projects either by engaging across all the different steps – namely definition, funding, implementation, and regulation – or by defining specific guidelines and priorities for funding. For example, in the case of Canada, the different rounds of funding for the Asia-Pacific Gateway and Corridor Initiative (APGCI) (2006), Gateway and Border Crossing Fund (GBCF) (2009), and National Trade Corridors Fund (NTCF) (2017, 2019) focus on specific strategies that aim to position city-regions within the global context and to contribute to the interconnectedness within Canada (and North America) via trade corridors.

Figure 2.1 provides a conceptual framework to explain how the governance of city-regions, through various forms of urban democratic practices and sites, shapes their positioning in GVCs while emphasizing a multilevel and cross-sectoral approach. Special attention was given to urban regimes and the need to include different types of stakeholders in any decision-making process.

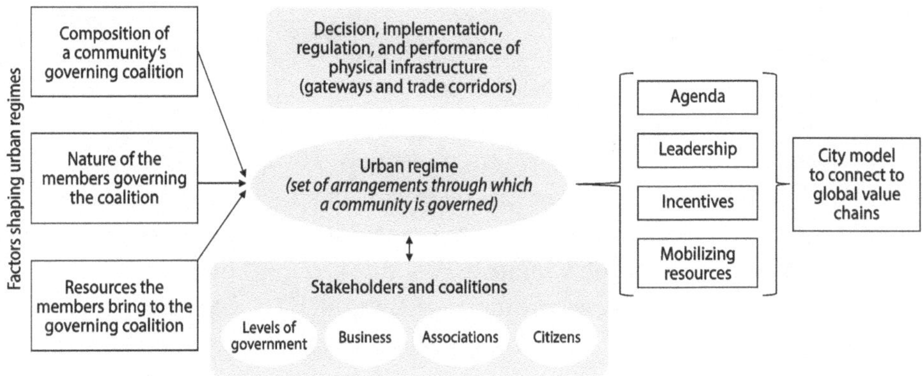

FIGURE 2.1 Framework, gateway regimes | *Sources:* Adapted from Brunelle et al. (2021), Evans and Hutchins (2002), While et al. (2004).

Our framework unpacks the institutional arrangements between private and public stakeholders that are context specific and respond to a set of complementary, but often conflicting, objectives. It emphasizes those market factors and governance factors that influence the formation of urban regimes and coalitions essential to the process of conceptualizing, developing, and implementing gateways and trade corridors that connect city-regions with GVCs/GPNs.

In line with contributions by Clemente Yáñez et al. (2008), we argue that the framework proposed explains the processes of governance and the processes of how and why coalitions are formed at the local level. We point out that the proposed framework must remain flexible and adaptable to be used to understand the complex fabric between global connectivity and the local specificities of city-regions – the specificities of the processes of governance, urban regimes, and coalitions.

Depending on the specificities of city-regions and their links to globalization and engagement in GVCs/GPNs, the views of stakeholders seeking to foster economic growth via participation in global trade and the engagement in GVCs/GPNs might widely differ from the views of stakeholders who are proponents of promoting sovereignty in the city-region.

CONCLUDING REMARKS

The four Canadian gateway cities under study are at the crossroads between what urban regime theorists characterize as an old phase, or model, of city structure and a new one (Short and Kim 1999, 117). They retain their "ordinary" connections to the hinterland economies that grew up with them (Cronon 1991; Robinson 2013), typified in flows of commuters and the local service-seeking migrations of students, patients, and vacationers and flows of perishable goods, water, and waste. Especially in the Canadian case, these local service hinterlands can be geographically expansive and were historically tied to the resource-processing and resource-exporting economies. These resource-export connections have never disappeared. However, two broad changes can be noted: the emergence of de facto city-states increasingly separated from their national economies and the creation of city-to-city connections across international boundaries. Recall that, in political terms, according to Veltz (2000), globalization forces are pulling cities away from the national economy and connecting them to the forces of globalization (or reglobalization, as the case may be). For Canadian city-regions, globalization has implied a complex mix of (re)engagement with established European and North American partners and increasing connections with various Asian partners (Norcliffe 2001).

The evolution of the city model in the four gateway cities discussed in this book reaches beyond questions of transportation intermodality and the multiple connections between the cities and their (provincial) hinterlands; it touches on the postindustrial vocation of the city itself, including a repositioning in the global knowledge economy and other high value activities in the service sector. Movement away from the Keynesian to the entrepreneurial state at both national and local levels has led to the negotiation of new compromises between political globalization and urban regimes. These forces have played and will continue to play themselves out in different ways in the four gateway cities for at least three reasons. First, each city's postindustrial – and industrial – basis is still regional, and its political economy is very much provincially oriented – if not determined – while its interplay with federal strategies is intermittent. Second, each city's role as gateway is subject to divergent and competing forces. And third, each city-region's political processes are highly fragmented. Gateway cities as economic transition zones (or economic transitional spaces) are becoming as important as the nation-state, but in the Canadian case, gateway cities have yet to acquire much leeway in facing the competing demands and expectations from either of the higher levels of government.

The notion of gateway regimes has allowed us to probe the relationship between cities (read: situated coalitions) and the global economy in a federal context where two competing political economies and social identities – pan-Canadian and regional/provincial – are at play, thus providing a different take on "the local and national political differences that are capable of exerting significant influence on the way globalization affects city development" (Leo 1997, 78). Exploring this dualism sheds light on the contradictory forces at play in the ongoing transformation of Canadian gateway cities as "urban societies" (Lefebvre 1974). In the Canadian context, urban regimes are "the formal and informal arrangements by which public bodies and private interests function together to be able to make and carry out governing decisions" (Stone 1989, 6) in conformity or not with the democratic institutions and processes sanctioned at the urban level.

Finally, considering that the Canadian government implemented its integrative commerce strategy as recently as 2007 to counteract effects of the ongoing financial crisis in the US at the time – and considering the highly nationalistic commercial policies applied by successive US administrations since 2016 – we find ourselves in an interesting situation. Canadian authorities have chosen to further globalize their city-regions without compromising the continental (read: United States) connection. Since this option is surely bound to impact governance schemes and new urban regimes "as products of complex struggles in networked and hierarchical interrelations among often entirely antagonistic actors" – as well as social market building at the urban level – our own study should provide another interpretation of a "post-neo-liberal regional governance regime" (Keil 2011; Keil et al. 2016, 9).

3

A History of the Federal Government's Approach to Gateways and Trade Corridors

The Confederation of Canada was explicitly designed to unite and connect the British colonies and territories of North America in support of one global trading empire after the United States suspended trade with the colonies at the conclusion of its civil war. As such, the confederation of disparate colonies was set up to engage in interprovincial and international trade and to provide the necessary transportation infrastructures. Local governments were relegated to a minor status in this governmental scheme. The relationship between federal and provincial governments has thus been understood as the defining feature of Canadian government since Confederation. However, that the national project of global trade integration depends first and foremost on city-regions has long been recognized in federal spending patterns, if not in formal policy. And cities, understood both as local governments representative of residents and as urban regimes operating within local governance schemes, have sought to insert themselves into the economic goals and infrastructure spending priorities of the federal government. In this chapter, we trace how federal economic and transport policy stances have converged over the past decades, and especially since the beginning of the millennium, in a trade-enabling vision of urban infrastructure investment.

Three milestones in the evolution of Canada's economic policy over the past 150 years or so can be traced through the tabling of three major royal commission reports (Brunelle 1997). Although social, financial, and other urban problems figured prominently in all three reports, cities were ignored in the first one, their financial predicaments and those of municipalities were the only focus of the second, while the third report did recognize that economic development increasingly depended on cities and local governments. However, another relevant aspect to these concerns over cities and local governments on the part of the two more recent royal commissions is the impact, direct or indirect, of their recommendations on intergovernmental transfers – not only from the federal to provincial governments but, more significantly, from the federal to municipal governments. In constitutional terms, this is known as the federal government's "power to spend" (Gauthier 2019).

We briefly present the three reports in question (Royal Commission on the Relations of Labor and Capital in Canada 1889; Royal Commission on Dominion-Provincial Relations 1940; Royal Commission on the Economic Union and Development Prospects for Canada 1985) as well as that of the Royal Commission on Transportation of 1961 to bring out the convergence between economic, urban, and transportation policies that occurred over previous decades in the federal government's approach to gateways and trade corridors.

The Royal Commission on the Relations of Labor and Capital (Freed and Armstrong Reports 1889) was set up some twenty-five years into Canada's second industrial revolution.[1] It deserves mentioning in the present context for two incidental reasons: One, because the commissioners shunned all form of government intervention on working hours, wages, or rent control and supported laissez-faire capitalism in the country, despite the prevalence of inadequate sanitary and safety working conditions in factories and mines, the reliance on child labour, and the exploitation of women in the labour force. Two, because the commission was set up on subjects that clearly came under provincial or municipal, or both, jurisdictions, which illustrates the early spillover effect of local economic and social issues at the federal level.[2]

Roughly fifty years later, the Royal Commission on Dominion-Provincial Relations – known as the Rowell-Sirois Commission – was set up at the height of the economic crisis of the 1930s. In its report, tabled in 1940, the commissioners proposed to relinquish laissez-faire and embrace Keynesian economics.[3] They recommended that Canada's political economy should be reorientated toward nation building through the import substitution strategy. To this end, the federal government would assume full responsibility for the provinces' debt and, in the case of Quebec, because its debt was low, for part of the municipal debt. However, as the federal-provincial conference of January 1941 would not come to an agreement on the commission's recommendations, Prime Minister Mackenzie King took the lead to secure a constitutional amendment transferring jurisdiction over unemployment to the federal level.[4]

The third commission, the Royal Commission on the Economic Union and Development Prospects for Canada – also known as the Macdonald Commission – tabled its report in 1985. In it, the commissioners took to task the political economy applied at the time, and criticized Keynes, "whose theories were written with a unitary-state model in mind [and] dealt primarily with the theory of a closed economy which neither traded nor engaged in capital-market transactions with the outside world; it indicated, to oversimplify, that contra-cyclical budgeting could level out aggregate demand and maintain full employment" (RCEUDPC 1985, vol. 1, 45). This approach was deemed particularly ill-suited for a federal system operating in an open economy. Henceforth, "the need for internal adjustments varies directly with the degree of integration in the world economy. The attainment of a necessary economic adaptability is hindered by domestic political forces and economic interests which resist changes demanded by increasing foreign competition" (RCEUDPC 1985, vol. 1, 30).

Entrusted with the mandate of stimulating the "economic union" of a federation hampered by its provinces' divergent claims,[5] and by Quebec nationalism in particular, and with an eye on the recently adopted Canadian Charter of Rights and Freedoms (1982), the report came up with three options. The first option was the status quo, which meant the continuation of the politics of import substitution – a path, the commissioners asserted, that would inevitably lead to the imposition of a planned economy. The second was trade liberalization under the auspices of the General Agreement on Tariffs and Trade – an option fraught with uncertainty that would require an extended amount of time. The third, which was the commissioners' main recommendation, was the negotiation of a bilateral free trade agreement with the US (RCEUDPC 1985, vol. 3, 271).[6]

This represented a fundamental policy change (Brunelle 2007), even a "paradigm shift" (McBride 2005),[7] since it meant that open markets and commercial policy should occupy the high ground in the government's political economy – a shift in priorities that was advocated and prescribed by the major international financial institutions at the time, notably the World Bank, the International Monetary Fund, and the Organisation for Economic Co-operation and Development (OECD).[8] Although neither municipal governments nor cities are mentioned in the Order-in-Council creating the commission, the commissioners were well aware of the negative consequences of the fiscal imbalance under which local governments operated in the federation. The report's ultimate chapter 24 on "unresolved problems" carries a most timely section on municipalities, to which we turn in due course.[9] Even if they were considered separate to begin with, political economy and urban affairs gradually converged and eventually represented the obverse of the government's gateway and trade corridor approach – a shift closely tied to the importance of infrastructure spending. It is therefore the main objective of this chapter to establish as close a link as possible between this new political economy, urban policy, transportation, and the evolution of the federal government's involvement with cities from the 1980s to 2006 and from 2006 onward. We analyze the impact of such initiatives on the formal and informal relations between and within the levels of government.

A HISTORICAL CONTEXTUALIZATION OF THE FEDERAL APPROACH

Political Economy

At the beginning of the 1980s, in line with Prime Minister Thatcher's and President Reagan's neoconservative agendas, the major advanced economies set aside nation building as a priority and sought to open and expand their markets. After signing its first free trade agreement with the US in 1989, Canada joined negotiations with Mexico and signed the North American Free Trade Agreement (NAFTA) in 1994. Even though the government negotiated other free trade agreements (FTAs) and numerous foreign-investment promotion and protection agreements with other partners, integration with its neighbour's economy grew inexorably, reaching 87 percent of its total trade in 2000. In other words, as far as Canada was concerned, the opening of its economy basically served to accelerate and deepen its continental integration with the US economy (Brunelle 2006).

But in 2001, two events in succession had a profound effect on the Canadian political economy outlook. The first was the terrorist attacks of September 11 on the World Trade Center and the Pentagon, while the second, on December 11, marked the entry of the People's Republic of China into the World Trade Organization (WTO).

In the aftermath of the terrorist attacks, President George W. Bush invoked security concerns to abruptly close the US's northern and southern borders, thus interrupting the north-south flow of goods. This decision had dire effects on the Quebec and Ontario economies in particular, where tighter border controls caused significant delays that were borne by exporting firms, especially smaller exporters, who could not take advantage of the smart border programs as readily as larger ones.[10]

The other important event, China's entry into the WTO, opened what some have called a "tectonic shift" (Lehmann 2012) within the world economy, whereby commerce with China and other countries of the eastern Pacific quickly overtook exchanges between countries of the Atlantic community. In the short span of ten years, between 2001 and 2011, China became a major trading partner for most of the larger economies of the world – in the Americas, Europe, Africa, and Asia.[11]

The events of 2001 were followed by disruptions from the financial crisis of 2007–08, when the US government devised ambitious assistance plans to facilitate the recovery of its economy. However, Canadian and Mexican firms were barred from submitting tenders for public works financed under the Buy American Act and Buy America requirements, against NAFTA's principles and provisions.

These episodes had an important cumulative impact on Canada's political economy outlook. On the internal front, taking heed of the economic globalization in progress – notably the pace of economic growth in countries in Asia – the government revised its commercial strategy. This led to a reappraisal of the export promotion strategy that had been adopted in 1985, as well as its revision and eventual replacement by the integrative commerce or integrative trade strategy of the Conservative government in 2007.[12]

On the external front, the government restored its multilateral strategy and launched a series of commercial negotiations to offset the sclerotic pace of global negotiations (WTO, Doha Round) and to counterbalance its economic dependence on the US market, starting with the Asia-Pacific Economic Cooperation (1989). After the failure of Free Trade Area of the Americas project (1994–2005), the government secured FTAs with twenty countries in the Americas in succession, the European Union (EU) in 2009, Morocco in 2011, and numerous others in Asia.[13] Finally, and most significantly, both the reappraisal and strategy were pursued without impairing commercial or political relations with the US in any way.[14]

Urban Policy

The British North America Act of 1867 established that municipalities fall under provincial jurisdiction,[15] but this reality never prevented – indeed could not prevent – the federal government and many of its agencies and corporations from having an impact on urban development, directly or indirectly. One need only mention the Canada Mortgage and Housing Corporation (1946), the port and airport authorities, policies on immigration and commerce, and investments in transport infrastructure, among many others (Graham and Andrew 2014). In fact, the federal government never shied from its role as a "promoter of globalization" by "subsidizing infrastructure investments designed to support a world's fair or Olympic bid, [enhancing] the position of its international cities through which trade is organized – particularly Montreal, Calgary, and Vancouver – at the expense of other urban areas" (Clarkson 2000).

On the other hand, municipalities and their quest to secure a measure of financial autonomy have been a recurring theme for at least half a century. In a brief presentation to the Special Joint Committee of the Senate and the House of Commons on the Constitution back in 1971, the Joint Municipal Committee on Intergovernmental Relations – set up for the occasion by the Canadian Federation of Mayors and Municipalities – "proposed that federal-provincial conferences should become trilateral meetings" (Tolley and Young 2001). The same year, a Ministry of State for Urban Affairs (MSUA) was created with an ambitious but vague mandate and little funding (Tolley and Young 2001).[16] It was subsequently abolished in 1979 due to the provinces' lack of participation in trilateral meetings and their constant opposition to federal meddling in municipal affairs.[17]

Although its mandate did not mention municipalities – an understandable omission given the failure of MSUA – the Macdonald Commission dedicated a section of its chapter 24 to the subject.[18] Summing up their findings, the commissioners advanced four proposals. One was to give local governments explicit constitutional status as a distinct order of government, with clearly defined powers and responsibilities – an idea that had been repeatedly set aside by many observers as it would only inject more complexity and rigidity in the system. Another was setting up trilevel conferences. A third was the improvement of intergovernmental relations through the (re)creation of a federal MSUA.[19] Finally, "an alternative to the creation of a new ministry might be the use of parliamentary processes to anticipate and to monitor the effect of federal measures on local administration" (RCEUDPC 1985, vol. 3, 376–79).

Even though the commissioners stated that "local governments, more than federal or provincial governments, are aware of urban issues and better able to deal with them [and] that in general, local governments can most effectively establish and carry out urban policy" (RCEUDPC 1985, vol. 3, 382–83), their sole recommendation on the matter was decidedly vague: "Recommendation: Although Commissioners do not recommend changing the constitutional status of local governments, the federal and provincial governments should increase the involvement and responsibility of local authorities. The federal government should review with the provinces the possibility of occasional trilevel conferences" (RCEUDPC 1985, vol. 3, 407).

During the subsequent Mulroney years (1984–93), the political debate on the status of local government waned, notably due to the priority given to, and ultimate failure of, getting Quebec to sign onto the Constitution of 1982 (Meech Accord 1987; Charlottetown Accord 1992). The federal government's cooperation with municipalities only picked up again with the Liberals' return to power in 1993 and with the adoption of a job creation initiative known as the Canada Infrastructure Works Program (CIWP) the following year. The program is noteworthy for two reasons. First, it introduced the concept of "collaborative arrangements,"[20] defined as "agreements between levels of government and, on occasion, the voluntary and private sectors, to share power, responsibilities, and costs in designing and providing services" (PACC 1999); and second, it involved significant funding. In the words of the Public Accounts Canada (PACC) Committee Report on its phases I and II, the program represented

> a major example of a collaborative arrangement [between] ... three levels of government – federal, provincial, and municipal – in an effort intended to boost employment and maintain and develop local infrastructure. The federal government was responsible for approving joint funding for projects proposed by the provinces. Provincial governments assumed responsibility for day-to-day operations and program delivery ... By the time the Program ended, in March 1999, the three levels of government had spent in excess of $8.3 billion. The federal government's contribution amounted to $2.4 billion. (PACC 1999)[21]

As Caroline Andrew and Jeff Morrison (1995, 133) wrote, "The program provide[d] funding to municipalities for water, sewer, and transportation projects, as well as for construction or improvement of community facilities and other special projects." One of the salient features of the program was that it operated in an atmosphere of notable intergovernmental harmony at all three levels.

Further actions were taken on infrastructure financing at the turn of the millennium at the instigation of Jean Chrétien's government. In October 1999, in the Speech from the Throne, the government outlined a plan to replace the CIWP with a new entity called Infrastructure Canada, with an allocated budget of $2.65 billion spread over six years "for the renewal of municipal and strategic highway infrastructure across Canada"

(Government of Canada 2000). The government then created four infrastructure and two complementary funds administered by the Federation of Canadian Municipalities (FCM).[22] Besides the Infrastructure Canada Program of 2000, the four include the Canada Strategic Infrastructure Fund, the Border Infrastructure Fund – both set up in 2001 – and the Municipal-Rural Infrastructure Fund, created in 2003.[23]

Why is the FCM involved in such a matter? Because,

> over time, the FCM assumed the role of primary interlocutor or broker, establishing a bridge between federal intentions and local government needs, and playing a central role in the aggregation, definition, articulation and advocacy of local government issues at the federal level. These FCM actions ... resulted in significant monetary transfers from the federal to local governments and large increases in FCM membership. (Chénier 2009)[24]

These initiatives led then minister of finance Paul Martin to propose "A New Deal for Cities"[25] in a speech delivered at the FCM in 2002.[26] The speech raised hopes but provided little practical comfort, until Martin himself was elected prime minister on June 28, 2004, at the head of a minority government. He then created the Ministry of State for Infrastructure and Communities (MSIC), which became responsible for the Office of Infrastructure of Canada, which in turn also included the Cities Secretariat.[27]

The lesson learned from the MSUA experience of the 1970s "allowed for a more conciliatory tone toward the provincial governments" and set up a new protocol: "Once a project was identified, it did not proceed without the establishment of a federal-provincial/territorial management committee. Memoranda of Understanding were signed to clarify the roles and responsibilities of both the provinces and the federal government. There were no surprises this time: it was made very clear the provinces were in the driver's seat" (Policy Options 2015).

Later on, "despite its record of relative success, MSIC was folded into the Ministry of Transportation in 2006" (Policy Options 2015) by the newly elected Conservative government.[28] The notion of "relative success" applied to the MSIC is contested by some, who faulted Martin for having redirected his initial program toward municipal governments instead of concentrating on larger cities or city-regions (Mau 2005, 32). In parallel,

> at the close of 2005, the FCM was poised to achieve its ultimate goal of establishing a joint federal-local mechanism for policy development as part of the New Deal. However, the election of the Harper government in 2006 led to a change in the federal position, leaving the FCM in a position reminiscent of 1982 and a way forward that was suddenly less clear. (Chénier 2009)[29]

Transportation Policy

Until the 1960s, although closely tied to national economic policy, transportation was dealt with on "a piece-meal or short-run basis" (RCT 1960, 8). The Royal Commission on Transportation, also known as the MacPherson Commission, had one major contribution in this regard, which was that the competition between modes of transport and within each mode should replace previous reliance on regulation. Five years later, in 1965, the National Transportation Act was finally adopted, based on the commission's findings, leading to the creation of the Canadian Transport Commission (CTC) – which became the Canadian Transportation Agency in 1996.

> The CTC absorbed most of the members from the previous boards – the Board of Transport Commissioners, the Air Transport Board, and the Canadian Maritime Commission ... It was created with a mandate to deal with all modes of transportation as a competitive whole with the object of coordinating and harmonizing the operations of all carriers engaged in transport by railways, water, aircraft, extra-provincial motor vehicle transport and commodity pipelines. (Canadian Transportation Agency 2017)[30]

After Prime Minister Mulroney's Conservative government accession to power in September 1984, transportation policy reform moved to the forefront of the agenda: reduced economic regulation and greater reliance on market forces were the order of the day. Many of the upcoming policy shifts toward deregulation and, chief among them, the opening of free trade negotiations between Canada and the US in 1986, were in no small measure influenced by pressure from the ongoing process in the US, where open markets were the order of the day.[31]

Following the successive waves of privatization – including Air Canada (1989) and rail services (CN 1995), airport (1992) and seaport (1997) governance reform, and the transfer of Canadian Coast Guard to Fisheries and Oceans – Transport Canada assumed a wide range of operational activities and became a department essentially focused on policy and regulation, while investments in transportation infrastructure were entrusted to various authorities. In parallel, this wave had a major impact on transport facilities. Whereas the federal government had built, operated, and maintained major seaports and airports, starting in the 1990s, as part of a new National Airports Policy and its National Marine Policy,[32] it divested itself of these facilities and established a new regime according to which it kept ownership but handed over responsibility for their management and governance to local authorities. From then on, "Canadian airports receive no subsidies from the federal government; they do, however, pay substantial rents to the government as the owner. Thus, the airports must fund the modernization of their infrastructure and their operating expenses by their own means ... It now falls to the Canadian airport authorities to ensure both profitability and the services adapted to users' needs" (Roy and Nadeau 2014, 7, 58).[33]

In 1996, adoption of a new *Canada Transportation Act* essentially reiterated the policy that had been declared in the earlier *National Transportation Act* and maintained the National Transportation Agency set up in 1988.[34] But the act introduced regulations that would transform the agency itself. As the agency's annual report for 1996 relayed, "What made these changes exceptional was the magnitude of their impact." Still, the *Canada Transportation Act*, as its name implies, is an independent entity acting as a quasi-judicial tribunal and economic regulator.

This agency operated in a shifting North American context. Free trade with the US stimulated a major repositioning in the development of transportation infrastructure within North America, affecting primarily road and rail transports.[35] Whereas, historically, national integration relied on the development of transportation facilities – roads, rails, waterways, and air routes – in a mostly east-west axis, new exchange patterns now called for the implementation of transportation corridors in a north-south axis. In 2002, the number of crossings of individuals at the Canada-US border stood at 200 million, over half a million each day. The same year, 11 million trucks crossed the border, or thirty thousand each day. A study made at the time came to the following conclusion: "The pace of growth is such that market forces, by themselves, cannot deal effectively with transportation as a system. Public-private partnerships are springing up, and government at all levels has an important role to play. Just what this role should be is still unclear because the problems of rapid transportation growth are so multifaceted, complex and incompletely understood" (Wirth 1999).

The North American Forum on Integration (North American International Trade Corridor Partnership n.d.)[36] defined the issue in these terms:

> Following the implementation of NAFTA, coalitions of interest have been formed in order to promote specific transport channels, to develop the infrastructures of these channels and to propose jurisdictional amendments to facilitate the crossing of borders. These coalitions include businesses, government agencies, civil organizations, metropolitan areas, rural communities and also individuals, wishing to strengthen the commercial hubs of their regions.

The solution contemplated for road transportation[37] was the creation of trade corridors – projects that were eventually abandoned in the wake of extended citizens' opposition.[38]

Meanwhile, following the implementation of a just-in-time production and distribution model spurred on by the extension of intrafirm trade, traffic congestion became a permanent concern on both sides of the Canada-US border. This issue goes a long way toward explaining the level of sensitivity the continental economy as a whole experienced following the events of September 11, 2001, and related closings of northern and southern borders in the US. The subsequent formation of long queues of trucks extending at least thirty kilometres inland has had an awakening effect on businesses in Canada, with the result that, since the terrorist attacks, security concerns have gained more urgency and tend to override other issues. This new approach was clearly spelled out in the National Security Strategy of the US of September 2002, and was taken up by former Canadian diplomat John J. Noble before the Standing Committee on Foreign Affairs and International Trade in 2003: "The US Ambassador to Canada has stated recently that US security concerns trump Canadian economic concerns. The challenge for Canadian policy makers is how to find a way to mesh these two objectives in a manner which both sides find acceptable."[39]

At the time, Canada quickly committed itself to maintaining a secure infrastructure as outlined in the Smart Border Declaration and Action Plan, signed December 12, 2001. The following year, Thomas d'Aquino, president of the Canadian Council of Chief Executives, launched the North American Security and Prosperity Initiative. This was followed by the setting up of a trilateral task force,[40] which later issued a statement calling for "the establishment of a North American Advisory Council that would prepare and monitor moves to further integrate the region over the next five years." The statement goes on to say: "The boundaries of the community would be defined by a common external tariff and an outer security perimeter. Within this area, the movement of people and products would be legal, orderly, and safe" (Council on Foreign Relations 2005).[41] Nevertheless, this did not imply free movement of people across borders; the US authorities even toyed with the idea of making visas compulsory for Canadian citizens as of 2008.

CANADA'S FEDERAL POLICY CONVERGENCE SINCE 2006

The Conservative Governments (2006–15)

At the turn of the millennium, growing impediments to the extension and deepening of economic integration within North America, on the one hand, and an accelerated globalization of the world economy, on the other, incited the Harper government to redefine Canada's commercial policy. This new approach became known as the "integrative commerce strategy," a strategy that was developed in two phases at the beginning of the government's first and second mandates, respectively.

In the aftermath of its first victory over the Liberal Party of Canada in January 2006, the Conservative government tabled its economic plan entitled *Advantage Canada. Building a Strong Economy for Canadians* (Government of Canada 2006). Among the many commitments made, six concern us here:

1 In a section entitled "New Ground Rules for Success in Global Markets," the plan recognized the notion of "global value chains" (GVCs), which will become a central component of its commercial policy.
2 The plan stated that the strengthening of the Canadian economic union – through fiscal balance, enhanced internal trade and labour mobility, and so forth – is a major objective.
3 The plan tied infrastructure spending to the gateway concept.
4 To retain a critical access to the US market, the plan proposed to increase "both security and border trade efficiency."
5 Given the difficulty of completing the Doha Round at the multilateral level, the plan also sought to open free trade negotiations at the bilateral and regional levels.
6 The plan developed a "new approach" to international trade policy through a comprehensive Global Commerce Strategy.

This policy shift reflects observations about the various approaches to internationalization. For instance, T.J. Sturgeon (2006, 35) indicates that an earlier era of internationalization, characterized by the simple geographic spread of economic activities across national boundaries, is giving way to an era of "globalization," which involves the functional integration of these internationally dispersed activities. It is this functional integration that drives our growing interest in "integrative trade."[42]

This is precisely the approach that was picked up by the newly elected federal government and defined in the following manner: "Commonly referred to as 'integrative trade,' this new international business model uses lower trade barriers to distribute production around the world through out-sourcing and off-shoring to maximize efficiency and reduce costs of each component – taking advantage of global supply chains" (Government of Canada 2012).

Simultaneously, as far as their dealings with municipal governments were concerned, the newly elected Conservatives brought together Transport Canada, Infrastructure Canada, and sixteen Crown Corporations and set up the Ministry of Transport, Infrastructure and Communities on February 6, 2006, thereby introducing a change of orientation regarding the integration of infrastructure policies with transportation issues (Champagne 2014, 175).

By the time the Conservatives secured their second electoral victory over the Liberals in October 2008, the ongoing financial crisis had spilled over to affect the EU's economic well-being, to facilitate a double-digit economic growth in China and in other emerging economies (India, Brazil, etc.), and had led to a renewed recourse to protectionism in the US. The latter had a direct negative impact on transborder crossings, while all these international developments called for the reinforcing of Canada's commercial strategy of 2006 (Lambert-Racine et al. 2010). The government devised a three-track response. The first track consisted in expanding trade with the US at all costs, and to achieve this, exportation of energy products (oil, gas, electricity) and raw materials were to compensate for the foreseen decline in the exportation of manufactured goods. The second track was the adoption of the Global Commerce Strategy in 2009, with the objective of diversifying Canada's reliance on the US market through the negotiation of FTAs and other agreements with a host of partners, as previously stated. Finally, the third track called for the adoption of a new commercial model, that of integrative trade relying on global supply chains with specific gateways and corridors, and the active involvement of Canadian municipalities.

Under the 2006 economic policy, the federal government formalized three gateways and corridors: an Atlantic gateway involving the four provinces of Atlantic Canada, a continental gateway involving the provinces of Ontario and Quebec, and a Pacific gateway involving British Columbia (see Figure 3.1). This is the backdrop against which one can understand the logic that the 2007 National Policy Framework for Strategic Gateways and Trade Corridors (revised in 2009) rests on. The introductory message from then minister of transport and infrastructure John Baird makes this quite clear: "[As] a comprehensive, integrated and strategic approach, this Gateways Policy framework represents an important new direction in transportation and trade" (Transport Canada 2009).

On May 3, 2007, the Government of Canada signed a Memorandum of Understanding (MoU) with the government of British Columbia on the development of an Asia-Pacific Gateway and Corridor. On July 30 of the same year, the governments of Canada, Ontario, and Quebec signed the Ontario-Quebec Continental Gateway and Trade Corridor, involving public and private sector stakeholders. Finally, on October 14, 2007, a similar MoU was signed with the Atlantic provinces of Nova Scotia, New Brunswick, Prince Edward Island, and Newfoundland and Labrador on the development of Canada's Atlantic gateway.[43]

During its first mandate (2006–08), the Conservative government sought to establish conciliatory relations with provincial governments, with Prime Minister Harper developing a one-on-one approach with premiers instead of relying on federal-provincial conferences. This way, he was able to secure the consent of Canadian provinces, which led to increased expenditures in health, social, and labour market transfers.[44] Later, in the wake of the 2007–08 recession, the newly reelected Harper government "decided to make the infrastructure file one of the mainstays in its policy arsenal and devoted $33 billion over seven years to the Building Canada Plan. This formed the base for later initiatives" (Dunn 2016, 5), notably Canada's Economic Action Plan, adopted with Budget 2009.

Under the plan, "the federal government established the $4 billion Infrastructure Stimulus Fund (ISF) to provide funding to provincial, territorial, and municipal construction-ready infrastructure projects. The ISF complemented existing federal infrastructure funding by focusing on short-term spending. This brought total infrastructure funding to $37 billion" (Dunn 2016, 5).

In this regard, the Conservatives took on "the policy tools of their predecessor in funding infrastructure expenditures at the local level" (Graham and Andrew 2014, 7), with the result that "the general nature of

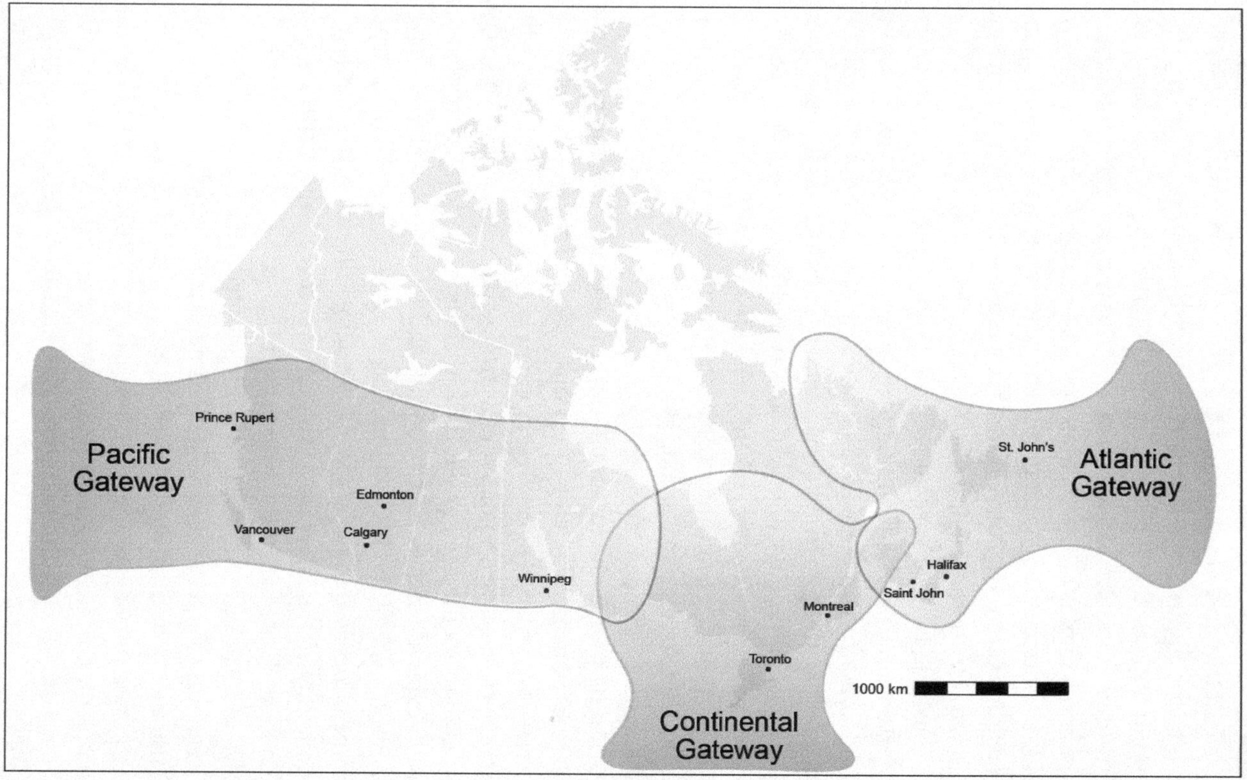

FIGURE 3.1 Canada's three gateways and corridors | *Cartography:* Steve Tornes. *Source:* Statistics Canada (2021a).

the municipal infrastructure program remained relatively stable over time" (Champagne 2014, 165), although the government had the reputation of being "indifferent to urban affairs" (Bradford 2018). In other words, although municipalities were increasingly relevant policy actors – and recognized as such under the numerous funds set up by successive federal governments – this failed to shift "traditional federalism toward a model of multilevel governance" (Bradford 2018). Even so, "since the beginning of the economic crises of 2008, the federal government has considered the municipalities as part of the solution to limiting the impact of the crisis on the Canadian economy, and infrastructure investments provide a good example" of this (Champagne 2014, 182).[45]

The Liberal Governments (2015–21)

After the Conservative government's defeat in November 2015, both the Global Commerce Strategy and the Global Markets Action Plan remained on Global Affairs Canada's website. However, the newly elected Liberal government's strategy was spelled out elsewhere. First, there are two chapters in the Budget 2017: chapter 1, which founds Innovation Canada with a mandate to develop six Economic Strategy Tables to create superclusters and to set up a New Strategic Innovation Fund; and chapter 2, which establishes a Trade and Transportation Corridors Initiative including, inter alia, a National Trade Corridors Fund (NTCF) "to address urgent capacity constraints and freight bottlenecks at major ports of entry, and to better connect the rail and highway infrastructure that delivers economic growth across Canada" (Government of Canada 2017).

Second, the Department of Infrastructure and Communities' Investing in Canada Plan is dedicated to new investments in infrastructure for cities and communities. It establishes the 2014 New Building Canada Fund, which earmarked $14 billion within its overall $53 billion fund to support projects of national, regional, and local significance that promote economic growth, job creation, and productivity. Table 3.1 shows the amount invested by the federal government per initiative, notably the Asia-Pacific Gateway and Corridor Transportation Infrastructure Fund (APGCTIF), the Gateways and Border Crossings Fund (GBCF), and the NTCF in each of the metropolitan areas of this book's focus.

In the main, even though the notion of integrative commerce has not been picked up in Liberal programs or initiatives, the notions of supply chains, gateways, and corridors are constantly referred to. The fact that Liberal policies centre on transportation corridors, ports and commercial infrastructures, maritime strategy, and the like – and that they reach down

TABLE 3.1
Federal investment via the APGCTIF, GBCF, and NTCF rounds of funding ($)

Metro with other	*APGCTIF*	*GBCF*	*NTCF 2017*	*NTCF 2019*	*Grand Total*
Halifax		32,500,000	38,400,000	47,500,000	118,400,000
Hamilton				11,000,000	11,000,000
Montreal		15,640,000	64,200,000	68,500,000	148,340,000
Toronto		53,419,000	17,700,000	828,000	71,947,000
Vancouver	125,427,092		224,920,000	131,000,000	481,347,092
Other	155,163,552	669,143,470	2,794,921,033	525,888,925	4,145,116,980
Grand total	280,590,644	770,702,470	3,140,141,032	784,716,925	4,976,151,072

Source: Authors' own calculations, based on Transport Canada (2021).

to city level – is an important indicator of the continuity between present and previous governments in a convergence approach to commercial, urban, and transportation policies.

In this regard, Justin Trudeau's government's approach to GVCs was not substantially different from the one prepared by its predecessor, except for the implementation process set up by Transport Canada's Trade and Transportation Corridors Initiative of 2017. The department now operates through calls for proposals that eliminate the signing of MoUs and the setting up of governance frameworks altogether.

The Liberal government's overall commitments are spelled out in its Investing in Canada Plan. Launched in 2016, the plan commits $180 billion over twelve years for infrastructure, "from public transit to trading ports, broadband networks to energy systems, community services to natural spaces" (Government of Canada 2016a). The plan set out to achieve three objectives[46] across five "investment streams," one of which, the fourth, on trade and transportation, should

> provide safe, sustainable and efficient transportation systems that will bring global markets closer to Canada to help Canadian businesses compete, grow and create more middle-class jobs. Through the National Trade Corridors Fund, $704 million has been committed to 16 air projects and 27 marine projects, leveraging total investments of $1.45 billion; and $1.09 billion has been committed to 19 rail and 21 road projects, leveraging total investments of $2.5 billion. (Government of Canada 2016a)

In the Transport Canada 2015 report, Transport Canada switched the terminology of gateways to corridors, thus referring to the Continental Corridor, Pacific Corridor, and Atlantic Corridor. Additionally:

> Through Budget 2017, the Government proposes to invest $10.1 billion over the next decade in trade and transportation projects. This investment will help build stronger, more efficient transportation corridors to international markets ... One part of the Government's overall investment in trade and transportation infrastructure is the Trade and Transportation Corridors Initiative, led by Transport Canada. This initiative will prioritize investments that address congestion and bottlenecks along vital corridors, and around transportation hubs and ports providing access to world markets. (Government of Canada 2016a)

Furthermore, in May 2017, the federal Liberal government introduced Bill C-49, the Transportation Modernization Act, which made significant amendments to the Canadian Transportation Act, notably in relation to rail and aviation modes of transport.[47]

A year earlier, in 2016, the House of Commons Standing Committee on Transport, Infrastructure and Communities, known as TRAN, adopted a motion to "launch a comprehensive study on the establishment of a Canadian Transportation and Logistics Strategy (using a regional gateway approach) with specific focus on [inter alia] ... an exploration, when practical, of the synchronization of federal plans and priorities with provincial, territorial and local government initiatives relating to transportation and infrastructure policies over the long-term" (TRAN 2019, 12). Even if municipalities and city governments are not mentioned in the thirty-one recommendations coming out of TRAN's February 2019 *Interim Report on Establishing a Canadian Transportation and Logistics Strategy*, under the heading "National Trade Corridors Strategy," Recommendation 24 states: "That the Government of Canada, in the context of the development of a National Trade Corridors Strategy, encourage enhanced dialogue with Indigenous communities, businesses, government agencies and international economic partners with the goals of strengthening strategic local, national and international trade corridors and ensuring long-term investments in needed infrastructure" (TRAN 2019, 12). This recommendation accredits comments from witnesses who insisted on the need for "greater coordination between all system stakeholders ... more specifically between port authorities and municipalities" (TRAN 2019, 30–31), and rightly so, since integrative trade and GVCs/GPNs involve and impact cities first and foremost rather than provinces. As nodes in value chains and gateways, cities are implicated both politically, as local governments responsible for public welfare, and strategically, as emplacement or location for ports, airports, and other transportation facilities.

Adapting to new events and international realities based on best practices, the Trudeau government has also made some investments in plans to mitigate the effects of the COVID-19 pandemic and related disruptions of global supply chains, as well as the "possibility" that, in the immediate short term, "localization or re-shoring will be the most dominant structural shift in the post-pandemic world" (Sahu 2020). If this should happen, such a disruption would certainly have detrimental effects on Canada's gateway and trade corridors policy. On October 1, 2020, Prime Minister Justin Trudeau "announced $10 billion in new major infrastructure initiatives to create jobs and economic growth [through] the Canada Infrastructure Bank's Growth Plan" (Government of Canada 2020). But these funds are dedicated to "investments in broadband, clean energy, retrofits and agricultural irrigation" (Government of Canada 2020), not on gateways or trade corridors.

Created in 2017, the Canada Infrastructure Bank was established to complement other rounds of infrastructure funding as an independent agency dedicated to routine investment in income-generating infrastructure projects, with a strategic, collaborative mission. As stated in the letter to the bank's inaugural chairperson of the board, the minister of infrastructure and communities explains that the bank's mission is "to help public dollars go further and be used more strategically by attracting private investment to help more infrastructure projects get built. The Bank will be an innovative financing tool designed to work collaboratively with public and private sector partners to transform the way infrastructure is planned, funded and delivered in Canada" (Sohi 2017). With $35 billion over ten years at its disposal, the bank was set up to favour public-private partnerships and investment in an ostensibly neutral and apolitical manner, but there have been numerous complaints that the public interest seemed sacrificed in decisions taken for the benefit of private interests, and many noted the slowness in the approval of submitted projects (Canadian Press 2021). In fact, since its creation, the bank had been mired in controversy, and opposition parties promised to abolish it (Curry 2019). Some municipalities, such as the town of Mapleton, Ontario, that have tried to take advantage of this source of funding have realized that the cost associated with the suggested public-private partnership might be too high (Canadian Union of Public Employees 2020). In May 2022, the House of Commons transport committee recommended that the bank be abolished.

According to Bradford (2018, 1):

> Since the 2015 election, the federal government has launched several programs that play out in Canada's biggest cities. The largest, the Trudeau government's 12-year Investing in Canada infrastructure plan, has a budget of $180 billion. Canada is, in effect, conducting national urban policy by other means. This significant, if implicit, urban agenda could be strengthened by expanding the mandate of the regional development agencies to include city-regions, and by establishing a Canadian cities innovation fund and a national urban policy observatory.

On June 29, 2021, the government announced that it was changing the name of the Gas Tax Fund to the Canada Community-Building Fund. The announcement clearly states that the fund does not "alter or modify the objectives or requirements of the program," which provides funding to provinces and territories, "who in turn flow this funding to their municipalities to support local infrastructure priorities" (Government of Canada 2021).

This initiative shows all too well that Bradford's assessment is overly optimistic. Even though the sums involved in the above-mentioned plan are impressive, the government's plan targets communities in general, not cities or city-regions, and nothing indicates that an "urban agenda" is forthcoming. In other words, no such urban agenda is in the offing and the issue has probably moved backward instead of forward since the Martin government of the early 2000s.

CONCLUSION

From the federal government's perspective, political economy, transportation, and urban affairs have indeed converged to the point that they can be said to represent the obverse of most of its infrastructure investments, including those on gateways and trade corridors. The fact that infrastructure has been tied to communities for quite some time now is a clear indication of the federal government's intention of reaching down to local levels first and foremost, and to sidestep cities and city-regions altogether. This is a far cry from a coherent urban policy. The UN-Habitat was conscious of this shortcoming when, in 2017, together with OECD, in their survey of thirty-five countries, they listed Canada as one of only five jurisdictions "where the urban policy landscape does not show any evidence of a National Urban Policy adoption." Such exceptional cases, they observed, "call for careful analysis in future work" (UN-Habitat-OECD 2017).

In the Canadian instance, the solution to this conundrum has already been devised by the Canadian Global Cities Council in a brief released in 2018:

> In our view, it is more reasonable to operate as if the legal *structure* of Canadian municipalities is wholly within provincial jurisdiction. On the other hand, the policy challenges of urban Canada are shared between all three orders of government, and roles should be defined and respected accordingly. Setting broad national goals for the overall fiscal, economic and physical resilience of urban Canada is legitimately within the national interest, at least to the degree that national governments should be free to cooperate directly with cities, metro-regions and provinces to ensure its funding is actually invested toward those goals. If this was not the case, provinces should not have spent the last two decades accepting and rerouting billions in federal funds intended for that purpose. (CGCC 2018, 23)

As full-fledged governments responsible for the well-being of millions of their inhabitants, municipalities, cities, and city-regions should be endowed with the political, economic, and social powers at least equivalent to those entrusted to higher tiers of government. In particular, they should be granted the financial means to pursue their own missions through an adequate fiscal regime to replace the outdated and unjust property taxation now in place (Coderre 2021, 138–48). This has not yet come to pass; instead, as we document in the following chapters on four city gateways and trade corridors, variations in factors such as the nature of the urban regimes and provincial-municipal relations create distinctive city models of engagement with GVCs and their supporting infrastructures.

In the case of Vancouver, we can observe a coherent industry-led coalition to develop a gateway to connect Vancouver to the rest of Canada and the rest of the world. This model served as a framework for the Halifax gateway, where a deliberate process was followed to build the coalition, coordinated by the Atlantic Canada Opportunities Agency, a federal agency operating at the regional level and working closely with the provincial Department of Transportation and Infrastructure Renewal. By contrast, we show that the continental gateway looks quite different if we compare Toronto and Montreal. On the one hand, Toronto is defined by a lack of centralized coordination; it is a place of intense growth, driven by the stakeholders pursuing local and sector-based interests. On the other hand, the Montreal model is defined by a clear strategic alignment with the presence of CargoM, a cluster, as a central stakeholder for the design and evolution of the Montreal gateway.

4

Vancouver and the Asia-Pacific Gateway

Greater Vancouver is a port city-region, but it was never inevitable that its gateway regime would enjoy success in pursuing its agenda for transportation-infrastructure development in the first decades of the twenty-first century – nor that it would secure substantial support and funding from senior governments. Various environmental, sustainable transportation, and community groups have mobilized against the various trade-supporting projects, especially those entailing the expansion of roads and highways. And the success of the trade-oriented gateway idea was achieved despite the fact that a competing urban development coalition was actively – and no less successfully – seeking to reorient the city-regional economy away from its resource control, processing, and export functions and toward a postindustrial development model that emphasized real estate development and residential amenity (Hutton 1997). The real estate–led coalition also espoused a notion of Vancouver as a gateway – for people and for financial capital; theirs too was enabled through senior government intervention in the fields of immigration (Hiebert 2000; Moos and Skaburskis 2010) and housing finance (Walks and Clifford 2015; August 2020).

There are, to be sure, points of overlap between the two competing visions of the Vancouver gateway. Both have sought to reorient the gaze of local actors away from the transatlantic and the continental and back toward the Pacific – without, we might add, necessarily embracing Indigenous and postcolonial perspectives on Vancouver as gateway (cf. Yu 2007). However, profound disagreements remain between the trade-and-transportation and people-and-real-estate visions of the Vancouver gateway regarding the nature and purposes of urban development. Put more concretely, container storage yards rarely make desirable neighbours for condominium developments. An implicit contention of this chapter is that, unlike the trade-and-transportation coalition that sought and found provincial and federal government support, the real estate coalition turned to municipal government to support its agenda. But interested readers will need to look elsewhere for that part of the story (Olds 2002; Punter 2010; Jacopo 2011; Regan and Hall 2018; Gurstein and Hutton 2019).

This chapter traces the evolving relationship in greater Vancouver between local, regional, and provincial governments; a trade-and-transportation infrastructure–promoting local growth coalition; and the federal government's gateway and corridor initiatives. Vancouver's case is distinctive in relation to the trade initiatives of the federal government because of the long-standing and activist role of the transport industry in infrastructure advocacy and planning. Although this legacy can be traced all the way back to the role of the Canadian Pacific Railway in the creation of the City of Vancouver in 1886, since at least the early 1990s, a coalition based in the Vancouver region has succeeded in producing a particular vision (or frame) of Vancouver as a trading gateway. On the strength of this vision, and the simultaneous expansion of trade with China, the gateway regime has secured substantial federal and provincial government support and financial resources for trade-enabling transportation-infrastructure development. Inevitably, these senior governments looked beyond Vancouver to the Port of Prince Rupert and the northern corridor to the American Midwest, but also to the corridor between Vancouver's port terminal and staging yards in central British Columbia and further to the east.

We focus on how the trade-and-transportation coalition has thrived through successive waves of coalitional reframing and institutionalization and how this was achieved with both tacit and active support of provincial and federal government actors. The coalition, comprising local actors and local representatives of nonlocal actors, has employed a mode of governance that involves alliances with provincial and federal government resource-providers. The post-2006 federal gateway programs in support of the integrative commerce strategy were an endorsement and elaboration of what this local coalition studied, proposed, and lobbied. In turn, federal funding of the gateway created various forums in which the coalition has institutionalized a role for itself in the infrastructure and land-use decision-making processes of regional government. Building on its success in convincing senior governments and agencies that gateway and corridor strategies could support larger commerce and trade strategies

(Government of Canada 2008, 2009), the coalition has also inserted itself in various regional governance bodies, thus institutionalizing a largely technocratic approach to infrastructure delivery. As such, tensions remain with democratically elected local governments, civil society actors with environmental and livability concerns, and those pursuing real estate–focused development strategies. These tensions revolve around general infrastructure, transportation, and land-use priorities, as well as concerns such as the role of Vancouver in energy exports.

With a significant interest in maintaining and expanding its saddle function between Asian and North American markets (rather than source or sink functions), gateway development in the Metro Vancouver region reveals how the tensions between global and local imperatives have been addressed by various stakeholders, including members of the gateway regime – its allies and opponents – and various fragmented local governments. At the outset, we recognize that global and local do not exist as disconnected absolutes. All actors respond to combinations of global and local attachment, affiliation, and dependency, and many occupy intermediary positions, including provincial and regional governments, industry associations, and labour groups. Our case study employs an approach focused on the internal workings and external relationships of this coalition. Interviews, policy, and archival data on earlier (pre-2015) waves of gateway development in Vancouver are supplemented by data on the most recent policies and strategies, especially the National Trade Corridors Fund (NTCF) launched in 2017.

We start with an overview of local and regional government arrangements in greater Vancouver before discussing the evolution of the local gateway coalition and its increasing institutionalization in various regional agencies and forums. We then discuss opposition to the gateway and the response of the regime, project funding arrangements, and the evolving network structure of the gateway regime.

REGIONAL AND MUNICIPAL GOVERNMENT IN GREATER VANCOUVER

There are several ways to describe the greater Vancouver region. Our focus is on Metro Vancouver Regional District (MVRD), but it is worth noting that other definitions are in widespread colloquial use and are relevant to understanding the functional region that hosts Canada's largest maritime port complex. The MVRD is one of twenty-seven such regional-tier jurisdictions in the province of British Columbia. Created by provincial law, they are governed as federations of member municipalities and are responsible for collaborative planning and regional services. The MVRD, or Metro Vancouver, is by far the largest such regional district by population in the province. According to the Census of Population, Metro Vancouver had a population of 2,642,825 in 2021, which accounts for just over half of the provincial population of 5 million people. Metro Vancouver is coterminous with the Statistics Canada–defined functional urban agglomeration, or what is known as a census metropolitan area (CMA). In other words, the regional district also captures a meaningful functional economic region defined by urban settlement and daily commuting patterns.

However, Metro Vancouver is also part of a larger and shifting geography. The term "BC Lower Mainland" describes the flatish lands around the lower reaches and delta of the Fraser River that lie between the United States border to the south and the Coast Mountains to the north. The Lower Mainland encompasses all of Metro Vancouver, as well as adjacent areas to the east and north. To the east of the Vancouver CMA lie the Abbotsford-Mission and Chilliwack CMAs. These form part of the geographically extensive Fraser Valley Regional District, although Abbotsford and Mission increasingly share economic, commuting, and settlement connections with Metro Vancouver and in time may be statistically incorporated into the Vancouver CMA. Logistics activities that are more or less related to port (and airport) activity in Metro Vancouver have been located on cheaper lands within Abbotsford and Chilliwack. And to the north of Vancouver, Squamish and Whistler in the Squamish-Lillooet Regional District are included in some expansive regional definitions.

The Lower Mainland is home to several Halkomelem-speaking First Nations, and the MVRD board acknowledges that it shares its territory with ten First Nations, namely the Katzie, Kwantlen, Kwikwetlem, Matsqui, Musqueam, Qayqayt, Semiahmoo, Squamish, Tsawwassen, and Tsleil-Waututh (Metro Vancouver 2022). Of these, only the Tsawwassen First Nation (TFN) has a settled land claim (the Tsawwassen First Nation Final Agreement). Of the nine First Nations without treaties, and hence without settled land claims, all but the Qayqayt First Nation have reserve lands within the region, although several other First Nations, tribal councils, treaty groups, and associations outside Metro Vancouver have acknowledged interests in the region (Metro Vancouver 2022, 26).

The TFN became a formal member of MVRD following ratification of its Final Agreement in 2009. TFN lands are adjacent to the Roberts Bank port complex south of the mouth of the Fraser River – the site of Westshore coal export terminal since 1970 and, since the mid-1990s, of

Deltaport – now the largest container terminal in the Vancouver port complex. The desire on the part of Port of Vancouver to expand Deltaport in the early 2000s and long-standing concerns on the part of the Tsawwassen people about the environmental and social impact of port development were central drivers of the negotiations between Canada, British Columbia, and the TFN leading to the land claim settlement.

The other members of Metro Vancouver – twenty-one municipalities and one electoral district – range considerably in size, economy, and social dynamics (see Figure 4.1). Table 4.1 shows the City of Vancouver as the largest municipality by population, with the City of Surrey closing in at second. Other fast-growing municipalities include the eastern suburban municipalities of Langley Township and Maple Ridge and the densifying New Westminster and City of North Vancouver. Together, Vancouver and Surrey account for almost half of the regional population, and only four other Metro Vancouver municipalities hold more than 5 percent of the population.

Population counts are important because of the weighted voting system the MVRD employs. When a majority vote is required and the interests of Vancouver and Surrey coincide, it is relatively easy for the two to find enough support to command a majority. However, given the very different interests and character of the two largest municipalities, and given that some decisions require a two-thirds super-majority vote, typically a high degree of consensus is required to move forward on most issues. While these voting details have been seen as an impediment to coordinated regional action on economic and other priorities, as explained below, the de facto preference for a high threshold of support has been looked to as a means to protect industrial, mixed-employment, conservation, and recreation lands from conversion to other uses (Metro Vancouver 2011).

Municipalities in British Columbia enjoy substantial freedom of control over land-use planning decisions, which is understandable since property taxes and development charges are essentially their only means of raising discretionary revenue. This freedom is somewhat limited by the agreed Metro Vancouver regional land-use strategy; all municipal Official Community Plans must include a regional context statement of how they are consistent with the regional plan or how they will become consistent over time, and some changes of use require the support of the MVRD board. Regional plans in greater Vancouver have for decades paid attention to green space and agricultural land protection (Harcourt, Cameron, and Rossiter 2007). Awareness of the loss of industrial lands in Vancouver was noted as early as the 1980s, particularly in relation to the rezoning and

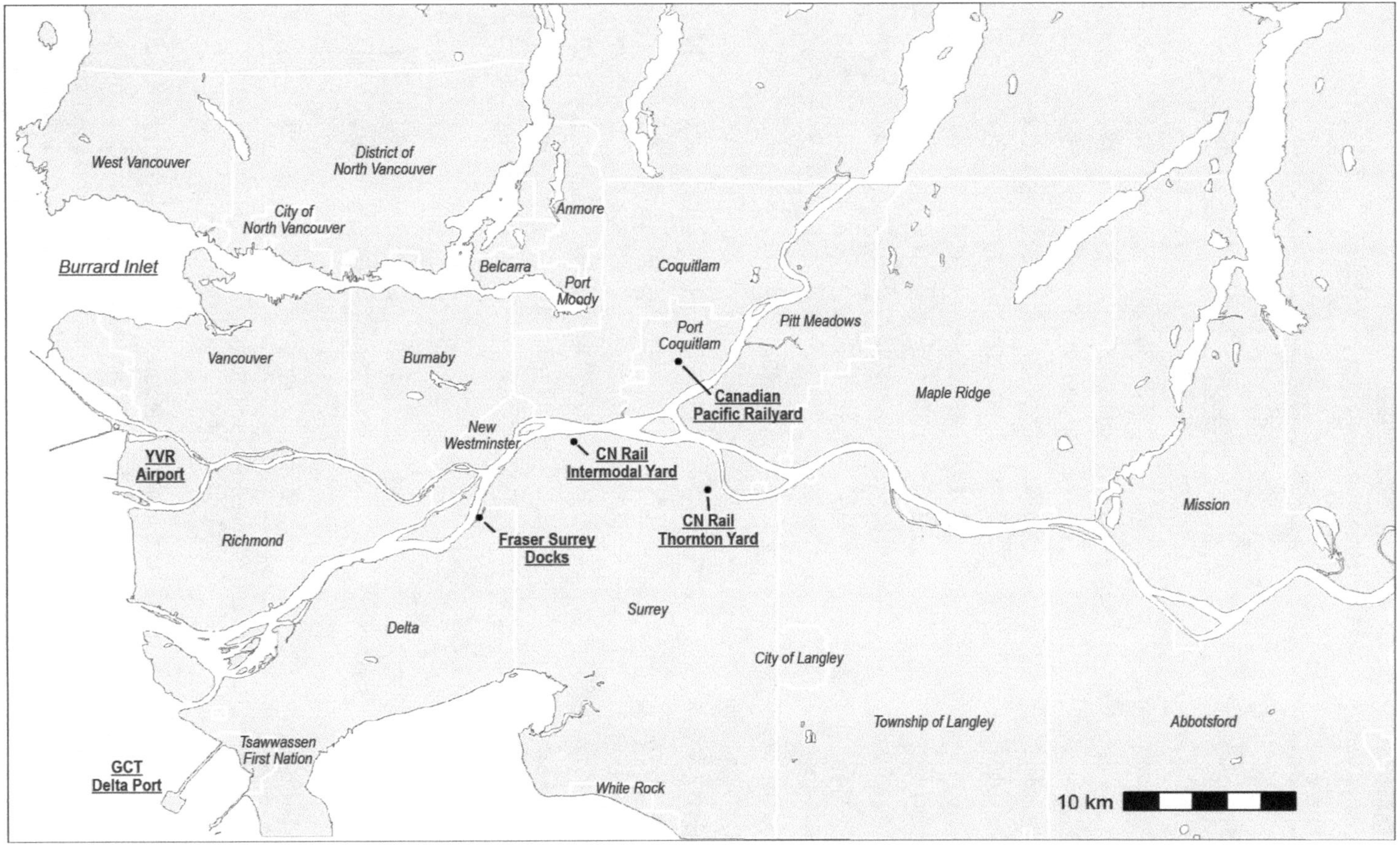

FIGURE 4.1 Metro Vancouver local governments and key trade nodes | *Cartography:* Steve Tornes. *Source:* Statistics Canada (2021a).

TABLE 4.1
Metro Vancouver and constituent municipal governments, by 2021 population

	Population		Growth (%)	Share (%)	
Municipal Area	*2006*	*2021*	*2006–21*	*2006*	*2021*
Metro Vancouver	2,116,581	2,642,825	24.9		
Vancouver	578,041	662,248	14.6	27.3	25.1
Surrey	394,976	568,322	43.9	18.7	21.5
Burnaby	202,799	249,125	22.8	9.6	9.4
Richmond	174,461	209,937	20.3	8.2	7.9
Coquitlam	114,565	148,625	29.7	5.4	5.6
Langley Township	93,726	132,603	41.5	4.4	5.0
Delta	96,723	108,455	12.1	4.6	4.1
Maple Ridge	68,949	90,990	32.0	3.3	3.4
North Vancouver District	82,562	88,168	6.8	3.9	3.3
New Westminster	58,549	78,916	34.8	2.8	3.0
Port Coquitlam	52,687	61,498	16.7	2.5	2.3
North Vancouver City	45,165	58,120	28.7	2.1	2.2
West Vancouver	42,131	44,122	4.7	2.0	1.7
Port Moody	27,512	33,535	21.9	1.3	1.3
Langley City	23,606	28,963	22.7	1.1	1.1
White Rock	18,755	21,939	17.0	0.9	0.8
Pitt Meadows	15,623	19,146	22.6	0.7	0.7
Greater Vancouver Electoral Area A	11,050	18,612	68.4	0.5	0.7
Bowen Island	3,362	4,256	26.6	0.2	0.2
Anmore	1,785	2,356	32.0	0.1	0.1
Tsawwassen First Nation	675	2,256	234.2	0.0	0.1
Lions Bay	1,328	1,390	4.7	0.1	0.1
Belcarra	676	687	1.6	0.0	0.0

Sources: Metro Vancouver (2017), Statistics Canada (2022a).

disposal of industrial lands in and around the False Creek and Coal Harbour areas of the regional urban core (Jacopo 2011). Metro Vancouver's Regional Industrial Lands Inventory – first released in 2005, and since then every five years, most recently completed for 2020 (Metro Vancouver 2021) – added an empirical base to the concerns. The inventory, together with studies commissioned by senior governments and trade proponents, as well as media reports about the high price and shortage of industrial lands, all added to a sense that the previous regional land-use strategy – the 1996 Livable Region Strategic Plan (GVRD 1996) – lacked the teeth required to halt the loss of industrial land to higher value real estate purposes.

Recognizing that previous regional plans had failed to protect the industrial land base of the region from conversion to residential and other amenity-enhancing developments, and at the prompting of the trade-promoting coalition described in this chapter, Metro Vancouver's 2011 Regional Growth Strategy set a threshold of 50 percent plus one in a regional weighted vote if a municipality wished to change the land-use designation of industrial or mixed-employment land (although amendments to some other regional land-use designations such as agricultural, conservation, and recreation, or rural require a two-thirds weighted vote) (Metro Vancouver 2011, 60). It also set a requirement to notify the port and airport authorities, the provincial Ministry of Transport and Infrastructure, and the Agricultural Land Commission of any change and to give them a chance to respond. The measures did not go far enough for some, with the Port of Vancouver CEO voicing concerns about the lack of appropriate space for logistics and other port-related use and calling for an industrial land bank (Bula 2012). Regional land-use policy, and specifically the designation and protection of trade-enabling industrial lands, remains a key objective of the gateway regime. The regional growth strategy was updated and enhanced in the form of Metro 2050, adopted in February 2023 (Metro Vancouver 2023). Metro 2050 includes a trade-oriented lands overlay policy designed to protect larger sites for "uses that support inter-regional, provincial, national, and international trade" (Metro Vancouver 2023, 2.2.9b).

Under the auspices of the 2011 Regional Growth Strategy, and at the prompting of trade promotion and industrial lands interests, Metro Vancouver (2020) approved the Industrial Lands Strategy. Through an Industrial Lands Strategy Task Force, the port and airport authorities, provincial and federal governments, Gateway Council, Greater Vancouver Urban Freight Council, Trucking Association, and private industry are all explicitly recognized in the strategy as stakeholders with roles and responsibilities related to industrial lands. For example, the Port of Vancouver, which has its own land-use plan for the federally owned lands it controls (Port of Vancouver 2020b), is recognized as having a role in efficient goods movement and also in that it "acquires and develops lands to support current and anticipated port-related operations" (Metro Vancouver 2020, 60).

All these concerns with industrial land protection are ultimately related to the Vancouver metropolitan economy's decisive turn from manufacturing and raw material processing to postindustrialism that began in the 1970s. Table 4.2 shows that in the period under consideration here, employment in Metro Vancouver continued a pattern of small and declining employment in primary and secondary production, with the notable

TABLE 4.2
Metro Vancouver sector of employment, 2006 and 2019 (thousands)

	Employment		*Growth (%)*	*Share (%)*	
Municipal Area	*2006*	*2019*	*2006–19*	*2006*	*2019*
Total employed, all industries	1,147.9	1,474.0	28.4		
Agriculture	9.9	7.6	–23.2	0.9	0.5
Forestry, fishing, mining, quarrying, oil, and gas	8.0	6.1	–23.8	0.7	0.4
Utilities	3.5	7.0	100.0	0.3	0.5
Construction	82.2	123.4	50.1	7.2	8.4
Manufacturing	101.1	96.2	–4.8	8.8	6.5
Wholesale and retail trade	185.4	230.5	24.3	16.2	15.6
Transportation and warehousing	65.1	88.4	35.8	5.7	6.0
Finance, insurance, real estate, rental and leasing	84.2	113.9	35.3	7.3	7.7
Professional, scientific, and technical services	108.8	154.8	42.3	9.5	10.5
Business, building, and other support services	52.3	69.3	32.5	4.6	4.7
Educational services	89.8	104.0	15.8	7.8	7.1
Health care and social assistance	112.3	160.6	43.0	9.8	10.9
Information, culture, and recreation	67.3	88.5	31.5	5.9	6.0
Accommodation and food services	84.4	103.4	22.5	7.4	7.0
Other services (except public administration)	51.3	68.6	33.7	4.5	4.7
Public administration	42.3	51.8	22.5	3.7	3.5

Source: Statistics Canada (2021d).
Note: Initial year of 2006 coincides with Census year reported elsewhere; end year of 2019 is the last year before start of COVID-19 pandemic.

exception of construction, and expanding employment in most tertiary and advanced services sectors. With a diversified services and advanced services economy, Metro Vancouver itself does not contain significant goods importing and exporting sectors. The value chains relying upon the Vancouver port cluster are continental in scope. At the same time, it is also worth noting that despite the successful infrastructure investment strategies of the gateway coalition since the mid-2000s, employment in the transportation and warehousing sector grew only a few percentage points more rapidly than overall employment. Substantial increases in cargo throughput have not translated into increases in direct employment, precisely because of the huge efficiencies gained through capital investment (Hall 2014).

TRANSPORT GOVERNANCE IN GREATER VANCOUVER

The small contribution of the transportation industry to regional employment stands in sharp contrast to the large and diverse cargo throughput of the Port of Vancouver. Table 4.3 provides one set of indicators of the extent to which the Port of Vancouver serves importers (of automobiles and containerized cargo, in particular) and exporters (of bulk and breakbulk cargoes, in particular) across Canada. In terms of cargo handled, Vancouver is the nation's largest port by far. In comparison, Canada's second largest port, Montreal, handled about 35 million tonnes in 2020, including 1.6 million TEU. Canada's second major West Coast port, Prince Rupert, handled about 32 million tonnes in 2020, including 1.1 million TEU.

The cargo profile underscores the fact that interests well beyond Metro Vancouver and British Columbia, including the other provinces and the

TABLE 4.3
Port of Vancouver operational activity indicators, 2019 and 2020

	2019	*2020*
Auto (units)	420,000	345,000
Breakbulk (metric tonnes)	17,165,000	16,731,000
Bulk (metric tonnes)	99,697,000	101,770,000
Containerized (metric tonnes)	26,907,000	26,649,000
Total tonnage (metric tonnes)	144,188,000	145,495,000
Containers (TEUs)	3,399,000	3,468,000
Cruise passengers	1,071,000	Pandemic, no cruise season

Source: Adapted from Port of Vancouver (2020a).

federal Government of Canada, have a stake in the development and success of the port and the functioning of the trade gateway. At the same time, the MVRD has a weak economic development mandate and no trade promotion mandate – although in 2020, Metro Vancouver created Invest Vancouver to act as a regional economic development service. Metro Vancouver has also undertaken policy and research work on industrial densification and e-commerce (Aderneck 2023; Colliers 2023). Nevertheless, it has clearly defined responsibilities around bulk services and parks, but when it comes to regional land-use responsibility, it relies on substantial consensus and a certain amount of deference to municipal preferences. This is why a succession of regional growth plans have struggled to protect industrial and other less desired land uses from acquisition by real estate development interest. Indeed, engagement with the regional land-use planning process has been a central objective of the gateway coalition actors to promote industrial land preservation and pursue trade transport projects.

In turn, the municipalities that comprise the regional federation have a range of exposure to, interest in, and tolerance for trade and trade-supporting infrastructure and the attendant externalities of goods movement that generate unhappiness among, and resistance from, residents (see Table 4.4). It is important to note that while industrial lands are well segregated from residential areas in many instances – Big Bend, Mitchell Island, and Annacis Island, as examples – the roads leading to them are not. And several important port terminals are near residential and commercial areas, including along the south and north shores of the Burrard Inlet in Vancouver and North Vancouver and at Fraser Surrey Docks. Of course, some neighbourhoods are more exposed to trade impacts (for example, Bridgeview in Surrey or Strathcona in Vancouver) than others. Some smaller, wealthier, and exclusively residential municipalities essentially have no exposure to trade infrastructure, including Anmore, Belcarra, West Vancouver, and Lions Bay.

The tug-of-war between municipal, regional, and provincial governments, federal agencies, and industry proponents that exists in relation to land-use planning is also present when it comes to transportation planning. The regional transportation agency, TransLink, was established in 1999 in a major consolidation and integration of transportation functions at the regional scale. TransLink is responsible for planning and managing the region's transportation system, including transit services, the major roads network, and goods movement.

TABLE 4.4
Trade exposure: Metro Vancouver municipalities, industrial areas, and trade infrastructure

Subregion	*Municipality*	*Main Industrial/ Warehousing areas*	*Trade Infrastructure*
Central	Vancouver	South Shore False Creek Flats South Vancouver	Port (Centerm, Vanterm, bulk) CN/CP Rail
	Burnaby	Burrard Inlet Big Bend Lake City Willingdon	Port (bulk) CN/CP Rail
	New Westminster	Braid Stewardson	CN/CP Rail SRY railyard
	Richmond	Mitchell Island Bridgeport Fraser Richmond Lands	CN Rail Airport (YVR) Port (Fraser River)
	Greater Vancouver A	n/a	n/a
Tri-Cities	Coquitlam	Fraser River	CP Rail
	Port Coquitlam	Mary Hill/Coast Meridian	CP Rail and yards
	Port Moody	Burrard Inlet	Port (bulk) CP Rail
	Anmore	n/a	n/a
	Belcarra	n/a	n/a
South of Fraser	Surrey	Bridgeview Newton Campbell Heights Cloverdale	Port (Fraser Surrey) CN Rail and yards Roberts Bank Rail Corridor Border crossings
	Langley City	n/a	Roberts Bank Rail Corridor
	Langley Township	Port Kells	Roberts Bank Rail Corridor
	Delta	Annacis Island Tilbury and North Delta	Port (Deltaport, bulk) Roberts Bank Rail Corridor
	White Rock	n/a	BNSF Rail
	Tsawwassen First Nation	TFN Industrial Park	Roberts Bank Rail Corridor
North Shore	West Vancouver	n/a	n/a
	North Vancouver District	North Shore	Port (bulk, dry dock) CN Rail
	North Vancouver City	North Shore	Port (bulk) CN Rail
	Lions Bay	n/a	n/a
	Bowen Island	n/a	n/a
Ridge Meadows	Maple Ridge	n/a	CP Rail
	Pitt Meadows	Golden Ears	CP Rail and yards

Initially known as the Greater Vancouver Transportation Authority, TransLink was at first directly accountable to the region's mayors, who held a substantial majority on the founding board. However, in 2007, the provincial government enacted a major governance reform, renaming the organization the South Coast British Columbia Transportation Authority. Conflict between the mayors and the provincial government over funding for transit network expansion factored considerably in the change, but it is also clear that the provincial government at that time was motivated to overcome resistance to some aspects of its highway-building agenda for the region – an agenda that also overlapped with the federal gateways and trade corridors agenda.

The 2007 TransLink governance reforms removed the mayors from their direct oversight role on the board; the board would instead comprise "nonpolitical" experts selected from a list of nominees provided by an industry-led screening panel. One of the five seats on the screening panel is held by an industry interest group, the Greater Vancouver Gateway Council, discussed below. The Mayors' Council was tasked only with appointing the board from the screened list of nominees and with endorsing the board's long-range plans. The provincial government's voice in regional transportation matters was further enhanced through the creation of the commissioner position, which carried oversight and advisory authority. Subsequent changes have returned a little influence, but no real power, to the region's elected politicians. The commissioner role was dissolved in 2014, and the mayors serving as chair and deputy chair of the Mayors' Council now serve on the board. In 2013, TransLink began work on a regional goods movement strategy, released four years later (TransLink 2017), and the agency is now an active participant in several gateway-promoting forums (see Table 4.7).

It is not only within TransLink that gateway proponents have secured an institutionalized voice. Reforms to Canada's port and airport authorities in the 1990s provided forums in which the local private sector has institutionalized influence on regional transportation planning and investment decisions. In the case of ports, the Canada Marine Act of 1998 created the Canada Port Authorities (CPA), which at first included three CPAs in the greater Vancouver area. In 2008, the Vancouver Fraser Port Authority – today known as the Port of Vancouver – was created out of the merger of the Vancouver, Fraser River, and North Fraser CPAs. The Port of Vancouver is governed by a board, a majority of whose members are appointed by the federal government from nominees provided by port users. It is probably correct to say that all the port users are trade gateway proponents and many are active in the gateway coalition. Vancouver International Airport is also governed by an appointed board, although here there is more balance between public sector appointees, including municipal and regional governments, and those representing private sector voices.

Table 4.5 shows the influence of various gateway coalition members in the appointment process of three public authorities responsible for gateway infrastructure: port, airport, and TransLink. Although there are important differences between these agencies, in each case, governance reforms since 1990 have tended to strengthen the voice of business and senior government partners, including gateway infrastructure coalition

TABLE 4.5
Board composition of gateway-related public authorities, 2023

Authority	*Number of board members*	*Appointing bodies*	
Vancouver Fraser Port Authority (Port of Vancouver)	11	1–4:	one each from Vancouver Region, BC province, western provinces, and federal government
		5–11:	seven appointed by federal government from port user nominees
South Coast British Columbia Transportation Authority (TransLink)	11	1–2:	chair and vice-chair of the Mayors' Council
		3–9:	seven appointed by Mayors' Council from the nominees of a screening panel of five representing BC Minister of Transport, Mayors' Council on Regional Transportation, Chartered Professional Accountants of BC, Vancouver Board of Trade, and Greater Vancouver Gateway Council
		10–11:	two appointed by the Province of BC
Vancouver Airport Authority (YVR)	14	1:	president and CEO
		2–8:	one each nominated by Association of Professional Engineers and Geoscientists of BC, Chartered Professional Accountants of BC, City of Richmond, City of Vancouver, Greater Vancouver Board of Trade, Law Society of British Columbia, Metro Vancouver
		9–10:	two nominated by Government of Canada
		11–14:	four appointed by the board

members, while reducing or constraining the voice of elected local government officials. In the next section, we trace how this situation came about, focusing on how the trade-and-transportation coalition evolved in relation to the various rounds of federal infrastructure funding.

TRACING THE RISE AND INSTITUTIONALIZATION OF THE TRADE GATEWAY COALITION

We can trace the evolution of the Vancouver-region trade gateway coalition to the formation, in 1991, of the Round Table on the Greater Vancouver Gateway. The round table itself was the outcome of a recommendation of an Industrial Commission of Inquiry that followed a major port labour disruption in 1986. Building on a suggestion from the union representing port workers, the International Longshore and Warehouse Union Canada (ILWU), Commissioner Weiler (1987) recommended the formation of a "Vancouver Gateway Container Traffic Council." While the ILWU was part of the initial round table (see Table 4.7), the formal involvement of the dockworker union in the regime did not survive a period of labour unrest in the early 1990s.

In 1994, the round table was replaced by the Greater Vancouver Gateway Council (GVGC), which has been the leading private sector membership organization in the coalition since then (McCalla 2009). Not all urban growth regimes have such formal institutional structures; indeed, the increasing formalization and institutionalization of the gateway coalition through the GVGC and related organizations are distinctive features of the Vancouver case. For example, as noted earlier, governance reforms at TransLink in 2007 formalized the role of the GVGC in board-member screening.

Table 4.6 shows that the Vancouver gateway infrastructure regime has pursued a distinctive and long-lived policy agenda built through advocacy, studies, consensus building, and securing funding. Although infrastructure funding announcements by the federal (and to a lesser extent, provincial) government are never a perfect mirror of prior proposals, there are, for example, direct connections between the projects identified in the Major Commercial Transportation Study (2001) and those funded by the Asia-Pacific Gateway and Corridor Initiative (from 2006). Similarly, infrastructure projects identified in Gateway 2030 Vision (2007) and Greater Vancouver Gateway 2030 Strategy (2016) feature prominently among those funded under the NTCF (from 2018).

The gateway coalition has proven remarkably unaffected by changes in elected governments. The right-hand column of Table 4.6 shows changes

TABLE 4.6
Gateway regime timeline

Year	*Selected events, reports, announcements*	*Government elections*
1991	Round Table on the Greater Vancouver Gateway formed	Canada: Conservative BC: NDP
1992	Vancouver Airport Authority (YVR) created Deltaport container terminal announced	
1993	International Maritime Centre opens	Vancouver: NPA Canada: Liberal
1994	GVGC formed	
1995	National Marine Policy Dockworker strike and Industrial Commission	
1996	"Transportation, Trade and Tourism" submission to Parliament (GVGC)	BC: NDP Vancouver: NPA
1997	Deltaport container terminal opens	Canada: Liberal
1998	Canada Marine Act, creation of three Vancouver-area Canada Port Authorities	
1999	TransLink formed Dockworker lockout, port trucking disruption	Vancouver: NPA
2000	Deltaport expansion	Canada: Liberal
2001	Major Commercial Transportation Study (GVGC) Phase 1 report	BC: Liberal
2002		Vancouver: COPE
2003	MCTS Economic Impact Analysis (GVGC) "Opening Up BC" program announced (BC government)	
2004	MCTS Lower Mainland Rail Infrastructure Study (GVGC)	Canada: Liberal minority
2005	Port trucking disruption	Vancouver: NPA
2006	Asia-Pacific Gateway and Corridor Initiative funding announced	Canada: Conservative minority
2007	TransLink governance reform (nonpolitical board) Gateway 2030 Vision (GVGC) National Policy Framework for Strategic Gateways and Corridors	
2008	North Shore Trade Area study Amalgamation of three CPAs to create Vancouver Fraser Port Authority (VFPA)	Canada: Conservative Vancouver: Vision
2009	Tsawwassen First Nation final land treaty ratified South Shore Trade Area study APGST begins	BC: Liberal

►

◄

Year	*Selected events, reports, announcements*	*Government elections*
2010	Deltaport expansion Roberts Bank Rail Corridor project begins	
2011	Regional Growth Strategy accepted (Metro Vancouver) Gateway Infrastructure Fee instituted (VFPA)	Canada: Conservative Vancouver: Vision
2012	Enhancing planning capacity (APGST)	
2013	Regional Goods Movement Strategy begins (TransLink)	BC: Liberal
2014	Port trucking disruption GTCF formed Port Land Use Plan (VFPA)	Vancouver: Vision
2015	Port 2050 Scenarios (VFPA)	Canada: Liberal
2016	Roberts Bank Terminal 2 EIA begins Greater Vancouver Gateway 2030 Strategy (GTCF)	
2017	GVUFC formed Regional Goods Movement Strategy released (TransLink) NTCF funding round 1 opens	BC: NDP minority
2018	NTCF funding round 1 results announced	Vancouver: NPA plurality
2019	NTCF funding round 2 opens and results announced	Canada: Liberal minority
2020	Roberts Bank Terminal 2 EIA ends (approved 2023) Regional Industrial Lands Strategy (Metro Vancouver) Gateway Infrastructure Fund 2022 announced (VFPA)	BC: NDP

in federal, provincial, and municipal (City of Vancouver) government. We have already noted the limited role of elected municipal governments in gateway-related planning processes, and it is fair to say that every municipal government in the Vancouver area has aggressively pursued a similar livability and real estate–based development agenda over the past thirty years. At the same time, however, Table 4.6 shows that the gateway coalition has successfully negotiated successive changes in the governing party at provincial and federal government levels.

One particularly notable event followed the 2006 federal elections in which the Harper Conservatives won a minority. The MP for Vancouver Kingsway, David Emerson, was elected as a Liberal, having previously served as minister of industry in Prime Minister Paul Martin's government. Despite being elected as a Liberal, he crossed the floor to join the new Conservative minority government, where he served as minister of international trade and minister for the Pacific gateway (and later as minister of foreign affairs). Emerson is credited by some in the gateway regime for ensuring support from the new Conservative government for the nascent Asia-Pacific Gateway and Corridor Initiative (Hall and Clark 2010).

The timeline in Table 4.6 also shows how the gateway regime has evolved in organizational terms; while the GVGC with its core private and public authority membership has remained influential, space has been created for new "permanent" bodies, with the formation in 2014 of the Gateway Transportation Collaboration Forum (GTCF) and in 2017 of the Greater Vancouver Urban Freight Council (GVUFC). Multiparty organizations with a time-limited existence were also created to pursue specific projects and funding opportunities related to the federal gateway initiatives, including from 2009 the Asia-Pacific Gateway Skills Table (APGST) and in 2018 the Gateway Infrastructure Program Advisory Committee.

Table 4.7 shows the membership of the key gateway regime organizations. It is noteworthy that the GVGC itself has had stable membership around a core group of public and private transport industry actors. However, a wider set of actors in a variety of sectors have become involved in the newer organizations (such as the APGST and GVUFC), which probably reflects the increasing complexity of the issues being handled (i.e., going beyond port infrastructure and into issues concerning regional labour market and skills, land use, and urban goods movement). It also reflects an increasing recognition within the gateway regime in the early 2010s of local opposition to some gateway infrastructure projects in the previous decade and the need to engage local stakeholders in planning processes (APGST 2012).

GATEWAY OPPOSITION AND REGIME RESPONSE

Opposition to the gateway, especially to the highway expansion projects pursued by the provincial government within and alongside the Asia-Pacific Gateway and Corridor Initiative (APGCI), came from a range of local actors. The opposition took a variety of forms, from protests at various construction sites around the region to formal motions and electoral politics. In the City of Delta, former councillor Vicki Huntington ran successfully for the provincial assembly as an independent candidate, campaigning against the loss of agricultural land for port and highway expansion (Hall and Clark 2010). Huntington secured support from the local Conservative member of Parliament John Cummins (2007, 1), who expressed his opposition to the policy of his own government in a 2007 mail-out to voters: "Quality of life is being sacrificed in communities south of the Fraser River as the federal and provincial governments push ahead with the Asia-Pacific Gateway Corridor project." Municipal politicians also expressed opposition and

TABLE 4.7
Gateway coalition organizational memberships and board composition

Organization	*Members*
Round Table on the Greater Vancouver Gateway (1991–93)	BC Maritime Employers Association
	BC Wharf Operators Association
	CN Rail
	CP Rail
	Chamber of Shipping of BC
	Fraser River Harbour Commission
	ILWU Canada
	Vancouver Port Corporation
GVGC (1994–present)	YVR (Vancouver airport)
	VFPA (Port of Vancouver)
	CN Rail
	CP Rail
	BNSF Rail
	Southern Railway of BC
	BC Trucking Association
	BC Marine Terminal Operators Association
	Vancouver Terminal Elevator Operators
	TransLink
	UBC Sauder
	Shipping Federation of Canada
	BC Maritime Employers Association
APGST – Asia-Pacific Gateway Skills Table (ca. 2009–17)	BC Construction Association
	Chamber of Shipping of BC
	BC Road Builders and Heavy Construction Association
	Association of Professional Engineers and Geoscientists of BC
	BC Chamber of Commerce
	ILWU Canada
	BC Trades Training Consortium
	TransLink
	Independent Contractions and Business Association
	Prince Rupert Port Authority
	Applied Science Technologists and Technicians of BC
	Initiatives Prince George
	Business Council of BC
	International Union of Operating Engineers
	BC Building Trades
	BC Maritime Employers Association
	Western Transport Advisory Council
	Greater Vancouver Gateway Council
	VFPA (Port of Vancouver)
	BC Trucking Association

Organization	*Members*
GTC – Gateway Transportation Collaborative Forum (2014–present)	Transport Canada BC Ministry of Transportation and Infrastructure Vancouver Fraser Port Authority TransLink Greater Vancouver Gateway Council
GVUFC (2017–present)	BC Business Council BC Ministry of Transportation and Infrastructure BC Trucking Association Boards of Trade Business Improvement Areas (BIABC) Greater Vancouver Gateway Council Insurance Corporation of BC Metro Vancouver Metro Vancouver Alliance NAIOP Vancouver Chapter Municipal CAOs VFPA (Port of Vancouver) Retail Council of Canada TransLink Transport Canada, Pacific Region YVR (Vancouver airport)
Gateway Infrastructure Program Advisory Committee (2017–18)	BC Chamber of Commerce BC Marine Terminal Operators Association Canadian International Freight Forwarders Association Canadian Manufacturers and Exporters Chamber of Shipping of BC Coal Association of Canada Fertilizer Canada Global Automakers of Canada Greater Vancouver Board of Trade Greater Vancouver Gateway Council Canadian Association of Importers and Exporters (IE Canada) Shipping Federation of Canada Vancouver Terminal Elevators Association Western Canadian Shippers' Coalition

concern; especially vocal was the City of Burnaby, which remained strongly opposed to the expansion of Highway 1 west of the Port Mann Bridge.

In 2004, a group of community, environmental, and sustainable transportation advocacy organizations, academics, and individuals came together to form the Livable Region Coalition (LRC). Anthony Clark (2010) convincingly argues that the LRC was never fully successful in overcoming the differences among opponents to the gateway. Although these differences were often more about what to emphasize and what tactics to employ, they mapped onto important subregional differences between those living to the north and south of the Fraser River. In its founding mission, the LRC (2004) explicitly referenced upholding the principles of the Livable Region Strategic Plan (LRSP; GVRD 1996). However, the route of what was to become the South Fraser Perimeter Road, a highway of great concern to gateway opponents in places such as Delta, had already been included in the LRSP. In the absence of truly united region-wide opposition to the gateway, the South Fraser Perimeter Road project went ahead without formal opposition from Metro Vancouver. In contrast, Metro Vancouver expressed the view that the replacement of Port Mann Bridge and related Highway 1 expansion were incompatible with the LRSP (Clark 2010), although both projects also proceeded.

In one regime response to local opposition, the APGST (2012, 7) "initiated a study to explore the level of awareness and understanding of the gateway – and the opportunities for integrating gateway planning with regional and municipal planning." The study focused on the Metro Vancouver region, described as the "southern corridor" of the gateway, since by then the Port of Prince Rupert was being identified as the gateway to the "northern corridor." More than thirty planners and professionals were interviewed, including many working in municipal government.

> The consultations identified that the majority of planners and professionals do not have a clear understanding of who represents the Gateway, what the network includes or who to contact for more information. The Gateway is more commonly associated with specific construction projects or with the actions of individual partners. As a result, the network that comprises the Gateway is generally not well recognized, understood or integrated into regional and municipal planning processes. (APGST 2012, 7)

The recommendations of the 2012 APGST study provide a template for much of the institutionalization of the gateway council and its member organizations – described in the report as "Gateway Partners" – in regional planning processes that have followed since 2012. Recommended action in five areas includes:

- "Establish the Greater Vancouver Gateway Council (the Gateway Council) as the entity responsible for providing leadership and guidance on behalf of the Gateway partners" (8).

- "Develop and communicate Gateway plans and projects within the context of the Gateway network" (8).
- "Establish a role for the Gateway partners in the development and management of regional plans and policies, with priority emphasis on engagement in a regional goods movement strategy, a regional economic framework and TransLink's Regional Transportation Strategy" (9).
- "Implement processes at the municipal level to work with local governments and communities to identify how the network and specific initiatives fit with municipal Official Community Plans, transportation plans and community development opportunities" (10).
- "Build awareness and understanding of the Gateway among planners, professionals and elected officials, and establish opportunities for knowledge and skill development" (10).

These recommendations are technocratic in the sense that they afford leadership to an unelected body (the gateway council) and they take the existence and importance of the gateway as uncontested. Hence, they seek to coordinate and integrate gateway infrastructure and other projects into the existing municipal and regional land-use and transportation- and economic-development planning processes without exposing them to political debate. At the same time, the report is reflective and realistic about the challenges. For example, it notes a willingness on the part of planners to learn more about the gateway from its proponent organizations but notes a "skepticism about the willingness of organizations to share information and to engage in open and constructive discussions about how Gateway plans fit with regional and municipal goals and priorities" (10). The report repeatedly points to the Roberts Bank Rail Corridor – initiated in 2010 with funding from the APGCI – as an example of a successful approach to integration of plans and priorities.

THREE ROUNDS OF GATEWAY FUNDING IN VANCOUVER

Vancouver-area trade transportation infrastructure has benefited from three rounds of federal funding: the 2006 APGCTIF and the 2017 and 2019 rounds of NTCF (the region did not benefit directly from the Gateways and Border Crossings Fund discussed elsewhere). With multiple announcements – often of the same projects with new titles and updated funding details – it is extremely difficult to keep accurate count of which of the many projects received how much funding. In many cases, federal funding leveraged funding from other government sources as well as the private sector.

Transport Canada's evaluation of the APGCI (and the Gateways and Border Crossings Fund) states that "in total, Government of Canada funding for the APGCI was $1.17 billion from October 19, 2006 to March 31, 2018" (Transport Canada 2017a, 4). The report identifies sixty-one projects approved by June 2016 and that the $817 million paid out by that date had leveraged projects worth over three times that amount ($2.76 billion). According to the Port of Vancouver, the APGCI resulted in approximately $7.5 billion of investment in gateway infrastructure (Port of Vancouver 2022). This count would include federal and provincial funding and private sector resources. Of course, it is almost impossible to say how much private sector funding would have been spent in the absence of the federal program; indeed, it is not even clear how much of the provincial gateway infrastructure spending would have been invested in the absence of the federal program. However, in the absence of a credible counterfactual, we can say that the federal program was associated with significant private and other public investments in trade-supporting transportation infrastructure.

The APGCI also leveraged funding from the provincial government. In early 2007, the Government of Canada and the Province of British Columbia entered into the "Asia-Pacific Gateway and Corridor Initiative, Transportation Component Agreement, 2006–2007/2011–2011." The agreement, later extended to the end of the 2013–14 fiscal year, funded a series of transportation projects that supported international trade on a fifty/fifty basis up to a maximum of $126.75 million. The agreement created a fund with a cochaired management committee consisting of senior Transport Canada and BC Ministry of Transportation staff, deepening the relationship between the respective government bureaucracies. The seven projects funded and implemented through this mechanism inevitably reflected their overlapping interests around a series of highway projects. These projects were not exclusively within the Lower Mainland; they included the Simon Fraser Bridge in Prince George and improvements in the BC interior to Highways 1, 16, and 97.

In Metro Vancouver itself, the federal-provincial funding was used for three projects, each of which tells important stories about the nature of the interaction between government interests. For local amenity and environmental opponents, these three projects, along with the provincial government's project to replace and expand the Port Mann Bridge, became emblematic of "the Gateway":

- Pitt River Bridge and Mary Hill Bypass, which provided additional road connectivity for the CP rail yards in Port Coquitlam and Pitt Meadows.

However, this project was but one part of what the GVGC's 2001 MCTS study had designated as the North Fraser Perimeter Road. Despite the completion of road expansion in the eastern portion funded through the APGCI, the western portion of the North Fraser Perimeter Road remains uncompleted due to municipal opposition to what was perceived as adding unwanted truck traffic.

- Environmental assessment for what became the South Fraser Perimeter Road, which provided direct highway access between the Deltaport complex, industrial sites in Tilbury and North Delta, the Fraser Surrey Docks, and the CN rail yards in Surrey. As indicated above, the South Fraser Perimeter Road follows a route first identified in the LRSP (GVRD 1996) that was a high priority for the Port of Vancouver and GVGC. The project proceeded despite significant environmental concerns about the impact of the road and associated industrial development on Burns Bog in the City of Delta.
- 41B Overpass at Deltaport Way, which separated a local roadway (41B) from the main road and rail corridors leading to the Deltaport complex. The project achieved improved safety and connectivity for area farmers, residents of the TFN, and the Ladner neighbourhood in the City of Delta. The project is also notable for having improved access to logistics and industrial land developments on the TFN territory. The 41B Overpass was one of six overpass projects, along with a whistle cessation project and rail crossing information system project that together comprise the Roberts Bank Rail Corridor.

The 41B Overpass project also serves to illustrate the role of the Port of Vancouver in creating a mechanism to collect infrastructure funding contributions from private industry – although this also highlights how difficult it can be for researchers (and the media and public) to trace the sources and use of funding in the federal infrastructure program.

For the $24 million 41B Overpass project, the Canada-BC agreement funded $5 million (on a fifty/fifty basis). The overpass was part of the Roberts Bank Rail Corridor project, originally budgeted at $307 million, making it one of the largest projects funded through the APGCI. Some of the key APGCI-funded projects in the Lower Mainland were included in what the Port of Vancouver identified as its seventeen Priority Gateway Infrastructure Projects, with a combined original budget value of $716 million. Of the original $716 million, the terminal industry agreed – apparently with some reluctance – to contribute $167 million. That amount was prefunded by the Port of Vancouver, which then recouped

90 percent of what it had paid through a levy on the cargo throughput on all the terminal operators. The levy was known as the Gateway Infrastructure Fee (GIF) (Port of Vancouver 2015).

The formula for recouping the funding also had its own nuances and complexities to reflect the mix of cargo and infrastructure needs of various parts of the larger port complex; agreement on, or least acceptance of, the formula and levy represents a remarkable achievement of collective action by the port authority. Arguably, the GIF also laid the foundation for a new understanding of the Lower Mainland's geography, one that does not respect municipal boundaries. The GIF formula divides the funding mechanism according to the local geography of key projects, which makes sense since this is a way to ensure a close match between the source of funding and the beneficiaries. In practice, this means that there are three different levy formulas for terminals on the north (North Shore Trade Area) and south (South Shore Trade Area) shores of the Burrard Inlet and for the Roberts Bank Trade Area – to which has been added (by the GTCF) the Fraser River Trade Area (see Figure 4.2). In essence, the gateway regime (GTCF 2014) has crafted a new subregional map of greater Vancouver, one that collapses twenty-three local governments into four trade areas.

Approaches taken, forums created, and funding mechanisms developed under the APGCI have provided templates and lessons for the subsequent rounds of federal infrastructure funding. For instance, in 2017, the Port

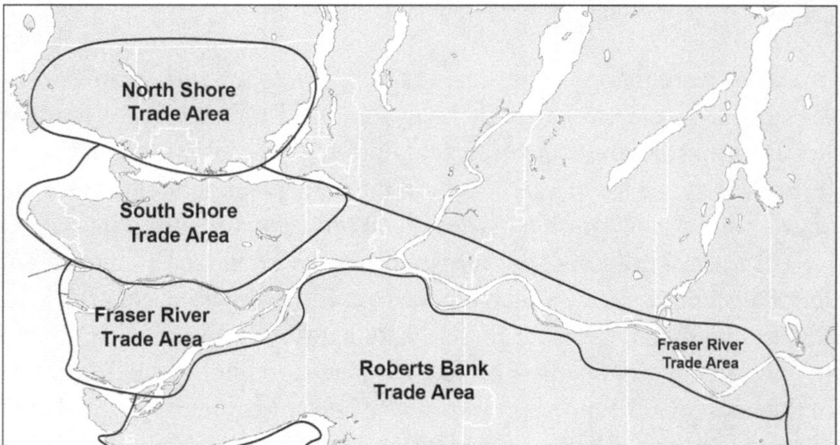

FIGURE 4.2 Metro Vancouver and Lower Mainland trade areas | *Cartography:* Steve Tornes, recreated based on GTCF (2014). *Source:* Statistics Canada (2021a).

of Vancouver convened a new industry advisory body, the Gateway Infrastructure Program Advisory Committee, to prepare for industry to fund its share of the projects being submitted to the NTCF. This consultation has led to the adoption of a second round of levy funding, known as GIF2022 (Port of Vancouver 2020c).

And despite the inclusion of more local and regional nonindustry voices in bodies such as the GVUFC, the sense of distance between the gateway and elected municipal government remains. The May 2019 media release from the Port of Vancouver (2019) regarding two rail crossing projects in the northeastern municipality of Pitt Meadows is instructive as to the ambivalent reception such infrastructure projects receive from local government. Pitt Meadows, along with its neighbour Port Coquitlam, accommodates the main CP rail yards in Metro Vancouver. The NTCF funding for these projects was initially announced in 2018; the 2019 media release was to confirm the funding agreement between the port authority and federal government.

Such rail crossing projects – sometimes referred to as grade separations – are generally popular (as was the Roberts Bank Rail Corridor) because, in the words of the press release (Port of Vancouver 2019), they help "improve public safety, emergency response times, and commute times, while reducing congestion and greenhouse gas emissions related to idling vehicles. These upgrades will help remove bottlenecks for trains, improving the flow of goods and helping accommodate growing trade." The media release noted that the project had been identified and prioritized through "a collaborative planning process called the Gateway Transportation Collaboration Forum. The forum is made up of the Vancouver Fraser Port Authority, Transport Canada, TransLink, the BC Ministry of Transportation and Infrastructure, and the Greater Vancouver Gateway Council." The media release included positive quotes from the CEO of the Port, the federal minister of transport, and the provincial government.

The mayor of Pitt Meadows was positive about the project, but note the unfinished business signalled in the last sentence of his quote, included here in its entirety:

> This important milestone represents the culmination of a great deal of work by each of the organizations over the past seven months. Rail grade separations in Pitt Meadows will mean that police, fire and ambulance services will be able to get to incidents faster and more easily. Public safety will be greatly improved. Commutes will be become more reliable and ultimately, drivers, cyclists and pedestrians will find it much easier

> to move around our community. Council will continue to advocate for the best interests of the community as we move toward finalizing the Memorandum of Understanding between the City and the project partners. Mayor Bill Dingwall, City of Pitt Meadows (Port of Vancouver 2019)

Even with an ostensibly popular project, even several months after the initial funding announcement, and on the occasion of the signing of the formal funding agreement, the municipal government was still working with the project partners to sort out the details. At the time of writing, the dispute over the rail separations remained unresolved. This is not a judgment on how worthy this infrastructure project is but rather to note the complexity of such arrangements. Here, the projects are first and foremost led by the gateway partners, and municipal governments are not equal partners, if they are at the table at all.

FUNDED PROJECTS AND THE NETWORKS OF GATEWAY PROPONENTS

In this last section of the chapter, we use network mapping and analysis to depict some of the coalitional dynamics described in the preceding sections. Figure 4.3 depicts the network of relationships surrounding selected APGCI-funded projects in British Columbia. Projects of interest include the APGCI general project (i.e., the various rail, road, and bridge projects within Metro Vancouver such as the Roberts Bank Rail Corridor, as well as projects in other parts of BC and Western Canada), the Skills Table, and the North Shore Trade Area study. It should be noted, however, that most projects directly assemble clusters of private sector actors, organizations whose singular connection is to these projects. More central to the network are industry associations led by the GVGC and major transportation services providers, the continental railroads and marine terminal operators (not labelled in the figure, but see Table 4.8). In contrast, municipal-tier governments are typically networked indirectly to the funded projects through singular connections to other governments and agencies, including Metro Vancouver, TransLink, and the Port Authority. Executive democracy is exemplified by the centrality of such senior governments (including the province and its Ministry of Transportation, Transport Canada) and public agencies in the Vancouver gateway regime. Civil society groups and First Nations are rather peripheral to this network.

Figure 4.4 depicts the network of relationships surrounding selected projects funded through the first (2017) round of the NTCF, while Figure 4.5 depicts the relationships surrounding the second round (2019) of the

NTCF. Notably, Metro Vancouver (the regional district government) occupies a more central role in both figures, with particularly close network connections to TransLink and the GVUFC. Metro Vancouver continues to provide a point of connection for municipal governments, although there are indications of some more direct involvement from individual municipalities in specific projects. This is in keeping with the technocratic engagement of local government in projects that have advanced to funding. Figures 4.4 and 4.5 reveal the continued centrality of the GVGC, as well as of government agencies such as Transport Canada and TransLink. Noting that this network analysis includes all of British Columbia, some First Nations located in and around the Port of Prince Rupert are now well connected to the projects funded in that part of the province.

Finally, the patterns depicted in Figures 4.3–4.5 are confirmed through network analysis presented in Table 4.8. Here we present the top ten network members in the three funding rounds, as measured by two standard network indicators. Degree centrality is a count of the total number of connections a node has with other nodes. It is taken as an indicator of the extent to which a node is connected to all the other nodes in a network. Betweenness centrality is a count of the number of times a node is on the

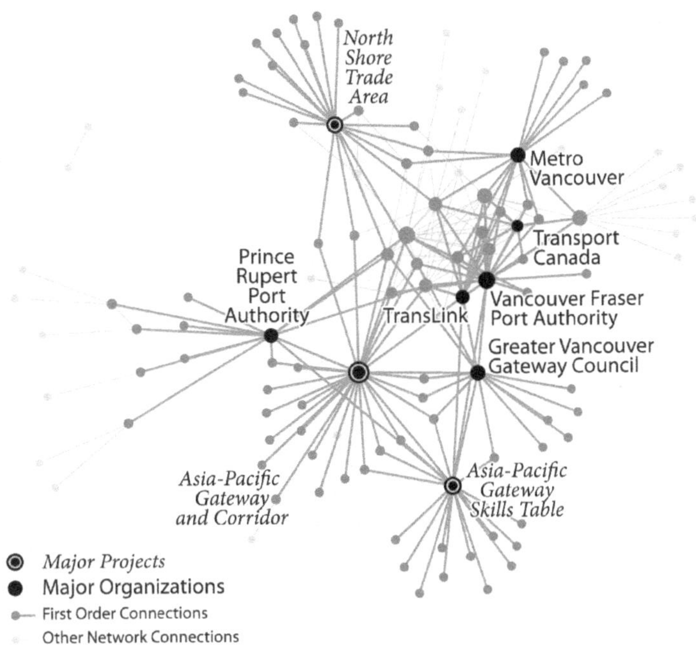

FIGURE 4.3 Network relationships around APGCI-funded projects in British Columbia

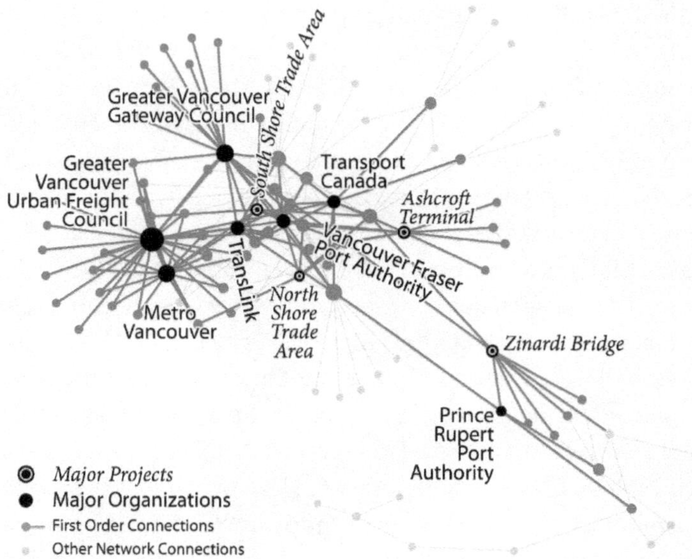

FIGURE 4.4 Network relationships around NTCF 2017-funded projects in British Columbia

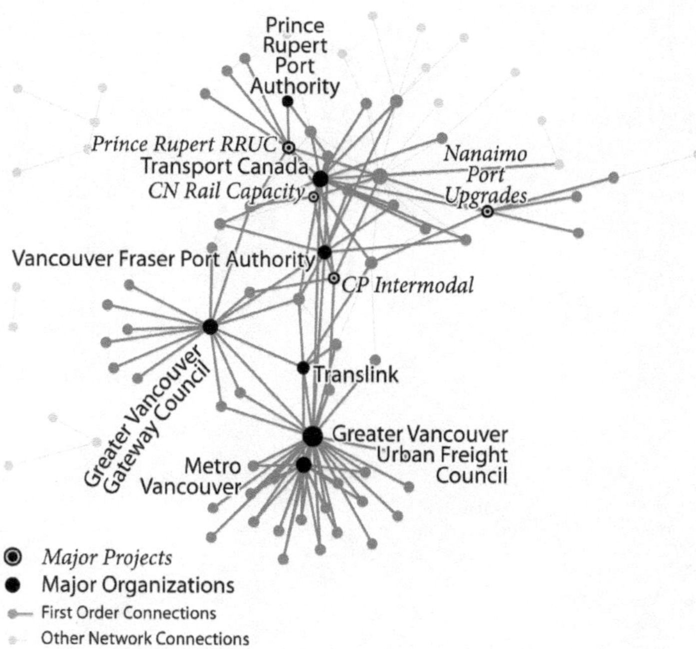

FIGURE 4.5 Network relationships around NTCF 2019-funded projects in British Columbia

TABLE 4.8
Top ten network members, British Columbia

Rank by Centrality score	*Asia-Pacific Gateway and Corridor Initiative projects*		*NTCF 2017 round projects*		*NTCF 2019 round projects*	
	Degree centrality	*Betweenness centrality*	*Degree centrality*	*Betweenness centrality*	*Degree centrality*	*Betweenness centrality*
1	Vancouver Fraser Port Authority	Prince Rupert Port Authority	Greater Vancouver Urban Freight Council	Greater Vancouver Urban Freight Council	Greater Vancouver Urban Freight Council	Greater Vancouver Urban Freight Council
2	Government of Canada	Government of Canada	Greater Vancouver Gateway Council	Greater Vancouver Gateway Council	Government of Canada	TransLink
3	City of Delta	City of Delta	Metro Vancouver	Government of Canada	Transport Canada	Government of British Columbia
4	Greater Vancouver Gateway Council	Greater Vancouver Gateway Council	Government of Canada	Prince Rupert Port Authority	Metro Vancouver	Greater Vancouver Gateway Council
5	City of Surrey	Vancouver Fraser Port Authority	Vancouver Fraser Port Authority	Transport Canada	Greater Vancouver Gateway Council	Metro Vancouver
6	Metro Vancouver	TransLink	TransLink	Canadian National Railway	Vancouver Fraser Port Authority	Government of Canada
7	Prince Rupert Port Authority	Metro Vancouver	Transport Canada	Coast Tsimshian Enterprises	TransLink	Transport Canada
8	District of North Vancouver	Canadian National Railway	Canadian Pacific Railway	Vancouver Fraser Port Authority	Government of British Columbia	DP World Canada
9	TransLink	District of North Vancouver	Canadian National Railway	Canadian Pacific Railway	Gateway Transportation Collaboration Forum	BC Ministry of Transportation and Infrastructure
10	Government of British Columbia	City of Surrey	BC Ministry of Transportation and Infrastructure	Metro Vancouver	BC Ministry of Transportation and Infrastructure	Vancouver Fraser Port Authority

shortest path between two other nodes. It is taken as an indicator of the extent to which a node is a connector between other nodes in a network.

The two network indicators applied to each of the three funding rounds confirm that municipal governments are not central in any of the networks. Two municipalities appear in the APGCI – Delta and Surrey – because of their importance to the Roberts Bank Rail Corridor. However, even though we did observe some direct municipal involvement in the NTCF-funded projects, no municipality occupies a central (top ten) role in these projects. This is one indicator that technocratic involvement of municipalities in specific projects does not create (or guarantee) a position of influence. At the same time, the emergence of the GVUFC as the most important actor in the NTCF network, and the associated heightened network importance of Metro Vancouver, provides some support for the conclusion that trade-and-transportation gateway proponents have learned about the importance of wider consultation – at least in comparison with the early days of the APGCI.

CONCLUSION

Our analysis of the changing practices of Vancouver's gateway regime from the APGCI to the recent rounds of the NTCF reveals some evolution in the network of relationships between actors pursuing trade gateway development. The most recent evidence shows an institutionalization of gateway-related perspectives in regional transportation, infrastructure, and land-use planning processes. As a result, pro-trade interests have become embedded in key local and regional institutions, alongside the creation of new forums for technocratic engagement with the representatives of municipal governments. In part, this reflects the depth of urban-based transportation industry engagement with federal and provincial governments and their trade agendas.

It is equally clear that the proponents of trade and its attendant infrastructures have followed a trajectory of responding to resistance and demands for greater local involvement without actually handing over decision-making power to local elected representatives. The Vancouver case is important in relation to the other Canadian cities discussed in this book because it inspired efforts elsewhere, most notably with the formation of the Halifax Gateway Council in 2004 (see Chapter 7). Vancouver does not provide a case of some external actor or actors imposing their view on the locality. Rather, this is the story of one group of local actors seeking to build support for their vision and successfully overcoming other local interests and opposition. At the same time that these local proponents were attracting support and resources from senior governments, they advanced a mode of technocratic engagement within various regional agencies and decision-making forums that promotes executive democratic practices by minimizing political engagement with local municipal democracy.

5

Toronto and the Continental Gateway

THE CONTINENTAL GATEWAY AND TRADE CORRIDOR: CONNECTING TORONTO AND MONTREAL

In the next two chapters, we discuss the engagement of Canada's two largest metropolitan regions, Toronto and Montreal, with the trade corridor and related policy initiatives. While the two metropolises formed part of the same federally designated gateway and corridor initiative that sought to forge a bi-provincial and international strategy, we devote a separate chapter to each because the particular circumstances were so different before, during, and after the federal intervention.

Following on the success of the Asia-Pacific Gateway and Corridor Initiative (APGCI), the federal government released its *National Policy Framework for Strategic Gateway and Trade Corridor* in 2007, one component of which was the creation of the Ontario-Quebec Continental Gateway and Trade Corridor (OQCGTC). This strategic designation reflected the region as "a vital component of Canada's multimodal transportation system," which "provides a critical link between all key gateway facilities and also to Canada-U.S. border crossings" (Transport Canada 2012). Building on the federal government's integrative trade strategy, a memorandum of understanding (MoU) was signed between the governments of Canada, Ontario, and Quebec "to develop, in partnership with the private and public sectors, a strategic, secure, sustainable and competitive multimodal transport system to support international trade" (Lévesque 2010).

In practice, the Continental Gateway has evolved to encompass the entire St. Lawrence–Great Lakes corridor – also known as the Quebec-Windsor corridor (see Figure 5.1). This territory is vital to Canada's

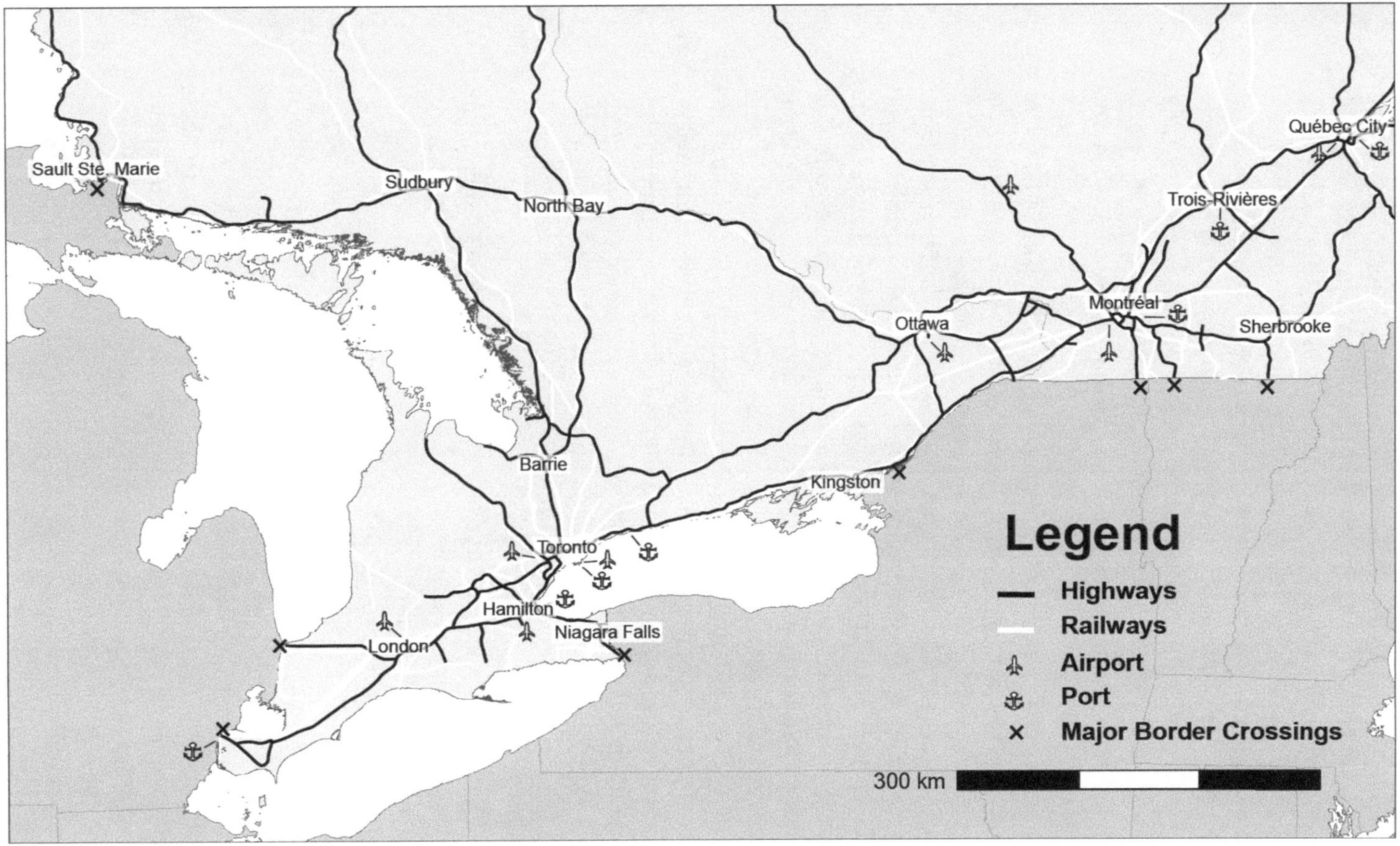

FIGURE 5.1 Ontario-Quebec Continental Gateway and Trade Corridor: Major transportation infrastructure and border crossings | *Cartography*: Steve Tornes. *Sources:* Commission for Environmental Cooperation (2022), Government of Canada (2021b), Statistics Canada (2021b).

economic heartland, shaping its ability to connect to North America's Midwest hinterland and a population of 135 million consumers (Lévesque 2010). As we shall see, this initiative had rather modest political and economic repercussions; but, as a mere recognition of the importance of this multimodal transportation system to Canada's economy, it helped draw attention to many of the infrastructural challenges facing the economies of central Canada. These included road congestion, lack of access to intermodal facilities, railway crossings, port capacity constraints, lack of policy harmonization, and a series of border crossing and security concerns (Lévesque 2010).

As such, the Continental Gateway was a government-initiated collaborative organizational structure between the federal and two provincial governments and a host of public and private stakeholders that aimed to identify "system efficiency, integration, capacity and condition, sustainability, as well as security and safety as areas where the three governments can focus their efforts" (Lévesque 2010). As represented in Figure 5.2, the Strategic Steering Committee was composed of three deputy ministers and three strategic advisors, and it received input from three units: a former Canadian ambassador to the US serving as strategic advisor, a Public Sector Advisory Committee, and a Private Sector Advisory Board. The Steering Committee's main responsibility was to supervise eight working groups set up under the MoU. Their agenda was determined through wide consultations with stakeholders, including business, university, and public sector experts. It included sustainability in the transportation sector, private sector involvement in public projects, and multimodal integration and border crossing (LNCPM 2008).

Although such a schematic governance framework does not highlight the (potential) organic connections to municipal actors, which are explored in both chapters, there are six important observations to make about the governance framework of the OQCGTC as a whole:

- The roles and responsibilities entrusted to the three transport ministers and deputy ministers are significant. It is they, and not the heads of the three governments or other departments with trade and economic mandates, who were tasked with the implementation of the government's new commercial policy. This is an important indicator of the prominence given to transportation infrastructure and systems in the entire gateway and trade corridor initiative.
- Related to the first point, with the Steering Committee or Secretariate drawn from either federal or provincial transport departments,

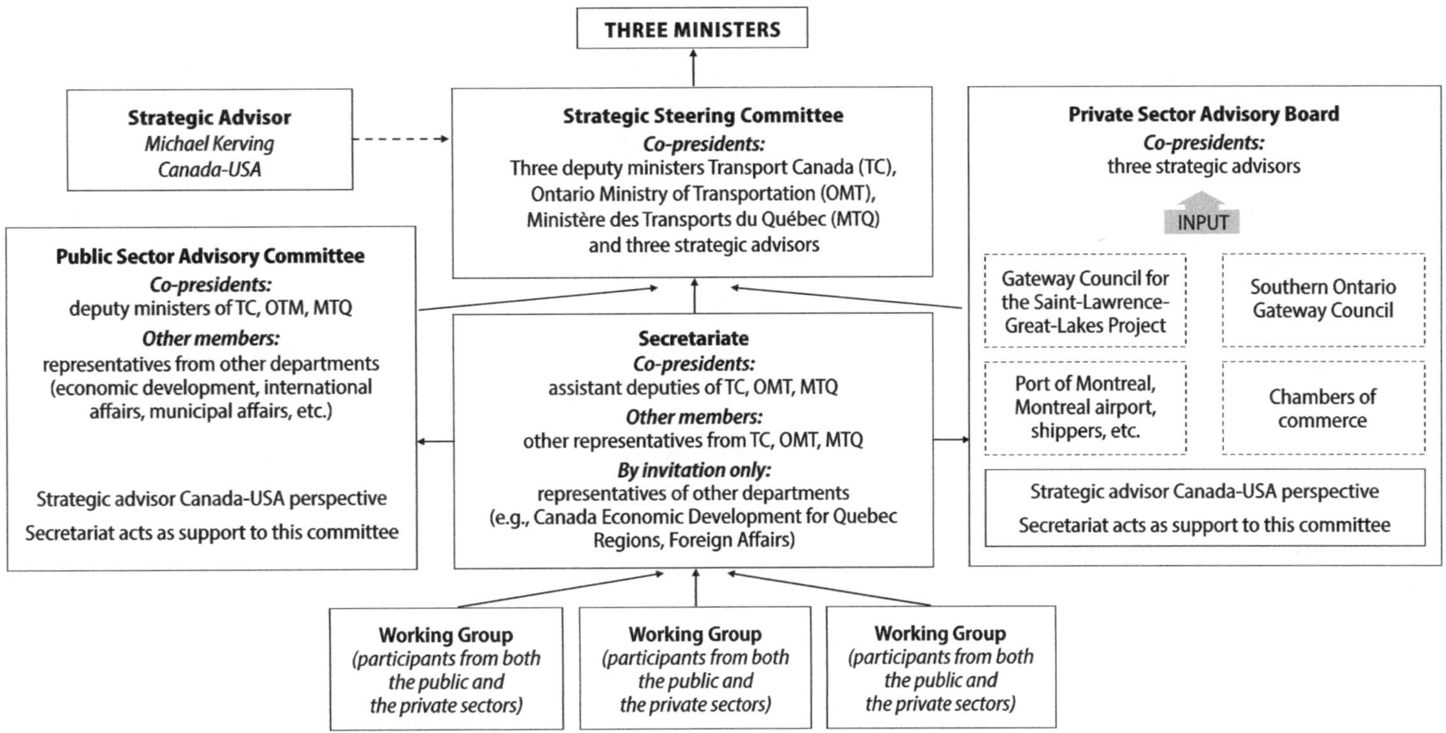

FIGURE 5.2 Governance framework of the Ontario-Quebec Continental Gateway and Trade Corridor | *Source:* Based on information in Governments of Canada, Ontario, and Québec, 2007.

representation from other departments was consigned to the Public Sector Advisory Board.

- While the Public Sector Advisory Board included the (provincial) departments of municipal affairs, lower tiers of governments, whether municipal or regional, enjoyed no direct representation at all.
- The eight working groups set up under the MoU carried out an impressive amount of research and published numerous reports. As such, if little came out of the MoU under the Conservative government in terms of hardware infrastructure investment for Quebec compared to Ontario, mostly for international border crossing projects,[1] the output for the Ministère des Transports du Quebec in terms of software (i.e., business, training) was significant (Evans, 2008).
- The Private Sector Advisory Board, which is tasked with bringing forward "the views of both shippers and transportation providers from all modes involved in international commerce, as well as the views of other key gateway and trade stakeholders" (Government of Canada 2007b), did so in a way that excluded consultations and perspectives from civil society actors.
- The strategic advisor providing insights from a "Canada-US perspective" appears to have enjoyed privileged influence, with direct access to the Strategic Steering Committee and a presence on the public and private sector advisory units. This illustrates the importance the federal and provincial governments confer on commerce with the US and on related investments in border crossing improvements.

Despite this structure, interprovincial coordinating efforts have been minimal, notably owing to the distinct functions and responsibilities imparted to both city-regions by superior governments. Since 1960 in particular, efforts by successive Quebec governments to integrate the economic development of the city-region of Montreal into their own national political framework to support their economic and social priorities have at times been at odds with the historical and national outlook promoted by successive federal governments (Polèse and Shearmur 2003). Nevertheless, regarding gateway-related projects in Montreal, both provincial policies and federal investments in infrastructure receive the support and backing of many stakeholders, including the private sector. In contrast, the economic development of the city-region of Toronto has proceeded in fragmented ways as a result of significant and increasing demographic and economic growth across an expanding territory, building on and transcending the historical industrial base of the Great Lakes region (Polèse and Shearmur 2003). In this context, gateway-related projects in and around Toronto are led by the private sector or local public authorities in municipalities outside of the City of Toronto, with the support of the Ontario and federal governments, but in less directive ways and without a cohesive vision for the city-region as a whole. The lack of interprovincial coordination on gateway projects can be partly explained by the distinct political culture of each province in approaching such initiatives, including a more *dirigiste* approach in the case of Montreal and a decentralized one for the city-region of Toronto (Brunelle et al. 2021).

Our network analysis confirms that stakeholders involved in the OQCGTC have not really bridged the interprovincial divide (see Figure 5.3). As the OQCGTC strategy was only one part of the collaborative effort to enhance the economic competitiveness of the Quebec-Windsor corridor, it built on projects facilitated by the federal government through the Gateways and Border Crossings Fund and the Canada-U.S.-Ontario-Michigan Border Transportation Partnership (Transport Canada 2008). At the provincial level, this strategy was part of broader efforts at that time to increase collaboration and harmonization, which included an Ontario-Quebec Economic Partnership Agreement for areas of increased collaboration as diverse as energy, labour mobility, public procurement, the Ontario-Quebec Climate Change Cap-and-Trade Initiative, and a Cooperation Agreement between Ontario and Quebec on Youth (Office of the Premier of Ontario 2008).

However, many of the stakeholders involved in the funded projects are not directly related to other actors, nor are urban-based stakeholders generally involved in infrastructure improvements outside of the boundaries of their city-region. Hence the network analysis depicted in Figure 5.3 reveals the central but separate role of both provincial governments in directing infrastructure improvement efforts across their province, alongside key metropolitan stakeholders such as CargoM in Montreal and Metrolinx in and around Toronto.

The success of the OQCGTC strategy is often framed by proponents in terms of the collaboration it permitted between Ontario and Quebec in managing a shared transportation and trade corridor. Our network analysis reveals limited success, as there was not a significant increase in collaborations between Quebec and Ontario due to this strategy. However, the strategy was successful in helping provinces determine their priorities, uses, and goals with respect to this federal vision. Moreover, it highlighted

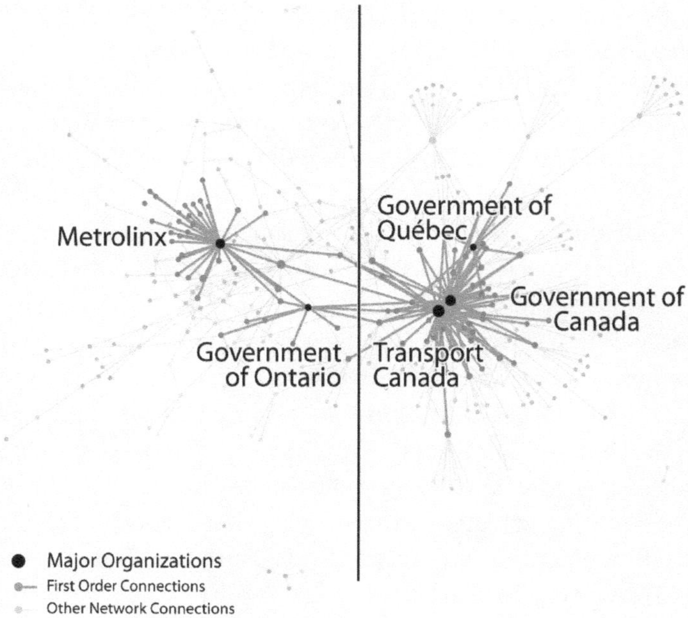

FIGURE 5.3 Network relationships around the Ontario-Quebec Continental Gateway and Trade Corridor

key differences in how each province relates to its main urban centre. While Quebec is more involved in integrating Montreal in its planning and priorities because of the city's central economic, political, and social role in supporting the province, the tense relationship between the Province of Ontario and the City of Toronto has contributed to a fragmented approach to regional planning. In practice, such an approach favours suburban municipalities and the interests of private sector actors.

As such, Montreal's municipal insertion in the federal gateway seems overly planned and aligned with provincial priorities. In contrast, both the city and the city-region of Toronto did not receive clear guidance from its province on how best to rely on gateway infrastructure funding to further its insertion in global value chains. Instead, the Ontario government saw this strategy as a means of securing infrastructure funding for particular border-crossing pinch points. In line with the importance of executive forms of democracy to guide such projects, the Continental Gateway has reinforced the position of each province in centring its role, priorities, and political culture in gateway transportation-infrastructure funding and planning. What all of this means for the dominant metropolitan areas of the two provinces is the substance of this chapter and the next.

SITUATING THE CITY-REGION OF TORONTO WITHIN THE CONTINENTAL GATEWAY

The history of transportation planning and related challenges in the Greater Toronto Area in southern Ontario, and more broadly in the Greater Golden Horseshoe, reveals how the priorities of the provincial government and selected municipalities intersect with the federal Continental Gateway Strategy and how transportation-infrastructure investments are framed and realized. Urban stakeholders in the Golden Horseshoe, such as municipalities and business proxies, have adapted their advocacy and implementation efforts in a decentralized and sector-based fashion across the region, with little to no attention to an overall regional, national, or continental approach. This is in line with the various gateway functions played by different municipalities and sectors, including complementary source (production), sink (consumption), and saddle (distribution) functions, across the region. Without the rise of a single urban coalition in the city-region of Toronto, various suburban and sectoral coalitions and business proxies play a key region-wide role in positioning the city-region in global value chains and fulfilling specific functions of the gateway.[2] From advanced manufacturing to transportation logistics, information and communication technology, and health technology, we reveal the role of secondary municipalities in Toronto's suburbs in establishing connections at subregional levels between transportation and economic development plans. At the same time, the City of Toronto is self-isolating from other regional stakeholders in trade corridor discussions to focus instead on urban livability for highly skilled individuals recruited to fuel the local knowledge-based economy.

The federal government's investment in transportation infrastructure in Ontario reflects the priority given to the Quebec-Windsor corridor, including the country's main border crossing area to the US and the vital economic importance of southern Ontario to Canada. However, the city-region of Toronto is difficult to define as a unit because it has shifting borders, depending on the stakeholder's position and perspective on its utility (Boudreau et al. 2006, 47). As Figure 5.4 illustrates, various expressions are used to describe this city-region, each with specific features, including select municipalities. While the population of the City of Toronto was just below 2.8 million in 2021, the Greater Toronto Area (GTA) – which includes the proximate regional municipalities of Halton, York, Peel, and Durham – was just above 6.2 million spread across twenty-one municipalities (see Table 5.1). The Greater Toronto and Hamilton Area's (GTHA) population exceeded 7.2 million across thirty different municipal entities, and the Golden Horseshoe's was above 9.7 million, divided into more than thirty-six municipal jurisdictions (Statistics Canada 2022a). Exceeding 10.2 million in 2021, the population of the Greater Golden Horseshoe – a designation that "includes the GTA as well as Peterborough, Kitchener-Waterloo, Guelph, and St. Catharines-Niagara" – is the broader geographical unit in which Toronto and its suburbs, as a city-region, can be understood. It is the preferred designation for provincial bodies in charge of planning, land-use, transportation, and economic development (Statistics Canada 2022a; Joy and Vogel 2015, 35), and it is used strategically by local stakeholders "as a means to access more power leverage in the federal arena" (Boudreau et al. 2007, 40) for advocates framing the regional relevance of particular local projects.

The importance of the city-region of Toronto is undeniable. As "Canada's Global City," it is the country's most important economic and demographic hub, with a consistent annual growth rate of 1.5 to 2.6 percent between 2011 and 2019. Approximately half of the province's population resides in the region and close to half of the population comprises immigrants to Canada (Joy and Vogel 2015, 37; Ontario Ministry of Finance 2020; Poiret 2017, 111–12; Statistics Canada 2022a). Besides the City of

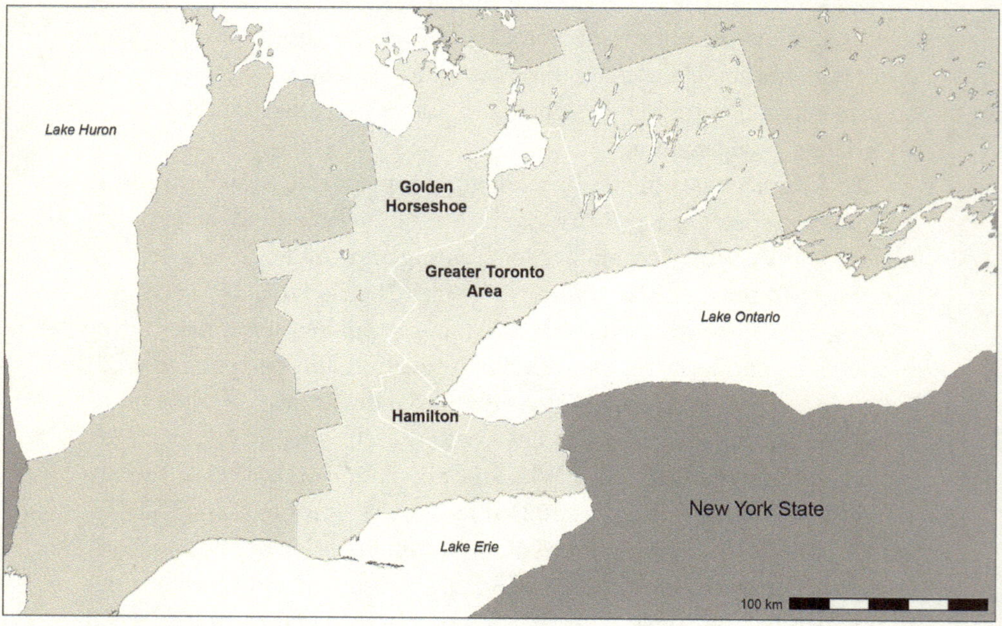

FIGURE 5.4 Greater Toronto region | *Cartography:* Steve Tornes. *Source:* Statistics Canada (2021a).

TABLE 5.1
Greater Toronto and Hamilton Area and constituent municipal governments, by 2021 population

	Population		*Growth (%)*	*Share (%)*	
Municipal Area	*2006*	*2021*	*2006–21*	*2006*	*2021*
Metro Toronto	5,112,796	6,202,225	21		
Toronto	2,503,281	2,794,356	12	49.0	45.1
Mississauga	668,599	717,961	7	13.1	11.6
Brampton	433,806	656,480	51	8.5	10.6
Markham	261,573	338,503	29	5.1	5.5
Vaughan	238,866	323,103	35	4.7	5.2
Richmond Hill	162,704	202,022	24	3.2	3.3
Oakville	165,613	213,759	29	3.2	3.4
Ajax	90,167	126,666	40	1.8	2.0
Pickering	87,838	99,186	13	1.7	1.6
Milton	53,889	132,979	147	1.1	2.1
Newmarket	74,295	87,942	18	1.5	1.4
Caledon	57,050	76,581	34	1.1	1.2
Halton Hills	55,289	62,951	14	1.1	1.0
Aurora	47,629	62,057	30	0.9	1.0
Georgina	42,346	47,642	13	0.8	0.8
Whitchurch-Stouffville	24,390	49,864	104	0.5	0.8
New Tecumseth	27,701	43,948	59	0.5	0.7
Bradford West Gwillimbury	24,039	42,880	78	0.5	0.7
Orangeville	26,925	30,167	12	0.5	0.5
East Gwillimbury	21,069	34,637	64	0.4	0.6
Uxbridge	19,169	21,556	12	0.4	0.3
King	19,487	27,333	40	0.4	0.4
Mono	7,071	9,421	33	0.1	0.2
Chippewas of Georgina Island First Nation	–	231	–		0.0
Metro Hamilton	692,911	785,184	13		
Hamilton	504,559	569,353	13	72.8	72.1
Burlington	164,415	186,948	14	23.7	23.8
Grimsby	23,937	28,883	21	3.5	3.7

Sources: Statistics Canada (2019, 2022b, 2022c).

Toronto itself, most of the economic activity is found in Toronto's suburbs and neighbouring municipalities, which bring in "a combined GDP of approximately $290 billion and are home to the majority of Canada's large domestic and multinational firms" (Joy and Vogel 2015, 37–38). Secondary cities such as Hamilton, Mississauga, and Vaughan in the regional municipalities surrounding Toronto have also been key in positioning the city-region in global value chains and in supporting its role in transportation logistics, as the movement of goods makes up 34 percent of the GDP of the Toronto-Waterloo corridor and 8 percent of Canada's GDP (Toronto Region BOT 2019). This is a good reflection of Ontario's economic reality, with exports to its five top markets – namely American, British, German, Chinese, and Mexican – in industries as diverse as transportation, primary metal, chemical, food, wholesale, and machinery manufacturing.

As a gateway city, Toronto's borders with its hinterlands have continually been redefined since the 1960s. With a constant incorporation of Toronto's suburbs and southern Ontario communities into the city's everyday operations, we witness a gradual shift in the organization of the hinterland from rural to urban affairs and from agricultural to industrial and postindustrial practices. Over the years and still today, the city-region of Toronto relies heavily on southern Ontario for the residential needs of the economic activity generated at the centre, including the City of Toronto and neighbouring municipalities (Polèse and Shearmur 2003; Zsolt 1993). More specifically, owing to sustained economic and population growth rates over the last twenty years (Joy and Vogel 2015; Poiret 2017), a shared everyday reality throughout southern Ontario pertaining to urban growth and transportation is the experience of "bottlenecks and gridlock at both the level of the globally oriented superstructure of airports, major highways, and rail corridors and at the level of the everyday infrastructure calibrated at the scale of the commuter shed, of individual municipalities, and of territorialized communities in the city and the suburbs" (Keil and Young 2008, 733).

Transportation challenges in the city-region of Toronto can be summarized in four main headings: the lack of efficiency and reliability of the current trade corridors caused by the amount of traffic (for local and international trade purposes), constant increases in activity that not only limit the ability to protect the current infrastructure but slow down any expansion projects, a lack of integration of the transportation system across the region, and logistical problems relating to intermodal transitions and multimodality – especially the accessibility of such facilities from roads (Montsion 2019).

Jean-Paul Addie (2013, 189) explains how the combination of a lack of capital investment, difficulties in creating a regional transportation network, and limited intergovernmental collaborations have been identified as the main impediments to finding solutions to these problems. Such problems are symptomatic of alignment issues between the various political units and jurisdictions involved in managing regional economic, demographic, and social processes, including growth. Specifically, the GTHA is based on a two-tier system of municipal government, with a division of labour between municipalities (lower tier) and regional municipalities (upper tier) determined on a case-by-case basis in all of its six regions. This is aside from powers given by the province to special-purpose bodies at the regional level, such as conservation authorities and the activities of federally mandated agencies on this territory (Government of Ontario 2021).[3] This political configuration results in jurisdictional fragmentation, confusion, and competition and heightens the difficulties in developing planning, institution building, and thinking at the regional level. As Meghan Joy and Ronald Vogel (2015, 49) indicate, "Although there is little support for a regional government for the GTA, there is still the need to develop a capacity for metropolitan or regional planning in economic development, transportation and related infrastructure. These plans need to address not just economic growth but also the social and human capital needs of the city-region."

The lack of regional planning has hindered the Golden Horseshoe's growth and its positioning in global value chains since the late 1980s, and it is expected that such trends will continue (Addie 2013). The Ontario Chamber of Commerce demonstrated that road congestion alone is responsible for "$3.3 billion annually in lost productivity, and despite a broad consensus regarding the need to develop new transportation infrastructure, political and financing mechanisms infringe upon the GTA's capacity to realize large-scale investment" (Addie 2013, 189). Meanwhile, the city-region's population is estimated to reach at least 13.5 million by 2041 (Ontario Ministry of Municipal Affairs and Housing 2021).

In this context, the City of Toronto does not provide regional leadership in planning the movement of goods and peoples, while secondary cities in Toronto's suburbs, and especially its neighbouring regional municipalities, have taken an increasingly important role in such matters. In this chapter, we highlight how the current deployment of the Continental Gateway Strategy in the city-region of Toronto has been shaped by the preferred province-wide approach to managing municipal affairs and urbanization in southern Ontario, namely to reinforce the control over transportation-infrastructure planning by the provincial Ministry of Transportation. In this view, transportation priorities are somewhat detached from local economic development plans, and so the positioning of the city-region in global value chains relies on a series of suburban coalitions coalesced around specific industry clusters. More concretely, we observe that Hamilton-Wentworth and Durham regions are playing a key role in mobilizing stakeholders of the Golden Horseshoe as it pertains to advanced manufacturing, while Peel Region is key in the transportation logistics sector, Halton region in information and communication technology and health technology for small and medium enterprises, and York Region in major information and communication technology companies. In contrast, the City of Toronto, in partnership with the Waterloo region, has focused on artificial intelligence, hence being more distant from regional discussions around urban freight and transportation logistics. This configuration of suburban interest in transportation logistics and niche industrial clustering for a better positioning in global value chains seems to set the city-region of Toronto apart from the other Canadian gateway city-regions: there is no leading urban coalition in the Greater Golden Horseshoe linking regional transportation-infrastructure discussions, economic development plans, and global value chains positioning. Rather, we find a decentralized series of sector-based and subregional coalitions led by urban stakeholders, including regional municipalities and private sector actors, building on historical patterns of fragmentary relationships between the City of Toronto, the Province of Ontario, and the federal government.

We explore the evolution of regional governance in support of local economic plans, in light of recent economic restructuring and repositioning of the city-region and the evolution of three distinct logics of regional governance, as currently deployed by local stakeholders. This sets the stage for a review of the configurations of these stakeholders through official rounds of federal funding based on a series of suburban and sector-based coalitions of local stakeholders. We conclude this chapter by contrasting the coalitions found in the City of Toronto with those in the suburbs, notably as it pertains to incorporating civil society actors and citizen voices into such projects.

THE HISTORICAL RELATIONSHIP BETWEEN THE PROVINCE AND THE CITY-REGION

In Ontario, a dialectical relationship can be seen between municipal reformism aimed at aligning social processes with democratic representation and a liberal conception of municipal affairs, looking at the territory through its economic value mostly, which has led to a decentralized approach to managing Toronto. Such an approach resulted in a significant influence of various business elites from particular economic sectors amid a drive for municipal consolidation into a service region, to the detriment of local democracy and autonomy (Poiret 2011). The history of relationships between the Province of Ontario and municipal governments in the Golden Horseshoe is shaped by tensions between the powers given to the City of Toronto concerning sustained urbanization over the years and the growing importance of its suburbs in meeting their own interest. Such tensions have been mediated by the various and often fragmented priorities of the provincial and federal governments for the city-region's economic, political, and social development, and they have opened the door to private sector leadership in providing coherence to the regional positioning in global value chains. As Addie (2013, 210) notes, "Toronto's structural capacity to employ its desired state spatial restructuring is greatly limited since the city, as with other Canadian municipalities, is subject to the political machinations of the Province" – a context in which most stakeholders "share an understanding of regional transportation development for future prosperity of the region, although the scale and form of this regionalization is contested." In this section, we discuss the historical relationships between the Ontario and municipal governments of the region to shed light on how regional transportation planning has developed in the city-region in ways that are fraught with tensions and contradictions.

The political geography of the Toronto region was shaped in the post-war period by the creation of the "two-tiered government framework of the *Municipality of Metropolitan Toronto*" in 1953, creating "a Fordist-Keynesian regime which proved (largely) adept to managing issues of urban growth" (Addie 2013, 198). The metropolitan government, or Metro Toronto, had the responsibility of "various local welfare state and collective consumption services with a number of local municipalities that had retained autonomy in many areas of municipal concern including fire and waste disposal services as well as water" (Boudreau et al. 2006, 31). Broadly defined, the establishment of this metropolitan entity made it possible to use "urban transportation as a spatial strategy to support infrastructure-led urban growth," with significant investments from both metropolitan and provincial governments and with the noted absence of federal investments (Addie 2013, 198). Using transportation as an engine of growth and accumulation, the strategy of both governments led to a "development-transportation nexus" in which Toronto's increasing economic importance resulted in a growing role for industry stakeholders to shape urban development (Addie 2013, 198).

The schism between the City of Toronto and its suburbs has its roots in the GTA's significant urban expansion of the early 1970s arising from "a lack of institutionalized regional governance," which "undermined Metro's growth region" as "suburban municipalities, growing in political strengths, resisted the extension of Metro's influence" (Addie 2013, 199). The Ontario government sided with the suburbs early on in limiting the planning authority of the metropolitan government, which set up a regional dynamic between the core and the suburbs fraught with tensions and leading to a general lack of regional integration over the years. As Julie-Anne Boudreau et al. (2006, 43) explain, "In the 1960s and 1970s, the Ontario government was much more active at that broader regional scale than it was in the 1990s. In the 1960s, it stripped Metro Toronto of its planning responsibilities and transferred them to a provincial agency that was working around the concept of a Toronto-centered Region." This reflects another important historical relationship still active today, whereby the provincial and federal governments have, from time to time, "attempted to influence the ways in which Toronto might grow" through a specific, top-down understanding of the city-region (Boudreau et al. 2006, 34–35). This brought the provincial government into conflict with urban civil society at times, as was seen in the case of resistance to the Spadina Expressway (Boudreau et al. 2006).

However, the Ontario government has regularly pushed for a more coherent governance model for the region, but this has never succeeded. In the late 1980s, the Office for the Greater Toronto Area was created with the purpose of offering and executing concrete regional plans and solutions, but it did not lead to much more than commission-style recommendations that were never fully realized (Boudreau et al. 2006, 35). Inefficiency in addressing the lack of regional coherence and integration led to a difficult situation at the end of the 1980s, as an incomplete metropolitan transportation system started to impede regional economic growth. Addie (2013, 199) explains that "as the spatial logic of transit investment had focused on the metropolitan scale, Toronto transit was disconnected from the GTA's globalizing infrastructure and emerging regional nodes, and lacked interregional governance integration." For instance, while Pearson International Airport currently connects with the transit systems of Toronto, Mississauga, and Brampton, a transit hub to connect the airport to the other transit systems of the region is not expected to be operational for many years.

Many efforts to address and redress the regional governance structure of Toronto – not only the recommendations of the Office for the Greater Toronto Area but also a provincial Royal Commission on the Toronto Waterfront – came to a halt in the mid-1990s with the election of Mike Harris's Progressive Conservative government (Boudreau et al. 2006, 35; Keil and Young 2008, 732). This election shifted the nature of provincial-municipal discussions for the Toronto city-region from regional integration to municipal mergers and amalgamation (Boudreau et al. 2006, 35). The 1998 "one-tier new City of Toronto" is the result of a fusion of the previous governance model into a single governance structure. "Driven by a civil service agenda not a political one" (Sancton 2000, 121), this technocratic reform was appealing to conservative government priorities because it was meant to dynamize the economic development of the region while "downloading significant social and physical infrastructure costs onto the city without commensurate revenue generating capacity" (Joy and Vogel 2015, 40–41). By creating relatively weak regional bodies like the Greater Toronto Services Board and by refusing to delegate significant powers to a metropolitan government, including for regional economic planning, this reform – part of Harris's Common Sense Revolution – led to an exacerbation of the tensions between the City of Toronto and its suburbs (Addie 2013, 199; Joy and Vogel 2015, 41). As Addie (2013, 199) puts it, "Megacity Toronto crystallized a rescaled, often combative relationship between the city and suburbs which fundamentally structures the politics of transportation in southern Ontario." Such a mindset, which fits well with the neoliberal precepts of the Harris government, also led to the reframing of ongoing regional initiatives along austerity lines, including making the King's Highway 407 a toll route, when the initial plan was to build a toll-free highway to alleviate traffic on the Toronto section of Highway 401.

At a time when "Metro Toronto government no longer corresponded with the city-region boundaries now extending to the larger GTA" (Joy and Vogel 2015, 40), such neoliberal restructuring also changed the landscape of local urban organizing and activism. Social protests, which were previously focused on federal and provincial governments' efforts to shape Toronto as an economic unit, were now relocated to the metropolitan level, in a context where such a regional level had become even more difficult to define owing to the disappearance of the GTA-scale in provincial public policy (Boudreau et al. 2006, 36–37, 43). These reforms led to an increasing democratic deficit in the city-region, as they resulted in "decreased local representation in transportation decision making, more

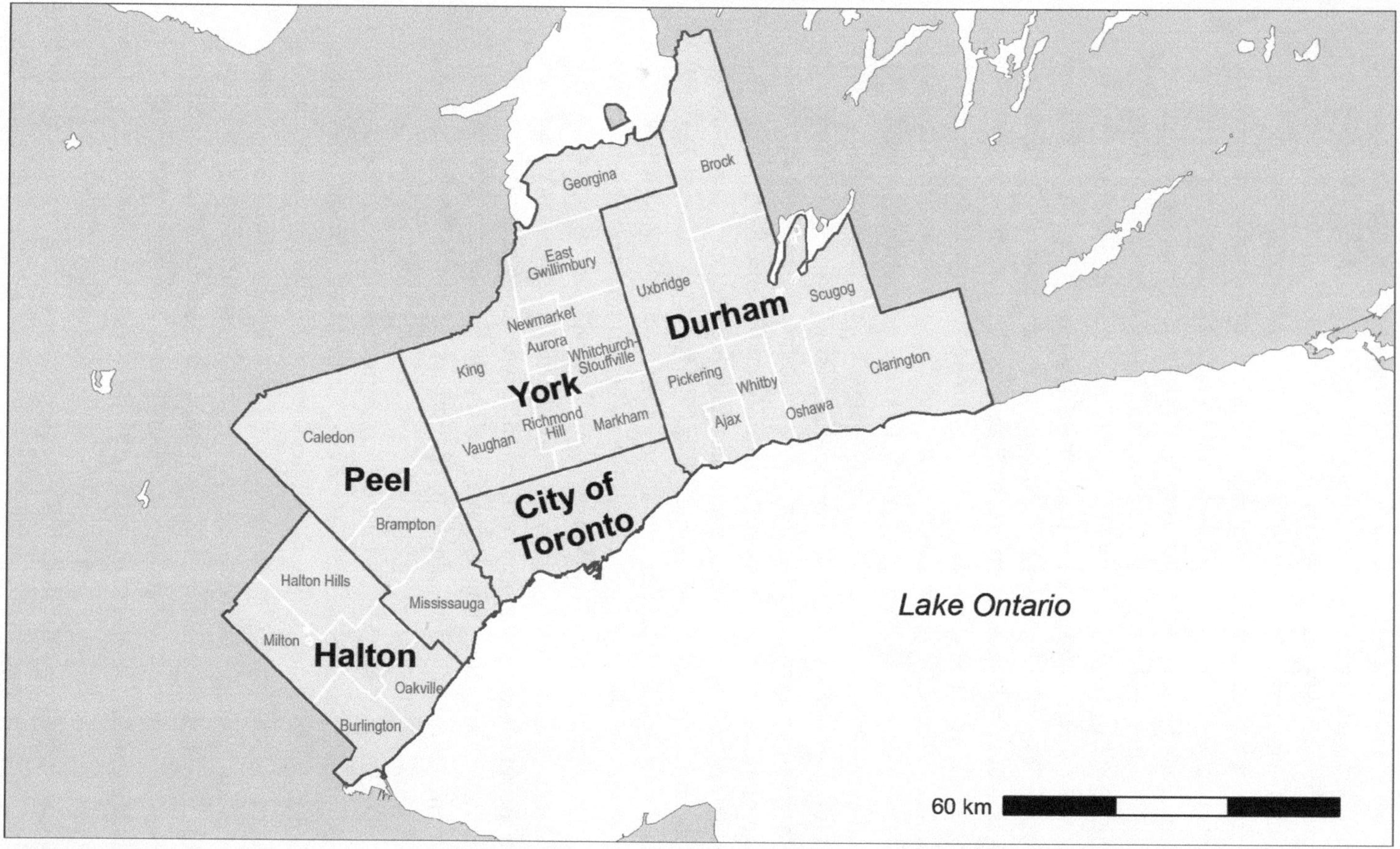

FIGURE 5.5 City of Toronto and the York, Durham, Peel, and Halton Regional Municipalities | *Cartography:* Steve Tornes.
Source: Statistics Canada (2021a).

hierarchical decisions (without overall coordination), more elected representatives in transit decision making (when GO transit, for example, was downloaded to municipalities between 1998 and 2001), and much more emphasis on the efficiency of systems and on the bottom line" (Keil and Young 2008, 745). In other words, restructuring efforts toward regional planning since the late 1990s resulted in a "bifurcated" system with "a premium network of transportation systems, on the one hand, and underserved community-based systems on the other hand" (Keil and Young 2008, 728).

Such a restructuring resulted in significant shifts in local governance plans in the early 2000s, notably for the City of Toronto and its relationship to the province. The city adopted an inward-looking strategy focused on service improvements, hence abandoning any significant role in regional transportation network development (Keil and Young 2008, 741). By privileging the important work of the Toronto Transit Commission (TTC) rather than procuring regional leadership to discussions such as urban freight, the City of Toronto developed a transportation strategy that put its municipal interests first, hoping that such a vision would inspire complementary efforts throughout the region: "The TTC strategy, which is so clearly linked to the municipality's expansion plans, is really a regional niche strategy that builds on the specific advantages of public transit in the built-up core of the GTA" (Keil and Young 2008, 742). This is in line with the City of Toronto's historical attempts at developing "a metropolitan-based spatial strategy grounded in the City of Toronto's territorial interests" (Addie 2013, 207). As explained by one participant involved in the city's municipal strategies, "There is always a recognition that we need to think regionally but we want most of it to come to us. There is always an element of competition" (Interview 5.9).

Similarly, such restructuring led local civil society actors to organize differently. In this case, the increasing divide between city-level and regional decision-making processes resulted in more systematic community organizing at a new regional scale, including with the creation of the Toronto City Summit Alliance in 2002 as "a coalition of over 40 civic leaders from the private, labour, voluntary and public sectors in the Toronto region" (TCSA 2003, 3). Renamed the Greater Toronto CivicAction Alliance in 2010, this coalition reflects a broader trend in local community organizing since the early 2000s, which remains true today: "Much of the civil society mobilization at the city-regional scale in Toronto does not come from progressive forces, but from globally oriented economic elites, who were able to integrate segments of community organizations and the voluntary sector in a coalition called the Toronto City Summit Alliance" (Boudreau et al. 2006, 37).

One of the core requests of the alliance in its 2003 policy document, entitled *Enough Talk: An Action Plan for the Toronto Region,* is for physical infrastructure and regional transportation to be understood as intricate parts of "a globally oriented agenda of local economic development," which will help transnational capitalists make the city prosper (Boudreau et al. 2006, 37–38). This role, given to business leaders in shaping local public debates about transportation and urban policy, is explained partly by a lack of regional political leadership following the municipal amalgamations and partly by the will of local business elites "for accessing the corridors of power at the federal and provincial levels, and consequently obtaining new public monies (for infrastructure development and increasing the urban quality of life) that will increase competitiveness and encourage private profits" (Boudreau et al. 2007, 41). The early role taken by the Toronto City Summit Alliance provided a space for other pro-business organizations, such as the Toronto Region Board of Trade, to take part in debates around the need for a regional approach to urban freight, notably as it relates to business development, strategic industrial clustering, and talent recruitment.

Municipal restructuring via amalgamation rather than regional governance also resulted in a perceived necessity to institutionalize direct provincial guidance of regional transportation. Without devolving any additional influence on the regional governance process, the provincial government opted rather for the creation of Metrolinx in 2008, "a new regional transportation institution ... with significant powers over the planning and management of transportation" in the GTA (Addie 2013, 205). Established by the province to bring some coherence to the regional transportation network – notably because of the inefficiency of the previous entity, the Greater Toronto Services Board (Boudreau et al. 2006, 42) – Metrolinx's initial regional transportation plan, The Big Move, demonstrated the importance of economic imperative to transportation projects by favouring a clustering of "transportation investments in key urban nodes" (Addie 2013, 210).

The Big Move plan highlights the importance of linking transportation to questions of land use and quality of life in local public discussions. In practice, however, the 2008 regional transportation plan lacked the necessary investments to be executed fully, and it also lacked local, bottom-up buy-in (Addie 2013, 205–7). Hence, it revived the long-standing tension in the region between the mobility of goods and the mobility of people.

As Roger Keil and Douglas Young (2008, 732) explain further, "This is essentially a contradiction between use value and exchange value, that is, between the quality of life of people as they travel in and through the region, and the efficient movement of commodities in and through the region." This tension was notably evident with Metrolinx "not being able to move (urban freight) forward" and having to design a forum for stakeholders to interact instead of a more centralized form of committee. The Urban Freight Forum was seen as "a means to an end" rather than the ideal solution in achieving a coherent regional vision on the movement of goods (Interview 5.4). Another participant indicated how Metrolinx was also restricted politically to the benefit of the Ontario Ministry of Transportation: "Its Urban Freight Strategy never really jelled, and Metrolinx moved out of the area. The government restricted their mandate" away from urban freight issues (Interview 5.9).

THE CURRENT FRAMING OF INVESTMENTS IN TRANSPORTATION INFRASTRUCTURE

With the city-region's transportation planning efforts being plagued by a lack of coherent regional governance framework, the current context for investments in transportation infrastructure seems best described as short-term, favouring locally interested projects to the detriment of larger, regional-based initiatives: "The anarchic governance model of the recent past, with its biases toward suburban road building, as an extension of the globalized post-Fordist 'just-in-time' economy to continue" (Keil and Young 2008, 729). This has led to significant competition and confusion over a relatively small territory close to the US border, as Figure 5.5 shows. On the one hand, subregional competition over priorities, transportation investment, and sustainable economic development projects can be seen between the core and the suburbs but also between regional municipalities and their constituent cities. On the other hand, this context is also confusing on account of the relationship between jurisdictions of the TTC and Metrolinx, which serves as a daily reminder of their parallel developments and adds to the inability to end the fragmentation of the system to the benefit of an overall regional strategy (Boudreau et al. 2006, 44–45). Moreover, the provincial approach to developing a regional strategy for transportation in the city-region has been influenced by the necessity to address other priorities, including quality-of-life indicators and environmental protection (Addie 2013, 207).

Throughout the 2000s and 2010s, the provincial approach to expanding transportation in the region within this framework was mostly timid.

Recently, this changed with the more forceful management of the Ford administrations (at the Toronto city level from 2010 to 2014 and provincial level since 2018), hence reviving tensions between the City of Toronto and its neighbouring municipalities in framing transportation plans and investments. Interestingly, no matter which political party is in charge at the provincial level, the necessity, for both Toronto and the region's secondary cities, for sustained investments in transportation-infrastructure protection and expansion receives a wide consensus, while the emphasis on specific modes of transport or plans will play to certain constituencies of the region and ideological preferences. Nonetheless, the problems are found in the execution of such plans. As Keil and Young (2008, 746) indicate, the provincial approach to transportation infrastructure fits a noninterventionist mentality: "Regulation has been mostly hands-off, and transfer payments to urban communities have lagged behind in international comparison." Moreover, transportation infrastructure is not funded holistically; rather, it is scattered through several provincial funds across municipal affairs, economic development, and transportation – from the 2011 *Building Together* vision and related 2012 Municipal Infrastructure Strategy, which lead to the Moving Ontario Forward consultations in 2014 and the creation of an Ontario Community Infrastructure Fund to which municipalities can apply, and other more indirect opportunities like the 2013 Going Global Trade Strategy, which supported increasing small and medium enterprises' exports to Asia.

Such a provincial context builds on the federal government's limited interventions and success in supporting regional governance and economic development plans in the city-region. Toronto's special needs have been caught between a selective and timid interest at the federal level to bypass provincial priorities, notably with Paul Martin's 2003 New Deal for Cities, and a general disinterest in getting involved, for instance during the government of Stephen Harper (Boudreau et al. 2007, 42–43). In line with the provincial approach of the last twenty years, the federal approach has generally favoured deregulation. This has not stopped the federal government from being "strategically interventionist" in recognition of Toronto's importance for the country and in world markets – nor from its need for a pragmatic investment approach to achieve economic targets including select physical infrastructure projects, following key economic sectors, such as in manufacturing, or key indicators, such as increased international trade with the US (Boudreau et al. 2007, 43–45; Keil and Young 2008, 743). As Boudreau et al. (2007, 43) state, "Toronto's weight in the federation results not only from its economic vitality. The proactive role of its political class who sees itself as endowed with a Canadian role ... certainly affects federal government's attitude toward Toronto."

As such, significant road and highway infrastructure investments were made to support the city-region's integration to the Quebec-Windsor trade corridor and the border crossing to the US. Since 2002, such post-9/11 collaborations gave priority to border security and global connectivity, including significant investments in the Detroit-Windsor-Toronto corridor, Gordie Howe International Bridge, the Queenston-Lewiston Bridge crossing renewal for shippers, Blue Water Bridge, Buffalo-Fort Erie Bridge, and the Windsor-Detroit border crossing. Such priorities were maintained through the 2013 New Building Canada Fund plan, which saw 129 projects funded in Ontario alone. However, the Ontario Ministry of Transportation remains the main driver for transportation planning, investment, and implementation – not necessarily an ideal configuration for investment in transportation. One participant involved in provincial discussions on the matter expressed frustration with the province, on the one hand feeling caught between the federal government and the need to compete at the national level for funding while investments are urgently needed in and around Toronto, and on the other hand with the lack of regional coordination in allocating investments where it makes more sense for regional development to the benefit of local and politically motivated investment. The participant explained that "the way the funding is structured makes it hard to apply for and to get investment ... while as a region, we are unable to masterplan" (Interview 5.3).

With the creation of the Continental Gateway Strategy, the provincial department's role did not diminish; rather, it was reinforced. The Continental Gateway Strategy was designed to increase regulatory harmonization between the provinces of Ontario and Quebec to optimize the efficiency of the transportation system. However, it never resulted in more than planning and coordination among the two jurisdictions, especially in that most of the funding followed border crossing priorities outside the GTHA, as Figure 5.3 demonstrates (Bareman 2015, 83–84; Guy 2013, 1188). As one participant involved in such discussions over the last twenty years opined, the problem with making the Continental Gateway Strategy work is that it was plagued by "a death by a thousand cuts." Even if it seemed promising at the time, "it was very hard to galvanize efforts when talking about a corridor from Windsor to Quebec City" while extending the focus of planning, coordinating, and funding to other places in Quebec and Ontario – and covering the interests of a plethora of actors from different modes of transportation, political levels, and geographical foci (Interview 5.9).

The lack of pan-provincial leadership was also owed partly to the failure of establishing a gateway council of users in both provinces to advance issues pertaining on both sides of the provincial border (Ditta 2015, 14). Many of the consultations, studies, and planning reports by Ontario's Ministry of Transportation were justified as part of the coordinating efforts of the Continental Gateway Strategy, but those recommendations only reiterated the centrality of the transportation department in setting up priorities and making decisions (Lawrence National Centre 2008). As such, the Continental Gateway cannot be "considered successful in terms of impact and results," considering the lack of interprovincial integration of the transportation system shared with the Province of Quebec (Ditta 2015, 14) and an inability of this strategy to be framed in conjunction with other provincial priorities, including environmental sustainability.

Interestingly, the Southern Ontario Gateway Council, created in 2006 to help advocate for cooperation between all modes of transport from a system user perspective, was effectively disbanded in 2015 because of an inability to serve as a catalyst on such issues, beyond transportation logistics and beyond outputs such as technical studies and reports. It remains active on paper but has limited reach and activities (Ferguson et al. 2012; Montsion 2019).

While the provincial and federal governments make investments in transportation infrastructure on their own terms, other stakeholders have emerged to fill the gaps in providing leadership at a regional level at the intersection of transportation logistics and economic development priorities. Bodies such as the Western Golden Horseshoe Municipal Network, created in 2014, allowed for cross-sectoral discussions, including municipal voices in Halton and Peel. Building on the 2005 Bi-National Transportation Strategy, the creation of such a network highlights the importance of, and centrality given to, coordinating transportation and economic development goals with US counterparts in the Great Lakes region.

The importance given to such forums adds to the complexity for planning and coordinating within Canada and through a gateway strategy with Quebec on transportation logistics. It also reinforces the centrality of the Ontario Ministry of Transportation in balancing local priorities with interprovincial and federal priorities, along with the ones coming out of international discussions (US Department of Transportation 2014, 47–48). Issues and priorities pertaining to the international border with the US

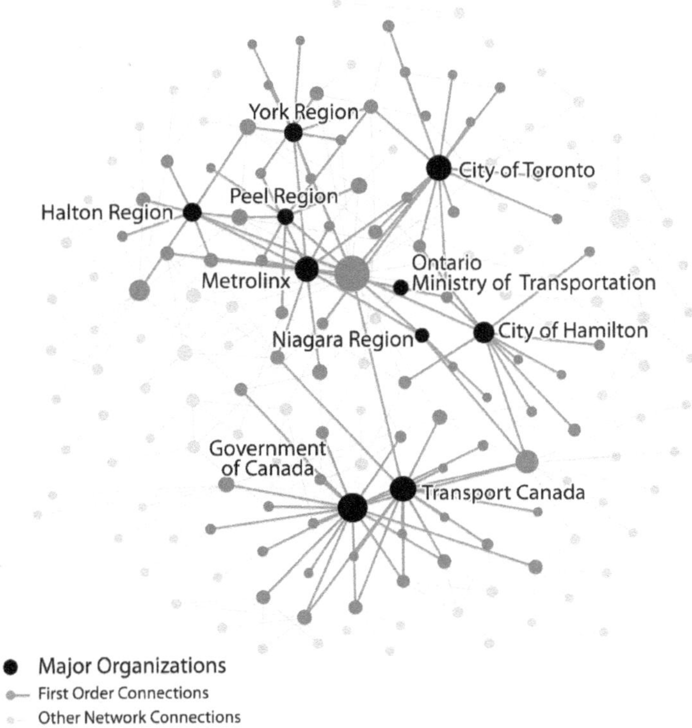

FIGURE 5.6 Ontario-funded projects

also produced studies and favoured investments outside the Toronto core while being framed as part of the Continental Gateway efforts, including in Sault Ste. Marie in northern Ontario and in Edwardsburgh Cardinal in eastern Ontario. Closer to Toronto, this includes investments in the Niagara-Greater Toronto Area Corridor study, ordered by the Ministry of Transportation in Ontario (US Department of Transportation 2014, 53), and the more recent launch of the Smart Freight Centre in 2019 out of Peel Region, which aims "to improve the economic vibrancy of business, environmental sustainability, and quality of life for residents of the Greater Toronto and Hamilton Area by providing innovative evidence-based research, decision support, advocacy, training, and monitoring in order to coordinate transportation infrastructure, land development, regulation, technology tools, and resources that improve goods movement activities" (Smart Freight Centre 2021).

By focusing on the main stakeholders involved in transportation-infrastructure projects funded in Ontario through the last federal investment rounds in 2008 and 2019, we observe in Figure 5.6 how the historical relationships between the Ontario government and the city-region of Toronto are structuring the current landscape of investments, starting with the important focus on border-crossing improvement and expansion projects outside the GTHA. Four more observations can be made on regional dynamics.

First, the network relations mapped in Figure 5.6 confirm the centrality of the Ontario Ministry of Transportation between the City of Toronto and federal investments, on the one hand, and Metrolinx and its interregional coordinating body, the Urban Freight Forum, on the other. The Urban Freight Forum has an eclectic list of members, from key corporations and universities to the usual suspects in terms of federal, provincial, and municipal governments, who are indirectly involved in these discussions:

- Canadian Courier and Logistics Association
- Canadian National Railway
- Canadian Pacific Railway
- Canadian Union of Postal Workers
- City of Hamilton
- City of Toronto
- Durham Region
- Greater Toronto Airports Authority
- Halton Region
- Hamilton Port Authority
- Hudson's Bay Company
- Intelligent Transportation Systems Canada
- Loblaws
- McMaster Institute of Transportation and Logistics
- Metrolinx
- Nulogx
- Ontario Ministry of Transportation
- Ontario Trucking Association
- Region of Peel
- Southern Ontario Gateway Council
- Supply Chain and Logistics Association Canada
- Toronto Atmospheric Fund
- Toronto Board of Trade
- TransCore
- Transport Canada
- University of Toronto
- York Region

Second, Figure 5.6 demonstrates that municipal and subregional stakeholders are involved in such funding requests, even more centrally than federally mandated agencies. Of note, regional municipalities such as Niagara – key to the trade corridor between Quebec and the US border crossing – and Peel Region, with two of its cities, Mississauga and Brampton, are key to transportation logistics projects throughout the Greater Golden Horseshoe. York Region – including two of its cities, Markham and Vaughan – is also significantly connected. While some cities such as Hamilton are less central to the network, they clearly play key roles in bringing together actors of different sectors around such projects. Third, railways and port and airport authorities are more secondary and insular, with input and collaboration with specific professional associations and pertaining to key projects. Fourth, and in terms of other types of stakeholders less present in Figure 5.6, postsecondary institutions play a supporting role in transportation logistics research while civil society actors are involved in linking such projects to questions of environmental sustainability, commuting, real estate development, and private sector interests through business proxies.

Figure 5.6 confirms that local and municipal actors of the city-region of Toronto were and are involved in transportation-infrastructure projects. Regional municipalities and their cities, as well as coordinating bodies like Metrolinx, are key connectors in these projects. Interestingly, the mapping of local stakeholders changes significantly if one focuses only on stakeholders involved in projects in more than one subregion of the city-region and in more than one sector of activity.

As Figure 5.7 highlights, only twenty-three stakeholders have inter-regional and cross-sectoral functions – mostly federally mandated agencies, civil society actors involved in representing and facilitating business interests, and research-based institutions. While being generally less central in Figure 5.6, these entities play a complementary and connecting role for cities and regional municipalities. They provide leadership geographically or by industry, notably confirming the key role pro-business civil society actors play in leading regional discussions about the city-region's positioning in global value chains. In Figure 5.7, the type of stakeholders represented also shows some of the tertiary economic development priorities of the federal government, including artificial intelligence, advanced manufacturing, and medical technologies. Toronto Global could qualify as a municipal-level stakeholder, but this not-for-profit agency was created to facilitate foreign direct investment and business in the region of Toronto as a whole (Toronto Global 2019). Shedding light on

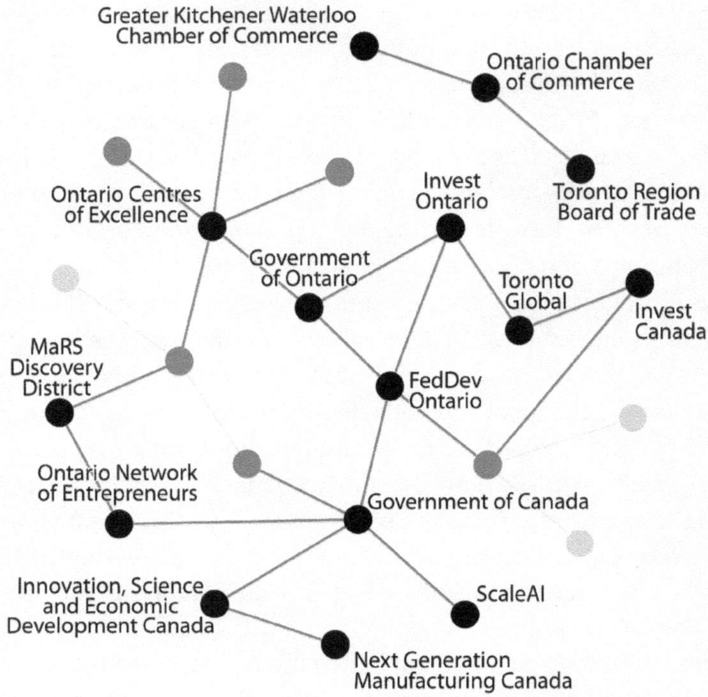

FIGURE 5.7 Greater Toronto stakeholders involved in gateway projects across regions and sectors

tertiary pan-regional economic development priorities, this second network map also highlights the lack of involvement of transportation actors like Metrolinx and even railways and port and airport authorities in more than one specific project or more than one sector of activity. In summary, the city-region of Toronto displays a lack of regional planning, institution building, and bringing together of transportation matters with economic development plans.

REGIONAL GOVERNANCE AND ECONOMIC DEVELOPMENT

One of the consequences of the absence of a regional approach to transportation is found in the lack of coordination among local economic development goals and the difficulties in developing a coherent positioning of the city-region in global value chains: "Global and local circuits of mobility are not well coordinated, and various scales of decision-making do not visibly interact for the regional good" (Keil and Young 2008, 279). One participant involved in provincial matters explained that the difficulty in finding a coherent and cohesive regional approach is owed partly to the geographical dispersal of economic activities throughout the city-region: "The balance to achieve is not an explicit and cohesive vision because of the make-up of business and geography across the region ... and there are significant subregional differences for business and people" (Interview 5.4).

In this section, we examine the parameters within which economic restructuring has occurred in the city-region and its consequences on regional governance, including on local urban democratic processes. We witness a regional governance scheme fragmented into three main logics, which helps to show how the positioning of the city-region in global value chains cannot be reduced to a single and unitary vision of the city-region. As Keil and Young (2008) note, such developments of a regional governance framework and regional sense of identity occur despite the inaction and paralysis from local political actors: "It is possible that the extant political system is structurally too inept to create a set of policies that would consolidate the region and would increase regional identity through transportation governance rather than in spite of it" (745).

Since the 1990s, the region's "gradual process of economic restructuring" has followed general trends of moving "from manufacturing to service orientation" (Joy and Vogel 2015, 38). The importance of manufacturing remains as significant as activities in finance, insurance, and real estate, even if it has been suffering significant losses (Keil and Young 2008, 733). There are strong subregional differential impacts, as Joy and Vogel (2015, 38) explain, "Economic restructuring has had significant spatial consequences. Although the downtown core has retained its primacy in the highest paid and skilled occupations associated with the global economy, there has been significant employment growth in the inner and outer suburbs of the GTA, particularly in manufacturing."

One finds significant negative impacts of this restructuring in cities and regions such as Hamilton and Durham Region, which were built on manufacturing. However, cities and regions that specialize in sectors of the knowledge-based economy, including the City of Toronto and the regions of Halton and York, are benefiting from such shifts. As one participant involved in provincial research and planning on these topics notes, "It used to be that the ones generating goods were the ones generating employment, but this is less the case now" (Interview 5.3). In a growing city-region with new economic and industry developments, cities in Peel Region have benefited the most, notably owing to the location of transport facilities and multimodal nodes (Keil and Young 2008, 735). As Keil and Young (2008, 733) indicate, the development of this sector of activity is also linked to major technological advances: "Of particular significance to this study of regional transportation is the development of specialized logistics and supply-chain-management firms supported by new information technology."

Such a changing landscape in terms of economic activity and related infrastructure projects has been characterized by the features of the regional rescaling of municipal affairs to the detriment of citizen involvement and awareness (Joy and Vogel 2015, 49). In such context, it is no surprise that the private sector actors have taken a key role in shaping the relationship between regionalization, urbanization, and economic restructuration. As Joy and Vogel (2015, 49) note, "Post-amalgamation Toronto operates like a private corporation, and participatory processes often appear as an afterthought rather than a space to let citizens proactively bring their issues to city staff before policies and plans are made." Such a political configuration has resulted in three interrelated observations. First, economic restructuring and related infrastructure funding do not necessarily follow demographic needs; while municipal governments may have the responsibility to provide social services, they do not have the required revenue to address them (49). Second, private sector actors and local civil society organizations have been able to influence and shape public sector projects and priorities, especially in the transportation sector. As Boudreau et al. (2006, 39) point out, the mindset of "transportation capital and its drive for global competitiveness" has been incorporated into the perspective of various stakeholders: "This is an indication of the ability of economic elites in steering the city-regional agenda in Toronto – something that their Montreal counterparts have not been able to achieve yet." Through the work of business proxies, private sector actors are well supported in advocating their vision to the public sector. Third, not only is the regional transportation system fragmented, there is also an increasing lack of awareness in how local transportation issues are related to regional economic restructuring trends and to plans for emphasizing the benefits of international trade through increased activity in and through the city-region, notably through the southern border. As Keil and Young (2008, 745) explain:

> In Toronto, regional transportation in the period of globalization has been both surprisingly uncoordinated and predictably contested. There seems to be a dramatic disconnect between the (specialized) knowledge and the experientially based (public) concern about problems that plague the region, on the one hand, and the political mechanisms through

which they can be addressed, on the other hand. To many, this disconnect is a direct consequence of the depoliticized and technocratic nature of transportation policy, where powerful interests (the automobile industry, air and rail service providers, road builders, developers, transportation officials, unelected agencies such as the Greater Toronto Airport Authority [GTAA], etc.) fight over various models of capital accumulation and rational service provision.

In sum, a public-led regional governance framework is not only impossible because of the lack of regional institutions and political will from existing municipal entities, but this vacuum has created a space in which private sector actors, in collaboration with particular municipal entities and with the support of provincial bodies, have taken the lead in shaping economic restructuring, transportation, and economic development priorities locally, away from citizen awareness and participation.

The Toronto regional governance, as it pertains to its positioning in global value chains and related movement of goods and peoples, is fragmented in three ways: a public logic characterized by the history of provincial-municipal relationships in the region as previously documented; a mode of transport logic determined by the priorities of federally mandated agencies including railways, ports, and airports; and a private sector logic, most notably made accessible by business proxies. This has been characterized by one of the participants from the City of Toronto as "bits and pieces of regionalization happening here and there" (Interview 5.10). First, public sector actors have played a key role in framing the importance of coordination and collaboration in transportation logistics, investments, and projects, especially as it related to road and highway management. Metrolinx is responsible for regional transportation concerns in the region. Although the main emphasis tends to be the mobility of people, Metrolinx's 2008 regional transportation plan The Big Move involved the movement of goods as well, with a key interest in the integration of management programs and improved multimodal transitions. Building on previous efforts and studies for the development of transportation logistics clustering, including consulting reports, Metrolinx launched its Urban Freight Strategy in 2011, which provided five directions and seventeen actions to be taken in the short term to facilitate goods movement in the region, in complement to the federal efforts surrounding the Continental Gateway. Despite sustained efforts of cross-sectoral coordinating groups such as Metrolinx's Urban Freight Forum, issues remain in most of the strategic priorities, notably in building collaboration across jurisdictions, relieving congestion, and reducing the environmental impacts of goods movement (Kriger 2016; Kriger and Gill 2016; Salsberg 2012). No matter the reasons for a reduced and more indirect role in urban freight, Metrolinx's focus on the mobility of people has displaced the visibility of, and public debates on, transportation logistics for actors and forums in regional municipalities, particularly in Peel Region around the Smart Freight Centre.

Second, depending on the mode of transportation, how it is governed, and the challenges specific to this mode, various priorities are being enacted throughout the city-region. This is the case for modes of transport under the jurisdiction of federally mandated agencies. For instance, one key player is the GTAA, which is

> a not-for-profit agency established by the federal government as part of its overall strategy of deregulation and privatization of air travel in Canada. Not being a branch of government or a publicly traded company means that the GTAA is not subject to public scrutiny, while at the same time it is vested by the federal government with tremendous power to raise money. (Keil and Young 2008, 734)

While crucial components of transportation logistics and economic development plans of the city-region, airport expansion and priorities are determined separately from local priorities by the GTAA (Keil and Young 2008, 736–37). Toronto is not in a unique position as it pertains to the role of airports in municipal and local development. Keil and Young (2008, 738) explain that "municipal governments, for example, get short shrift in the administration of the airport's business, and their policies are often just appendices to decision-making processes that have already been made at higher levels of authority both public and private." Nonetheless, the GTAA plans are determined by distinct facts and trends, such as increases in air cargo of 7 percent annually and of international volumes of 10 percent annually (GTAA 2018, 21). Through the Southern Ontario Airport Network, and despite the fragmented governance model at play, a regional division of labour among the region's airports is emerging, if only to meet the demand. This includes a role for the Munro Hamilton Airport in the movement of goods, especially overnight express freight, as well as a key function for the Billy Bishop Airport in Toronto (governed by Ports Toronto and not GTAA) and Kitchener-Waterloo Airport in the movement of service workers throughout the region (Metrolinx 2016, 12–14; Montsion 2019). Related regional planning includes an airport in Pickering in Durham Region to replace the executive airport of Oshawa, in association with plans for a Pickering Innovation Corridor (City of Pickering 2018; Montsion 2019).

A similar but distinct regional governance logic can be found with other modes of transport governed by federally regulated industries. While railways have focused on the efficiency of intermodal facilities – including CN Brampton Intermodal Terminal, CP Vaughan Intermodal Terminal, CP Milton Expressway Terminal, and CN Logistics Hub in Milton (Metrolinx 2016) – these agencies' efforts are mostly coordinated through the Toronto Terminal Railways, a joint subsidiary of CN and CP responsible for rail operations and planning in the region. The Toronto Terminal Railways is tasked with balancing the sheer amount of traffic in the corridor and the needs of other users of the system – including commuters and passengers – and executing renovations and expansion projects without significantly impeding daily activities (Montsion 2019; TTR 2019).

For maritime freight too, we see coordination between some of the ports in the Great Lakes and St. Lawrence Basin, most notably with the merger of the port authorities of Hamilton and Oshawa (Hamilton 2021). While there is a need to balance usage of ports between recreational activities, transport of cargo, and storage, activity levels have remained relatively stable, with Hamilton remaining the most active port and the Port of Toronto focusing mostly on recreational activities and serving the city itself – the latter a key entry point for the City of Toronto, with 2.2 million metric tonnes passing through in 2017 alone (Metrolinx 2016, 14; Ports Toronto 2019). All in all, federally mandated agencies responsible for the regional governance of a mode of transport have developed independent mechanisms to connect with regional transportation concerns and provide leadership in their own ways for the city-region's positioning in global value chains. As one participant involved in such matters indicated about their agency, "How we see our role is that we should play a role; we should take on the responsibility of leadership role in the region" (Interview 5.5).

Third, private sector actors, historically permitted to lead regional discussions on transportation and economic development owing to the lack of public leadership, have been involved in such discussions. The importance of a transportation logistics cluster has been pushed by private sector interests since at least 2012, notably through the Toronto Region Board of Trade. One report sponsored by the board argues that such cluster would "grow in this evolving global business environment, given its size, firm density and infrastructure assets like the Toronto Pearson Airport and the Toronto Port" with focus on addressing "inadequate transportation infrastructure in road and rail, and skill shortages across T&L sub-sectors like trucking" and "looking at creative IT solutions, identifying efficiencies in work processes and having effective talent development and management strategies" (KPMG 2012, 5). As with recent plans for a more efficient and comprehensive planning of urban goods movement in the region, the Toronto Region Board of Trade (2019) highlights the inherent links between urban freight and economic growth, including talent recruitment and retention. With a mandate "to make Toronto the most competitive global region it can be" (Interview 5.1), the Toronto Region Board of Trade (2021) has worked for years in branding local expertise in a few clusters of activity – namely advanced manufacturing, energy, food and beverage, human health, transportation logistics, and information and communication technologies. The way these can be mobilized and branded to give coherence to the regional positioning in global value chains is by expanding on these clusters to develop a series of innovation corridors throughout the region, building on existing distribution networks and trade corridors. An idea advocated by the board as well as the World Trade Centre Toronto, the Canadian Global Cities Council, and the Innovation Corridor Council – endorsed by eleven chambers of commerce – the intent of such business proxies in leading the city-region's branding through the idea of innovation corridor is "to go bolder." While in the past "there was no coherent vision across sectors," such business proxies see their work and the use of innovation corridor in supporting this branding locally and globally as "reflecting the region to itself," hence offering not one substantive vision but a framework through which distinct industrial clusters can emerge (Interview 5.1). The goal is to attract the necessary capital, talent, and economic activity to specific regions in the Golden Horseshoe, depending on local strengths (Montsion 2019). In a context in which a single substantive regional vision is impossible because of political competition and fragmentation, the idea of having many innovation corridors to position the city-region in global value chains is gaining momentum.

The strongest example of such an innovation corridor can be found in the proposal for the Toronto-Waterloo Innovation Corridor (Toronto Region BOT 2017b). This is the "country's first global innovation supercluster," building on available resources in Waterloo and Toronto such as a pool of talent in high technology professionals and artificial intelligence business (Toronto Region BOT 2017a, 10). This innovation corridor is meant to brand some parts of the region in global value chains (for example, Quantum Valley in Waterloo) based on existing computer and artificial intelligence expertise from the private sector, building on partnerships to research institutions and counting on investments for a more efficient connection in terms of the movement of goods and people between Toronto and Waterloo (City of Kitchener 2018; Toronto Region BOT 2017a, 11). Such a model can be replicated based on various place-based expertise and local economic development priorities. In all cases, the positioning and development of the region in global value chains is directly linked to the ability to remain competitive through efficient use of its transportation infrastructure. As such, the Board of Trade remains key in mobilizing local urban actor coalitions advocating for more efficient transport infrastructure.

SUBURBAN COALITIONS AND TORONTO'S DIFFERING CONFIGURATION

As Guillaume Poiret (2017, 121–22) notes, the schism developing in the city-region of Toronto since the 1960s between the downtown core and the suburbs remains a significant political reality of the region, especially for the suburbs in Toronto's outer ring. This categorization of the city-core and suburban-periphery is harder to justify in contemporary times since many of Toronto's neighbouring cities are centres in themselves. However, the centre-periphery dynamic between the City of Toronto and other municipalities in the region is a helpful heuristic tool to examine how a series of suburban coalitions (read: coalitions organized outside the City of Toronto) are developing, each around particular sectors of activity. By analyzing and comparing various network arrangements, we identify a model of the suburban coalition in contradistinction to the configuration found in the City of Toronto itself, where a general disconnect between the city and regional discussions on transportation logistics for international trade purposes is explained by the distinct importance of civil society actors and their priorities.

A historical competitor to the City of Toronto, the City of Hamilton (2016) has repositioned itself as a complementary node to high value activities in Toronto and the region since its de-industrializing phase of the 1970s (Hannah 2012; Phillips and Bouchier 2014; Terpstra 1985). As gateway to the city-region, the City of Hamilton has been trying to brand its infrastructure advantages, such as its port and airport and its geographical position between the US border crossing and the rest of the Golden Horseshoe, as part of a trade facilitation agenda that benefits the regional municipality and the city-region as a whole (Montsion 2019). Since the mid-2000s, the City of Hamilton has developed plans to improve the efficiency of its multimodal facilities and increase freight-friendly land-use and regional coordination with the rest of the city-region, with the idea of developing a freight village that can cater to advanced manufacturing and incorporate innovations in automation, computation, sensing, and networking into conventional manufacturing processes (City of Hamilton 2018; Hannah 2012; Montsion 2019).

In line with the findings of the Continental Gateway working groups and in collaboration with other stakeholders through Metrolinx's Urban Freight Strategy, the city elaborated a truck route action plan in 2014, while the Port of Hamilton pursues its efforts to remain a key node in the distribution networks of the Great Lakes region, and while the Munro Airport specializes in domestic cargo, as Canada's fastest growing airport in 2017 (City of Hamilton 2010, 2018; Hamilton Port Authority 2017). Such strategies follow a roadmap provided by the McMaster Institute for Transportation and Logistics in 2011 to encourage the clustering of specific knowledge-based and manufacturing activities in the region – with the hopes for a hub of transportation logistical skills, expertise, and training – for smaller firms that need shared facilities, equipment, and services to prosper (MITL 2011). As one participant familiar with such municipal discussions and plans put it, "It is about addressing supply chain efficiency issues locally that are not under the radar of main agencies" to build this local synergy between transport, knowledge-based industries, and a conventional industrial base (Interview 5.12).

The link between transportation logistics and local economic development plans is well represented in Figure 5.8. It shows how the City of Hamilton, directly linked to the airport, transit, and port network, is as central as Metrolinx's Urban Freight Forum in coordinating and actively participating in public conversations and activities to improve transportation logistics on its territory. Figure 5.8 depicts the city and the forum as mediators, conveners, and interlocutors to connect with other regional municipalities and regional, provincial, and national bodies including railways, research institutions, ministries of transportation, and business proxies. In this configuration, the City of Hamilton is the main link between environmental stakeholders, local transit agencies, (air)port authorities, transportation logistics bodies, and economic development priorities, above all in advanced manufacturing (Next Generation Advanced Manufacturing 2019). Representing a suburban coalition, Figure 5.8 demonstrates the key role a municipal government like the City of Hamilton can play in regional transportation planning and in collaboration with bodies like the Urban Freight Forum to bring together actors of different types

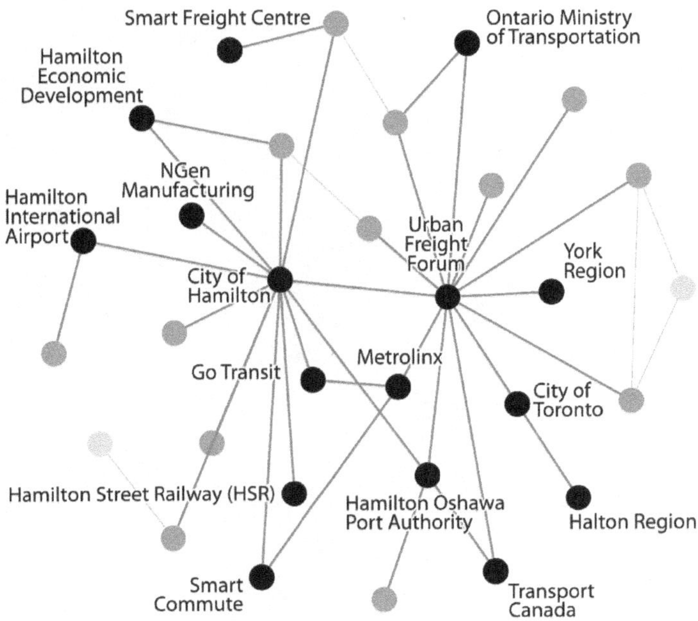

FIGURE 5.8 Hamilton stakeholders involved in discussions linking regional economic development and transportation priorities

to address transportation logistics in ways that connect to economic development priorities.

The composition of such a coalition is similar to the one found in the region of Peel. With Pearson International Airport and extensive warehousing for transportation purposes within its borders, Peel is also the locale of cities such as Mississauga and Brampton, which have seen significant economic activity increases in recent years; some even call for making such cities independent from a regional municipality (Woudsma 2012).[4] A regional municipality situated between the cities of Hamilton and Toronto, Peel Region has significant saddle functions in transportation logistics for urban freight in and through the city-region. Characterized by one local public official as "the champion of freight" in the city-region and by another as "the influencer" in transportation logistics, Peel Region can leverage its geographical advantages and unique integration to the regional transportation system to take on regional leadership functions (Interview 5.2; Interview 5.4). As Figure 5.9 shows, the regional municipality of Peel is key to coordinating local economic priorities, as determined by its municipalities and regional agencies. It is notably supporting

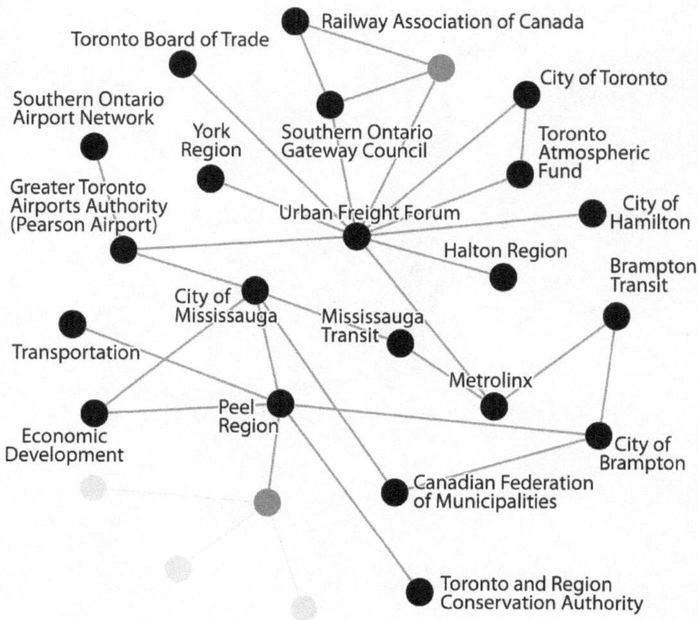

FIGURE 5.9 Peel stakeholders involved in discussions linking regional economic development and transportation priorities

a Smart Freight Centre to support transportation logistics throughout the city-region. This role is somewhat complementary to coordinating efforts of the Urban Freight Forum and Metrolinx, with their interest in transit issues and their connection to urban freight for international purposes (Region of Peel 2016; Smart Freight Centre 2021).

Although Figure 5.10 seems to depict a less complex configuration in the Halton region, the model of the suburban coalition remains quite similar. Key differences are explained through the division of powers that exists between each regional municipality and their cities, as well as their own economic development goals and priorities. Also located between Hamilton and Toronto, Halton includes significant agricultural lands and activities, but it also represents municipalities such as the City of Burlington, which depends on manufacturing, and others such as Oakville that are prioritizing higher-value industries, including the fields of digital media and biosciences (Halton Region 2019). Connections to neighbouring regional municipalities are seen through the central role played once again by Metrolinx's Urban Freight Forum and also the region's focus on HalTech and its Global Business Centre as ways for the region to position

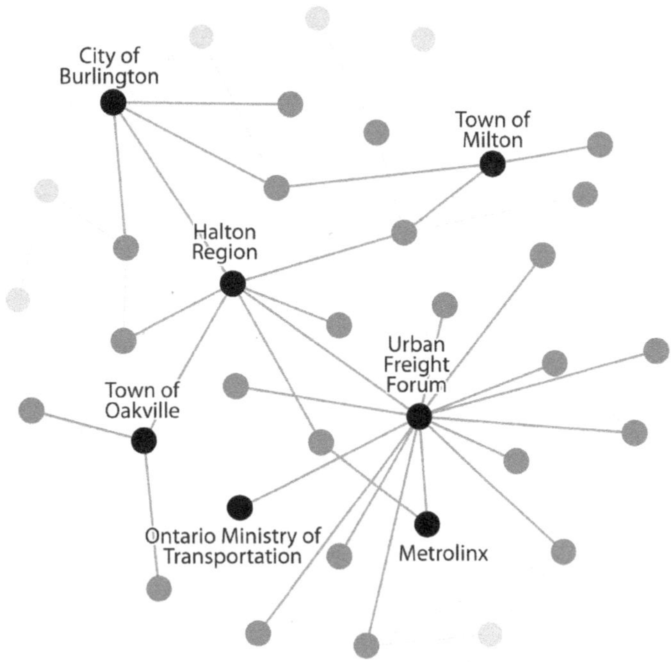

FIGURE 5.10 Halton stakeholders involved in discussions linking regional economic development and transportation priorities

itself within the city-region and to support a global positioning in global value chains, focused on start-ups, especially in digital media, information and communication technologies (ICT), and health technologies (HalTech 2020; Halton Region 2019).

The connections to York Region highlight, both through indirect coordination efforts with its cities and in terms of economic development priorities targeting ICT, a complementary positioning of Halton Region toward the most important role York Region plays in the ICT sector. From its industrial base in manufacturing to becoming a residential relief space for the City of Toronto, York Region's economic development strategy has changed significantly in recent years, developing secondary knowledge-based clusters away from Toronto, with global firms like KPMG and GM moving to it with the intent of developing new innovation hubs (York Region 2018). Figure 5.11 highlights the importance of growing municipalities such as Markham and Vaughan in coping with transportation challenges related to sustained growth, including a series of initiatives that links subregional transportation options for commuters and trucking to

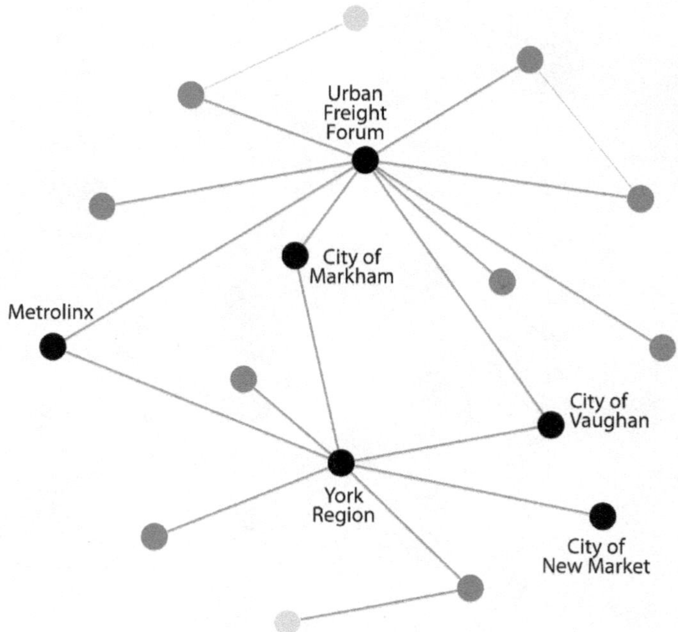

FIGURE 5.11 York stakeholders involved in discussions linking regional economic development and transportation priorities

other modes of transport and destinations in the region (York Region 2022).[5] As a participant familiar with the regional municipality explained, the more systematic focus on talent recruitment and retention in recent years, especially for people working in knowledge-based industries, is meant to follow the advice and research from regional business proxies, and the regional municipality's economic development goal "has very close parallels with their priorities" and that "building regional capacity through innovation is key" (Interview 5.8).

Figure 5.12 shows how Durham is a regional municipality focused on being a transport corridor to the city-region. The region's economic development is currently highly dependent on road infrastructure and the trucking industry; hence many local actors are looking into diversifying the means of transportation used and boosting local production. For instance, Oshawa's historical importance as a centre of manufacturing and industrial activities is continuously being mobilized to stimulate local growth, especially around its port (more than its airport) and in collaboration with the Port of Hamilton (Invest Durham 2023). More recently,

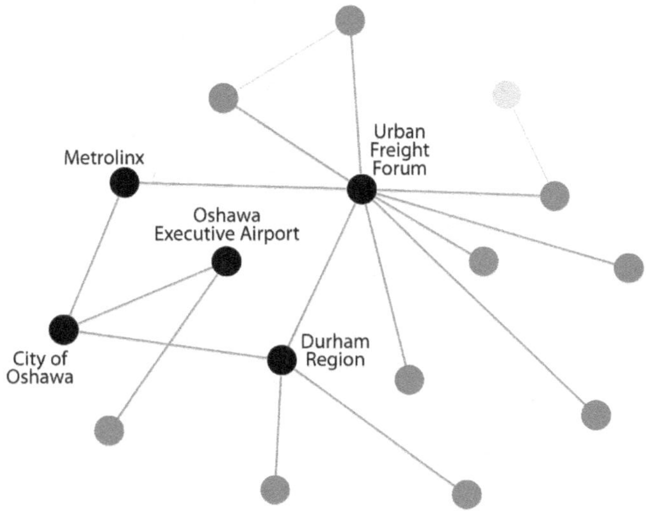

FIGURE 5.12 Durham stakeholders involved in discussions linking regional economic development and transportation priorities

and not captured in Figure 5.12, are plans to envision a Pickering Innovation Corridor. Even if this vision does not seem to be moving forward, the proposal is to leverage its airport and location close to the city-region's road infrastructure for the development of a research and innovation park (City of Pickering 2017, 2018).

In sum, we observe a similar type of coalition out of the network maps for Durham, Hamilton, Peel, Halton, and York as it pertains to integrating transportation logistics discussions and initiatives into their local economic development priorities. In all cases, we see suburban configurations involving local government stakeholders, transportation actors, economic development actors, and research or postsecondary institutions to help meet local economic development plans. In each case, we also observe that the centrality of a city or regional municipality is relatively matched by the role of the Urban Freight Forum and Metrolinx, as key integrating nodes for said region. Key differences observed from one suburban coalition to another are based on the unique geographical and infrastructural features of each region, which shaped the strategic sectors of activity they are supporting and related economic development priorities.

However, the model of the suburban coalition in the city-region stands in sharp contrast with the configuration found in the City of Toronto. In this case, it seems like local discussions and initiatives around transportation challenges and economic development priorities have evolved in distinct ways. Building on the works of Metrolinx, the TTC, and the Greater Toronto CivicAction Alliance, the city held a series of public consultations in 2014 that confirmed the need for sustained investment in transportation infrastructure to address local road congestion issues. Even if some of the priorities and connections revealed in such consultations are similar to the ones expressed in the suburbs, there are key differences in how to frame such priorities, especially in relation to economic and social development goals (City of Toronto 2014).

As such, some of the transportation priorities to solve road congestion reflect regional concerns and priorities. For instance, local investments were made in the protection and expansion of the 400-series highways and in more reliable freight distribution – in line with what other cities and regional municipalities were working on (Montsion 2019). After calls for increased collaboration among local jurisdictions, the City of Toronto worked in a complementary fashion with the City of Hamilton in making improvements to Highway 427 to support a more reliable road connection to the US border crossing (City of Hamilton 2010; City of Toronto 2016). The City of Toronto also collaborated with Toronto-based stakeholders such as Waterfront Toronto to create dedicated trucking routes and improve transportation access and efficiency in and out of the port lands (City of Toronto 2017). Despite some collaborations with proximate cities and regional municipalities in improving the 400-series highways, the goals behind such improvements were mostly for the city itself and meant for its population and businesses. This is in line with a historical policy agenda focused on using Toronto-based interests to guide a wider involvement in regional transportation matters.

More importantly, the City of Toronto's economic priorities and their relations to transportation issues differ significantly from what is found in the suburbs. As one participant involved in municipal affairs in Toronto asserted, "There is a recognition that the city is a bit lagging behind." They ascribed this to the internal division of files between city planning, economic development, and transportation services, as "there is not one centralized function or place where this is addressed at the city" (Interview 5.9). Through Figure 5.13, it is clear that the result is how the city prioritizes high value industries in innovation and knowledge-based economies while framing its engagement with regional transportation discussions through a locally and quality-of-life-oriented lens. Even the City of Toronto's support of pro-business stakeholders, such as Toronto Global,[6] seems intended to

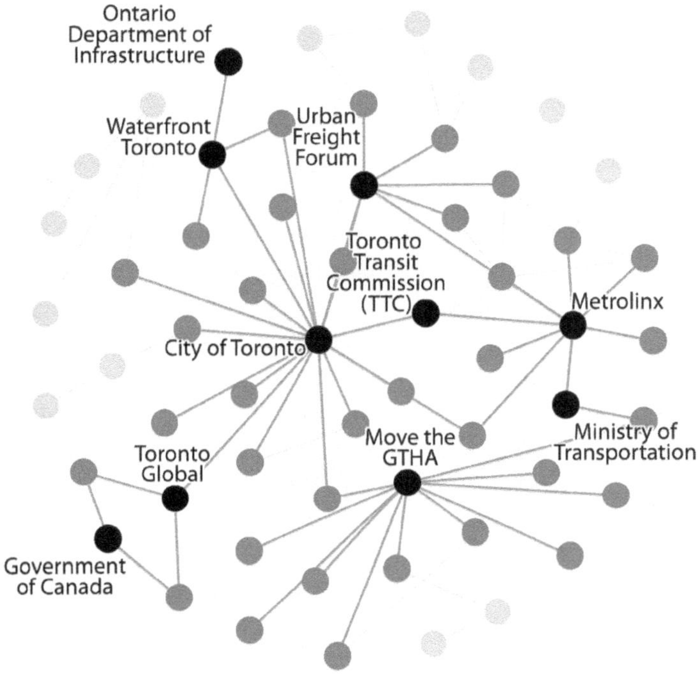

FIGURE 5.13 City of Toronto stakeholders involved in discussions linking regional economic development and transportation priorities

address quality-of-life indicators for the recruitment and retention of global talent, experts, and investors and to address issues raised by organized civil society actors such as transit advocacy groups – including Move the GTHA and the other dots below it on Figure 5.13, like TTC Riders and CodeRedTO – toward a more integrated, sustainable, affordable, and accessible regional transportation system (CodeRedTO 2019; TCSA 2010; Toronto Global 2019). As explained by a representative of the city, the focus is on knowledge-based economic development, including cultural innovation, and having a transportation plan that is more concerned with people as talents and innovators than the movement of goods per se:

> Cultural development is as important as economic development. Today, internet connectivity is as important as roads and rails, if not more. You need a strong cultural frame for successful innovation economically ... I would argue that the transportation of people is more important than

> the transport of goods for us. There is no grand vision for the region but there is a grand view of the way we should work: being inclusive, technology driven, adaptative and tolerant. (Interview 5.10)

In this context, Figure 5.13 portrays an urban coalition around Move the GTHA in which civil society actors are a lot more present than in previous suburban configurations, including the David Suzuki Foundation and other local environmental groups and alliances. Metrolinx and the Urban Freight Forum are less central, and proximate cities and regional municipalities are also less important. Based on Figure 5.13, we can see that the City of Toronto's concern about transportation logistics are threefold: (i) commuting, social, and environmental concerns; (ii) land use for economic purposes around ports, airports, and railways; and (iii) regional coordination. Even in the latter case, urban freight is represented only indirectly and is mediated through various bodies to coordinate with neighbouring regions and cities.

Such a contrast between the two models of coalition found in the city-region is confirmed when one examines the work of these coalitions through specific sectors of activity. Looking at the involvement of these local stakeholders based on their involvement in strategic industry clusters, such as advanced manufacturing and artificial intelligence, reiterates how coalitions are coalesced through specific sectors of activity. This structures their interactions with proximate regional municipalities and cities, as shown in Figure 5.14. As one person involved in Next Generation Manufacturing explained:

> Today's value chains are more than supply chains. They include knowledge supply, talent, IP ... what we're calling an advanced manufacturing ecosystem ... to scale up technology in manufacturing, to adopt technology in the manufacturing sector, and to support new technology options ... and in connecting start-up[s] with existing companies to develop effective ways for technology solutions to reach customers who can use them. (Interview 5.6)

As represented in Figure 5.14, the two central federal bodies – Next Generation Manufacturing and Innovation, Science and Development Canada – work in relationship with regional municipalities or cities including Hamilton, Markham in York Region, and Oshawa in Durham – somewhat bypassing the City of Toronto to focus on suburban cluster activities that fit subregional priorities. Both Hamilton and Oshawa are

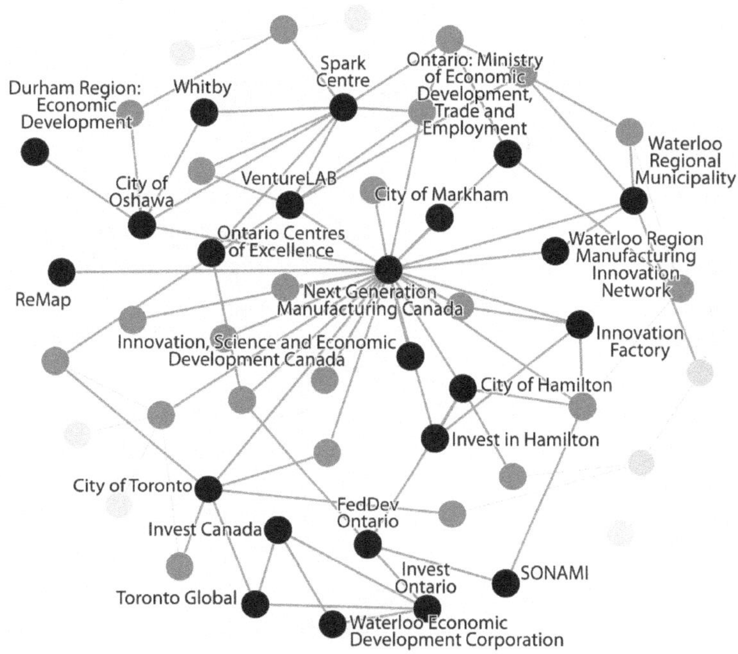

FIGURE 5.14 Advanced manufacturing as a regional economic priority in the city-region of Toronto

known for their local manufacturing activities and for having faced challenges in recent years, making them key interlocutors in this sector of activity. Advanced manufacturing structures the relationships between said locales and other sectors of activity and regional municipalities specializing in these activities (Myers 2019).

This is in line with the Toronto Region Board of Trade's 2018 Southern Ontario Advanced Manufacturing supercluster (Interview 5.11). Figure 5.14 illustrates the centrality of the City of Hamilton and Durham Region as key investment sites and stakeholders in realizing advanced manufacturing goals; goals that complement and support the key economic development goals of neighbouring regional municipalities. Within the framework of the Toronto Region Board of Trade, and in light of the recent merger of Hamilton and Oshawa port authorities, one could imagine the development of an advanced manufacturing innovation corridor bringing together Durham and Wentworth-Hamilton (Hamilton 2021). A key challenge in thinking of advanced manufacturing through the idea of an innovation corridor is noted by a participant from Next Generation Advanced Manufacturing: "We need to raise awareness and connect more across the ecosystem, which remains for now disjointed. We have a world-class ecosystem, but we need to connect across supply chains and across the ecosystem (throughout) the GTHA, because this is where the concentration of the ecosystem is" (Interview 5.6).

In contrast, one can look at artificial intelligence, an industry cluster that, for a few years already, has been organized and thought of through the notion of an innovation corridor. In this case, the geographical priority is given to the City of Toronto and, to some lesser extent, the Waterloo region. While Figure 5.15 demonstrates the connections structuring the relationship between both entities, it also echoes the City of Toronto coalition, having little to no involvement from other regional municipalities and their cities in the process. As such, the coalition emerging from the artificial intelligence sector finds anchors in municipal realities in Toronto and Waterloo regions. This picture is consistent with a regional development model based on specific subregional entities leading particular industry clusters semi-independently. In the case of artificial intelligence, we can see the role of the city at the centre of discussions and initiatives with business proxies, including the Toronto Region Board of Trade, and

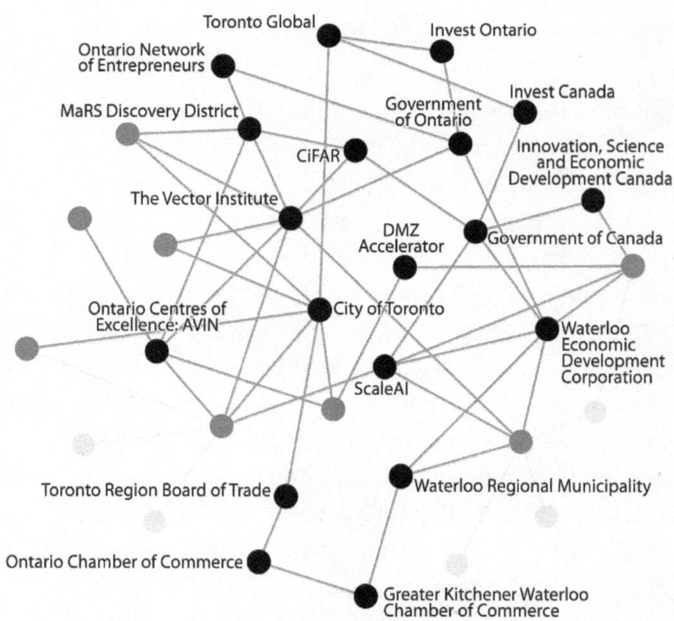

FIGURE 5.15 Artificial intelligence as a regional economic priority in the city-region of Toronto

with research institutions and pro-business organizations such as business incubators and membership associations, along with the direct support of provincial and federal bodies and programs.

Reflecting the model of innovation corridor as proposed by the Toronto Region Board of Trade to interpret such clustering of activities and pairing of Toronto and Waterloo, it is important to note the similarities between Figures 5.14 and 5.15 as a configuration of actors in which pro-business actors and research institutions are more numerous – and centrally represented. Drawing on their historical role in leading regional discussions around transportation and economic development, private sector actors are serving as the connectors between various official political bodies and structures, at different scales. In contrast with their role in figures representing region- or city-based coalitions, such stakeholders are a lot more present and key in guiding the discussions and initiatives supporting a better positioning of the city-region in global value chains through their own sector of activity. Finally, this analysis also confirms the limited role of civil society organizations in these configurations, even when the City of Toronto is a central actor. Such actors are not represented in industry-specific coalitions, with the exception of business proxies. In fact, civil society organizations might be in relation to municipal governments on transportation concerns and issues, but in the industry-sector coalitions, even municipal governments' representation is less central.

CONCLUSION

The implementation of the federal government's Continental Gateway Strategy in the city-region of Toronto has built long-standing tensions between the City of Toronto and the Ontario government – and a sustained schism between Toronto and its suburbs. While transportation and economic development are usually treated separately, we can see the emergence of a series of suburban coalitions around certain sectors of activity to support a better positioning of the city-region in global value chains. A series of decentralized suburban and sector-specific coalitions using executive democratic practices to advance their interests can be identified with the regions of Durham and Hamilton-Wentworth specializing in advanced manufacturing, Peel Region focusing on transportation logistics, Halton Region on start-ups in specific technology fields, and York Region on ICT. Some of these articulated directly with the gateway strategy and its associated funding programs. In contrast, the City of Toronto's focus on artificial intelligence – in partnership with the Waterloo Region – portrays an urban coalition a lot more interested in talent recruitment for high-value knowledge-based sectors and the local aspects of transportation, especially as they intersect with quality-of-life indicators. As such, there is not one singular urban coalition to organize, mobilize, and represent the city-region of Toronto in global value chains, which only adds to the challenge of intergovernmental collaborations and alignment with the other city-region identified by the Continental Gateway Strategy, namely Montreal in the neighbouring Province of Quebec.

6

Montreal and the Continental Gateway

In the words of author and inspector-general of the Protestant schools of the province of Quebec John Campbell Sutherland (1922, 83):

> Montreal became the chief city of the Dominion on account of its position at the head of ocean navigation, and, in the railway period, owing to its direct connection south with New York through the Champlain-Hudson valley's "gap." These advantages, together with the nearness to the hydro-power furnished by the rapids of the St. Lawrence, have made Montreal the greatest industrial centre in the Dominion.

In 1978, Jean-Claude Lasserre wrote that Montreal had always been a *ville-seuil,* a gateway city first and foremost – an attribute to which higher tiers of government have rarely failed to give full credence. If the westward expansion of the North American economy and the decline of industrial activity have diminished Montreal's importance relative to other Canadian urban areas, its position as a gateway is still as consequential today as it was yesterday. In this way, Montreal's gateway has always combined different source (production), sink (consumption), and saddle (distribution) functions in international networks, most notably around its port infrastructure.

In this chapter, we address two questions: (i) To what degree does integrative trade influence Montreal's economic strategy? (ii) How are its impacts managed? In other words, how does Canada's commercial policy percolate down to city level, and how are its constraints managed locally? How do Montreal's elected officials and planning bodies pay heed to the impacts of GVCs on the city's environment? We are also interested in exploring how and when citizens' inputs, preoccupations, and claims on these matters are taken into account. As we will see, the city-region's numerous municipal governments and their multiple governance frameworks constitute a complex system that poses a number of challenges for citizens who wish to express their needs and make their voices heard.

The chapter is divided into three sections. The first provides a description of Greater Montreal's political and administrative institutions followed by an analysis of their respective planning documents to establish if and how the impacts of GVCs make it into their respective economic development and planning strategies. The second follows the path of federal policies on integrative trade and GVCs, normally relayed by the province, to the city-region and borough level. The third section centres on the political scene. It summarizes two major municipal party platforms and discusses various urban consultation mechanisms, with a focus on the consultations held in a borough most impacted by the federal government's commercial policy. A correlation is established between the failure of municipal party politics to fully engage with the externalities that accumulate in a gateway city immersed in a globalized economy, the absence of city-wide mobilizations on these issues, and the role that social acceptability at district level plays in this context.

GREATER MONTREAL'S POLITICAL AND ADMINISTRATIVE INSTITUTIONS

The Island of Montreal's Municipal Governments

There are sixteen municipal governments on the main island of the Hochelaga Archipelago – the City of Montreal and fifteen municipalities – that also have jurisdiction on half a dozen smaller isles (see Figure 6.1).[1] The city itself is divided into nineteen boroughs, with each borough having its own mayor, so there are thirty-four mayors in all. City council is composed of the mayor and sixty-four councillors elected by direct universal suffrage,[2] with an executive committee of eleven members.

With each borough having between five and eight councillors, there are a total of 103 elective offices at the city level for a population of 1.8 million in 2021. To this we must add 106 elected officials for the other fifteen municipalities that have a total population of 243,000. Consequently, the sum of elected representatives on the island reaches 209 for a population of a little over 2 million. By comparison, Toronto, with a population of 6.2 million, has one mayor and twenty-five councillors.

The sixteen municipal governments on the Island of Montreal come together in the Agglomeration Council (AC), which is made up of fifteen

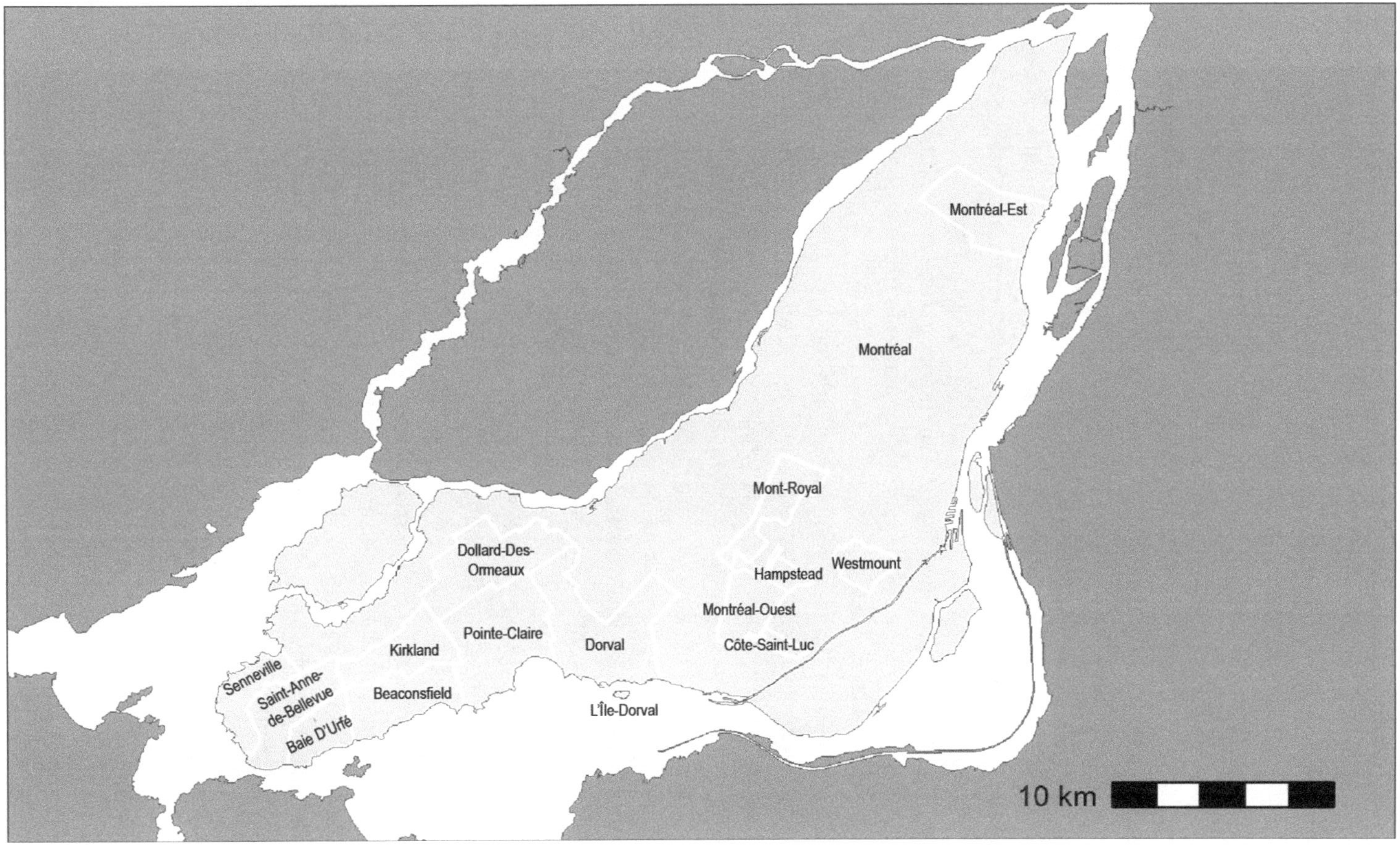

FIGURE 6.1 Montreal and neighbouring islands: The city and its fifteen municipalities | *Cartography:* Steve Tornes. *Source:* Statistics Canada (2021a).

elected representatives from the city council as well as fifteen representatives from the other municipalities.[3] The thirty-first member and head of the council is the mayor of the city. The weighting of votes in the council is established according to demographics and grants 87 percent to the City of Montreal and 13 percent to the other municipalities on the island.

Finally, at the regional level, the Greater Montreal, or the Montreal metropolitan region is administered by the Montreal Metropolitan Community (MMC), which comprises eighty-two municipalities divided into five geographic sectors: the Montreal Agglomeration, the Longueuil Agglomeration, Laval, the North Shore, and the South Shore (see Figure 6.2).[4] In 2021, the MMC had a total population of just over 4 million (see Table 6.1). The MMC is run by a council of twenty-eight members and an executive committee of eight.[5] However, the eighty-two municipalities are each also part of a Regional County Municipality (RCM),[6] with the result that Greater Montreal encompasses all or part of fourteen different RCMs or equivalent territories.[7]

As far as distribution of responsibilities is concerned, borough councils in the city have jurisdiction, powers, and obligations in seven fields. These are, according to Article 130 of the Charter of Ville de Montréal: (i) urban planning; (ii) exceptions to the prohibition from converting immovables to divided co-ownership; (iii) fire safety and civil protection; (iv) the environment; (v) local economic, community, cultural, and social development; (vi) culture, recreation and borough parks; and (vii) local roads.

The AC has competence, inter alia, over the following nine common services: public transport, police, municipal evaluation, public housing, fire prevention, drinking water, wastewater treatment, arterial road network management, and the municipal court. However, some of its powers are shared with the MMC, notably on land use. Finally, the MMC "has jurisdiction over what are referred to as the strategic functions of a region, such as land-use planning, economic development, environment, transportation and social housing. The MMC is therefore able to carry out an integrated planning and development strategy for its territory" (Cahiers métropolitains 2016, 23). It also relies on the recommendations coming out of five standing committees: urban planning, economic development, environment, transportation, and social housing.

Further complicating matters, each local government level is responsible for the adoption of a development plan in accordance with the Quebec government's orientations. Since 2005, the MMC has adopted four five-year Metropolitan Economic Development Plans (MEDP),[8] the last covering the years 2022–31,[9] and one Metropolitan Land Use and Development

TABLE 6.1
Montreal Metropolitan Community, by 2021 population

	Population		*Growth (%)*	*Share (%)*	
Municipal Area	*2006*	*2021*	*2006–21*	*2006*	*2021*
Montreal MMC	3,532,006	4,029,332	14	100.00	100.00
Agglomeration (Montreal Island) = 16 municipalities	1,854,442	2,004,265	8	52.50	49.74
Montreal	1,620,693	1,762,949	9	45.89	43.75
Dollar-Des-Ormeaux	48,930	48,403	–1	1.39	1.20
Côte-Saint-Luc	31,395	34,504	10	0.89	0.86
Pointe-Claire	30,161	33,488	11	0.85	0.83
Westmount	20,494	19,658	–4	0.58	0.49
Mont-Royal	18,933	20,953	11	0.54	0.52
Kirkland	20,491	19,413	–5	0.58	0.48
Beaconsfield	19,194	19,277	0	0.54	0.48
Dorval	18,088	19,302	7	0.51	0.48
Hampstead	6,996	7,037	1	0.20	0.17
Montreal-Ouest	5,184	5,115	–1	0.15	0.13
Sainte-Anne-de-Bellevue	5,197	5,027	–3	0.15	0.12
Montréal-Est	3,822	4,394	15	0.11	0.11
Baie-d'Urfé	3,902	3,764	–4	0.11	0.09
Senneville	962	951	–1	0.03	0.02
L'Île-Dorval	–	30	–	0.00	0.00
Couronne nord = 20 municipalities	493,956	615,339	25	13.99	15.27
Laval = 1 municipality	368,709	438,366	19	10.44	10.88
Longueuil = 5 municipalities	385,533	436,785	13	10.92	10.84
Couronne sud = 40 municipalities	429,366	534,577	25	12.16	13.27

Sources: Statistics Canada (2012b, 2021c).

Plan (MLUDP)[10] adopted on December 8, 2011, to cover the years 2012–17, and subsequently maintained in force until 2022. Within two years of the MLUDP's coming into force, and in conformity with it, the AC adopted its own Land Use Planning and Development Plan (LUPDP)[11] in 2015, the contents of which are prescribed by law.[12] Finally, the City of Montreal (2004) adopted its Master Plan (MP) – Plan d'urbanisme – which was substantially modified January 25, 2016, to conform with the LUPDP, while the nineteen borough councils are responsible for the adoption of

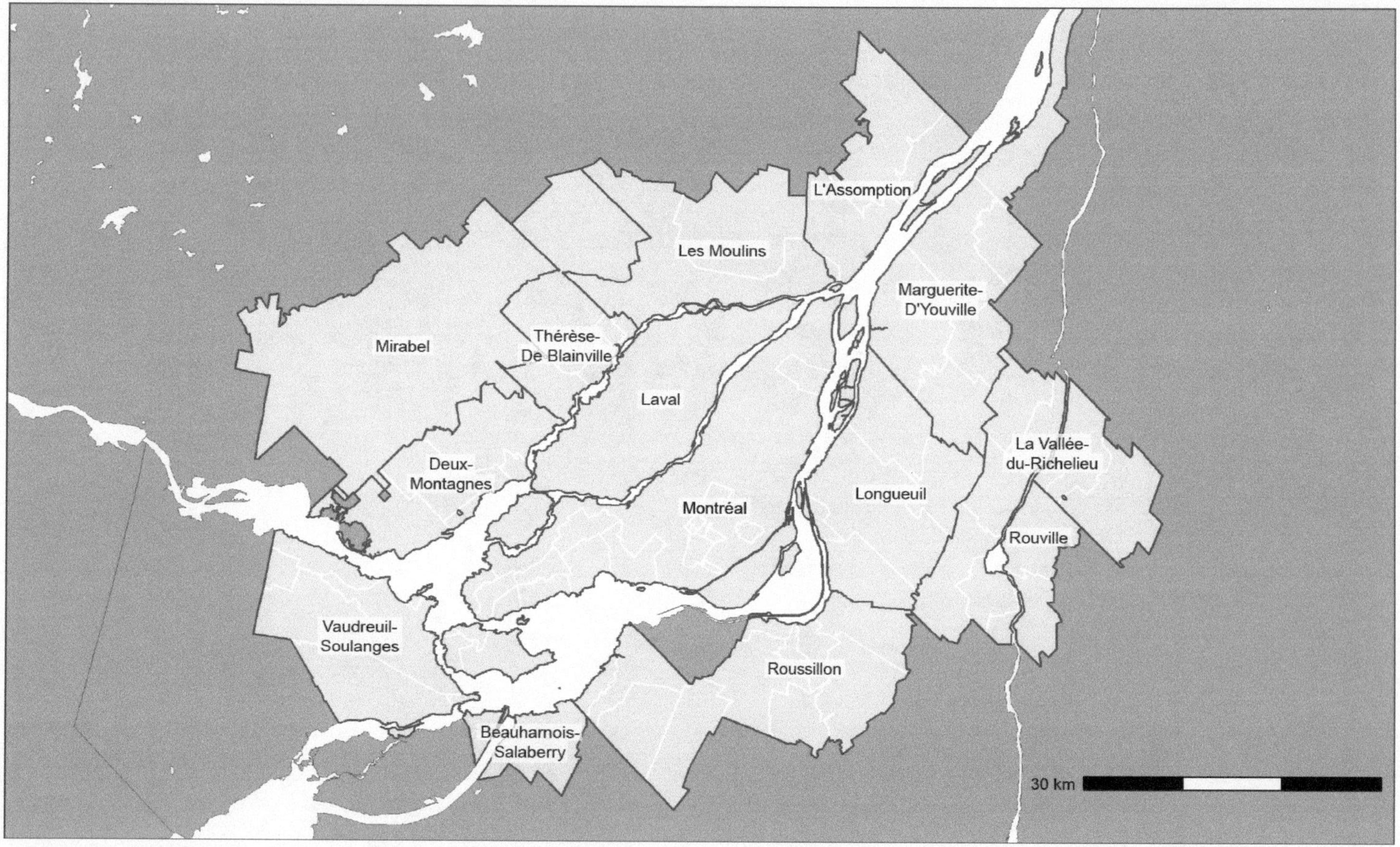

FIGURE 6.2 Greater Montreal and its five geographic sectors and eighty-two municipalities | *Cartography:* Steve Tornes. *Source:* Statistics Canada (2021a).

TABLE 6.2
Planning on the MMC's territory and deliverables

Levels of intervention	*Deliverables*
Quebec government	Strategies and policies *Loi sur l'aménagement et l'urbanisme* (LAU)
Montreal Metropolitan Community (MMC)	Metropolitan Economic Development Plan (MEDP) Metropolitan Land Use and Development Plan (MLUDP)
Agglomeration Council (AC)	Land-Use Planning and Development Plan (LUPDP)
City of Montreal	Master Plan (MP) Special Planning Programs (SPP)
Boroughs	Planning bylaws

planning bylaws in accordance with the LUPDP and the MP. The city also adopted numerous Special Planning Programs (SPP) – Programme particulier d'urbanisme – that complement the MP and provide detailed planning in specific areas. Table 6.2 describes the five levels of land-use and development planning with their deliverables.

A more complete – if more complex – description of the institutional framework for economic development in the region is the one coming out of the MMC's MEDP (2015–20), which takes into account five levels of intervention. But the chart places the City of Montreal at the local level alongside the eighty-one other municipalities – thereby ignoring its boroughs – and places the AC alongside thirteen other RCMs, even though six of these are only partially in the MMC (see Table 6.3).

The MEDP 2015–20 offers this explanation about its chart:

> The institutional framework for economic development above includes five levels of intervention. The Government of Québec intervenes at the provincial level, the [MMC] at the metropolitan level, the agglomerations, the RCMs and the RCM-cities at the regional level, and the municipalities at the local level. Also, the regional conferences of elected officers (CRÉs), the ministries and a number of organizations intervene at the administrative region level. Each level has its own planning tools. (MMC 2015, 67)

Here again, each level has its own agenda, but as in the previous table, the implication is that every effort should be made to plan in accordance with the orientations coming from above. Commenting on the city's organizational structure, the Chamber of Commerce of Metropolitan

TABLE 6.3
Planning on the MMC's territory according to the MEDP 2015–20

Level of intervention	*Organizations and Tools*
Provincial	Government of Quebec: Strategies and policies
Metropolitan	Montreal Metropolitan Community: Metropolitan Economic Development Plan
Administrative regions	7 regional conferences of elected officers: Five-year development plan
Regional	14 Regional County Municipalities: Local economic and employment action plan
Local	82 municipalities: Economic development strategies

Source: MMC (2015, 67), reproduced with permission.

Montreal (CCMM) has this assessment to offer on its website: "A total of 103 mayors within the territory of the [MMC], powers split between cities, boroughs and the urban agglomeration, a city divided into five administrative regions by Quebec: Montréal's governance is enough to make your head spin!" (CCMM n.d.).

In its *Rapport Côté-Seguin*, tabled in 2010, the working group on the challenges of governance and taxation in the Montreal region had already documented these difficulties and showed that Montreal's internal problems were such that the larger perspective was lost (CCMM 2010). The report underlined that Montreal and its region were losing ground quickly: the Montreal region accounted for 11 percent of the Canadian economy and would continue to decline unless something was done. The report also pointed to the fact that there existed at the time no coordination at the ministerial level in Quebec regarding government action vis-à-vis its metropolis. Responsibility for the region was divided between three ministers: one for the Island of Montreal, one for Laval and the Laurentians, and a third for the South Shore. The report concluded that, with so many actors involved, the main challenge was better coordination between activities and the promotion of a coherent economic development – two objectives that should be reached through the rationalization and simplification of the mandates of all organisms involved. Some minor shortcomings were eventually resolved with the adoption of Bill 121, an act to increase the autonomy and powers of City of Montreal, the metropolis of Quebec, in January 2017, although the act had nothing to say about the fifteen so-called reconstituted cities or the agglomeration, thereby probably compounding the complexity alluded to earlier instead of reducing it.

Turning now to the city-region's major planning documents, we want to see how these contradictory forces are taken into account.

MMC's, AC's, and the City's Major Planning Documents

To explore the linkages between different levels of administrative and political responsibility in the region as far as economic development and global value chains (GVCs) are concerned, a close reading of the numerous planning documents and action plans drawn up respectively by the MMC, the agglomeration, and the city is in order. We follow chronological order here, and since the lower levels are required to adapt their own planning instruments according to the guidelines coming out of the level above, we start off with the MMC's two major documents, the 2015–20 MEDP and the MLUDP, before moving on to the AC's LUPDP and the city's MP.

It should be underlined at the outset that these plans, especially the ones coming out of the MMC, were submitted to extended public consultations. In this regard, the MMC prides itself on its democracy and transparency, and it is why the Agora métropolitaine figures prominently in the governance framework.

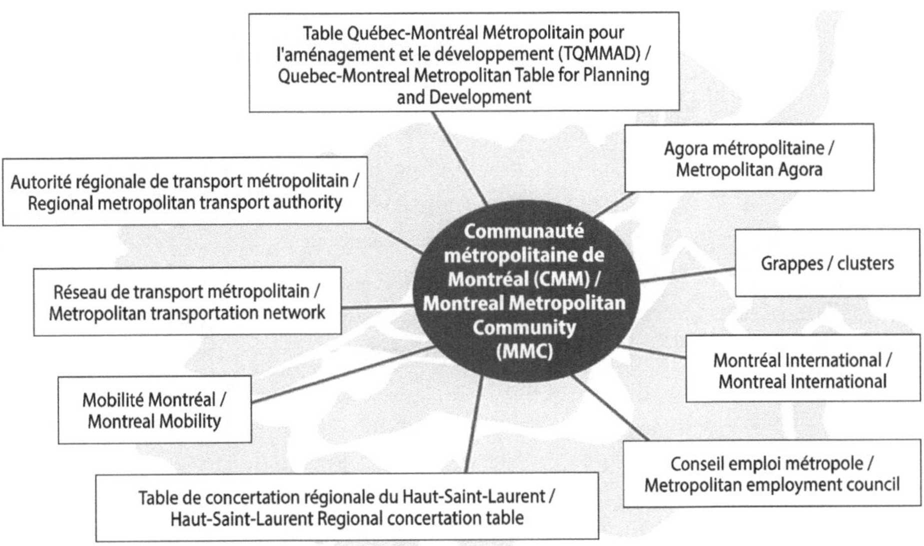

FIGURE 6.3 Montreal Metropolitan Community (MMC) governance framework | *Source:* Adapted from MMC (2018, 18).

Nevertheless, the transparency and inclusiveness of this framework is open to question for at least two reasons. First, the status of one of its stakeholders, the Table Québec-Montréal métropolitain pour l'aménagement et le développement, which figures prominently at the top, is unclear. Second, and more importantly, some of the major stakeholders are also involved in another selective and extended governance framework known as the "Montreal model." Here, select stakeholders are called upon to play an extensive and significant role in economic matters.

Coming now to the 2015–20 MEDP (MMC 2015), adopted by the MMC on April 30, 2015,[13] it confirms the two-pronged approach spelled out in its previous versions: the first being the contribution of its clusters to the city's global standing,[14] and the second, the role of Montreal International (its lobbying arm in attracting foreign investors) as the city's promoter at the international level.[15] These reiterate the objective of establishing Montreal as a "smart metropolis" (18, 57). Furthermore, to promote collaboration between key economic partners, a "Montreal model" is introduced that involves the Government of Canada, the Government of Quebec, Montreal International, the Board of Trade of Metropolitan Montreal and other boards of trade, Conseil emploi métropole, as well as the city's ten clusters, the MMC, and other chambers of commerce (see Figure 6.4).

The model's partners are responsible for the identification of issues and challenges that should boost the role of all clusters, with CargoM identified as the cluster specifically involved in transport, logistics, and hubs. The action plan sets up a committee called MEG-Mtl (Metropolitan Economic Governance-Montreal),[16] made up of the aforementioned stakeholders who are responsible for following up on the implementation of the strategy. And to better fulfill its mandate, the committee relies on the data provided by the Greater Montreal Observatory, an entity set up at the instigation of the MMC in November 2008.[17]

The juxtaposition of both frameworks supports the argument that Hamel and Keil's (2017) idea of deliberative democracy as well as Mayer's (2017) "unfettered operation of the market" could be pursued in parallel through two distinct and, we may add, highly asymmetrical governance frameworks, as we see here. We return to this point later in the chapter.

Coming now to its content, the MEDP 2015–20 identifies eight major challenges, defines three sets of objectives, and proposes three strategic axes.[18] The first axis, "focus on our economy's strength," has three components: the development of clusters, the consolidation of a creative economy, and the promotion of a logistics hub with CargoM.[19] The second

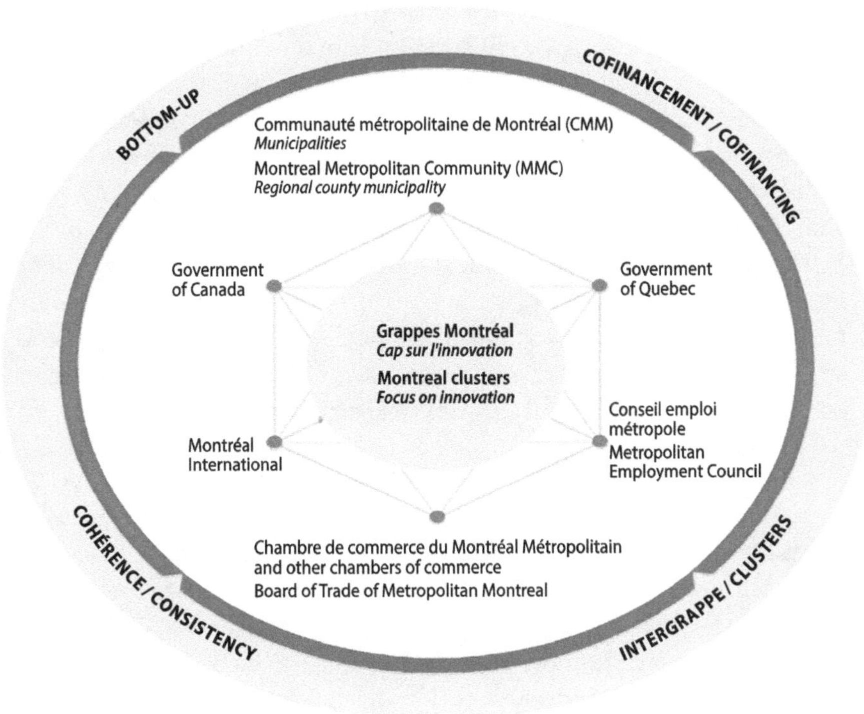

FIGURE 6.4 The "Montreal model" | *Source:* Adapted from MMC (2015, 16 [figure 3]), reproduced with permission.

axis, "optimize our production factors," has two components: attracting private investment and the development of a high-quality workforce. The third, "provide metropolitan coherence," also has two components: support smart city initiatives and mobilize metropolitan economic stakeholders to foster coherence and avoid "inconsistent results."[20] If the reliance on clusters and on the Montreal model are two salient features of the metropolitanization of Greater Montreal, the central role entrusted to Montreal International characterizes its internationalization as interpreted and applied by the MMC.

In addition to the MEDP, the law obliges the MMC to "adopt and maintain in force a Metropolitan Land Use and Development Plan" (MMC 2012, 5). The plan was finally adopted in 2011 and was also submitted to an extensive consultation process involving the MMC's partner bodies, the public, and the Quebec government to ensure it was consistent with the direction of government policy (MMC 2012, 5).[21] It was followed by the adoption of the Action Plan 2012–17.

There are three items in the MEDP 2015–20 (MMC 2015) that most concern us: (i) logistics, (ii) collaboration with other tiers of government, and (iii) follow-up and consultation. Concerning the first item, logistics, the plan underlines Montreal's historic role as a transport hub for North America on account of its well-developed transportation infrastructure, including the Port of Montreal, the Trudeau and Mirabel Airports, CN and CP continental rail networks, and an established highway network (MMC 2012, 140). It then introduces the three notions of intermodality, intermodal centres, and logistic hubs. The importance of intermodality for Montreal and its region, and the impact of GVCs on the city's road and rail infrastructures, are made quite plain in the following statements on the Port of Montreal and the Montreal airports:

> The Port of Montréal ... [is] one of the largest inland ports in the world, the ninth largest container port in North America in 2009 and the main gateway into the specific sector of transatlantic trade. In 2009, 24.5 million metric tonnes of merchandise passed through the Port of Montréal, of which 11.2 million tonnes were containerized cargo, for a total of over 1.2 million containers per year. Half of the containerized cargo was transported by rail, and with trucking accounts for 50% of total traffic. Approximately 2,000 truck movements linked to container traffic were recorded in each direction, ... without directly using the nearby highway network ... The port's facilities will soon reach capacity. To meet the anticipated demand, the Montréal Port Authority is currently evaluating expansion scenarios ... [arguing that] it is possible to develop additional container treatment capacity on the Montréal site to accommodate up to 2.2 million containers; the port's current capacity is 1.6 million ... Improved road access to the Port of Montréal constitutes a priority investment for numerous stakeholders ... In the medium term (5 to 10 years), ... the Port of Montréal's total processing capacity [might increase] to 3 million containers. This increase in capacity will probably require the addition of an intermodal terminal. (MMC 2012, 142)

The MEDP notes that in 2009, 174,000 metric tonnes of merchandise passed through Montreal's air cargo facilities (half through Trudeau International Airport and half through Mirabel). And "in terms of value, these goods represented a fifth of all goods transported in 2007. The market value of products transported by plane is much higher ($45/kg) than that of products shipped other ways ($0.32/kg)" (MMC 2012, 143).

The MEDP goes on to describe the pivotal role played by the road networks and the concentration of jobs in industries that generate the movement of goods in the *centre* of the Montreal census metropolitan area (CMA)[22] – that is, the Island of Montreal proper (MMC 2012, 138). Because the City of Montreal and the agglomeration are majorly affected by the movement of goods, they are also the ones most concerned with issues of intermodality and the creation of logistics hubs. However, lumping Regional County Municipalities (RCMs) and the agglomeration together, as in the quotation below, dilutes this core urban reality instead of prioritizing it:

> New logistics hubs must guarantee the efficiency and capacity of the transportation infrastructure providing intermodality between the various modes of transport (marine, rail, air and road). The PMAD encourages RCMs and agglomerations to consider sites with the following characteristics when selecting locations for logistics hubs: (i) direct access to the metropolitan road network; (ii) direct access to the rail network; (iii) located near a port or airport facility; (iv) able to accommodate a buffer zone to minimize the impact of the site's activities (e.g., noise, hazardous materials). (MMC 2012, 164)

Notwithstanding their relevance, these recommendations failed to make it into the MMC's Action Plan 2012–17.

Regarding collaboration between governments, the MEDP 2015–20 mentions the July 2007 Memorandum of Understanding (MoU) signed between the governments of Canada, Ontario, and Quebec on the development of the Ontario-Quebec Continental Gateway and Trade Corridor.[23] It then reiterates the reliance of the plan and the action plan on cooperation with the Quebec government (MMC 2012, 201). This cooperation between governments and the MMC is entrusted to the newly created Quebec-Greater Montreal working table on land use and development, which "will bring together key ministers and elected officials of the MMC, as well as major regional stakeholders" to

> suggest major policy directions and priorities for action to ensure consistent government actions with regard to the sustainable land use and development of the metropolitan region. The interdepartmental committee ... will be in charge of planning and implementing these policy directions, ... foster[ing] better synergy between government actions and the major players ... as well as a more efficient use of public funds. (MMC 2012, 202)

Despite recognizing the complexity of the make-up of Montreal, the plan does not call for a municipal reorganization, though it does recommend clarifying the roles and responsibilities of each governing body to ensure the pursuit of common actions and goals (MMC 2012, 202). Yet, there is no sign that this clarification will be forthcoming any time soon. This probably goes a long way to explaining why the MEDP has chosen to lump together the *centre* of its CMA – the Island of Montreal and its Agglomeration Council – with the surrounding agglomerations and the RCMs that represent second-tier stakeholders when issues of logistics, intermodality, and GVCs are raised.

Finally, concerning the third item, follow-up and consultation, the MEDP 2015–20 document assigns political responsibility for the implementation of the plan, and for "many aspects of the PMAD's action plan," to the MMC's commissions before describing the consultation process that is set up. The MMC commissions are "called upon to play a major role in implementing the PMAD" and their responsibilities are defined in the following terms:

> Each commission will be supported by the administration of the MMC. Technical committees made up of representatives from each of the MMC's five geographical areas (RCMs and agglomerations) will support the commissions' work. The representatives from the provincial ministries involved and civil society will also be called upon to collaborate. *If necessary, public consultations will be organized* [emphasis added]. The MMC Executive Committee and Planning Commission will be in charge of monitoring the activities of the PMAD. (MMC 2012, 206)

In short, the commissions assume a "major role," while the Montreal Agglomeration in particular is relegated to technical committees with the four other "geographical areas." As for the consultation process, to involve the maximum number of stakeholders, a biennial metropolitan "agora," or assembly of elected officials and citizens, is convened to provide and share a "supralocal and regional vision" of the MEDP (MMC 2012, 206). The Greater Montreal Observatory, a website, offers free access to relevant information.[24]

Coming down one tier to the agglomeration level, it is interesting to note that its comments on the MEDP are positive – approving, notably, of the plan's creation of logistics centres to ensure efficient intermodal access. In its concluding remarks, the AC gives its full support to the

MMC's first metropolitan plan. It also supports the proposal to create a consultation mechanism to facilitate concertation between the government and the elected officials at the municipal level and to establish better co-ordination and more coherence among the Quebec government's interventions at the regional level.[25]

We already noted that the AC adopted its own LUPDP in 2015.[26] But as the AC has no administrative structure as such, the plan was prepared under the guidance of the City of Montreal's Planning Division (Arteau 2014). The plan outlines the broad parameters that should guide the council in its decisions pertaining to land use over the coming years. It covers the agglomeration's territory and carries the obligation for the urban plans and planning regulations adopted by all the municipalities, to be drafted in compliance with the plan.

The *Loi sur l'aménagement et l'urbanisme* (Law on planning and urban development) (RLRQ, chapitre A-19.1) (Gouvernement du Québec 1996) provides that the AC's own LUPDP should cover the eight following subjects: (i) the broad guidelines concerning land use on an agglomeration's territory; (ii) the major land-use zones on such territory; (iii) the urbanization perimeter; (iv) the determination of areas subject to special restrictions for public safety reasons (inundation, erosion) or for reason of environmental protection (shores, coasts, floodplains); (v) the determination of roads along which land use is subject to major constraints (public security, public health, general well-being); (vi) the determination of the parts of the territory with a historical, cultural, patrimonial, aesthetic, or ecologic interest; (vii) the organization of land transport; and (viii) the nature and approximate location of infrastructure and important equipment.

To realize its objectives, the LUPDP's strategic vision relies heavily, as it should, on the MLUDP's own analysis and vision. It proposes, inter alia, to achieve major road projects to boost access to intermodal platforms (Agglomeration Council 2015, 21), to dynamize intermodality through investments in logistics hubs, and to develop specialized sectors in logistics. Most interestingly, it proposes the establishment of a committee, bringing together all the partners to pursue three objectives: (i) analyzing the dynamics of the employment sector related to logistics in the region and its fallout for the Montreal Agglomeration; (ii) exploring new distribution channels, especially regarding urban logistics (home delivery); and (iii) supporting efforts on the part of Aéroports de Montréal to increase the number of direct connections with Asia and South America to support economic development (Agglomeration Council 2015, 69). However, the

AC's approach to these issues does not consider the environmental impacts of its options, although the notion of "sustainable development" figures prominently in the plan.[27]

At city level, the Montreal MP was first adopted by city council in November 2004, but – as mentioned earlier – was substantially modified in January 2016 to bring it into conformity with the MLUDP. The objectives stated in the MP are supported by a series of concrete actions, for instance, the rehabilitation and optimization of the Metropolitan autoroute or the redevelopment and extension of major arteries.[28] In turn, some among these concrete actions have been the object of nineteen SPPs, one of which, "Assomption Nord," deals specifically with land development in a district of the Mercier-Hochelaga-Maisonneuve (MHM) borough. Quite surprisingly, the adjoining district, Assomption Sud, which includes Port of Montreal, is not the object of an SPP but of a tailor-made project to which we turn in a following subsection.

Meanwhile, to complete our overview, mention should be made of the Montreal Development Plan, which, notwithstanding its title, is a policy paper for future guidance rather than an economic development plan as such. An English summary of the plan entitled "Montréal for Tomorrow" (City of Montreal 2013, 2) states that its measures will "be implemented in conjunction with the Metropolitan Land Use and Development Plan (PMAD) of the MMC." Further on, it states that the city plans "to develop integrated management of goods transportation" and "to strengthen Montréal's economic role as a shipping hub, by encouraging freight transportation logistics, near the airport and the port, and relying on rail and highway infrastructures" (City of Montreal 2013, 4). Although longer (ninety pages vs. twelve), the full version in French dedicates half a paragraph to the integrated management of goods' transport and to the implementation of an intermodal logistics system – subject matters that the recently established cluster on transport and logistics should address in partnership with concerned stakeholders, and its action plan itself presents no concrete actions in this regard.

Finally, following the municipal elections held November 5, 2017, the new mayor, Valérie Plante, expounded her party's own vision of economic development in a document, tabled April 2018, entitled *Montréal Geared Up for Tomorrow* (Ville de Montréal 2019),[29] which, as its title reveals, is not substantially different from its predecessor mentioned in the previous paragraph. This economic plan is built around five strategic sectors: creative and cultural industries, life sciences and health technologies, the digital industry, transportation/mobility, and clean technologies. Recalling the status of Quebec's metropolis granted to the city by the provincial government in 2017, allotting it new powers and responsibilities, the plan stresses the importance that the challenges of economic integration and the competition between cities represent at a global level. It specifically mentions the importance of intermodality, the revitalization of economic and industrial hubs, and the challenges of employment and merchandise transportation.[30]

To conclude this overview, a few comments are in order. First, and most obviously, even though the historical role of Montreal as gateway and the importance of intermodality are ritually reasserted in the six planning documents we have reviewed, none make any reference whatsoever to the economic or commercial policies adopted by the higher tiers of government, with the sole exception of a cursory reference in the MLUDP-PMAD to the 2007 signing of an MoU on the Continental Gateway. Small wonder that no reference is made to integrative trade – or GVCs either. Nevertheless, the MEDP spells out an economic strategy that proposes an interesting compromise or mixture between a Keynesian and a post-Keynesian perspective, with a notable preference for the latter. The Keynesian dimension is dealt with in its reliance on the Quebec government's economic policies, but the post-Keynesian dimension is most apparent in its double-pronged approach, relying, on the one hand, on a host of cluster initiatives, while on the other, on Montreal International. In this regard, the MMC's approach to both metropolitanization and internationalization is decidedly post-Keynesian. However, before concluding that integrative trade and GVCs are irrelevant in the present context, we look into these policy trajectories to find out how the terms of this agreement percolated down to the urban level. This approach allows us to uncover the path taken by said policies.

INTEGRATIVE TRADE, GVCs, AND SOCIAL ACCEPTABILITY

This section is divided into two subsections. The first deals with the two trajectories through which the federal government's commercial policy of 2007 (Government of Canada 2008) percolated down to city level and beyond. The second concentrates on a district specifically targeted for the implementation of a project aimed at complying with the exigencies coming out of integrative trade and GVCs.

Two Successive Trajectories for the Federal's Policies

If a new commercial policy does not percolate down from the federal government to city level, it could simply be because the government does not have jurisdiction over cities, which are governed by their province. This explains why federal policies tend to be ignored in recent literature on Canadian city-regions (Hamel and Keil 2017, 182). But it is worth repeating that while the federal government has no formal jurisdiction over cities, it has jurisdiction over ports and airports, whose dependence on the government's commercial policies has a growing impact on cities. In the present instance, when the federal government released its new commercial policy, the Quebec and other provincial governments followed suit and signed the MoU in 2007 (see the Continental Gateway and Trade Corridor).

If the MMC placed little emphasis on the policies, this could simply be because, in its own reading, these policies had little bearing on its strategies. After all, with Montreal being a major hub in North America since its foundation almost four centuries ago, no new commercial policy should be deemed to have a paramount impact on its historic mission. Consequently, our own hypothesis would not hold and, at best, integrative trade would be a mere extension of an export promotion strategy – a conclusion that would also invalidate the thesis according to which integrative trade and GVCs impact city-regions as never before (Brenner 2004; Dicken 1992; Sturgeon 2006, 2008). If we are to validate our hypothesis, we must resort to another approach: instead of relying on documents, we propose to follow these policies' trajectories from the federal to city level.

The first trajectory follows on the heels of the federal government's 2007 adoption of the integrative strategy – and the signing of an MoU that same year between the ministers of Transport Canada, Ontario, and Quebec. In Quebec, the Ministère des Transports du Québec (MTQ) was made coresponsible for the research that the working groups set up under the MoU. This work carried on through 2011, two years beyond the duration of the MoU itself.[31] The second trajectory is the Quebec government's Maritime Strategy of 2015 (Gouvernement du Québec 2015), which adapted the federal government's commercial strategy and relayed it down to city level. This strategy, it should be noted, was duly taken up by the Coalition avenir Québec (CAQ) after its victory over the Parti libéral du Québec (PLQ) in the provincial elections of October 1, 2018.[32]

If the MoU of 2007 did not provide for an extension of its governance framework down to municipal or city levels, the MTQ did take the initiative in that direction and joined forces with the Interregional Committee on the Transport of Goods (Comité interrégional pour le transport des marchandises, CITM) to set up the Greater Montreal Working Group on the Ontario-Quebec Continental Gateway and Trade Corridor (OQCGTC) that published its report in 2009 (Working Group on the OQCGTC 2009). The CITM was an initiative that predated both the MoU and the Conservative government's promotion of the integrative trade strategy at the time. It had been set up in 1999 at the instigation of Montreal's Elected Officials Conference – CRÉ de Montréal – to bring together some seventy leaders from public and private sectors involved in transportation and logistics, including a few union representatives. The committee tabled its first five-year strategic plan in 2001, aimed at consolidating Greater

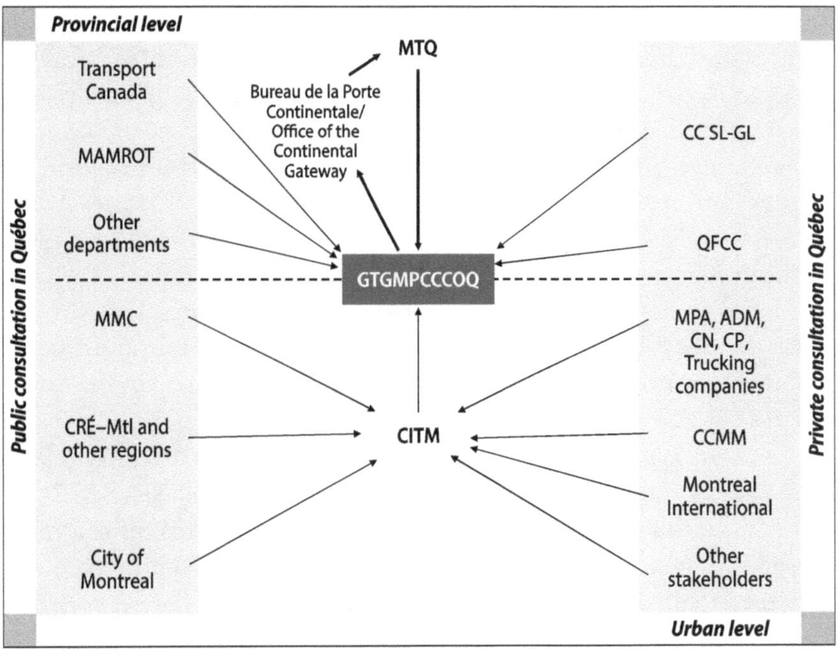

FIGURE 6.5 Stakeholders in the framework set up under the MoU in Quebec

Note: The following abbreviations are used: ADM = Aéroports de Montréal; CC SL-GL = Conseil du corridor pour le projet St-Laurent-Grands Lacs; CCMM = Chamber of Commerce of Metropolitan Montreal; CITM = Comité interregional pour le transport des marchandises / Interregional Committee on Transport of Goods; CN = Canadian National; CP = Canadian Pacific; CRÉ–Mtl = Conférence régionale des élus / Regional Conferences of Elected Officials (abolished in 2014)–Montreal; GTGMPCCCOQ = Groupe de travail du Grand Montréal sur la Porte continentale et le corridor de commerce Ontario-Québec / Greater Montreal Working Group on the Gateway; MAMROT = Ministère des Affaires municipales, des Régions et de l'Occupation du territoire; MMC = Montreal Metropolitan Community; MPA = Montreal Port Authority; MTQ = Ministère des Transports du Québec / Quebec Ministry of Transport; QFCC = Quebec's Federation of Chambers of Commerce

Montreal's position as a North American hub for the transportation of goods, and its second action plan explicitly mentioned its participation in the OQCGTC project (CITM 2001, 2008). This joint initiative brought together an array of stakeholders from the public and private sectors, including Transport Canada, the MMC, and the City of Montreal, among the former – the major players in transportation – as well as Montreal International and the CCMM, among the latter. Here again, no organization or group from civil society was involved.

The centrepiece in this framework, the Greater Montreal Working Group on the Gateway, had the responsibility of bringing together these stakeholders to advise the OQCGTC bureau on forthcoming investments. In turn, the bureau's findings were to be integrated in the MTQ's strategy. As Figure 6.5 illustrates, this framework confirms MTQ's pivotal role in relaying the federal government's commercial policy to the Greater Montreal level, on one hand, and as centralizing agent for the propositions coming out of the consultation process, on the other.[33] However, the Conservative government withheld investments in the Montreal region, so the group's action plans were not acted upon. Furthermore, the CRÉ de Montréal was abolished by the Liberal government in 2014, with the result that the follow-up on these issues at the metropolitan level was left to CargoM, the cluster on transportation and logistics set up by the MMC in 2012.[34]

A network analysis of the stakeholder relationships around projects funded under the Gateway and Border Crossing Fund and National Trade Corridors Fund programs in the Montreal region confirms the centrality of CargoM and, to a lesser degree, of the Chamber of Commerce, along with the Montreal Port Authority (see Figure 6.6). While the network diagram puts an emphasis on specific projects and not provincial bodies, this is deceiving. Provincial bodies have designed and institutionalized CargoM as a pillar of their provincial economic strategy and as the main entry point to using gateway infrastructure funds, a position that appears quite clearly in Figure 6.7. Identified both as an industrial cluster itself and a facilitator to supporting other industrial clusters, transportation logistics through CargoM are put at the centre of the local and provincial gateway economic plans, which is reflected here through the importance of the Port of Montreal and to a lesser extent the railway companies and trucking association. In this visualization of stakeholders involved in gateway infrastructure funding, we observe a relatively small number of them and a strong representation from the private sector. These actors are put in relation to public bodies at the various levels of government through

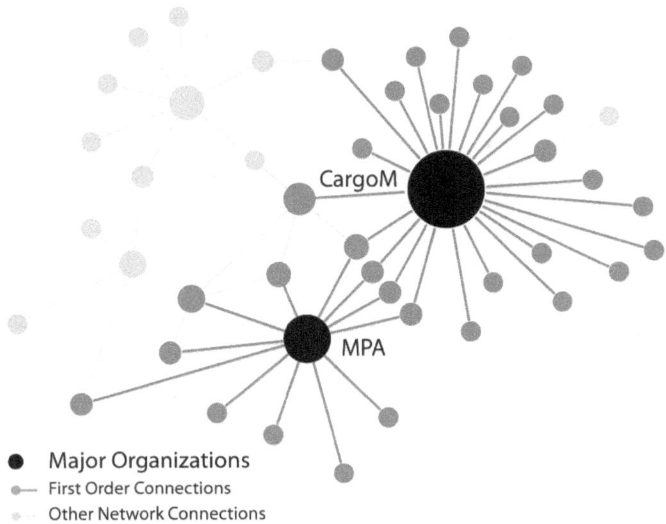

FIGURE 6.6 Network relationships around Montreal-funded projects

forums like CargoM and the Chamber of Commerce, highlighting once again the centrality of the institutionalized approach of the provincial government in transportation logistics.

Figure 6.7 illustrates the five tiers of responsibility and planning starting with the federal, the provincial, the MMC, the city, and one of its boroughs. A sixth level was added in anticipation of our argumentation in the following subsection, a district of the MHM borough called Assomption Sud. This district encompasses the Port of Montreal, which set up a Committee on Good Neighbourliness, an initiative aimed at smoothing relations between port authorities and residents, given the mounting negative externalities induced by the port's activities and its transportation.[35]

Concerning CargoM's stakeholders, the left side of the figure lists the representative from Transport Canada and the three from Quebec's ministries who are either observers or members of CargoM. The Quebec rectangle also includes a box labelled SAM, the Secretariate for Maritime Affairs, which is responsible for the implementation of Quebec's Maritime Strategy (MS), the policy that adapted and transposed the federal's blueprint in commerce, infrastructure, and industrial port zones at the provincial level. The MS explicitly mentions CargoM as the vector of its policies in the Greater Montreal area. On the figure's right side are listed members of CargoM's board of directors, comprising the major players in transportation and logistics on the Island of Montreal and beyond, including two

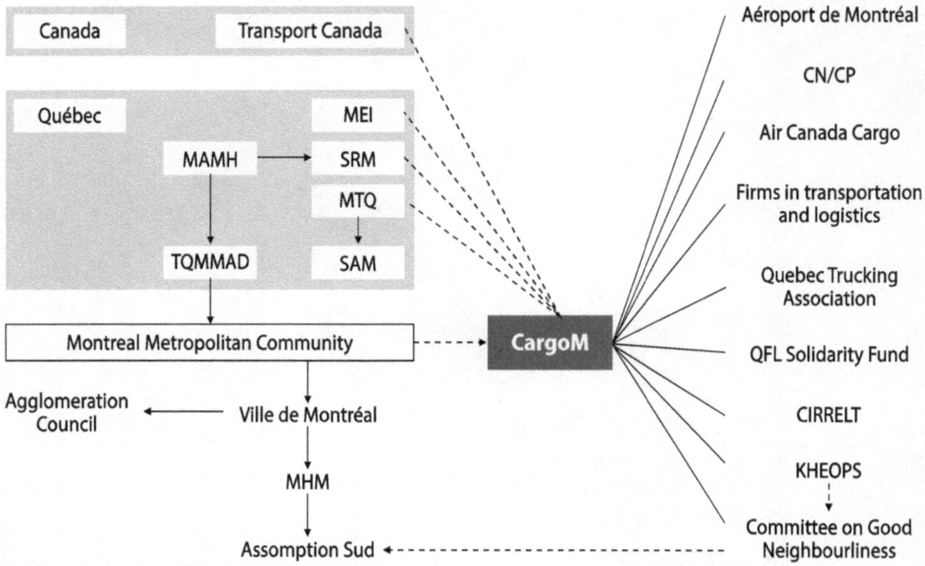

FIGURE 6.7 Montreal's multilevel organization chart with CargoM's major stakeholders

Note: The following abbreviations are used: CIRRELT = Interuniversity Research Centre on Transportation and Logistics; CN = Canadian National; CP = Canadian Pacific; KHEOPS = International Research Consortium on the Governance of Large Infrastructure Projects; MAMH = Ministère des Affaires municipales et de l'habitation / Ministry of Municipal Affairs and Housing; MEI = Ministère de l'économie et de l'innovation / Ministry of the economy and innovation; MHM = Mercier-Hochelaga-Masionneuve borough; MTQ = Ministère des Transports du Québec / Quebec Ministry of Transport; QFL = Quebec Federation of Labour; SAM = Secrétariat aux aAffaires maritimes / Maritime Affairs Secretariat; SRM = Secréteriat à la région métropolitaine / Metropolitan Region Secretariat; TQMMAD = Table Québec-Montréal Métropolitain pour l'aménagement et le développement / Quebec-Montreal Metropolitan Table for Planning and Development. CargoM includes board of directors as observers/members. Assomption Sud is a district of MHM borough.

research centres (CIRRELT and KHEOPS) and the Quebec Federation of Labour's Solidarity Fund.[36]

What is most significant about this figure is that both the federal government's new commercial policy and the MTQ's own redefinition and implementation through its MS occupy an ancillary position compared to that of the contingent of private stakeholders. In other words, these policies are taken for granted by all concerned. The only remaining question is, what practical means, facilities, and investments will be made available by their promoters to set in motion their implementation and matching action plans? This is consistent with the fact that CargoM's board of directors is made up of representatives from the private sector, while the two governments and the MMC act as either observers or simple members. The City of Montreal's marginal position in Figure 6.7 could explain the disregard on the part of municipal parties vis-à-vis commercial policy, integrative trade, and GVCs.

Social Acceptability

Greater Montreal is identified as one of fifteen industrial port zones in Quebec's MS, while Assomption Nord – not Assomption Sud, where the Port of Montreal is actually located – is specifically earmarked in one of the city's Special Planning Programs.

It was therefore as a relay for the MS and as a representative of the transportation and logistics sector's interests that CargoM, in tandem with the City of Montreal, gave group CAI Global the mandate to prepare an economic position paper for the Assomption Sud district in the wake of the new trade agreement between Canada and the European Union and its impact on the expansion of the Port of Montreal's activities (CAI Global 2015). The authors of the report underlined the importance of the MS, the creation of industrial port zones, and the coming expansion of the Port of Montreal's activities as factors that call for the economic positioning of Assomption Sud as a transportation and logistics hub. They also mention that the project's social acceptability will probably represent a challenge. Subsequently, CAI Global's confidential study was turned into a short report tabled by the city's Economic Development Department in August of 2016. The report mentions that the coming into force of the Canada-European Union Comprehensive Economic and Trade Agreement and the Trans-Pacific Partnership, as well as the Quebec government's MS, should be seen as opportunities for Montreal to consolidate and further develop its competitive advantage. It adds that "the Assomption sector and the neighboring industrial port zone are identified as 'strategic planning sectors' in the AC" (Ville de Montréal 2016, 7). This explains why a project of "Cité de la logistique" (logistics city) was prepared for Assomption Sud.

It is notable that this is the first time a report coming out of the City of Montreal makes any kind of reference to the federal government's commercial policies and the province's MS. However, in January 2017, the city's project was duly rejected by the local population after a one-day consultation made by the Institut du Nouveau Monde at the request of the MHM borough. The report on the consultation listed the citizens' complaints and preoccupations and asked that the promoters prepare a new version (Ramacieri and Dorais Kinkaid 2017). A petition was subsequently circulated that amassed over 6,600 signatures, again asking for a new project to be drafted and demanding that the next public consultation be organized under the aegis of the Office de consultation publique de Montréal (OCPM), Montreal's Public Consultation Office.

PARTY PROGRAMS AND CONSULTATION MECHANISMS

We resume the story of Assomption Sud below, but we first pause to consider the nature of political party platforms and the repertory of consultations offered to the public by the City of Montreal.

Parties and Their Political Programs

Although many candidates belong to established political organizations, as a general rule there are no outright political parties at the local level of government. But this rule does not apply to the City of Montreal, where provincial and federal party affiliation has always played an important role. The relations between municipal parties and their provincial or federal counterparts, however, are mixed, at best. A recent illustration shows the extent to which a Montreal mayor can be close to the provincial Cabinet, as when, on June 18, 2015, Mayor Denis Coderre (2013–17) gave an important speech on Montreal's economic strategy at the Metropolitan Montreal Chamber of Commerce in which he emphasized the significance of the MS for the city, eleven days before the official launching of the MS by the prime minister on June 29.[37]

An analysis of the programs prepared in view of the November 7, 2021, elections shows that questions related to international commerce and global supply chains were not mentioned by either of the two major parties.[38] Projet Montréal, the party of the incumbent Valérie Plante, first elected in 2017, recognizes the importance of the transportation of goods for the city's economic development but does not go into any further detail. Rather, the party's program promotes environmental issues and sustainable urbanism. For instance, its strategy "for a mobile and dynamic city" rests on the reduction of nuisances owing to freight transport. To this end, a review of truck routes and delivery schedules, the improvement of transport logistics, the creation of urban distribution centres, and the regulation of freight transport by train are mentioned. Traffic fluidity and road safety should be improved. In addition, the party's program draws attention to noise pollution as a result of maritime, air, and road transport and calls for the cooperation of all actors, especially in the collection of appropriate data.[39] But these issues are treated without any connection made to the decisions and strategies adopted and implemented at the agglomeration, city-region, provincial, or federal levels. As for Ensemble Montréal,[40] the party of former mayor Coderre, who challenged Plante in the 2021 municipal elections, its program does not explicitly mention these issues.[41]

There is a net contrast between municipal and provincial party politics in this regard. Going into the provincial elections of 2018, the CAQ and the PLQ addressed the fluidity of the transportation system on the island, especially in the area around the port, while Québec solidaire committed itself to reducing heavy traffic by establishing new logistic chains and the creation of consolidation centres. The CAQ and the Parti Québecois highlighted the importance of the construction of a container terminal at Contrecoeur on the south shore of the St. Lawrence, a project spearheaded by the Port of Montreal. These commitments and numerous others of the same nature contrast with the lack of engagement or even support in municipal party programs on these matters, a lacuna that has significant consequences for civil society.

Public Consultation

Democracy came late to the city, since universal suffrage was first established for the municipal elections of November 1970. Before then, some councillors were appointed by the archdiocese and others were elected, primarily by homeowners. But this did not prevent groups and community movements from mobilizing against a host of projects coming out of city hall or private promoters and from calling for independent consultation mechanisms.

The political system was opened to citizens' participation at the instigation of the Ralliement des citoyens de Montréal (1974–2001), a decidedly leftward-oriented party, at the end of the 1980s after more than thirty years of Mayor Jean Drapeau's (1986–94) autocratic – albeit progressive – regime. One significant innovation came in 1986 with the establishment of a public oral question period whereby citizens were allowed to address members of city council during council meetings. Later, the administration organized public consultations with citizens to discuss specific land-use and development projects, as well as the democratization of the city's political system (Hamel 2008, 110). New institutional mechanisms emerged in this context thanks to a redefinition of the relations between the city and civil society, notably the Bureau de consultation de Montréal (or Montreal Consultation Bureau) in 1989. The objective of the rapprochement with citizens, according to one observer, was "to increase legitimacy and to improve the management of municipal programs" (Hamel 2008, 105).

In this regard, Montreal has a recent and varied tradition of concertation, including a significant "anarchist interpretation of local democracy" (Boudreau 2003, 800). Urban movements have contributed to democratizing local management and compelled decision-making processes to be more inclusive. Several mechanisms have been introduced over the last decades. For instance, Article 16 of the Montreal Charter of Rights and Responsibilities (a bylaw that came into effect on January 1, 2006) highlights the city's commitment to informing citizens on city matters, encouraging public participation, and providing transparent and effective public consultation tools. In a document entitled *The Challenge of Participation* (Le défi de la participation), the city identifies three basic components of participatory democracy: information, consultation, and participation, accompanied by monitoring and evaluation. While the term "information" is defined as a unidirectional relationship, "consultation" implies an exchange of information between the administration and the citizens, while "participation" refers to the active engagement of citizens in the policy-making process (Ville de Montréal – Service du greffe 2017).

Beginning in 2002, a question period was instituted in all borough council meetings (Ville de Montréal, 2013), and since 2010, citizens can obtain a public consultation in their borough or at city level by exercising their Right of Initiative (Ville de Montréal 2012). After the filing of a draft petition, the admissibility of the petition is reviewed. If approved, fifteen thousand signatures are required for petitions addressed at city level and five thousand or fewer – depending on the size of the borough – for questions relating to a borough matter. At the borough level, the consultation is under the authority of the borough council, a committee or other groups designated by the council. For consultations concerning a city-wide matter, the executive committee charges either a council committee or the Office de consultation publique de Montréal[42] with organizing the consultation process.

A further possibility for citizens to make their voice heard is the ombudsman, who constitutes "a last resort recourse for those who believe that they are adversely affected, or likely to be, by a decision of Ville de Montréal."[43] The ombudsman is independent from the administration and elected officials. As mediator, the ombudsman can request the intervention of the Executive Committee, the Municipal Council, or the borough council to resolve the problem. For instance, in 2011, residents close to a viaduct complained about the vibrations triggered by the passage of heavy trucks. To limit this nuisance, the borough banned trucks from using the viaduct and redirected them to another road.

In addition, the MMC can charge its five standing committees with organizing consultations on issues of concern for citizens. However, as noted previously, major governance frameworks such as the Montreal model, or clusters such as CargoM, the logistics and transportation cluster, provide no representation for civil society organizations.

Back to the Assomption Sud–Longue Pointe District

No fewer than three successive consultations were organized in 2017 concerning the future development of the sector. First, the MHM borough held a public meeting to inform residents and give them the opportunity to voice their reactions and make suggestions. Second, a consultation was set up on the Plan d'implantation et d'intégration architecturale (Architectural integration plan) for the district, which led to the publication of a report in December (Ville de Montréal 2017a). Third, a public consultation was organized in May, following a petition presented to the borough by citizens making use of their Right of Initiative to public consultation. The petition, "regarding a request for a public consultation concerning the development of industrial port activities in the industrial sector of the borough and their cohabitation with the residential districts" (Ville de Montréal 2018), contained the following requests:

> This consultation aims at ensuring that the borough adopts development policies that are viable for the community and include development orientations regarding land use, intensity of activities, active transportation networks and infrastructures. This planning must also take into account the management of nuisances related to industrial port activities such as noise, air quality, and truck traffic. Finally, it must propose improvements to the interfaces between the Port, the industries and the city. (Ville de Montréal 2017b)

The citizens' group at the origin of the petition, Mobilisation 6600, explicitly referred to the MS and noted that the sector was part of an industrial port zone (ZIP), two indications that made their way into the report submitted to the borough in September 2017.

During the first public meeting of the consultation process, many questions surfaced concerning, among other issues, the noise level of port activities, truck and railway traffic, health risks linked to transport activities in the planned Cité de la logistique, and the expansion of the Port of Montreal (Ville de Montréal 2017a). Several participants pointed out that earlier plans for the redevelopment of the sector had been drafted without providing room for the citizens' viewpoints, ideas, and concerns. Thus, two opposing viewpoints came to the forefront: an urban point of view held exclusively by an elite who sees the project as an important investment for the competitivity of Montreal, and a local point of view expressed by residents directly affected by the project. The asymmetry between the two perspectives was reinforced by the fact that the original policy and its offshoots had been carried by the federal government, the province's MS, the MMC, the city's economic development plans, Port of Montreal, CargoM, and others.

As a case in point, the brief submitted by the Port of Montreal stated that the implementation of a Cité de la logistique would have positive effects for the district thanks to the creation of jobs, adding that the project would help consolidate the "logistic and freight transport chain of Montreal" (Port de Montréal 2017). In a similar vein, the letter submitted by the general director of CargoM highlighted that "Montreal was a unique logistics and freight transport hub in North America" and that the Cité de la logistique would send a strong signal to investors (CargoM 2017). This positive vision, which draws attention to the positioning of Montreal in the larger economic context, stands in stark contrast to the briefs submitted by individual citizens or groups, which concentrate on concrete negative consequences for residents.

In response to citizens' numerous criticisms of its Cité de la logistique project, the municipal administration prepared a new version of its project relabelled an "ecopark" (Ville de Montréal 2020). The consultation process was scheduled for September 2018 but was postponed due to the provincial elections. After a visit by the new premier Francois Legault, the creation of a joint working group for the east of Montreal with representatives of the provincial government and the City of Montreal was announced – an initiative that raised the question of the provincial government's increased involvement in urban affairs without any consideration given to citizens' participation.

Finally, consultations on the ecopark plan were held in March 2019, preceded by an information session organized by the city and its "external partners": Administration portuaire de Montréal (APM; Montreal Port Authority), Hydro-Québec, MTQ, and the Montreal transport commission (OCPM 2019, 19). Neither the city nor the MHM borough were involved in the consultation, even though the city's project and the borough's regulations are mentioned in the OCPM's final report. Figure 6.8 shows, in the top line and on the left, the promoters of the project for the district, and

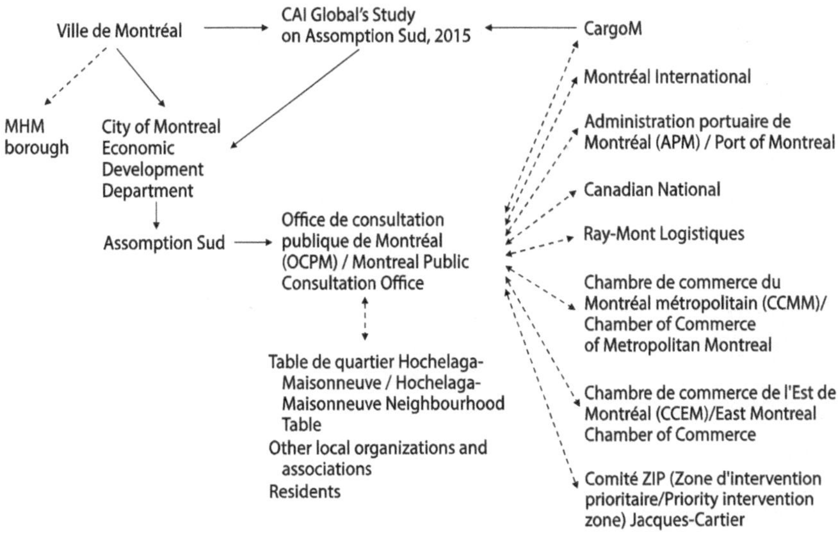

FIGURE 6.8 The promoters of a project for Assomption Sud and the participants in the OCPM's consultation

on the right at the bottom, the participants in the consultation organized by the OCPM.

The participants in the consultations on the right side of the figure are from the private sector, while the three in the middle of the figure (Table de quartier, Other local organizations, and Residents) are from the area concerned. The APM, the CN, and Ray-Mont Logistiques – all members of CargoM – as well as the two chambers of commerce, Montréal International, and the ZIP Jacques-Cartier Committee were favourable to the project,[44] while the residents, their organizations, and associations were at best reticent if not outright critical. In its report, tabled in September 2019, the OCPM (19) duly noted that the dividing line between the two was tied to "a metropolitan versus a local level of analysis and interpretation" but failed to mention the extent of their prior involvement on the part of representatives from the private sector – or even their basic economic interest in the project. In its opening remarks, the report omits any reference to the global context, to trade agreements, or GVCs, and merely mentions the fact that "the City of Montreal wishes to requalify the Assomption Sud-Longue-Point district" (3, 8) without providing any further explanation. Nevertheless, the report does underline the crisis of confidence that prevails at the local level and lists several interesting comments coming out of its consultation. These cover an array of questions running from the reduction of pollution (emissions and noise), the establishment of green spaces, opening a public access to the river (45), the lack of transparency on the part of the MTQ (57), the fact that social acceptability comes late in the overall process since the project itself is already finalized (59), the implementation of an environmental management system or establishment of a permanent governance framework involving all stakeholders at the local level (60–61), among others.[45] Some of these comments were picked up in the report. For instance, Recommendation #1 proposes that the project's nuisances should be reduced; Recommendation #6 suggests the creation of a permanent consultation mechanism for the ecopark; Recommendation #14, that the SPP for Assomption Nord be applied here; and finally, Recommendation #3 gives the city a go-ahead with its ecopark project (66, 73, 78, 69).

But for all that, the Quebec government's Ministère de l'Environnement, de la Lutte contre les changements climatiques, de la Faune et des Parcs granted permission to Ray-Mont Logistiques on November 4, 2022, to build its container transshipment platform despite citizens' and many organizations' opposition to the project.[46]

CONCLUSION

We started off with the premise that a government's political economy has a significant impact on a city's development. This led us to the hypothesis that integrative trade and GVCs, as promoted by the federal, and relayed by the provincial, government – notably through its MS – should have a significant impact on Greater Montreal and the City of Montreal's development strategies. In the past, an export promotion strategy relied on the adaptation or elimination of norms and regulations. Provincial authorities were involved when subject matters came under their jurisdiction, while cities were kept at bay. Today, integrative trade is less concerned with norms and more with physical gateways and corridors that necessitate investments in infrastructure, soft and hard. This calls for two major innovations: (i) setting up governance frameworks between federal and provincial transportation departments, and (ii) the involvement of city-regions in these schemes. In other words, economic globalization ushered in through integrative trade and GVCs calls for resorting to a multiscalar strategy on the part of governments – a strategy that was duly applied at the instigation of the MTQ in the two governance frameworks presented earlier (Figures 6.3 and 6.4). For its part, the MMC, as the city-region's governing body, acts as both facilitator and vector in the implementation of policies coming out of the higher tiers of governments, particularly those relating to the positioning of Montreal as the most important of the fifteen industrial port zones identified in Quebec's MS.

All things considered, we can conclude that the federal government's new commercial policy does indeed have an impact on Montreal as a city-region – an impact taken into account by the MMC's commissions and the city's planning department. At the same time, these policies and plans bypass many public administrations – notably the AC – and are ignored in terms of municipal party politics. In fact, not only city hall but the borough councils downplay the effects of commercial policies and GVCs on their constituents' well-being, except in the latter case, when their citizens are directly impacted. And yet, these same policies are openly circulated and diligently acted upon among private stakeholders. Here, the MS plays a pivotal role in relaying the provincial government's investment strategies in infrastructure at city level. Furthermore, closely tied to this absence of a large public awareness – and in full accordance with it – is the concentration of public consultation in the smallest geographical area possible. In the present instance, the ecopark project was prepared for a mere section within the MHM borough without even considering the experience of a previous initiative applied to another section in this same borough, Assomption Nord (Ramacieri and Dorais Kinkaid 2017, 16; OCPM 2019, 77).

This is even more telling since, as we saw, there is a profusion of consultations processes set up under the numerous planning documents reviewed. But the two major governance frameworks introduced by the MMC essentially rely on a collaboration between public and private economic actors, as is the case for the Montreal model and the CargoM cluster. Neither model nor cluster are open to the political process or to civil society, which shows that the MMC applies in these matters – as it does in others – a selective top-down interpretation of metropolitanization. By contrast, if we look at the city and borough levels, we could expect to have an "internal reconstitution of the political sphere and its articulation with civil society" along the lines set forth by Boudreau et al. (2007, 34–35), but such is not the case. If the city is open to consultations with civil society on a host of topics, the subjects and questions that interest us here are not among them, even though their importance is alluded to in planning documents and studies tabled upstream. Significantly, in the case of the Assomption Sud, a district most impacted by integrative trade and GVCs, these issues were set aside and mere social acceptability was called for.

Coming back to Hamel and Keil's (2017) analysis, which equates resorting to governance framework vis-à-vis private-public stakeholders as a feature of a deliberative democracy, we are now in a position to establish, with regard to the commercial policy and strategy coming out of the federal and provincial governments, a clear-cut distinction between the co-operation and deliberation mechanisms entrusted to governance frameworks and the public consultation processes per se. On the one hand, at the city-region level, we have a pair of major governance frameworks organized around the Montreal model and the CargoM cluster, both involving public and private stakeholders from the economic sectors in pursuit of many of the Continental Gateway's objectives. These actors are provided with all the necessary information and analysis that allow them a full grasp of the national political economy and its implications downstream at the local levels, and they act accordingly. On the other hand, the consultation processes set up under the auspices of either the OCPM or other citizen-led initiatives (Agora métropolitaine, Forum Urba 2015, Institut de politiques alternatives de Montréal, etc.) involve exchanges between citizens in the aftermath of a presentation by a few officials – not necessarily elected – from the city or from the borough, or both. These exchanges are concerned with a planning document that, as we saw, is centred on a given sector or subsector – not even on the entirety of a borough, let alone on its larger urban setting – and that provides no clue as to the political economy implemented by both federal and provincial governments with their economic partners.

In the first instance, governance frameworks involving public and private sector actors are decidedly deliberative but not democratic, whereas in the second instance involving civil society actors and local government, the consultation processes are indeed democratic but based on truncated or partial information. The notion of partiality refers to two shortcomings here: not only are deliberations bounded in their scope by the lack of contextualization in the documentation provided, but they are limited in their reach since the appropriate representatives in the political and economic spheres are not involved in the consultations set up at the local level. The main objective of this approach is tied to the central purpose of the public consultation itself, which is simply to reach "social acceptability" – a fallout of the depoliticization process at play here.

Our incursion into the development policies elaborated at the city-region level offers another perspective on a Montreal regime that, according to Boudreau et al. (2007), aspires to consolidate statehood while safeguarding a social-democratic tradition. As for the impacts of integrative commerce and GVCs at the city-region's level, our study shows that the Montreal regime has to deal with a number of competing forces. Veltz (2000) opposes a proximity network linking cities vertically to their hinterland, to a horizontal network between megacities forming an archipelago economy. In the present instance, the outward pull exerted by the global economy impacts a proximity network involving three competing forces: the city-region, the Quebec economy, and the Canadian economy. This array of forces provides an interesting explanation for the complexity of city politics and strategies in and around Montreal. And in terms of the model's social-democratic content, here again, seen from the viewpoint expounded here, this dimension is ill-served indeed. There is certainly no preoccupation with social democracy within the governance frameworks set up by the MMC – and little if any contribution on the part of the public consulted to the political debate on the impacts of the global issues that affect it.

Contrary to what the OCPM's mandate suggests, there are virtually no interconnections between representative and participatory democracy on the topics presented here, either in the city or its boroughs. Not only are urban political parties and their programs mute on these questions, but in the eyes of the political representatives and elected officials at the municipal level, Canada's and Quebec's commercial policy, integrative trade, free trade agreements, and GVCs and their impacts on urban development strategies fall into a blind spot. The central and incidental issues tied to these policies, as well as their impacts at the local level, are sheltered from the citizens involved in participatory democracy, while their social acceptability is solicited on changes brought about on their immediate environment by forces unidentified.

Finally, our study partially confirms the validity of Dani Rodrik's (2007) "inescapable trilemma of the world economy," according to which national sovereignty, global economic integration, and democracy cannot be pursued concurrently. In the present instance, the implementation of an integrative trade strategy does bypass both electoral and citizen democracy, relying instead on an executive democracy.[47]

This leads us back to Hamel and Keil's (2017) claim concerning deliberative democracy, on the one hand, and Mayer's (2017) argument about urban policy making hinging ever more on business "to facilitate the unfettered operation of the market," on the other. These interpretations are not mutually exclusive because, as we have noted several times, there exists a plethora of consultation mechanisms applied within Greater Montreal. At the same time, there are numerous paramount issues, notably in matters of commerce and GVCs and their enabling transportation infrastructures, that bypass electoral and deliberative democracy and that, in this respect, induce a democratic deficit.

7

Halifax and the Atlantic Gateway

International trade has been a major driver of economic development, technological development, and innovation (De Fuentes et al. 2021). International trade does not refer only to the exchange of final goods; intermediate inputs represent an important percentage of its total. Concepts like global supply chains (Gereffi and Lee 2012) and global value chains (GVCs) (Gereffi 1995) are central to understanding the interactions between firms and countries shaping international trade and transportation patterns.

A gateway is an entry or exit point supporting a transport corridor for the movement of international freight and passengers to and from key markets. In this chapter we discuss the evolution of the strategy on gateways and trade corridors with a focus on Halifax. We study the role of the coalition, which was set up to attract federal and provincial funding for investments in infrastructure that support engagement in GVCs. While serving mainly as Canada's Eastern saddle gateway between international (i.e., Europe, Latin America) and North American markets, it was set up also to contribute to the attractiveness of the City of Halifax via investments in city infrastructure and knowledge across specific sectors, including the ocean, biotechnology, and IT, with the hope of expanding its source (production) and sink (consumption) functions. We discuss the role played by the Atlantic provinces in the Atlantic Gateway Strategy, analyze the different levels of stakeholders in this process, and connect this discussion with the notions elaborated on earlier of urban governance and GVCs. Finally, we describe the different rounds of funding by the federal government to support infrastructure projects as well as the major stakeholders involved in each round of funding. We also look at how these infrastructure projects connect to regional needs, contribute to the region's growth, and stimulate both the city's and the Atlantic provinces' development.

The Atlantic Gateway connects Atlantic Canada with markets in Europe, Africa, Asia, and the Americas. The Atlantic Gateway and Trade Corridor Strategy, released in March 2011, was developed through collaboration between the governments of Canada, Nova Scotia, New Brunswick, Prince Edward Island, and Newfoundland and Labrador, involving public-private partnerships (Transport Canada 2011, 120).

Discussions and initiatives to set up the Atlantic and Halifax gateways were tied to the improvement of GVCs, which in turn involved the infrastructure required to export goods produced in Canada and the Atlantic provinces, thus contributing to the economic growth of the region. The City of Halifax and the Atlantic provinces created bodies whose main mandate was to oversee and identify specific shortcomings to strengthen the Halifax and Atlantic gateways. These bodies did so in consultation with all levels of government and included business organizations, academic institutions, and the community at large. In the process, they commissioned a number of reports that provided information on the specific gaps and suggested strategic infrastructure investments. Indeed, many initiatives promoted collaboration between stakeholders to further economic growth in the region.

In addition to infrastructure measures, several noninfrastructure measures have been implemented, including the marketing of the Atlantic Gateway, trade missions, regulatory measures to improve rail service, alternative models of port and supply chain governance, alliances with inland ports and distribution centres, development of the transload facilities and long combination vehicle transport, and an integrated approach to human resources in the transport sector.

The Atlantic Gateway and the Halifax Gateway play an important role in international trade and domestic trade. Most of the imports to Canada through the Halifax Gateway include manufacturing, clothing, machinery and equipment, auto parts, and furniture, while exports from Halifax include wood pulp, seafood, vegetables, newsprint, and paper (see Figure 7.1). Trade with Europe, South America, and South Asia represents a high percentage of trade to and from the Halifax Gateway (Transport Canada 2011).

The chapter is divided into five sections. It begins by providing a historical background before discussing the context of the Halifax Gateway by elaborating on the main transport stakeholders. It then describes the initiatives that have been implemented to shape the Halifax and Atlantic

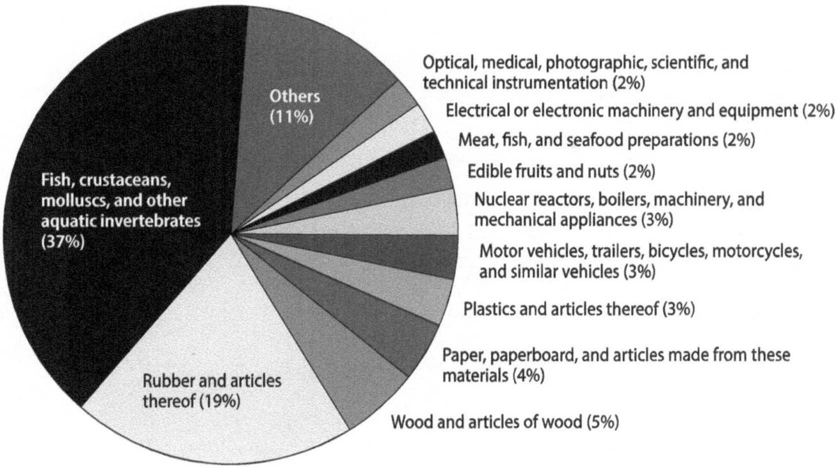

FIGURE 7.1 Main exports from Nova Scotia, 2021 | *Source:* Government of Canada (n.d.).

Gateways as well as their stakeholders and presents the different rounds of investments in gateways and trade corridors, elaborating on the specificities of each. The chapter ends with some concluding remarks.

ATLANTIC CANADA AND THE HALIFAX GATEWAY

Nova Scotia and Halifax played an important role in the founding of Canada. Annapolis Royal, in western Nova Scotia, was home to early French and British settlements and a number of forts were built throughout Nova Scotia and in Halifax, which was a strategic location. However, for the last five decades, Nova Scotia has been underperforming in terms of economic growth, innovation, attraction, retention of talent, and the ability to retain its younger population, as indicated in *Now or Never: An Urgent Call to Action – The Report of the Nova Scotia Commission on Building Our New Economy* released in 2014 (Ivany et al. 2014). Strategies were called for to tackle a long list of challenges, notably immigration, retention of its younger population, creation of new business and venture capital, support for exports and firms participating in exports, domestic and international markets for fisheries and agriculture products, increasing the employment rate, and strengthening postsecondary education and training, postsecondary research, and research and development partnerships. The report's analysis was well received by Nova Scotians and many initiatives were promoted. In fact, both the Atlantic Gateway Strategy and the Atlantic Growth Strategy, discussed later in this chapter, are well in line with the report's key recommendations, notably the ones promoting exportation, supporting firms involved in exports – especially those in the aquaculture and agriculture sectors – and the attraction and retention of talent. The Atlantic Canada Opportunities Agency (ACOA), the Halifax Partnership, the Nova Scotia Department of Transportation and Infrastructure Renewal (TIR), and many other public and private organizations have been key stakeholders in this regard, since they gave their full support to the development of the Atlantic Gateway Strategy and the establishment of the Halifax Gateway Council (HGC).

MAIN INDUSTRIES IN NOVA SCOTIA

As noted by Gary Gereffi (1995), the size of an organization tells us something important about the prevailing context in a region. For example, larger firms employ more financial and human resources and have a more direct impact on the governance of GVCs (Gereffi et al. 2005). Their location and whether they are part of a larger group, as well as their position within that group, also provide this context. Organizations that are part of a group have access to internal sources of knowledge, for example, and most strategic decisions are made in their headquarters. Several large enterprises, including Clearwater Fine Foods, Farmer's Co-op (food), and Irving Shipbuilding, have headquarters in Nova Scotia and Halifax (HGC 2012). Some of the key industries in Nova Scotia include the biotech and life sciences sector, information and communication technologies, ocean technologies, fisheries, and agriculture – sectors that have played a pivotal role in the decisions related to gateways and trade infrastructure.

The life sciences sector has been identified as a key driver of competitiveness in the region and multiple initiatives have been implemented to attract investment in the sector. ACOA has played the role of funder, enabler, and facilitator for over ten years to develop and foster this sector in Nova Scotia (Interview 7.1). Incumbent firms from Nova Scotia have contributed to the development of nutraceutical research, thanks to the transformation of fisheries, aquaculture, and agriculture products. Acadia Seaplants and Clearwater, for example, have invested in research and development for value-added products originating from aquaculture and fisheries. The report from HGC (2012) indicates that many of these local companies are partnering with multinational companies, in particular the pharmaceutical sector, including Bayer, Johnson & Johnson, Novartis, Pfizer, and Schering-Plough. This industry has been a key stakeholder in the discussions on gateway infrastructure and the identification of what is holding back exports from this sector.

The ocean tech sector has also been identified as a key sector in Nova Scotia. In 2012, Gary Gereffi was commissioned to conduct a study on the ocean tech cluster in the region (see Gereffi et al. 2012). The companies that operate in the ocean tech supercluster include professional service providers and advanced manufacturers for offshore energy, security and defense, transportation, and earth observation (HGC 2012). Some of the key organizations that conduct research in this field include the Bedford Institute of Oceanography, the National Research Council, the Institute for Marine Biosciences, and Dalhousie University (HP 2018). One of the major drivers for the industry was the multibillion-dollar contract awarded to Halifax in 2011 to build fifteen warships and eight arctic patrol vessels (HGC 2012). This project is considered a "super project" given its magnitude and the economic spillover effects. In addition, the Centre for Ocean Ventures and Entrepreneurship supports the ocean technology industry by promoting public-private partnerships and connecting talent that supports the commercialization of ocean technologies. Building the ocean tech supercluster is of high importance to Nova Scotia, as highlighted by key stakeholders: "We should be focusing all our energies on the research and commercialization of research around green technologies and ocean technologies" (Interview 7.2).

The agriculture and agri-food sector and fisheries and aquaculture sector have contributed to the gross domestic product and exports from the region (Interviews 7.1 and 7.3). These sectors also played a key role in the push to build better gateway infrastructure in Halifax and Nova Scotia, with stakeholders from the industry taking part in the discussions. For example, the aquaculture and fisheries sector was one of the main industries behind the adaptation of cold chain technology to export products from the south shore of Nova Scotia to Asia, and by doing so, to export lobsters and shellfish to Asia and Europe. As indicated by provincial stakeholders, the planning took over fifteen years and trade agreements that lowered tariffs contributed to higher exports to Europe. "Part of the value chain built with the federal government and the province in the last fifteen years focused on developing this value chain [to export] to Europe and China ... it changed the whole game, and that's a policy decision" (Interview 7.3).

The information and communication technologies, or digital sector, has also played a key role in Nova Scotia, with many firms providing support to aerospace, defense, financial services, online learning, software development, and gaming industries (HGC 2012). Figure 7.2 illustrates the evolution of exports for the main industries in Nova Scotia. It shows

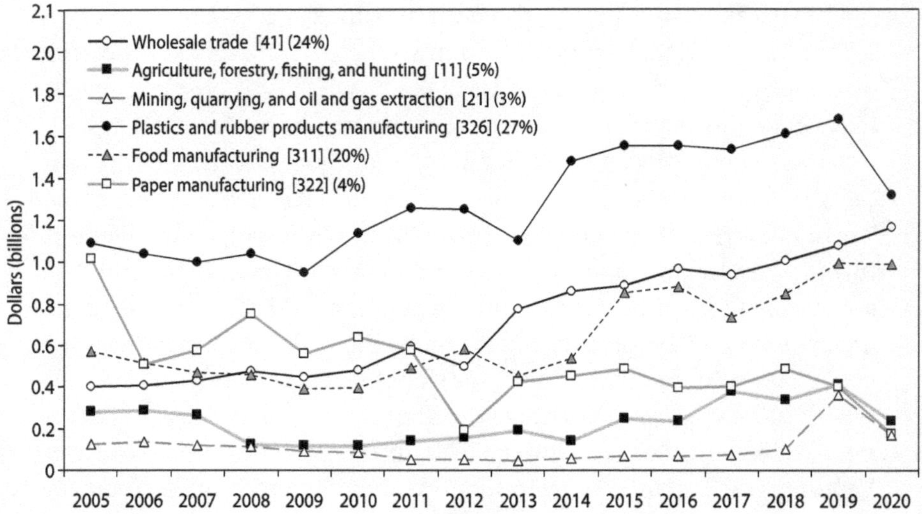

FIGURE 7.2 Nova Scotia top six exported commodities, 2020 |
Source: Statistics Canada (2024, 2025b).
Note: Percentage of total exports is shown in parentheses.

the increase of exports from Nova Scotia in all top six commodities, with the exception of paper manufacturing.

These sectors have played a pivotal role in the development of trade infrastructure, supporting both exports and imports in Canada. Exports from the Halifax Gateway reach US, Asian, and European markets (APEC 2016). The gateway infrastructure has contributed to both the development of the industries in the region, by supporting their exports, and as argued by the Halifax Port Authority (HPA), the appeal (marketability) of the city (HPA 2017).

HALIFAX GATEWAY INFRASTRUCTURE

The Halifax Gateway infrastructure includes the Port of Halifax, the Halifax Stanfield International Airport, and the rail and road infrastructure that connects the Port of Halifax and the Halifax Stanfield International Airport to the rest of Canada and North America (HGC 2010) (see Figure 7.3). As underlined in the two reports made by the HGC (2010) and the Atlantic Provinces Economic Council (APEC 2006), the transportation infrastructure has contributed to the expansion of trade in Nova Scotia and the Atlantic region, and "building Canada's transportation gateways and corridors has been an important national priority" (InterVistas 2007). Several stakeholders emphasized the strategic vision from the government

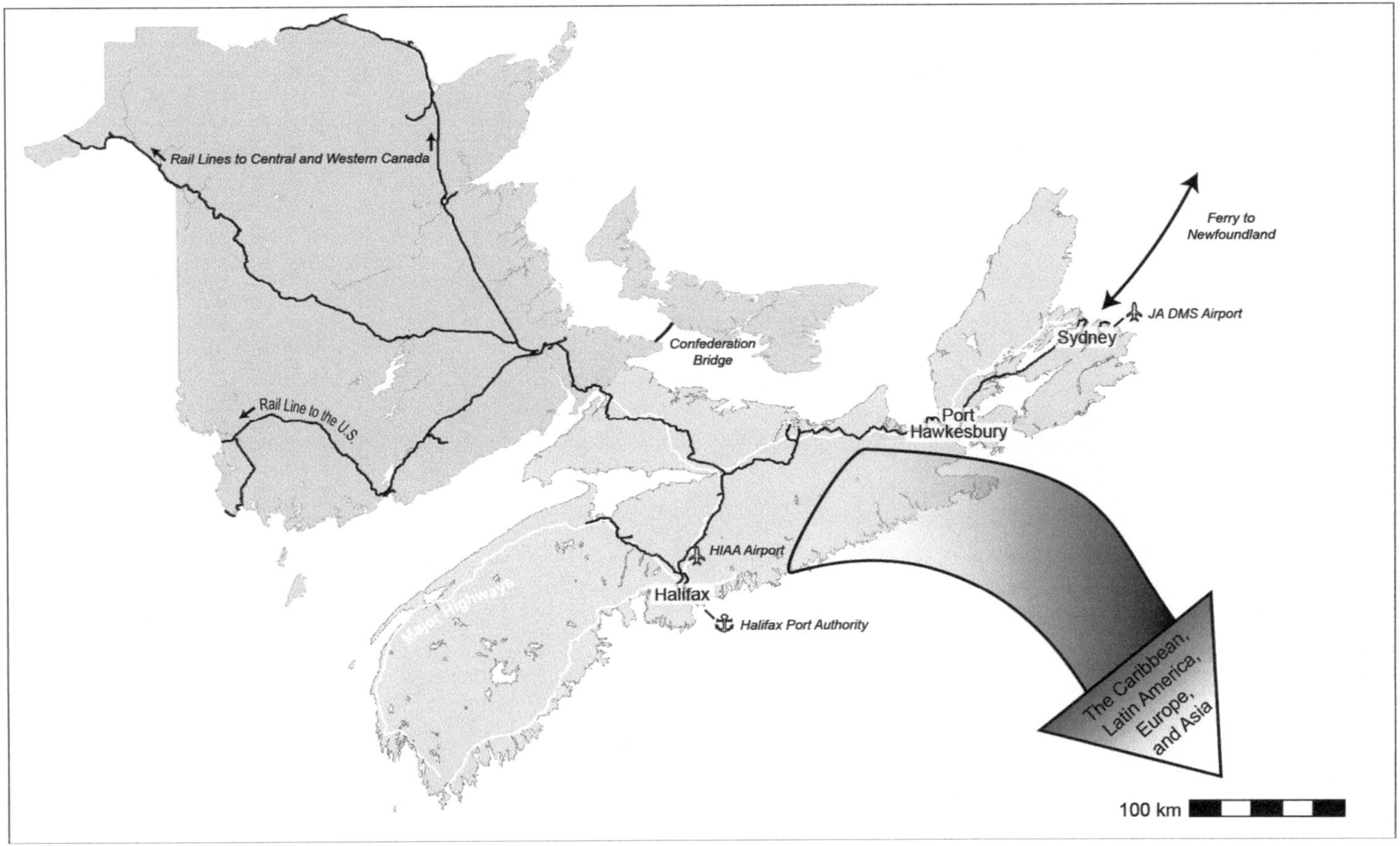

FIGURE 7.3 Nova Scotia Gateway and Trade Corridor | *Cartography:* Steve Tornes. *Sources:* Government of Canada (2021b), Statistics Canada (2021a, 2021b).

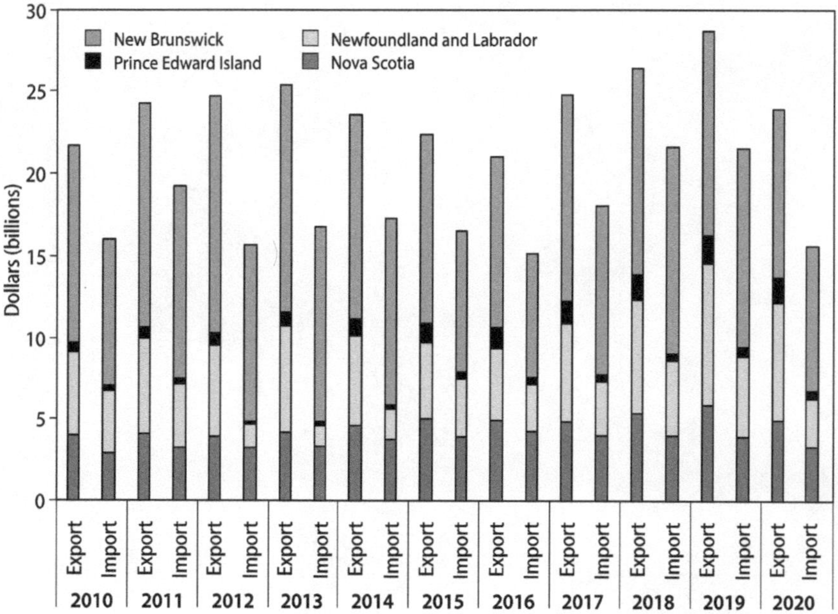

FIGURE 7.4 Evolution of trade to and from Atlantic Canada, 2010–20 | *Source:* Statistics Canada (2025a).

to invest in gateway and trade corridors infrastructure that contributes to connecting Canada with the rest of the world (multiple interviews). "The Atlantic Gateway is a fluid concept that incorporates all transportation infrastructure and related operations that support the movement of international freight and passengers, through entry and exit points in Atlantic Canada to and from key markets" (Access to information and privacy [ATIP], pers. comm., April 15, 2021).

The transport infrastructure acts like a well-tuned system, and one of the most critical challenges is distortions at any point in the trade corridor system, which can disrupt the whole supply chain. The trade corridor has been affected by several factors, many of them external, such as strikes at CN and truck blockades, such as those during the COVID-19 pandemic. These disruptions remind us that the supply chain is complex and fragile (Interviews 7.1, 7.3, 7.4, 7.5).

Airport Infrastructure as Part of the Halifax Gateway

The Halifax International Airport Authority (HIAA) was incorporated on November 23, 1995, as a corporation without share capital under Part II of the Canada Corporations Act. On February 1, 2000, HIAA signed

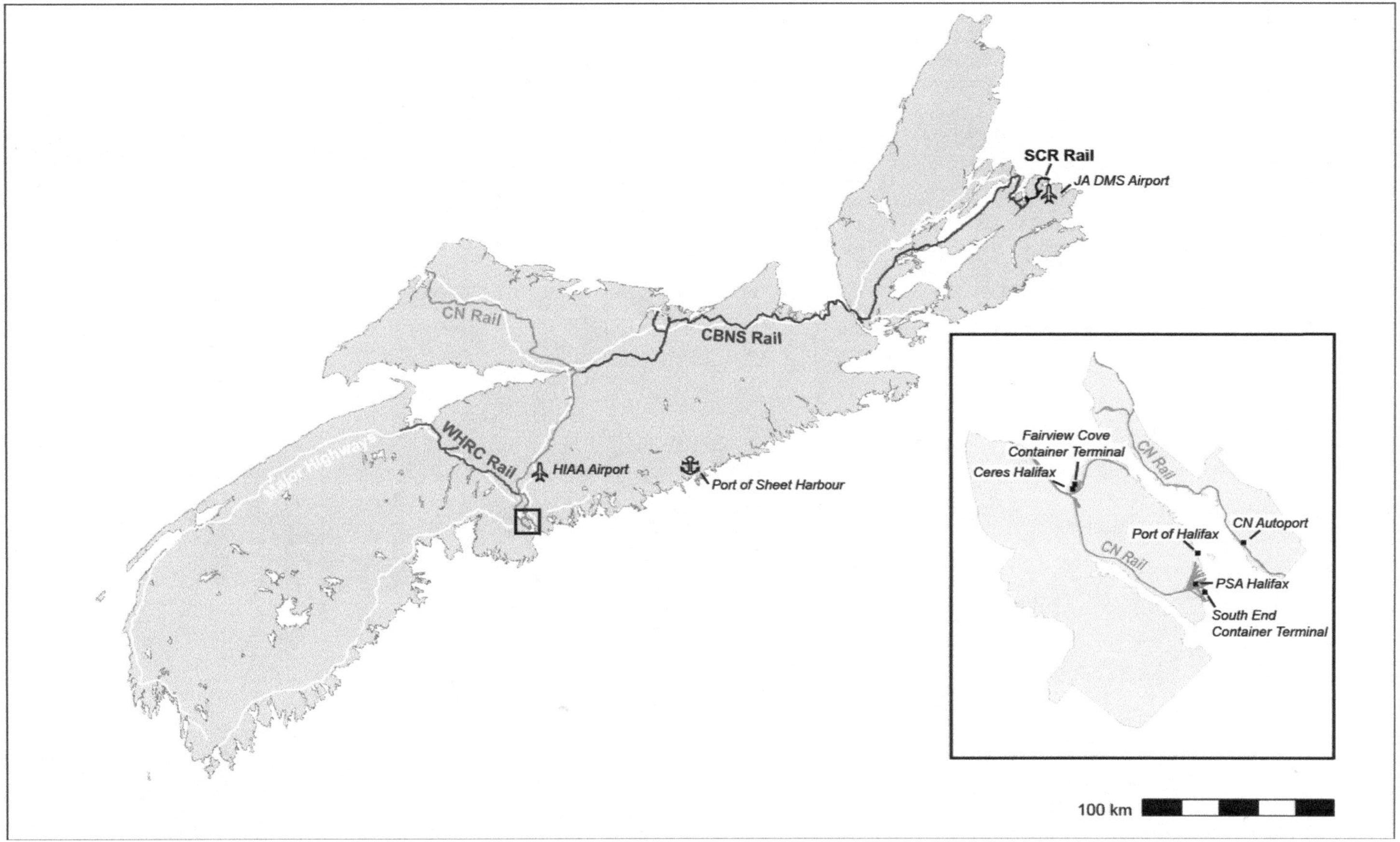

FIGURE 7.5 Nova Scotia's Trade Corridor Network | *Cartography:* Steve Tornes. *Sources:* Government of Canada (2021b), Statistics Canada (2021a, 2021b).

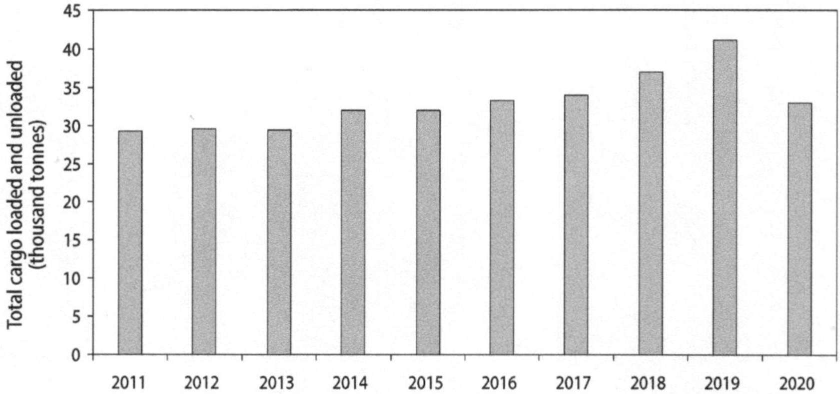

FIGURE 7.6 Total cargo loaded and unloaded, Halifax Stanfield International Airport | *Sources:* HIAA Annual Reports, 2011–20.

a sixty-year ground lease with Transport Canada and assumed responsibility for the management, operation, and development of HIAA. In 2014, they received an extension of the lease for an additional twenty years, to January 31, 2080 (HIAA 2017). The HIAA is governed by a board consisting of fourteen directors whose members are nominated by the Halifax Regional Municipality (four), the Province of Nova Scotia (one), the Government of Canada (two), the Halifax Chamber of Commerce (three), and the Airport Authority board of directors (four). The nominated members can also appoint additional members (HIAA 2017).[1] Figure 7.6 shows the increase in air cargo between 2014 and 2019 and the decline in 2020.

In 2016, seafood exports from the airport valued at $176 million were the largest category of exports, 86 percent of which was live lobster. The Nova Scotia market is now directly reaching markets in Europe and Asia. "Before the facilities [cold chamber] were designed, Nova Scotia used to truck lobster through the ferry system to Boston or New York, and it would be flown out to England and Asia. Now Nova Scotia flies it directly" (Interview 7.3). HIAA works closely with the HPA, the provincial and federal government, and the private sector to diversify product exports. During 2017, exports in aerospace parts and services represented over $74 million (HIAA 2018).

Port Infrastructure as Part of the Halifax Gateway

The HPA is one of the major players in the Halifax Gateway for intercontinental transport. According to HPA (2017), Halifax is Canada's fourth largest port measured by container volume, after Vancouver, Montreal,

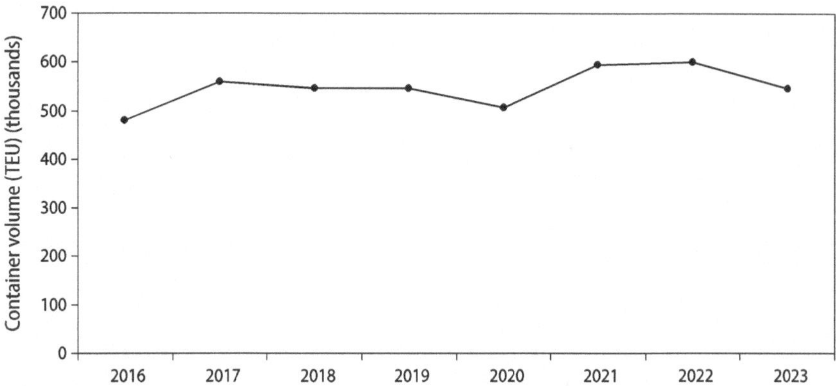

FIGURE 7.7 Port of Halifax container volume | *Source:* Data from Port of Halifax operations.

and Prince Rupert (see Figure 7.7). The main container terminals in Halifax are Fairview Cove, Richmond, South End, a terminal for crude oil and refined energy products, and a terminal for automobiles (APEC 2006; HPA 2017).

The HPA is governed by a board of seven directors whose members are nominated by the Province of Nova Scotia (one); the Halifax Regional Municipality (one); the minister of transport (one), who is appointed the Governor in Council; and the minister of transport in consultation with Port User groups (four), who are again appointed by the Governor in Council (HPA 2017). It reports to Parliament through the minister of transport and plays an important role in connecting Canada with Europe, the Mediterranean, the Middle East, and Southeast Asia via the Suez Canal. The HPA is responsible for ensuring the infrastructure, docks, and terminals follow international standards and respond to international pressures, including pressures involving the capacity to handle larger vessels. For example, the HPA and private operators have invested in infrastructure to accommodate larger container ships known as Post-Panamax.

The HPA has invested in infrastructure capacity to service the largest ships in the world and in dock expansion to be able to take two ultra-class vessels simultaneously – up to 24,000 TEU capacity. The investment includes longer and deeper piers and super Post-Panamax cranes (HPA 2017),[2] however, most of the ships coming into Halifax have fewer than 10,000 TEU capacity. "Some of the customers that use the Port of Halifax ship to the Caribbean, England, and Singapore. By 2010, the port had sufficient infrastructure to handle about eight hundred container ships a

TABLE 7.1
Port of Halifax cargo

		2020	2021
Container throughput at HPA facilities (TEU)	Import	259,403	302,912
	Export	249,798	292,839
Container throughput at HPA facilities (metric tonnes)	Import	1,766,510	2,298,981
	Export	2,064,439	2,050,104
Noncontainerized cargo at HPA facilities (metric tonnes)	Import	199,190	360,921
	Export	186,603	192,888
Noncontainerized cargo at non-HPA facilities (metric tonnes)	Import	1,835,061	1,892,284
	Export	2,221,654	2,167,258
Port-wide cargo at HPA and non-HPA facilities (metric tonnes)	Import	3,800,761	4,552,186
	Export	4,472,696	4,410,250

Source: Port of Halifax, n.d.

year, about fifteen hundred commercial vessels in the port, two hundred cruise ships, two hundred ships at the auto port, and about three hundred general ships that are multipurpose tankers" (Interview 7.4).

Table 7.1 includes the cargo at the Port of Halifax for the years 2020 and 2021. As emphasized by several stakeholders, the HPA plays a central role in positioning Halifax in the GVC. "The port is making significant investments to accommodate new Post-Panamax ships. If not, then there's a threat of obsolescence of the port infrastructure. The port is a key engine in the harbour and the economy. Ships are getting bigger and the ports of the future need to be able to accommodate them; that means infrastructure investment" (Interview 7.6).

Rail Infrastructure as Part of the Halifax Gateway

There are four operating railways in Nova Scotia: the Canadian National Railway (CN), Cape Breton and Central Nova Scotia Railway, Sydney Coal Railway, and Via Rail Canada (CPCS 2016).[3]

To improve the rail in support of the Atlantic Gateway, and given the critical role of the CN network infrastructure to connect the Atlantic Gateway and Trade Corridor, the Atlantic Gateway Advisory Council made a recommendation to the National Rail Freight Service Review Panel in 2016: "To facilitate and encourage the development of service level agreements between CN Rail and Atlantic Canada ports and stakeholders. The service level agreement would describe a series of service level benchmarks that are important to port users to monitor and evaluate services to its clients" (extracted from Rail Freight Service Review Panel Submission).

A study by the Canadian Pacific Consulting Services (CPCS 2016) suggests that since CN faces no competition in Atlantic Canada, they have limited incentive to reduce rates or improve service. The study also suggests that increased service to and from Halifax could have a negative impact on CN operating ratio. The report highlights that the success of the Port of Halifax is highly dependent on CN.

Road Infrastructure as Part of the Halifax Gateway

The Atlantic Gateway has two main truck corridors: one that links Atlantic Canada with the northeastern United States, and one that links Atlantic Canada with central Canada (APEC 2006). The Atlantic Trucking Association is the major lobbyist on specific needs related to infrastructure, regulations, and cooperation for trucking companies in the region, which include Clarke Transport, Midland Transport, Armour Transportation, Consolidated Fastfrate, Western Logistics, Day and Ross, M&O, Conrad's, and Guysborough Transfer (HGC 2012). Table 7.2 indicates the share of trucking shipments to and from Atlantic Canada.

Several highways in the province need capacity increases, and since the beginning of 2010, the province is assessing the feasibility, or is already in the process, of twinning eight sections of Highways 101, 103, 104, and 107, covering 301 km (CPCS 2016). A CPCS study in 2013 on truck mobility and performance found truck congestion points in downtown Halifax on the route to Halterm Terminal along Lower Water Street and Barrington Street (ATIP, pers. comm., April 15, 2021). Congestion on the bridges to Dartmouth have also been identified as problematic. As we describe later, these studies were instrumental in a proposal that seeks to reduce congestion points in downtown Halifax.

TABLE 7.2
Truck share in Atlantic Canada, 2017 (billions of tonne-kilometres)

	From Atlantic Canada by destination		*To Atlantic Canada by origin*	
Atlantic Canada	9.2	31%	9.2	29%
Rest of Canada	11.9	39%	18.4	58%
United States and Mexico	9.1	30%	3.9	12%
Total	30.3	100%	31.5	100%

Source: Statistics Canada (2018).

BUILDING PARTNERSHIPS AND COALITIONS FOR GATEWAY INFRASTRUCTURE

Stakeholders Relevant to the Halifax Gateway Periods 2007–13 and 2014–19

The main stakeholders in the Halifax Gateway that played a key role in building the strategy for the gateway and trade corridor include those directly connected with the gateway infrastructure: HIAA, HPA, CN Railway, and highway and logistics infrastructure. Additional stakeholders that have played a key role in the discussions regarding gateway infrastructure include the federal, provincial, and municipal governments, the private sector, and non-for-profit organizations. We present the different stakeholders that played a key role in shaping the strategy for the Halifax Gateway and Trade Corridor.

Federal Level

At the federal level, Transport Canada has played an essential role in emphasizing the importance of international trade and connectivity in the GVCs to support economic growth and development as well as to ensure the infrastructure that supports connection within GVCs remains relevant according to the needs of global trade. It can be argued that the federal government used a mission-oriented approach (Mazzucato 2021).

As a federal economic development agency, ACOA has played a key role in the Atlantic and Halifax gateway and trade corridor. It funded strategic initiatives and played an important role in advocacy and enabling interoperability (Interview 7.2).

ACOA has close interactions with Transport Canada, the trade commissioner, and Global Affairs at the federal level. ACOA also interacts closely with TIR at the provincial level and with the Halifax Partnership, Port and Airport Authorities, industry associations, firms, and not-for-profit organizations at the municipal level. Through the National Gateways and Border Crossings Fund (GBCF) and the National Trade Corridors Fund (NTCF), ACOA has played a key role in the gateway and trade corridors since the end of the 1990s (Interview 7.1).

ACOA commissioned several studies to examine the importance of supporting a gateway strategy in Halifax, in Nova Scotia, and in Atlantic Canada. These reports underlined the Halifax Gateway's potential in increasing exports in manufacturing products and in agri-food, fisheries, and energy (InterVistas 2007). The report from InterVistas (2007) recommended the adoption of an Atlantic Gateway Action Plan, with investments in gateway infrastructure, and mentioned the role of regulations in contributing to the Atlantic Gateway.

Some of the studies emphasized the need to establish trade relations with potential trade partners. Trade missions and marketing strategies were implemented toward this end; for example, ACOA led an Atlantic Gateway and Trade Corridor Mission to India in 2008.[4] This initiative was one of the first examples of government and private sectors coming together to promote the Atlantic Gateway and Trade Corridor's value proposition (Transport Canada 2010, 15). The ACOA action plan for the Atlantic region, linked to the Atlantic Gateway Objectives and aligned with Halifax Regional Municipality initiatives (HRM 2007), focused on improved marketing for the city, gateway infrastructure improvements and protection, security and border efficiency improvements, stakeholder collaboration, and policy initiatives to improve competitiveness and development of the region's human resources.

Provincial Level

At the provincial level, TIR is responsible for the public sector infrastructure. It works with federal and local stakeholders to support infrastructure-funded projects (Interview 7.3) and has close interactions with ACOA, especially on gateway and trade corridor infrastructure. At the provincial level, TIR interacts with Develop Nova Scotia and, at the municipal level, with the Department of Municipal Affairs.

The Department of Business (DOB) and its crown corporations – Develop Nova Scotia,[5] Tourism Nova Scotia, Halifax Convention Centre Corporation, Innovacorp, Invest Nova Scotia, and Nova Scotia Business Inc. (DOB 2018) – have played an important role in the gateway strategy. For example, the mandate of Develop Nova Scotia is to expand the physical infrastructure that contributes to economic growth in the province in an effort to make Nova Scotia attractive for people and investment (Interview 7.6). The DOB works in close collaboration with other provincial agencies to prepare initiatives that, according to the 2018–19 annual plan, contained an inclusive economic growth agenda, innovation and entrepreneurship acceleration programs, a rural internet strategy, and an export accelerator program. DOB supports economic growth and international competitiveness by providing policy oversight, accountability, and connections between the private sector and different levels of government. The province works closely with the federal government and the other Atlantic provinces to advance the Atlantic Growth Strategy. In 2016–17, the DOB promoted pan-Atlantic and federal collaboration by working with Tourism Nova

Scotia to renew the Atlantic Canada Agreement on Tourism. The department also worked with Nova Scotia Business Inc. to establish the Atlantic Trade and Investment Growth Agreement (DOB 2017).

Develop Nova Scotia has been a contributor to the attractiveness of both Halifax and Nova Scotia in terms of skills, talent and innovation, and real estate infrastructure. For example, they are one of the main stakeholders in the implementation of the Centre for Ocean Ventures and Entrepreneurship, which built the ocean tech supercluster in Halifax.

Municipal Level

The Department of Municipal Affairs supports municipalities in Nova Scotia to build community and encourages municipal governance to improve economic growth. The HRM is a significant economic development stakeholder in the city (see Figure 7.8). The City of Halifax has experienced renewed growth since the 2010s (see Table 7.3). The HRM "manages industrial parks, regulates businesses and land development, invests in major infrastructure, establishes and supports Business Improvement Districts, collaborates with other levels of government and agencies on economic development issues, and provides financial and in-kind support to community organizations and special events" (ATIP, pers. comm, April 15, 2021). The municipality played a very active role during the Halifax Gateway initiative. The HRM, in collaboration with the HGC, provided a municipal focus in three areas: facilitating the growth of new business opportunities through improved marketing and development of regional infrastructure and business parks, supporting the development of transportation systems and infrastructure, and supporting gateway infrastructure improvements and protection (HRM 2007). In addition, during the NTCF round of funding, the HRM actively supported the development of the Distripark/Transload Sector, the air cargo facility, Home Port Cruise Strategy, and the Windsor Street Exchange two-phase project. All these activities were identified as key for the Halifax Gateway and Trade Corridor. Communications between the municipal government and stakeholders are essential for considering the different perspectives coming out of the latter (Interview 7.3).

The HRM provides operational support to three organizations that contribute to the development of the Halifax Gateway and Trade Corridor: Destination Halifax, the Halifax Convention Centre Corporation, and the Halifax Partnership. In addition, the Community Planning and Economic Development Standing Committee's Terms of Reference, section 6(b), states that the committee

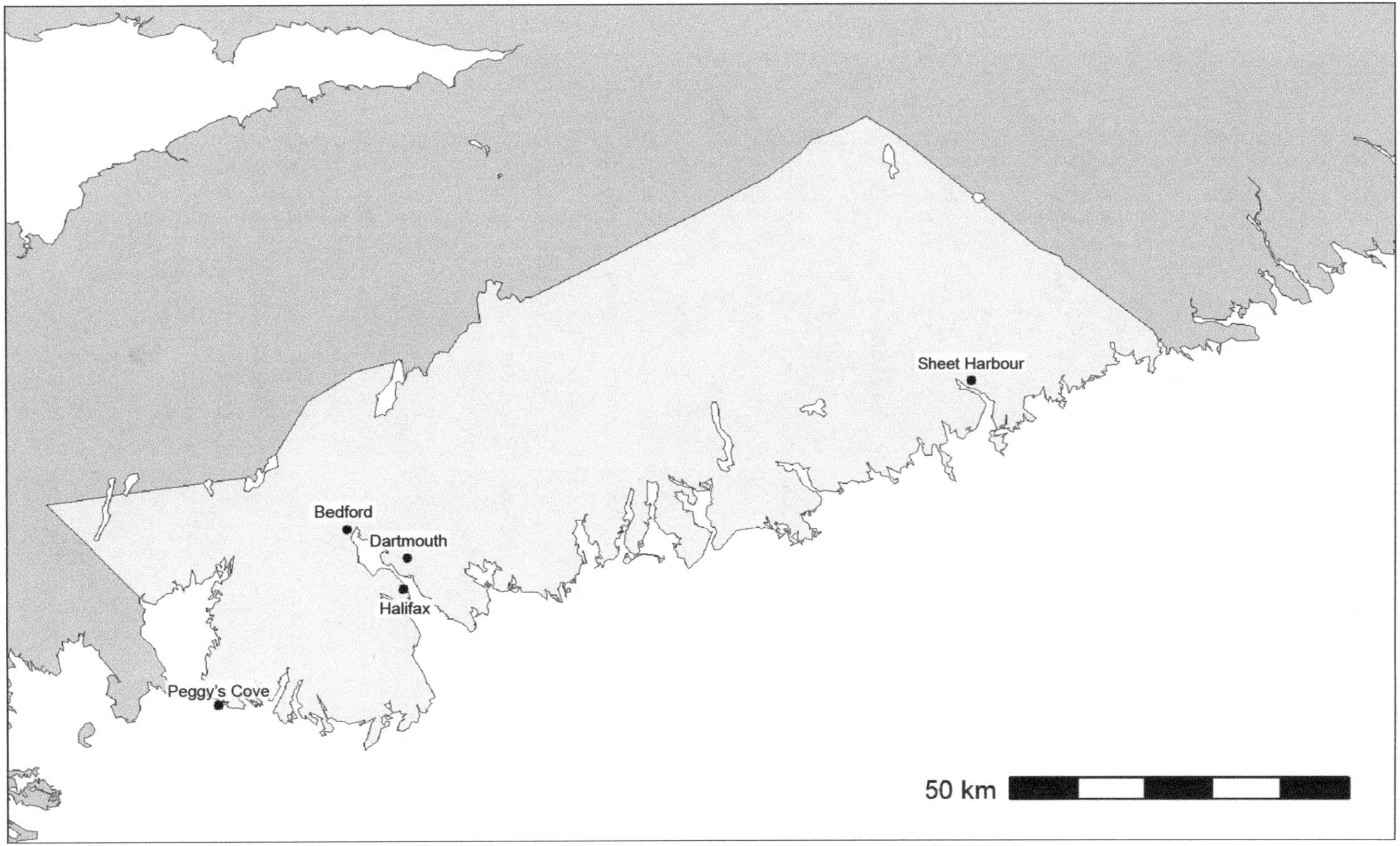

FIGURE 7.8 Halifax Regional Municipality | *Cartography:* Steve Tornes. *Source:* Statistics Canada (2021a).

TABLE 7.3
Halifax CMA and constituent municipal governments, by 2021 population

	Population		*Growth (%)*	*Share (%)*	
Municipal Area	*2006*	*2021*	*2006–21*	*2006*	*2021*
Halifax CMA	372,858	465,703	25	0	0
Halifax	372,679	439,819	18.02	99.95	94.44
East Hants	–	22,892	–	–	4.92
Indian Brook 14	–	2,739	–	–	0.59
Cole Harbour 30	128	208	62.50	0.03	0.04
Beaver Lake 17	21	20	–4.76	0.01	0.00
Wallace Hills 14A	–	15	–	–	0.00
Sheet Harbour 36	30	10	–66.67	0.01	0.00

Sources: Statistics Canada (2012a, 2021c).
Note: East Hants was added to the CMA for the 2021 population census.

> shall have an active interest in the Agencies and Initiatives that support community and economic development throughout the municipality by engaging, at a governance level, the agencies, boards and committees funded by the Municipality and under the mandate of the Standing Committee to ensure they meet community needs and expectations including: the Greater Halifax Partnership, Destination Halifax, Trade Centre Limited, Community Boards and Arts Boards and the broader Arts Community, HRM Business Districts and organizations, and others as identified by the Committee and approved by the Council. (Halifax Regional Council meeting, November 28, 2017)[6]

The Halifax Partnership is the economic development arm of the HRM. It works toward the promotion and marketing of the city worldwide and has been a key stakeholder for the development of Halifax. The Halifax Partnership has implemented and actioned several measures that tackle the challenges brought by the *Now or Never* report, and it has been instrumental in leading private, public, and community sectors involved in the social and economic development of Halifax, as well as the Halifax Gateway via the HGC, which is under the umbrella of the Halifax Partnership (HP 2017).

Industry associations have played a key role in discussions on the gateway and trade corridors, including the Halifax Chamber of Commerce, the Lobster Council of Canada, and Canadian Manufacturers and Exporters.

For example, early in 2009, the Chamber of Commerce's Transportation Committee developed recommendations for further action regarding infrastructure specific to air, port, rail, and highways (HCC 2009).

The stakeholders from the business sector that have been actively involved or have benefitted from better gateway infrastructure include ACL, Zim, Hapag-Lloyd, Michelin, Oxford Frozen Foods, the fishing industry, the agricultural industry, pulp and paper, Acadian seafood, the two major terminal-operating companies that lease the container terminals from the port authority – PSA International in the Halterm terminal and Ceres[7] at the Bedford base terminal – the Longshoremen's Association, Armored, Midland, FedEx, and Cargo Jet (all interviews).

Both the provincial and federal governments own and operate transportation facilities. Their roles are to regulate and support partnerships (Transport Canada 2010) and to develop policy frameworks and strategies that contribute to the development of a transportation system geared at both national and international trade. The most recent frameworks include the National Policy Framework for Strategic Gateways and Trade Corridors (2007), the Atlantic Canada Transportation Strategy (2008–18), the Atlantic Gateway Business Case (2007), and the NTCF (2017–27).

Partnerships and Coalitions for the Halifax Gateway, and Capacity Building

In the early 2000s, the federal government launched the GBCF initiative, and a number of gateway-related initiatives, organizations, and advisory councils were established in Halifax and Atlantic Canada to contribute to the development of the Halifax and Atlantic gateways. In response to the GBCF federal initiative, the four Atlantic provinces participated in the elaboration of the Atlantic Gateway and Trade Corridor Strategy. This collaborative partnership was formalized with the signing of a Memorandum of Understanding (MoU) on October 14, 2007, between the governments of Canada, Nova Scotia, New Brunswick, Prince Edward Island, and Newfoundland and Labrador (Transport Canada 2010). The main purpose of the MoU was to develop the Atlantic Gateway Strategy, which stimulated a coordinated approach between private and public sector stakeholders that was necessary for the development of major infrastructure projects. The Atlantic Gateway MoU of 2007 established the Atlantic Gateway Advisory Council and the Nova Scotia Gateway Secretariat and Advisory Council in 2009 (HGC 2010). The Atlantic Gateway Federal-Provincial Officials Committee was established as the primary forum for collaboration between governments in the development of the Atlantic Gateway (InterVistas 2007). These bodies were mandated to further develop gateway opportunities in Atlantic Canada, Nova Scotia, and Halifax (HGC 2010).

The HGC, which was modelled on the Greater Vancouver Gateway Council (Interviews 7.3, 7.4), provided a forum for transportation providers and stakeholders in the Halifax region and included representatives from the port, airport, rail, and the Halifax Logistics Park to improve the competitiveness of the Halifax Gateway. "There's been a lot of planning going on for the last five years and everybody is there, just to contribute and give feedback. All they wanted was feedback so they can have a strong business case ... Communication with everybody is important, especially with the city, the port, sea and rail, Transport Canada, Ministry of Transportation in Nova Scotia" (Interview 7.7).

The main mandate of the HGC is:

1 Ensuring the Halifax Gateway offers efficient transportation networks to meet shipping and travel needs.
2 Improving Halifax Gateway infrastructure to capitalize on gateway-related business opportunities.
3 Ensuring government policy supports gateway development and that barriers to trade and travel are minimized.
4 Establishing the Halifax Gateway brand nationally and internationally.
5 Coordinating with other gateway councils and organizations in Atlantic Canada and supporting the Atlantic Gateway Strategy (HGC 2010).

The HGC was under the umbrella of the Halifax Partnership (HP 2017) and included senior executives from industry and government.[8] Provincial and municipal governments worked closely with the HGC to identify and move opportunities forward. One example is the proposal for the Halifax Logistics Park, a key piece of infrastructure for logistics and warehousing (TIR 2016; HGC 2010). Two strategic plans were prepared, one in 2005 and another in 2010 (HGC 2010).

With support from the federal government, the New Brunswick Gateway Council was created in 2007 and the Atlantic Gateway Advisory Council (AGAC) was established in September 2009 (HGC 2010). They provided advice to governments on issues and priorities relating to the Atlantic Gateway. The AGAC was made up of private sector representatives from all four Atlantic provinces to supply regional perspectives in support of the development of Atlantic Gateway initiatives (HGC 2010). The council included thirteen private sector representatives from different industries in Atlantic Canada who worked with governments to identify issues necessary to support domestic and international trade to and from the Atlantic region (Transport Canada 2011, 120). The AGAC complemented existing gateway councils in Atlantic Canada by ensuring wide representation of private sector interests in the region in the development of the Atlantic Gateway and Trade Corridor Initiative.

In October 2009, the Province of Nova Scotia announced the establishment of the Nova Scotia Gateway Secretariat and Advisory Council. Its main priorities included the preparation of a vision and strategy for the Nova Scotia Gateway and leadership in engaging and facilitating co-ordination among gateway stakeholders. Other gateway-related initiatives in the region included the Sydney and Area Gateway Council and Corner Brook Gateway Committee (HGC 2010).

Figure 7.9 shows the key events relevant to the Halifax gateway and trade corridor. The Atlantic Gateway Federal-Provincial Officials Committee is chaired by ACOA and represented primarily by representatives from the four provincial departments of transportation, ACOA, and Transport Canada. The committee was set up in January 2007, and "now it's merely an information sharing committee" (Interview 7.3).

The development of the Atlantic Gateway helped build consensus, governance, and accountability among stakeholders in the region, as well as collaboration with the Asia-Pacific Gateway and Corridor Initiative, the Ontario-Quebec Continental Gateway and Trade Corridor, and international gateways and corridors (InterVistas 2007). ACOA played a key role in the Atlantic Gateway Strategy as a facilitator, helping to foster consensus between stakeholders. Based on many interviews, ACOA was central to the process as "the facilitator for the Gateway strategy [and] convener of the four provincial governments, Transport Canada, and some of the key stakeholders, like the airport and the port authorities, and industry" (Interviews 7.1, 7.3, 7.6, 7.7).

Within this governance structure, each level of government had a specific role to play. The federal government established the infrastructure funds that contributed to the gateways and trade corridors, and, in many instances, the provincial government provided matching funds (Transport Canada 2010). However, funding is not the only role federal and provincial governments play. According to ACOA, the federal government also played a key role as facilitator and enabler of the collaboration between public and private organizations that together strategized the investments

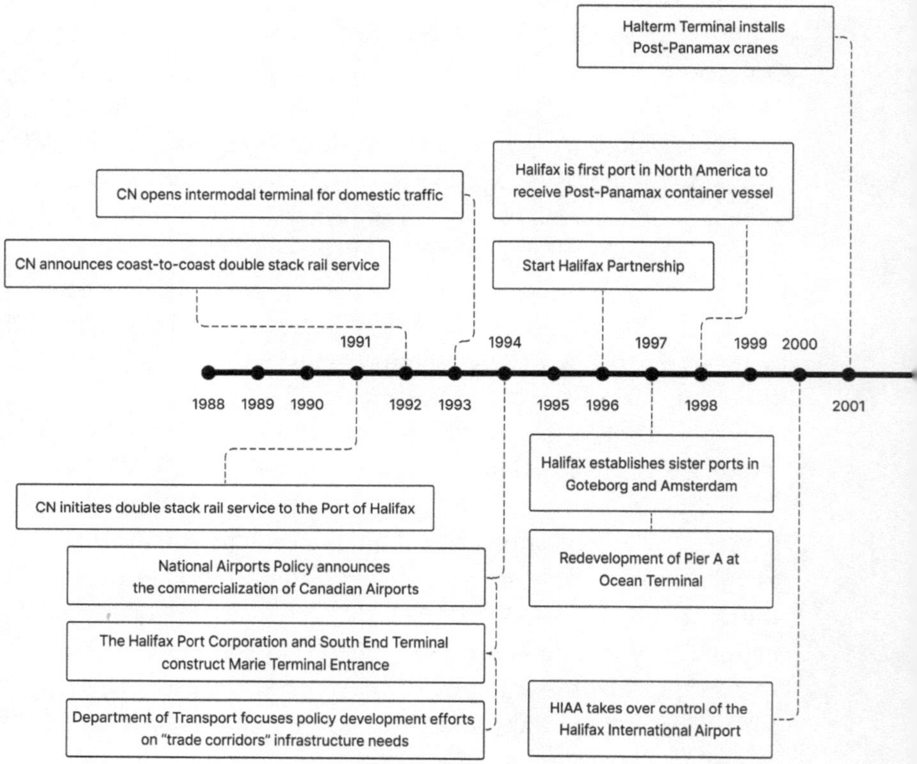

FIGURE 7.9 Gateway and Trade Corridor timeline, 1990–2020 | *Drawing:* Fariba Seyedjafarrangraz.

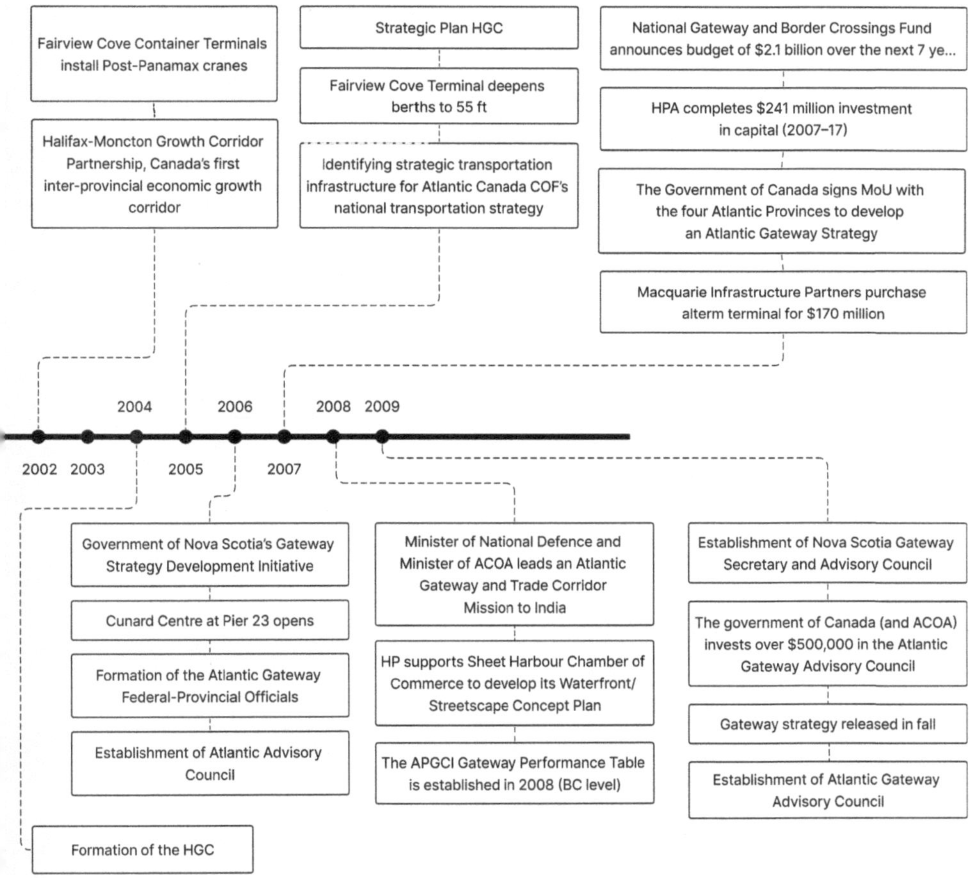
Fairview Cove Container Terminals install Post-Panamax cranes
Halifax-Moncton Growth Corridor Partnership, Canada's first inter-provincial economic growth corridor
Strategic Plan HGC
Fairview Cove Terminal deepens berths to 55 ft
Identifying strategic transportation infrastructure for Atlantic Canada COF's national transportation strategy
National Gateway and Border Crossings Fund announces budget of $2.1 billion over the next 7 ye...
HPA completes $241 million investment in capital (2007–17)
The Government of Canada signs MoU with the four Atlantic Provinces to develop an Atlantic Gateway Strategy
Macquarie Infrastructure Partners purchase alterm terminal for $170 million
2002
2003
2004
2005
2006
2007
2008
2009
Government of Nova Scotia's Gateway Strategy Development Initiative
Cunard Centre at Pier 23 opens
Formation of the Atlantic Gateway Federal-Provincial Officials
Establishment of Atlantic Advisory Council
Formation of the HGC
Minister of National Defence and Minister of ACOA leads an Atlantic Gateway and Trade Corridor Mission to India
HP supports Sheet Harbour Chamber of Commerce to develop its Waterfront/ Streetscape Concept Plan
The APGCI Gateway Performance Table is established in 2008 (BC level)
Establishment of Nova Scotia Gateway Secretary and Advisory Council
The government of Canada (and ACOA) invests over $500,000 in the Atlantic Gateway Advisory Council
Gateway strategy released in fall
Establishment of Atlantic Gateway Advisory Council

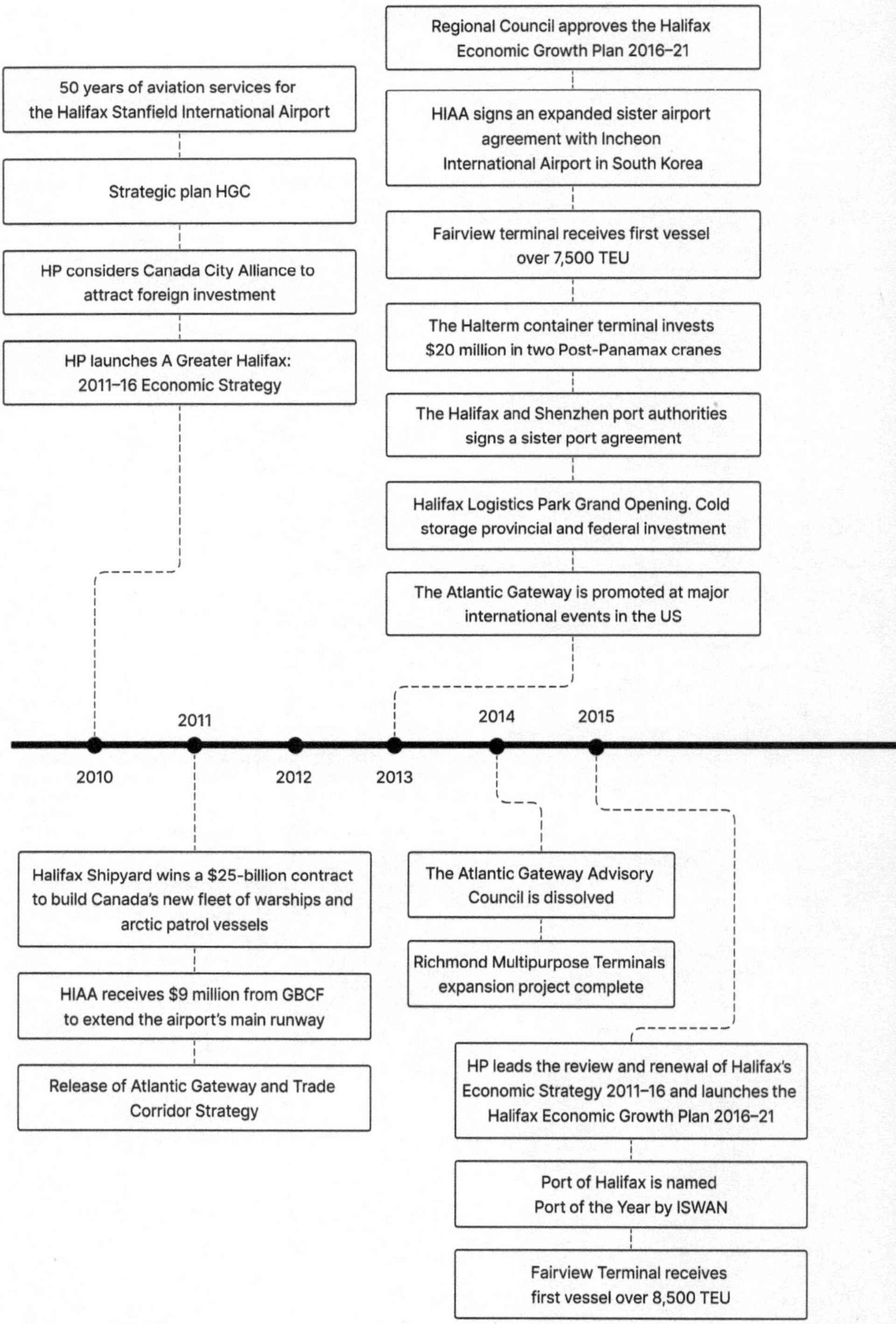

FIGURE 7.9 (continued)

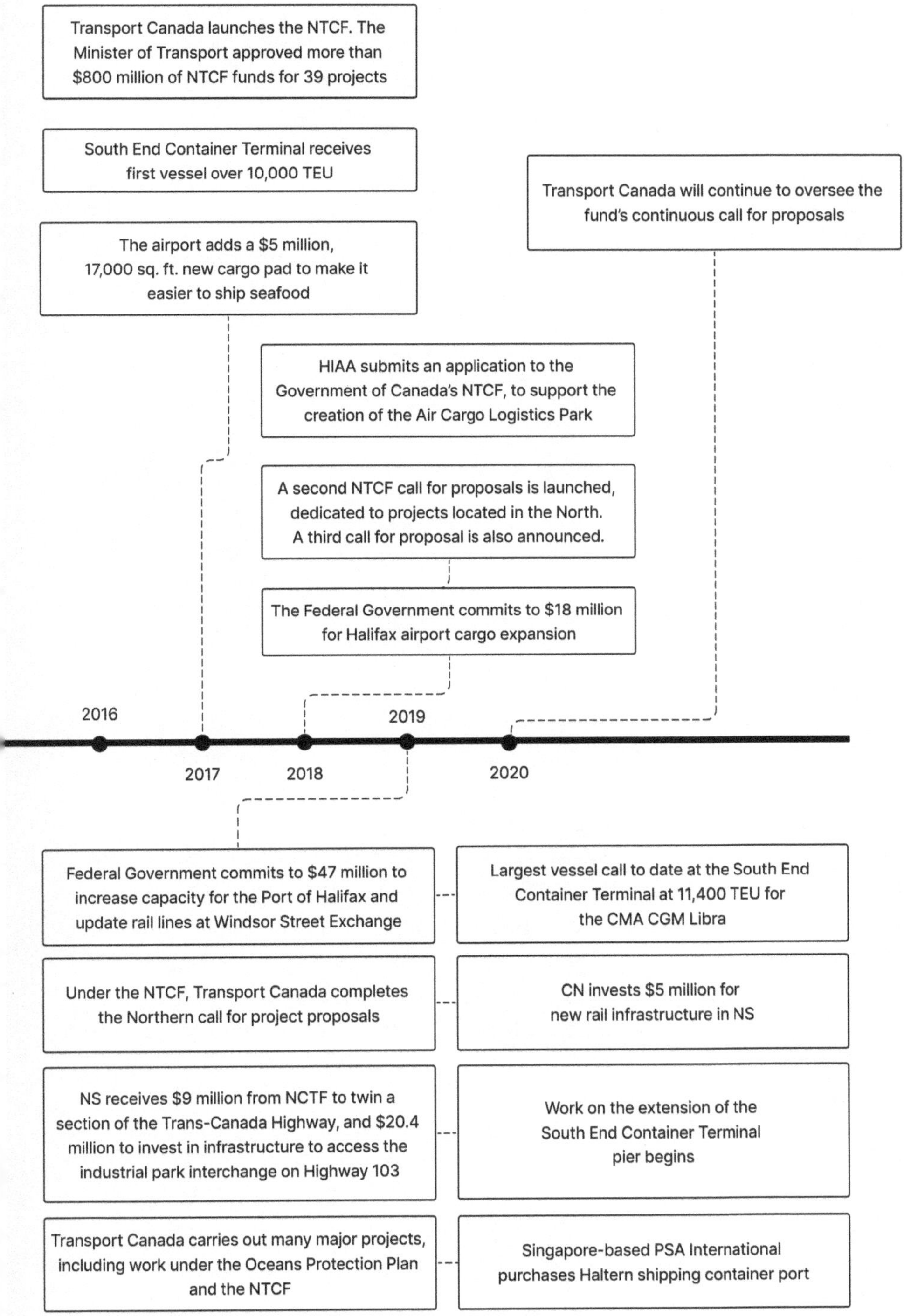
Transport Canada launches the NTCF. The Minister of Transport approved more than $800 million of NTCF funds for 39 projects
South End Container Terminal receives first vessel over 10,000 TEU
The airport adds a $5 million, 17,000 sq. ft. new cargo pad to make it easier to ship seafood
Transport Canada will continue to oversee the fund's continuous call for proposals
HIAA submits an application to the Government of Canada's NTCF, to support the creation of the Air Cargo Logistics Park
A second NTCF call for proposals is launched, dedicated to projects located in the North. A third call for proposal is also announced.
The Federal Government commits to $18 million for Halifax airport cargo expansion
2016
2017
2018
2019
2020
Federal Government commits to $47 million to increase capacity for the Port of Halifax and update rail lines at Windsor Street Exchange
Largest vessel call to date at the South End Container Terminal at 11,400 TEU for the CMA CGM Libra
Under the NTCF, Transport Canada completes the Northern call for project proposals
CN invests $5 million for new rail infrastructure in NS
NS receives $9 million from NCTF to twin a section of the Trans-Canada Highway, and $20.4 million to invest in infrastructure to access the industrial park interchange on Highway 103
Work on the extension of the South End Container Terminal pier begins
Transport Canada carries out many major projects, including work under the Oceans Protection Plan and the NTCF
Singapore-based PSA International purchases Haltern shipping container port

in infrastructure for the Halifax and Atlantic gateways. The municipal government also supported the proposals to the GBCF and NTCF. "The elected officials have a role to understand the port dynamic. So yes, they have a role of dialoguing ... they have the responsibility to have both sides of the story [i.e., the city and gateway]" (Interview 7.4).

Halifax Gateway and Trade Corridor, NTCF

According to the complexity of the infrastructure and the number of stakeholders that play a key role as users and decision makers, decisions around gateways and trade corridors require public and private sector partners interacting to identify the gaps, needs, and opportunities to support domestic and international trade. The HGC was instrumental in bringing together the relevant stakeholders to build the case for the first round of infrastructure funding; however, the council no longer operates. "Part of the council's responsibility was to look for and identify infrastructure projects, provide advice, in particular to Transport Canada around that funding and where would be the best spots to put it. That funding ran out and there was a change in government and there wasn't as much interest to continue or revitalize it" (Interview 7.1).

The Atlantic Growth Strategy (AGS), launched in 2016, was a plan designed to drive economic growth in the Atlantic region through targeted, evidence-based actions that included a comprehensive understanding of the different drivers of growth, including innovation, productivity, trade, and attractiveness of the region. The strategy required the coordination and involvement of different levels of government and a variety of stakeholders. At the federal level, the Department of Intergovernmental Affairs worked with the Government of Canada and the Atlantic provinces to advance economic growth in the region through the AGS (Department of Municipal Affairs 2019). To contribute to the development of international relations, the department also worked with Nova Scotia Business Inc. to develop international engagement strategies and with the Council of the Atlantic Premiers, meeting on a monthly basis.

On April 5, 2016, the Regional Council approved the document *Halifax Economic Growth Plan 2016–21,* as a five-year economic strategy for Halifax. The economic growth plan had four overarching goals: (i) promote and maximize growth, (ii) attract and retain talent, (iii) make Halifax a better place to live and work, and (iv) align economic development. "Align economic development" included increased awareness of the role cities play in economic development in the context of Nova Scotia and Canada and improved coordination in the development of economic activities. As did the AGS, the Halifax Economic Growth Plan emphasized the collaboration between different levels of government and a variety of stakeholders. Many of the public policy themes and sectors of activity targeted by the economic growth plan and gateway strategies for Halifax are at least partly outside of the purview and jurisdiction of local municipal governments, including immigration and social integration of newcomers, tourism, and business facilitation (Ivany et al. 2014). With a Halifax gateway vision that puts front and centre provincial and federal priorities, municipal plans and interventions in the region are mostly logistical building blocks to achieving these goals. Rather than being an abdication of responsibility at the municipal level, the division of labour among governments of all three levels highlights convergence of their perspectives for this vision.

ROUNDS OF INVESTMENT, FROM GBCF TO NTCF

Table 7.4 and Figure 7.10 indicate the Halifax Gateway and Atlantic Gateway projects that were supported under the GBCF and NTCF. During the GBCF round of funding, Nova Scotia received approval for four projects. Many of them focused on conducting studies to market the Halifax and Atlantic gateways and to organize forums and trade missions. In terms of magnitude, the amount received from Transport Canada under the GBCF initiative was over $41 million. From a historical perspective, funding for the Halifax and Atlantic gateways recognized the potential benefits of increased market access and the potential for related transportation-infrastructure improvements in the region (Transport Canada 2015, 4). This support from the GBCF contributed to capacity building and to forming the coalition required to design the case of the Halifax Gateway:

> Under the National Gateway and Border Crossing Fund there were a number of projects funded in Atlantic Canada and also a number of trade missions that Transport Canada led. Then that fund ran out, and there were no funds and there was no program in place, until Transport Canada announced the NTCF in 2017, and they implemented it in 2018. So, there was a gap of a number of years. The Atlantic Gateway fund concluded in 2013. (Interview 7.3)

In July 2017, Transport Canada launched NTCF. Funding allocation under this initiative was based on merit, with a focus on trade corridor efficiency and reliability. The NTCF had three objectives: easing capacity constraints, increasing resilience, and adapting to new technologies (Transport Canada 2017b). Eligible projects included construction, rehab,

TABLE 7.4
Projects supported by the GBCF and NTCF (CAN$)

Year	*GBCF*	*NTCF 2017*	*NTCF 2019*	*Grand Total*
2011	9,000,000			9,000,000
2013	32,500,000			32,535,000
2014				42,500
2015	110,500			110,500
2016				73,041
2017			23,500,000	23,500,000
2018		108,000,000		108,000,000
2019		20,400,000	24,000,000	44,400,000
Halifax Regional Municipality	32,500,000	38,400,000	47,500,000	118,400,000
Other Nova Scotia	9,110,500	90,000,000		99,110,500
Grand Total	41,610,500	128,400,000	47,500,000	217,510,500

Source: Authors' own calculations, based on Transport Canada (2021).

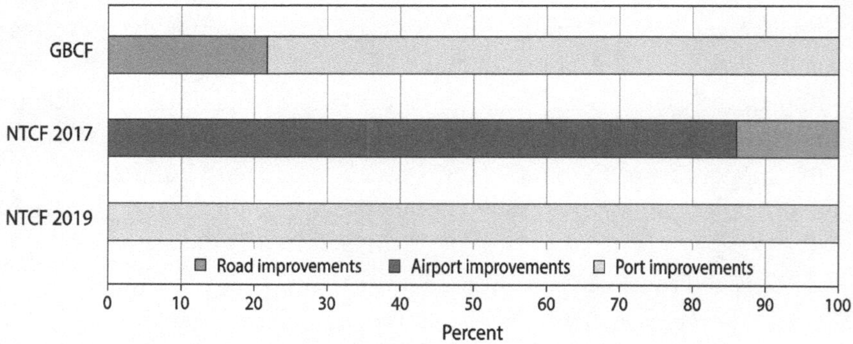

FIGURE 7.10 Projects supported by the GBCF and NTCF by type of investment | *Source:* Data from Transport Canada (2021).

and improvement of hard infrastructure assets; acquisition of new technologies related to traffic and trade monitoring; and studies and research on efficiency and resilience of transportation systems or efficiency barriers.

> The previous program and the current program had focused around international trade, and because our geographic position is the closest mainland link to the EU and, by the Suez Canal, to Asia, we benefit from

> the federal government's focus around international trade infrastructure funding. In the last ten years, there's been a fair number of infrastructure investments in Nova Scotia, both at the airport and ports around the region. (Interview 7.3)

The first call opened in summer 2017. Funding agreements for the first round of NTCF took place in 2018. During the NTCF, four large projects have been supported by Transport Canada, most of them capital investments over $151 million.

> Halifax is really showing leadership in positioning themselves as a true competitor on the global market ... For the cities, the gateways of St. John's and Halifax have to make significant investments in their terminals to play in the big leagues in the world market. And the cities need to make commitments because there's going to be more traffic going through their city. (Interview 7.7)

Some of the projects are important because they address climate change threats, as with the study on the Chignecto Isthmus that seeks to mitigate threats from storm surge, rising sea levels, and the effects on railway and highway infrastructure connecting New Brunswick and Nova Scotia. The study involves a comprehensive engineering assessment of existing infrastructure, consultation with stakeholders, and options to protect and sustain the trade corridor that includes the CN Rail line connecting the Port of Halifax to the rest of Canada. This project is led by the Government of New Brunswick in partnership with the Government of Nova Scotia.

NTCF rejected one HPA proposal for $275 million. Many speculated that different stakeholders' concerns about the increased truck traffic in downtown Halifax had a negative effect on the decision. "Given significant federal funds for other ports and over $90 million for road building in Nova Scotia, that the Port of Halifax expansion be rejected on grounds of land use and traffic suggests ... [some municipal stakeholders] ... had an influence on a decision that works against the interests of [the] constituency" (Ziobrowski 2018). Failures of consultation in this case are significant and contributed to a public backlash against increased traffic on already inadequate infrastructure linking the 100-series highways with the Port of Halifax. It can be argued that failures in consultation prevented this major port expansion in 2017 and 2018.

Even though the HPA was not successful in the application, they proceeded with the expansion of the Halterm terminal with a $35 million berth extension (piers 41 and 42); the funds came from private investment and loans from banks. The HPA engaged in significant public consultation regarding the extension or the option to build another terminal in Dartmouth.

In 2019, the federal government came up with the support of $100 million for a Windsor Street Exchange two-phase project in Halifax. This is one of the largest projects in terms of amount and impact for Halifax and involves a new rail connection between the South End and the Fairview Cove port terminals. The project includes additional rail tracks within its existing footprint and the acquisition of four new rail-mounted cranes to load and unload containers, addressing one of the biggest challenges in Halifax related to traffic in the city (Interview 7.7). This particular project involved the city, the province, the federal government, CN, and the Port Authority – all identifying the Windsor Street Exchange and the rail shuttle concept as integral to allowing Halifax to improve its engagement in the GVCs and for the city to remain appealing to its citizens. The project required years of background studies and numerous consultations between stakeholders and the city (Interviews 7.3, 7.4).

Another relevant project under the NTCF is the twinning of Highway 104, which received funding under a public-private partnership model. The responsibilities for designing, building, financing, operating, and maintaining the highway was given to a single firm through a bidding process.

The HIAA submitted a project that was rejected during the first submission but was later resubmitted and awarded. The CEO of HIAA said after being debriefed by Transport Canada, the airport made an unsolicited second bid, which was accepted (Interview 7.1). The investment represents a $36 million cargo handling facility, $18 million of which is provided by the NTCF, and the rest by the HIAA and the province. This facility aims to support fresh seafood exports from Nova Scotia to Europe and Asia. The project includes a cargo building, taxiways, and an expansion of deicing facilities on ten hectares of forest land adjacent to the existing cargo facility.

Governance structures need to be maintained at all levels. As indicated by several stakeholders, trade corridors across Canada need to be connected to avoid bottlenecks. "If you're investing $500 million in Halifax and your key market is Montreal but it all slows down because that forty kilometres is not four lanes, then you are questioning the process ... trying to make sure the entire supply chain is a ... chain" (Interview 7.7). Figure 7.11 illustrates the different partnerships and coalitions associated with the projects supported by the different rounds of funding for Nova Scotia.

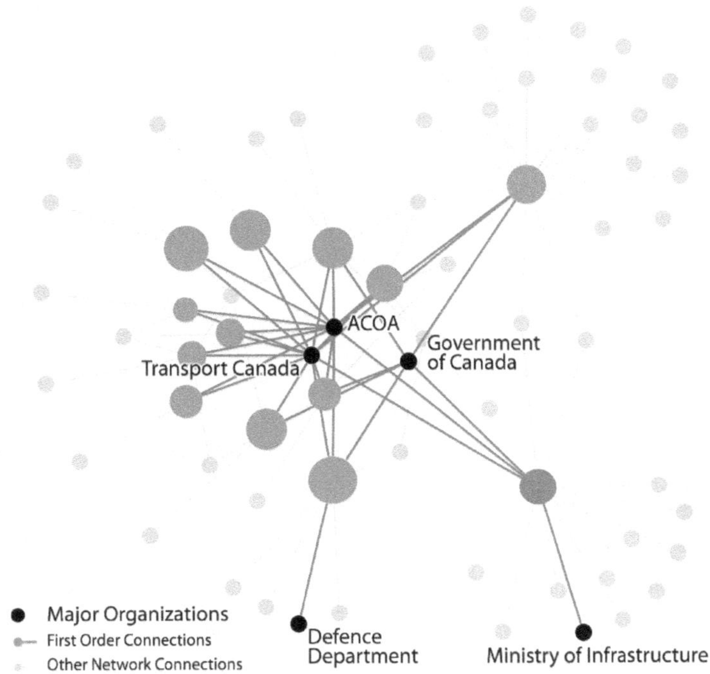

FIGURE 7.11 Network relationships around Halifax-funded projects

The Atlantic Gateway was viewed as a key gateway to North America, China, India, Thailand, Malaysia, Indonesia, Bangladesh, Pakistan, Singapore, and the Middle East (InterVistas 2007; APEC 2015), which explains why, in addition to the federal funding, the Atlantic Gateway has experienced significant private sector investment since 2007. Private sector investment has also played a key role in the development of gateway infrastructure (Transport Canada 2010). "In terms of funding, for first extension in 2009, 2010, the Canadian government matched HPA investment for a total of $35 million; the HPA put $17 million, and the federal government gave us a special grant of the other half. This second one, which is a $35 million extension, we're 100 percent financing that from our cash flow" (Interview 7.4).

CONCLUSION

The federal government, through the different rounds of funding for infrastructure projects related to gateways and trade corridors, made a positive contribution to the economic and social development of Halifax and Nova Scotia. The rounds of funding set an important precedent that acknowledged the significance of infrastructure in a complex globalized economy.

The funds also contributed to capacity building and the formation of coalitions that brought together different stakeholders. Several forums were created where the stakeholders came together to contribute their expertise and points of view. For example, the Atlantic Gateway Federal-Provincial Officials Committee, the AGAC, and the HGC were instrumental during the first round of funding for the GBCF. Most initiatives supported by this round were associated with intangibles necessary to bring the stakeholders together and create awareness of Halifax in the international context via trade missions and marketing efforts. With the second round of funding via the NTCF, more capital projects were supported in Halifax and significant efforts were made to build coalitions that facilitated dialogue between stakeholders. This was an important element in the plan to identify the key projects for gateway infrastructure. In line with the notion of executive democracy, stakeholder engagement was based on inviting industry representatives to cocreate the plans for gateway infrastructure and not as a way to empower residents and local communities in shaping the design of such projects.

The interplay between levels of government is complex, in particular because of their respective responsibilities and missions. The interviews and the reports studied have shown that ACOA was one of the most important and central organizations and brought stakeholders together and contributed to the capacity building required to form sustainable coalitions. ACOA was an enabler and facilitator throughout the different rounds of funding. Having offices in all the Atlantic provinces, the ACOA is deeply rooted in the region.

We know that consultations with communities played an important role, probably more during the round of NTCF funding than in the round of GBCF funding, with the HPA regularly engaging in consultations to identify areas of interest and development as prioritized by the residents of Nova Scotia and, more specifically, the residents of Halifax. We also know the effects of gateway and trade corridors infrastructure on job creation, wages, and salaries. What is harder to conceptualize, however, is the effort and work that was necessary to identify and decide what projects to build and to create partnerships and build the cases for the federal government.

8

Canadian Gateways, City-Regional Governance, and Executive Democracy

As urban spaces partly structured by and for international trade purposes, Canadian gateway cities have developed similar, yet distinct, governance models related to meeting global value chain (GVC) requirements. In this chapter, we contrast the cases of Vancouver, Toronto, Montreal, and Halifax to draw out the specificities of each gateway governance model, especially how trade transportation proponents interact with local governments and civil society actors. Such insights shed light on the various stakeholders involved in these gateway regimes, despite their distinct priorities and mandates. Focusing on how gateway regimes frame citizen engagement, we highlight the ways conventional urban governance processes and structures have been transformed to meet the requirements of GVCs. The result is that urban democracy is bypassed, replaced by the technocratic pursuit of community buy-in and social license, which may also be referred to as a form of executive democracy.

Canada's main gateway cities have developed distinctive urban coalitions or regimes through which the particular challenges of transportation-infrastructure delivery are governed. Such regimes are characterized by a broad multisectoral support of stakeholders, sharing broad goals and specific agendas that endure over time, hence offering some stability to the shared vision and interests (Stone 2001). These arrangements, whether formal, informal, or a combination of both, are the basis on which an urban governance model is consolidated. Each urban regime relies on such a governing structure, devised and negotiated by a set of stakeholders, to achieve shared objectives. Gateway regimes, by definition, share the objective to better position a city-region in GVCs and global production networks through trade and transportation-infrastructure development.

In this concluding chapter, we contrast the governance models of four Canadian gateway cities to highlight the evolution and relative stability of their respective gateway regime. While the core objective of each gateway regime is similar – namely better integrating a city-region into global distribution and production networks – local historical, geographical, and jurisdictional conditions have resulted in four distinct gateway regimes, establishing four different governance models to reconcile the requirements of GVCs, physical assets, and institutional arrangements with local and social considerations (Brunelle et al. 2021). That these differences have persisted and were in some ways further entrenched after more than a decade of city-shaping federal government intervention in the form of trade-enabling transportation-infrastructure spending underscores the importance of these local conditions.

In this sense, each of our case study city-regions reveals a unique set of interactions and social relations among members of the gateway regime – between these stakeholders and other parts of the local, provincial, and federal institutional landscape – hence leading us to identify four distinctive models of gateway city governance. Our use of the term "model" to describe each set of governance arrangements is comparative and does not imply normative approval of any particular approach. The Vancouver model reveals the role of a long-standing, private sector–led regime behind the Asia-Pacific Gateway. The Continental Gateway reveals the importance of provincial bodies, especially Ontario's and Quebec's transportation departments, in shaping the nascent gateway regimes; but comparing the two provinces exposes opposite styles of governing. Whereas the Montreal model shows proactive public sector leadership and highly planned stakeholder integration, the Toronto model, or lack thereof, stems from Ontario's relatively laissez-faire approach. This has allowed the development of several suburban coalitions to form as partnerships focused on certain sectors, creating a correspondingly fragmented city-regional vision. Lastly, the Halifax model shows a governance approach consolidated and led by federally mandated agencies and priorities to further Canada's Atlantic Gateway.

No matter the governance model, in all four cases the same types of actors are involved. While they develop a distinct role in each case, they also have a similar pro-trade rationale for being involved in gateway regimes. Each governance model has distinct sets of practices of incorporating (or not) community concerns to their plans. Key stakeholders, and the urban coalition of which they are a part, are all advocating for a better positioning of each gateway city in GVCs. This requirement puts some distance between them and urban democratic praxis, moving toward an executive form of democracy, most notably by adopting citizen engagement strategies that are separate and technocratically mediated away from conventional political and citizen forums. Global economic requirements are thus built into projects in ways that cannot be opened for political opposition or compromise. Whether framed as consultations and accommodations or, conceptually, as community buy-in or social license, this type of outreach offers only minimal engagement with urban democratic processes and institutions designed to represent residents and local communities. Those pursuing global trade corridor–development strategies require the buy-in of local stakeholders to secure GVC attachment and upgrading, yet they simultaneously seek to bypass conventional mechanisms of democratic decision making and accountability. This dual requirement to secure support without ceding control results in an uneven set of acceptances and resistances to trade-supporting transportation-infrastructure investments that are shaped by and through multiscalar processes of coalition and regime building.

In this chapter, we first present four distinct gateway governance models. In discussing the Vancouver, Toronto, Montreal, and Halifax models separately, we draw out the specificities of each to examine how the gateway regimes have been formed and mobilized and how arrangements have emerged. We then explore the contributions for the same types of stakeholders in all four cases to assess some of the parameters structuring the operations of the gateway regimes – and potentially limiting its cohesiveness. We continue the reflection by examining how gateway regimes have engaged with their local communities to address social concerns and accommodate such priorities within their activities. This allows us to shed light on how these community outreach strategies intersect, or not, with established urban democratic practices to establish what we call an executive democracy. Finally, we discuss the normative and conceptual framings of these citizen engagement strategies, centred on community buy-in and social license as a form of diminished urban democratic praxis.

GOVERNANCE MODELS: ARRANGEMENTS AND STAKEHOLDERS

The governance models in place to better position Vancouver, Toronto, Montreal, and Halifax in GVCs both reflect and reinforce the geographically shaped accumulations of gateway functions present in each. In other words, location matters over time to shape the range of possible gateway functions local regimes can and do pursue. In this section, we compare the governance model of each of the four Canadian gateway cities to highlight distinct models. In each case, we reprise the historical roots of the urban coalition, its composition, arrangements, and relations to the local social polity.

Vancouver: A Private Sector–Led Model

Historically, Vancouver's repositioning in GVCs is rooted in a broader internationalization process of systematically opening the Canadian economy to the Asia-Pacific region. Since the 1980s, a coalition of private sector stakeholders has formed, grown, and set the stage for the Asia-Pacific Gateway vision. In line with its business interests, this coalition advocated for reorienting the economic priorities of the city-region away from its long-standing reliance on trade in resources with the US. It created mechanisms to help its lobbying efforts, notably the Greater Vancouver Gateway Council (GVGC), established in 1994. Working through various forums and networks, private sector and not-for-profit stakeholders involved in international transportation and trade made the case to government officials for advancing Vancouver's gateway functions. This activity began well before the federal designation of the Asia-Pacific Gateway and Corridor Initiative in 2007. With official provincial and federal support secure, the gateway regime has expanded, shifting its approach from lobbying efforts outside of government to advocating from within institutions and agencies. Despite this evolution, core elements of the governing structure and related arrangements remain the same, as the agenda is still being shaped outside local government and civil society.

The gateway governance model of Vancouver affords a private sector–led coalition a central and institutionalized role in setting the agenda. Its members convey their priorities to key regional agencies and decision-making forums, where the actions of port and airport authorities and regional transportation planning and transit priorities are discussed. In the midst of considerable institutional complexity, which includes multiple local governments and agencies each with a certain degree of autonomy, the gateway regime has found its niche in proposing a regional vision to bring dispersed interests together and to advocate for a more centralized approach to solving issues affecting GVCs. This regime had the support of provincial governments and the ability to provide payoffs to local actors through infrastructure mitigations. As the private sector–led coalition has evolved, it had to incorporate additional partners and stakeholders, including local actors and interprovincial partners across Western provinces, which further complicated the commitments and outcomes of its vision for Vancouver.

The constellation of stakeholders and related arrangements to push new projects and initiatives forward involve a core group of private sector actors, industry associations and lobbying bodies, senior governments, and regional port and airport authorities. Focused on initiatives that will support trade diversification, this core group will incorporate municipalities and not-for-profit and civil society organizations from time to time – always strategically and differentially – in ways that support its broader normative vision for the gateway. For instance, labour unions were originally part of the coalition but have never been part of the GVGC, and some coalition members have advocated for antistrike legislations at particular gateway sites. Similarly, municipal governments are consulted if directly affected by the plans and projects of the gateway regime; otherwise they are ignored. Interestingly, the discursive framings of the Vancouver gateway have evolved to seek broad public support while not incorporating institutional champions related to these causes. For example, over the years, environmental considerations have been increasingly part of the public positioning of the gateway regime, but local environmental groups generally have not been included.

Toronto: A Fragmented Model

The Continental Gateway was designed by the federal government to help address transportation issues such as congestion and border-crossing effectiveness for international trade purposes in the Quebec-Windsor corridor. The city-regions of Toronto and Montreal have their distinct positioning in GVCs, and each has independent governance models. In the case of Toronto, there is wide consensus among local stakeholders as to the nature of several transportation problems impeding further growth and the lack of local solutions. Historically, a strong divide between the City of Toronto and the suburbs, fuelled by provincial decisions against the city's leadership in regional transportation matters, has led to the impossibility of having a public and coherent city-regional governance structure. Despite some provincial mandated institutions like Metrolinx, with relatively reduced powers and legitimacy, the gateway city governance model of Toronto is characterized by its fragmentation, the plurality of suburban coalitions, and a widespread unawareness of the key role of transportation infrastructure in pushing for a better positioning of the city-region in GVCs. Any support from the Continental Gateway Strategy has been mediated by provincial bodies, notably the Ministry of Transportation.

Enacting a province-wide decentralized approach to managing municipal affairs and urbanization in southern Ontario, transportation priorities have been conceived as separate from local economic development plans, which partly explains why the City of Toronto did not provide regional leadership on planning the movement of goods and peoples. Instead, secondary cities in the suburbs of Toronto took a leadership role. Ontario's approach made room for business elites and secondary and regional municipalities to fill the gap, with the development of several suburban coalitions around specific, sectoral, and subregional gateway projects and priorities.

In this context, each suburban coalition comprises a mix of public stakeholders from the three levels of government and private sector actors from specific industries, with some relationship to neighbouring municipalities or regional actors. Federal and provincial bodies are integrated in various pro-gateway arrangements across the city-region, all with different local actors and in support of particular industries, including advanced manufacturing in Oshawa and Hamilton and transportation logistics in Peel Region. The City of Toronto is less involved in these projects and does not serve as the locus for mobilizing the efforts of various suburban stakeholders. The City of Toronto is rather interested in advancing its own transportation plans, focused on local transit efficiency, while its plans for better positioning in GVCs are directly connected to other localities, such as Waterloo, for an innovation corridor specialized on artificial intelligence and to the competitive networks of global cities. Similarly, and without being part of a regional urban coalition, key civil society associations organized at a city-regional scale are involved in these arrangements across the city-region, often in line with the requests and the support of business proxies and private sector actors operating at that level.

In these suburban coalitions, network arrangements tend to be limited to municipal, provincial, and federal stakeholders and private sector actors, including local chambers of commerce and other business proxies, as they are organized around key projects, initiatives, and industries. Local civil society organizations are mostly excluded from these suburban coalitions, notably because these coalitions are less known in local circles and less stable. In contrast, civil society organizations are involved in transportation discussions in the City of Toronto, but they are mostly interested in public transit, livability, and environmental considerations. Overall, most civil society organizations are involved in local discussions, but these are institutionally separate from considerations for transportation infrastructure and from most GVC decisions made in the suburbs.

At the same time, regional business and civil society organizations such as the Toronto Region Board of Trade and CivicAction Alliance have developed a similar diagnosis of the issues and problems affecting the city-region of Toronto, notably when it comes to transport. There is wide agreement among these stakeholders and public bodies, such as Metrolinx, on the importance of better positioning in GVCs, but these realizations are met with the impossibility of developing a cohesive regional approach to solving these issues.

Montreal: An Institutionalized Model

Montreal's urban coalition is shaped by a more state interventionist political culture than any of the other cases, rooted in Quebec's nationalist history, social-democratic traditions, and more recent overlays of neoliberalism (Keil and Boudreau 2005a, 100). This historical context resulted in a strong institutionalized alignment of provincial and public interests with local urban coalitions. This multilayered governance model in Montreal is led by the Montreal Metropolitan Community (MMC), the city-region's governing body. The MMC acts as both facilitator and vector in the implementation of policies coming out of federal and provincial as well as the lower tiers of governments – the city, the agglomeration, and the region. It plays a key role in projects and matters relating to the positioning of Montreal as the most important of the fifteen industrial port zones identified in Quebec's Maritime Strategy.

While on paper there is a metropolitan governance framework, in which the MMC is predominant, the so-called Montreal model centred on the city's ten economic clusters is more salient to understanding this gateway regime. The general Montreal model involves a complex urban coalition, has extensive formal and informal connections at all levels of activity and across multiple sectors, and plays a significant role in economic matters, beyond mere consultations. CargoM, the logistics and transportation cluster, is a major player in this model. While the model is characterized by a constellation of stakeholders and institutionalized relations among them, this governing structure does not include direct representation from civil society organizations.

Interestingly, the City of Montreal and the borough councils downplay the impacts of commercial policies and GVCs on their constituents' well-being, choosing to assume the role of informant rather than participant in the few and far-between consultations organized by the Office de consultation publique de Montréal (OCPM) on these issues. As an independent organization whose mission is to carry out public consultation mandates entrusted to it by Montreal's city council or its executive committee, the OCPM is a key feature of citizen participation in Montreal. It is not implicated in any governance structure and its consultations on gateway issues are limited to the nuisances suffered by citizens at the local level. A comparable office does not exist in any of the other cases under study. It is an institutional body responsible for all public consultations for the city, which reveals how the city is quite prone to consultations with civil society actors on a host of topics. The OCPM is a key mediator in the governance model between the urban coalition and civil society. However, this applies marginally to gateways and GVCs even though their importance is alluded to in most planning documents and studies tabled upstream. Closely tied to this absence of a large public awareness, public consultation on the impacts of GVCs is concentrated in the smallest geographical area possible, and other actors including the Port of Montreal have designed and implemented their own consultation process with local citizens. At city and borough levels, the consultation processes set up under the auspices of the OCPM or other citizen-led initiatives (i.e., Agora métropolitaine, Forum Urba 2015, Institut de politiques alternatives de Montréal) largely involve exchanges between citizens in the aftermath of a presentation made by a few officials – not necessarily elected – from the city and/or the borough. The degree of institutionalization of the coalition means that it has remained relatively stable over time. Even with changes in governments and elected positions, there is an institutional persistence to the network arrangements.

Halifax: A Model Led by Federal Priorities

The gateway regime on the West Coast and related Asia-Pacific Gateway strategy were inspirations to institutional and political developments on the East Coast. In this case, the urban coalition was consolidated only after the federal designation of 2007, with the official Atlantic Gateway Strategy released in 2011. In the Eastern case, a coherent trade gateway and corridor strategy that encompasses all four Atlantic provinces needed to be developed first. As such, federal and provincial interests were instrumental in consolidating the Atlantic Gateway regime. Due to declining local and regional economic development indicators, both international transportation and trade and a stronger integration of the local infrastructure into global distribution networks were identified as important for the region. The Atlantic Canada Opportunities Agency (ACOA) – the federal government's regional economic development organization for the Atlantic provinces – was tasked with expanding the Atlantic Gateway vision to explore various avenues through which this designation can serve for a better positioning in GVCs, most notably by working with stakeholders in the city-region of Halifax.

The Halifax model of gateway city governance reveals the importance of federal priorities and highlights the role of ACOA in convening key regional stakeholders. Specifically, ACOA has helped with local efforts to form the coalition, in close collaboration with provincial governments and select provincial and municipal bodies such as the Nova Scotia Department of Transportation and Renewal and the Halifax Partnership. With a focus on stakeholders from the different levels of government, the private sector, and representatives of each mode of transport, ACOA played a significant role in identifying potential coalition stakeholders and inviting them to rounds of discussion so that projects and a shared vision could be developed. During the capacity-building phase of the coalition between 2007 and 2011, ACOA notably supported the establishment and work of the Atlantic Gateway Advisory Council, which helped the development of local gateway institutional infrastructure such as the Halifax Gateway Council, which was based on the Vancouver model but included more city stakeholders in these discussions. Moreover, ACOA led many activities and initiatives with local private and public sector actors to develop shared gateway initiatives that go beyond transportation issues, including trade, education, talent recruitment, and industry-specific strategies.

Federal leadership requires many informal network arrangements to gather the support necessary for the success of gateway initiatives. Informal networks and coordination were seen as the best way to incorporate social considerations and concerns that contributed to elaborating the Halifax case. Due to the relatively small size of the region and the small number of stakeholders interested and involved in the gateway regime, the prevalent use of strategically appointing the same people or colleagues from the coalition to select boards and key official positions has significantly helped in consolidating the urban coalition and ensuring that its vision is discussed in various forums. Interestingly, these network arrangements were supported through the federal rounds of funding, notably during the National Gateways and Border Crossings Fund (GBCF) round, when support to council bodies was considered a form of capacity building. Such efforts were deemed successful. During the subsequent National Trade Corridors Fund (NTCF) round of funding, we observe that communication and connection among key coalition stakeholders continue, despite significant changes to the institutional landscape, including the disbandment of the Atlantic Gateway Council. Significant progress has been made for some exporting sectors. A gateway regime focused on Halifax, with a vision for a more integrated role for Atlantic Canada in GVCs, has evolved into a relatively stable and multisectoral local buy-in with provincial, city, and private sector actors.

TOWARD A TYPOLOGY OF GATEWAY STAKEHOLDERS

Each Canadian gateway city governance model reveals a similar set of stakeholders participating in the shared vision and projects in the positioning of each city-region in GVCs. Table 8.1 identifies the leading stakeholders based on network positionality in each of the four gateway regimes, classified according to the typology developed below. Despite similar types of actors, stakeholders across the four cases have taken different roles in supporting the agenda of the gateway regime. An examination of key stakeholders by type – based on their similar mandates across the four city-regions and their differing contributions – provides an opportunity to better assess some of the parameters and constraints through which these gateway regimes operate. By identifying distinct types of stakeholders, their interest in such coalitions, and the ways they relate to their local community, we seek to avoid creating an illusion of rigid cohesiveness among an urban coalition. In what follows, we explore four types of stakeholders that are proponents of Canada's gateways across the country – namely federally mandated agencies, provincial bodies, business proxies, and municipal and regional governments – and contrast their contributions across all four cases.

Federally Mandated Agencies

Many federal government departments, agencies, and initiatives have been part of the urban coalitions pushing for a better positioning of their city-region in GVCs. Whether through direct involvement of federal departments such as Transport Canada or via regional economic development agencies including Pacific Economic Development Canada and ACOA, the federal perspective is well represented in all four cases. Aside from funding initiatives such as APGCI, GBCF, and NTCF, which make various federal departments responsible for implementing the federal vision, federally mandated agencies that include port and airport authorities have also been significant stakeholders in all four cases. With some independence from other federal bodies, they develop their own plans in

TABLE 8.1

Leading gateway stakeholder organizations in four Canadian city-regions

Organization (and Type)			
Vancouver	*Toronto*	*Montreal*	*Halifax*
Greater Vancouver Urban Freight Council (*Regional*)	Urban Freight Forum (*Regional*)	Transport Canada (*Federal*)	Transport Canada (*Federal*)
Greater Vancouver Gateway Council (*Association*)	Government of Canada (*Federal*)	Government of Canada (*Federal*)	ACOA (*Federal*)
Metro Vancouver (*Municipal*)	Transport Canada (*Federal*)	CargoM (*Regional*)	Government of Nova Scotia (*Provincial*)
Government of Canada (*Federal*)	City of Toronto (*Municipal*)	Government of Quebec (*Provincial*)	Government of Canada (*Federal*)
Vancouver Fraser Port Authority (*Authority*)	Metrolinx (*Regional*)	Greater Montreal Area (*Municipal*)	Halifax Port Authority (*Authority*)
TransLink (*Authority*)	City of Hamilton (*Municipal*)	Canadian National Railway (*Private*)	Halifax Gateway Council (*Association*)
Transport Canada (*Federal*)	HalTech Regional Innovation Centre (*Regional*)	Chamber of Commerce of Metropolitan Montreal (*Association*)	Halifax Stanfield International Airport (*Authority*)
Canadian Pacific Railway (*Private*)	Halton Region (*Municipal*)	Montreal Port Authority (*Authority*)	Halifax Regional Municipality (*Municipal*)
BC Ministry of Transportation and Infrastructure (*Provincial*)	York Region (*Municipal*)	Quebec Ministry of Transport (*Provincial*)	Nova Scotia Department of Transportation and Infrastructure Renewal (*Provincial*)
Government of British Columbia (*Provincial*)	City of Brampton (*Municipal*)	Quebec City (*Municipal*)	Air Canada (*Private*)

Note: Organizations ranked by centrality score in networks surrounding federally funded gateway and trade corridor projects, 2006–19.

support of city-regional growth. For instance, in Toronto, we have observed the creation of the Southern Ontario Airport Network and the Hamilton-Oshawa Port Authority. Similarly, the 2008 merger of three port authorities to become the Vancouver Fraser Port Authority (also known as Port of Vancouver) created a federal body with a region-wide perspective on infrastructure development; as such, the Port of Vancouver has assumed a leadership role in the gateway regime. Collaborations such as those with the GVGC are institutionalized in the case of Montreal, where the Administration portuaire de Montréal as well as Aéroports de Montréal, Air Canada Cargo, CN, and CP are all members of CargoM. CargoM also acts as a major partner for the province's Maritime Strategy in the Greater Montreal area. Interestingly, the ways these agencies operate can provide them with additional strength within the local urban coalition, notably in smaller gateway cities such as Halifax, where local and regional stakeholders have relatively low negotiating power vis-à-vis CN, CP, and the port and airport authorities.

These federally mandated agencies are clearly visible and sought after to participate in forums for local, regional, and national transport issues, while their own plans and actions may also be at a distance from the urban coalition. The federal agencies typically have their own mechanisms to determine the perspectives of business, residents, local communities, and other stakeholders, and to consult with them. Their advantage over federal departments is that they are often aware of local issues and concerns. They can also convey such concerns to various stakeholders in the private or public sector – hence defining their role in part as a medium for specific messages, an advocate and lobbyist on behalf of local interests (often as employers themselves), and a resource for educating and training the local community with new developments in their sector of activity. In contrast to other types of stakeholders, their structure, centrality, and contributions to the four gateway regimes is mostly similar, with the exception of the emphasis put on relationships to other types of actors, depending which actor is leading the coalition (i.e., private sector on the West Coast or ACOA on the East Coast). Federally mandated agencies are somewhat institutionalized, relatively independent members of gateway regimes with specific concerns related to their transportation mode and mandate.

In this respect, they are an inadequate substitute for democratic government, and herein lies a problem. They are seen by some in higher levels of government as a form of community stakeholder, hence obviating the need to engage with other, more local, stakeholders. At the same time, they are perceived from outside the gateway regime by other urban actors as key champions of trade transportation and as federal actors that are difficult to engage with and often unmoved by local civil society and resident concerns.

Provincial Government Bodies

In all four cases, the prominence of provincial departments and agencies as partners to infrastructure projects for international trade purposes is to be expected. In part, this reflects the Canadian constitutional order in which provinces have authority over local government and are responsible for intraprovincial infrastructure, including most highways. Another reason is that the movement of goods and peoples in geographically distributed economies is rarely limited to the jurisdictional boundaries of the city-region; in three of the four Canadian cases, Halifax being the exception, the metropolitan areas are internally fragmented.

Provincial bodies have advocated for various projects that were seen as key to the effectiveness of the city's gateway functions, including those located outside the city along the trade corridor. In theory, provincial stakeholders play a key role in mitigating the tensions across regions, competition between municipal governments, and demands from the private sector. In British Columbia, the provincial government has directly managed major highway projects within the Vancouver region and has indirectly sought to shape decision making through governance reforms at TransLink, the regional transport agency. In Ontario, provincial departments have been actively involved in planning to avoid such tensions, notably the need to balance the considerations for commuters in the Greater Toronto and Hamilton Area – a key concern of municipalities – with the establishment of an efficient urban freight network. In practice, this has mostly meant support for activities at the US border crossings, hence putting their efforts into supporting the city-region of Toronto and often outside the region itself. In contrast, Quebec's Ministère des Affaires municipales, des Régions et l'Occupation du Territoire, Ministère de l'Économie et de l'Innovation, and, most importantly, Ministère des Transports du Québec support the government's overall economic development strategy centred on Montreal as its metropolis. Similarly, in Nova Scotia, the Department of Transportation and Infrastructure Renewal has been one of the key stakeholders for the identification of projects that contribute to the development of the Atlantic Gateway, collaborating closely with ACOA since 2007.

Provincial governments nevertheless face a balancing act to support local city-regional economic activity and residential amenity while not impeding international trade activity going through the gateway. Depending on the importance of the saddle function of the gateway city-region, provincial bodies have varying levels of involvement in ensuring coherence between local, domestic, and international uses of transportation infrastructure. Such provincial considerations are less prominent in Montreal and Toronto, where local urban freight is proportionally more important to the economy than in Vancouver and Halifax, where hinterland freight predominates. The result is that the movement of goods has less political traction at the provincial level within the Continental Gateway compared to the other two gateways. In the case of specific industry clusters related to and depending on gateway functions, the provincial bodies find a lot more political traction to support key sectors, such as advanced manufacturing in the Greater Toronto and Hamilton Area and marine produce in the greater Halifax region.

Nevertheless, provincial bodies are limited in many ways in their capacity and legitimacy to take a leadership role to better position their city-region in GVCs. As significant supporters and key members of the coalitions, their alignment with the coalition goals may yet be limited by the considerations, demands, and requests of many other regions and municipalities on their territories. While federal investments are seen as one-off and necessarily selective initiatives, local public officials constantly compete for provincial attention. Hence, provincial politicians are loath to invest in a sole region, even if it is their gateway city, since it comes at a political cost and risks critiques of favouritism. Provincial government bodies are, paradoxically, heavily invested in gateway city governance but act mostly from the margins.

Business Proxies

Chambers of commerce, boards of trade, as well as industry-specific, executive, and transportation-user professional associations have a strong presence in the institutional landscape of each gateway city governance model. While they are more visible to gateway discussions when it comes to transportation – or if they represent the transportation business – business proxies of all stripes have been involved in advocating for a value chain integration of their city-region on behalf of their membership. They have commissioned reports, convened public officials, and contributed to public debates from a pro-business perspective on GVCs and on the need to strengthen the ability of local private sector actors to compete globally. In this view, the Toronto Region Board of Trade has been at the forefront of consolidating the business component of the urban coalition

– or rather filling the gap left by the lack of a cohesive urban coalition by bringing together the various municipal, sector-specific priorities under the umbrella of innovation corridors. The clearest example of this is the proposal for the Toronto-Waterloo corridor for artificial intelligence. In much the same way, the Chamber of Commerce of Metropolitan Montreal has played a major role in promoting the city's strategic functions, most notably infrastructure development, economic growth, environment, transportation, and social housing. The Chamber of Commerce of Metropolitan Montreal, with other regional chambers, is one of the seven key partners in the Montreal model set up to promote collaboration between economic partners in the region.

In the case of the Atlantic Gateway, the demands from private sector actors, especially in targeted industries, are directly incorporated in planned projects. For instance, the creation of cold chambers infrastructure in the Halifax International Airport has been instrumental in linking the transportation of agri-food and agricultural products to Europe and Asia. The Vancouver gateway regime began with a membership almost exclusively drawn from the transportation industry – trucking, rail, marine terminals, and shipping – and these remain core members of the Gateway Council. Groups with wider business membership have assumed a more prominent role over time, including the BC Chamber of Commerce, which first became involved in the Asia Pacific Gateway Skills Table funded under the APGCI.

The involvement in gateway regimes of associations and proxies that represent businesses beyond the transportation sector arises because the transportation challenges of and within a gateway city are not assessed distinctly from other types of considerations. When advocating for a regional perspective on any action to better position in GVCs, the business case necessarily involves branding, marketing, research and development, legislative and human resources measures, as well as physical transportation infrastructure – or at least, it should. At the same time, business proxies are often perceived to be invisible or marginal in the formal governance models of gateway regimes. This can be explained by the reliance on informal networking and lobbying by and between business actors. It can also be explained by the ways such stakeholders create institutional forums and organizations in support of their agenda. For instance, very much in line with the GVGC, the Toronto Region Board of Trade has created a goods movement council to address the transportation challenges of the city-region, as part of the business case for a better positioning in GVCs. This council is composed of the large companies in the region, transportation stakeholders such as CN and CP, and public officials from key ministries and levels to address issues beyond hard infrastructure, including technology-enabled connectivity and harmonization of municipal bylaws. The influence of such business proxies is found when they advocate on behalf of their members (often with a city-regional perspective and operations) and lobby local and municipal stakeholders on the benefits of a regional approach to solving such issues and for planning with the aim of positioning Canada in the global political economy.

Municipal and Regional Governments

Municipal governments, including regional municipal governments, are also incorporated in various capacities in the four gateway city governance models, albeit differentially. One reason for the differences we observe across the four cases is that the projects they are involved in or affected by vary in important ways. Municipal involvement also depends in part on the willingness of other actors to engage, notably provincial government and private sector actors. Equally important, the limited and differentiated involvement of municipal actors in such governing structures can also be explained by internal motivations, or lack thereof, for getting involved in projects related to transportation infrastructure for international trade purposes. Not only are the linkages between transportation and economic development files not always established within such organizations, in some cases active disengagement strategies are being employed.

In the cases of Montreal and Toronto, gateway projects were both caught at the intersections of the priorities of various desks and branches and distant from the core municipal foci. Although traffic congestion and transport system reliability are frequently mentioned in municipal discussions, the focus for future development is not put on urban freight but on human mobility to support cultural production, innovation, and a knowledge-based and postindustrial economy. As such, the disengagement from both city halls is explained by the priorities of its residents. The priorities of municipalities in greater Vancouver are the same, although this is somewhat ameliorated because goods movement is part of the mandate of the regional transportation agency, TransLink. In contrast, we found significant channels to involve local stakeholders in the case of the Atlantic Gateway, whether through the Halifax Partnership or the Halifax Gateway Council. Of course, some municipalities, such as Peel Region in the Greater Toronto Area and Delta in greater Vancouver, are directly involved in gateway projects. Their incorporation in the gateway regimes is project-based, but this does put them in direct contact with various stakeholders operating on their territory, from federally mandated agencies to private sector actors.

The result is a variegated picture of municipal involvement in gateway regimes across all four cases. Municipal governments are also caught in a logic of coopetition with neighbouring municipalities, as cooperation leads to significant synergies and opportunities notably around strategic clustering activities, while competition drives their desire to host new initiatives on their territory. The dialectical nature of municipalities in interacting among themselves reveals the limits to their engagement with a shared regional vision. Hence, other actors, such as provincial bodies and business proxies, must factor in this competitive reality when seeking to advance projects with municipal partners.

FRAMING URBAN DEMOCRACY AS CITIZEN ENGAGEMENT

In this section, we discuss the ways municipal and urban democracy intersect with gateway city-regional governance. While elected officials and local governments are involved in some public-private forums where gateway-related plans and discussions occur, across all four cases we find that urban democracy has been reduced to a limited form of citizen engagement around the implementation of projects and plans already determined by the gateway regime. Citizen engagement strategies are instead focused on community buy-in and social license, resulting in the incorporation of local concerns in a mediated way. While citizens are aware of the implementation of specific projects, they are rarely involved in discussions on the inherent merits of such initiatives and alternatives to them. We explore how urban democracy is bypassed in gateway city-regional governance and executive democracy is resorted to in its stead, whereby councils and committees, or both, composed of a small number of elected officials are set up. In turn, these officials have little or no accountability to their constituents. Sometimes, membership extends to nonelected actors (as in the Montreal model, for instance) but, here again, with little or no accountability.

At the Margins of Urban Democracy

In each of the four cases, we can identify specific sites, institutions, and processes by which citizen concerns are expressed to the gateway regime, typically via their elected officials. Likewise, provincial and federally mandated agencies have their own consultation processes with the local population. Such consultations may be more informal or temporary in some settings and more institutionalized in others, like Montreal, but they are usually quite fragmented by geography, economic or transportation sector, and issue.

In each locale, specific topics have galvanized urban public conversations and debates at intersections of transportation, economic development, and city planning priorities. Whereas the ports of Halifax and Vancouver are central to the gateway regime in each city-region, they have also been a key concern for residents, notably around questions of livability, as the increased activity of the port equates with less citizen access to the waterfront and increased rail and truck traffic through the city. Engagement with the urban public, including the Halifax Regional Municipality, was central for the design of one of the NTCF-funded projects for a new rail connection between the South End and the Fairview Cove port terminals. In Vancouver, the gateway regime has focused on trade-supporting transportation infrastructure and has underplayed broader but related issues around transit, livability, and urban planning. This is despite being pushed to do so by municipal, environmental, and civil society interests. However, concerns over industrial lands have pushed senior government agencies and business proxies to engage more directly with regional and municipal governments.

Similarly, in Montreal, there has been a growing schism between local dynamics and concerns related to GVCs and gateway infrastructure. Even if the public apparatus of consultation is firmly institutionalized with the OCPM, most concerns address urban planning and renovation, traffic congestion, and transit-oriented development. Questions related to the port development projects are rarely raised. However, there are citizen-led initiatives that take on discussions about such projects, often after they are publicly presented by officials. The Agora métropolitaine (2013), for example, plays a unique institutional role within the metropolitan governance model.

In Toronto, the schism between local concerns and matters related to gateway infrastructure is lived geographically, with varying degrees of awareness from the City of Toronto to the suburbs. Some secondary municipalities and related regional governments are deeply involved in integrating transportation infrastructure for international trade purposes into their economic development goals, including Hamilton, Mississauga, and Vaughan. However, concerns from the core, in Toronto, are mostly focused on land use for local purposes and environmental and livability considerations.

Sites where regional transportation infrastructure for international trade purposes are discussed are distinctly separate from the regular municipal and urban democracy forums. In Vancouver, the initial trade and transport gateway vision was forged by an industry and government agency lobby group. Subsequently, the same evolution can be noted with the GVGC, which has remained focused on representing trade transportation logistics and usage, leaving economic development discussions for others to address, such as the provincial and federal governments. In Halifax, the regional vision for the gateway came out of a series of commissioned reports (i.e., consulting firms like InterVistas and think-tanks like Atlantic Provinces Economic Council) and the convening power of federal agencies like ACOA. Although the Gateway Council was established as a site to connect to local concerns, it was disbanded and replaced by informal discussions between key stakeholders such as ACOA, the Department of Transportation and Infrastructure Renewal, and port and airport authorities.

The Montreal model and its formal constellation of industrial superclusters bureaucratizes this distance even further. This structure provides opportunities for provincial and federal actors to be exposed to discussions and concerns with transportation users but not directly from citizens. In contrast, the several suburban and subregional gateway interests of Toronto have resulted in competition within the city-region rather than a strong regional gateway vision. While the connections between transportation infrastructure and economic development are taken up by municipal governments, stakeholders operating at the regional level such as the Toronto Region Board of Trade (2016) are the main actors pushing for a truly regional discussion over these connections.

In all these contexts, the local gateway regimes have mostly relied on consultation mechanisms and community mitigation to obtain local buy-in in planned initiatives rather than discussing the project rationale itself. For instance, consultations have been systematically conducted by the Port of Halifax and Develop Nova Scotia, with several consultations focused on how to solve the bottlenecks by the port while it commits to community projects like the Halifax Seaport Farmers' Market. In Vancouver, consultations have often led to small concessions to planned projects in the form of parks, bikeways, flood improvements, and grade separations to make infrastructure projects locally acceptable. Such consultations have resulted in mitigation measures rather than opening consideration for underlying drivers of gateway economies. This is also the case in Montreal and in Toronto. On the one hand, transportation-infrastructure projects in Montreal were influenced by local considerations, which led to the use of vacant lots in Assomption Sud and the modernization of the Notre-Dame Est corridor. On the other hand, increased local demand and activity through the region of Toronto has required major transportation expansion projects, notably the CN Milton logistics hub to improve truck-rail intermodality in Halton Region. Despite significant protest and mobilization against the project, a series of community consultations helped frame opponents as not-in-my-backyard, self-interested citizens.

The Limiting Effects of Consultation

Talking with broad publics about trade-supporting transportation infrastructure is difficult at the best of times. Most members of the public have not thought about these issues; those that have views tend to be polarized in camps strongly opposed or in favour. It is hence perhaps not surprising that the main strategy of citizen engagement by the gateway regimes is not with residents directly but through buy-in sought via port or airport authorities or city-regional and municipal governments. But consultation after an agenda has been set reduces the act to a technocratic consideration of implementation; in this way, consultation itself can serve to limit or depoliticize public debate (Purcell 2006).

Indeed, one mark of the success of the gateway regimes documented in this book is that no successful social movement has yet arisen to contest their trade promotion precepts, nor the massive investment of public funds they have secured. The closest thing to an urban social movement opposing the federal trade corridor program arose in Vancouver in the mid-2000s, where a coalition of environmentalist, residential livability, and sustainable transportation activists coalesced in opposition to the provincial government's highway-building gateway program. According to some sources, this opposition caused some consternation among federal officials and the local transportation industry. However, such opposition has receded, both with attention to local planning matters by gateway proponents and with a change in provincial government in 2017.

Pierre Hamel (2008, 65), who has studied urban social movements in Montreal with a focus on deliberative democracy, noted that these movements were greatly influenced by institutional changes such as the introduction of a public consultation policy in the 1980s and the metropolitan reform at the end of the 1990s. But the numerous and complex metropolitan governance models impede citizen consultation at the urban planning and development levels with the result that mobilizations are centred on local or district-wide issues. In Montreal, it seems very difficult for social and political actors to imagine collective action at the scale of the amalgamated city or the city-region, even if the political opportunity structure for such mobilization is wide open given the many (often contradictory) institutional reforms implemented (Boudreau et al. 2006, 49). Consequently, despite the increased importance of both city-wide and city-region levels in the elaboration of strategies to promote economic development and to tackle environmental problems, local actors mobilize mostly at the borough, or even at the district, level and are less inclined to voice their demands at higher levels. These actors tend to "focus their energies to alleviate social problems where their expression is most obvious, that is to say at the scale of the borough or the neighborhood, instead of taking part in political and social conflicts or challenging the authority of elected officials" (Boudreau et al. 2006, 49). In the highly institutionalized Montreal model, residents are not part of the configuration of international trade and gateway stakeholders, hence leaving city-regional and municipal governments playing this role.

We have noted parallel challenges to region-wide social mobilization in relation to the gateway agenda in both Toronto and Vancouver. In Vancouver, the private sector-led coalition has mostly tried to stay away from publicizing its presence and has instead used municipal and provincial government support to build legitimacy for its projects. Therein lies one of the contradictions of the Vancouver gateway regime, which wishes for more regional scale discussion and coordination but which works pragmatically only with the affected municipalities on specific projects. In Toronto, fragmented municipal government structures likewise militate against region-wide collective civic action. In the city-region of Toronto, many citizen engagement strategies involved not-for-profit actors operating at the regional level, including CivicAction and the Toronto Region Board of Trade. These are elite groups led by economic interests, and they participate in gateway discussions as representation for citizen groups, notably because citizen concerns are generally considered separate from transportation for international trade purposes and are limited to local transit concerns. The Halifax Gateway Council was located under the umbrella of the Halifax Partnership, which in turn works closely with the municipality; but the council relies on even closer connections and communication channels with ACOA, the federal agency that affords the bridge to government funding.

In other words, in all cases, public and private elites still dominate city planning related to gateway infrastructure. Laurent Viel et al. (2012) have illustrated this phenomenon by analyzing the role of stakeholders in the planning of the Quartier des Spectacles in the centre of the City of Montreal. Despite the opening to civil society participation throughout, the planning process of this large-scale project was dominated by the urban elites who controlled all strategic decisions. This has led many to argue that the main objective and actual impact of the tools elaborated for civil society actors are information and consent. Jonathan Durand Folco (2016, 89), researcher, activist, and administrator at the Institut de politiques alternatives de Montréal, analyzed the participation instruments provided at the metropolitan level. He concludes that the institutionalization of participation in Montreal has led to the emergence of top-down strategies that inhibit progress toward the ideal of participatory democracy. He denounces this "trivial participation" as part and parcel of a managerial model in which citizens have little impact, a consequence that can lead to disillusionment and demobilization.

Bypassing Urban Democracy

Urban democracy has often been defined to reflect some of the conceptual and practical tenets of Henri Lefebvre's (1974) "right to the city" as a way to fight disenfranchisement and re-empower residents and local communities affected by the consequences of economic processes (Purcell 2006). However, it is increasingly impossible for urban democracy to achieve this goal when Western liberal democratic apparatuses adapt to operating principles to meet global economic requirements (Goodhart 2001; Falk 2000; Purcell 2006). For instance, proponents of major economic projects, notably around GVCs, have often advocated against deliberative democracy to approve their projects. From their perspective, deliberative democracy is too slow and rigid to efficiently address the evolving needs of private sector actors – leading to other forms of private-public governing arrangements and public engagement strategies (Purcell 2006). In this section, we discuss how urban democracy has failed by being predominantly framed as citizen and public engagement, where social license and community buy-in have led to the default consolidation of an executive form of democracy in which the value of projects themselves is not open for discussion.

Executive democracy can be understood as a shift in current democratic practices toward addressing global economic requirements first rather than centring citizen perspectives. While the notion has been used to refer to "elective dictatorship" and other forms of democratic institutions evolving away from constant and active citizen engagement, we consider it as the locale of negotiations for considerations of stakeholders acting at different levels, from the local to the global (Deblock and Brunelle 1998; Lever 2010). For John Dryzek (1996), the need to accommodate global economic requirements locally has led to several shifts in the discursive and practical components of deliberative and participatory democracy, with citizens being increasingly framed through a consumer or user lens and various institutions being inserted between global requirements and local resident concerns to facilitate decision-making processes. In this context, local urban democracy has been seen as a site to fight against undue external influence in city-regional developments. However, any automatic assumptions between what "good" urban democracy praxis looks like and a specific scale of activity may lead to what Mark Purcell (2006, 1925) calls "the local trap": "The local trap in the urban democracy literature is founded on the assumption that devolution of authority will produce greater democracy ... More specifically, the assumption is that the more autonomy local people have over their local urban area, the more democratic and just decisions about that space will be."

Uncritically championing the most localized site as "good" democratic praxis might not take into question the various political forums that are part of the process of metropolization (Lefèvre 2010). Similarly, when the metropolitan scale is framed as the best level at which a balance between urban democracy and global economic requirements can be achieved, we fall into another scalar trap (Tomàs 2012). As such, when locating urban democracy, the best scale cannot be predetermined. City-regional governance involves an ensemble of norms about local democracy, how it translates into multiscalar governance arrangements, and more importantly, what it ought to do in terms of priorities.

City-regional governance arrangements in Canadian gateway cities locate urban democracy at the level of municipal and regional governments, where their role is often reduced to considering a set number of options when deciding on projects, and not discussing their value per se. As Purcell (2006, 1922–23) explains, "Urban governing institutions have been restructured so that they are better able to respond to the needs of capital. They are becoming a less democratic forum for citizens to make decisions and more of a tool to ensure the area competes effectively for capital investment."

To facilitate the local implementation of projects that will facilitate global economic processes, such institutions are preferred because they require stakeholders involved in these projects to address citizen perspectives, which has led many to associate the detachment from local urban democracy praxis as a democratic deficit or failure (Lefèvre 2010). The increasing importance of executive democratic practices in the Canadian context is not specific to urban democracy. Rather, this trend is an extension of practices seen more commonly at other levels of government. A featured tension of the Westminster system, the dominance of the executive over the legislative branch sets the stage for and legitimates more executive forms of democracy, here seen in action in local governance arrangements for transportation-infrastructure projects (Arter 2004).

As Roger Keil and Julie-Anne Boudreau (2005b, 18) have observed, city-regional restructuring in Canada involves unique challenges in expanding, improving, and addressing transportation needs:

> We can assume there are major contradictions between various user groups and speeds: while much "global city"-related transportation of people and goods both internally and externally supports the city's international competitiveness, it actually endangers the social and environmental sustainability of the region. Whereas the globalized travel and trade patterns of the world city explode the regional coherence of production and consumption patterns, urban transportation planning discovers the region as the real scale of solution.

In this view, city-regional governance in Canada, especially when it comes to transportation, requires a clear normative intervention and priorities to be negotiated and determined between opposing priorities, leading to preferred and unique scalar configurations of governance where conventional urban democracy praxis might not be directly incorporated.

Transportation is not the only city-regional matter in which conventional urban democracy praxis is replaced by executive democratic processes. As Vincent Béal (2011) indicates, the management of environmental issues at that scale has evolved from incorporating the citizen perspective more directly between the 1960s and 1980s to being reduced to technical discussions about the management of environmental issues to economic development plans in the 1990s. This change has been accompanied by a turn to the private sector to find sustainable solutions and to elite-led efforts to solve environmental issues. Since the 2000s, they are framed as risks to growth rather than in broader normative terms. Designated as either postdemocratic regimes (Béal 2011) or postpolitical coalitions (Carr and Hesse 2020), many city-regional governance models, for a variety of topics and projects in Canada, have a detached, mediated, or indirect connection to local urban democracy praxis. For Constance Carr and Markus Hesse (2020, 70), this speaks to a "cleft between politics and the political, and is evidenced by the strategic behaviour and the lack of communication on the part of governing authorities in charge of land use and urban planning."

In the case of Canadian city-regional governance, we observe how political opposition to gateway projects is marginalized within technocratic consultation and accommodation processes. This is done by framing opposition and contradictions as technical problems to be addressed outside the public sphere and by legitimating these bureaucratic decisions through a series of public engagement strategies (Carr and Hesse 2020; Wilson and Swyngedouw 2014). For transportation planning, public engagement strategies involve hosting interactive and feedback events that target key stakeholders for consultation and are more generally open to the public to inform residents of upcoming projects. As outcome-oriented processes, these events are not meant to change desired outcomes but to gather information to frame said project as reflecting local community values (Wagner 2013). In many of such public engagement strategies, the consultation processes are framed as "citizen-centric" even if they are not led by citizen concerns or requests (Goodman et al. 2020, 421).

Looking at the smart city technocratic governance arrangement, Rob Kitchin (2014) explains that public engagement strategies are meant to stifle opposing views, as part of a top-down approach to consultation. As Nicole Goodman et al. (2020, 421) indicate, "Examinations of smart city projects show that consultations are mostly top-down and not as citizen-centric as governments would have residents believe despite the citizen-focused framing of smart projects." In their framework, public engagement strategies are found on a spectrum of degrees of local stakeholder involvement in projects, from informing to consulting, involving, collaborating, and empowering residents and local communities (422). As their study reveals, for most projects, the information and consultation strategies are the most utilized. This is notably done by targeting key local public officials and stakeholders rather than the public at large (428).

Such strategies are helpful for proponents of projects to gain a social license to operate or for the reputational capital within the community to achieve the project in ways that are socially acceptable. As Michael Ircha (2014, 5) explains in the case of port authorities in Canada:

> A social license is based on the beliefs, perceptions and opinions of the local community; it is granted by the community ... a social license has to be earned by a port and then maintained through constant vigilance and community involvement. A social license reflects the community's desire for a measure of control over its own future. In other words, the community often wants to participate in the port's development.

A social license is part of a broader goal toward social sustainability or any arrangement that provides an "ability of different kinds of citizen organizations to come together and act on the political system to achieve greater sustainability, particularly in the area of transport" (Sagaris et al. 2017, 733).

In this view, whether it is through official municipal or regional governments or organized by independent entities like port and airport authorities, consultation and accommodation processes for gateway projects are meant to provide legitimacy and some community buy-in to these projects and the stakeholders leading them. Bypassing urban democracy, such processes allow project leads to target key, selected stakeholders for extensive feedback rather than letting broader city forums discuss the projects' value. Urban democracy is replaced by an executive form of democracy focused on technocratic citizen engagement strategies and often limited to discussion of project implementation matters outside of conventional democratic institutions. This means that opposition to these projects struggles to mobilize the public to directly protest the gateway agenda, hence making the link between the city-regional governance models and urban democracy praxis difficult to establish.

Notes

INTRODUCTION

1 We use the terms "integrative trade" and "integrative commerce" interchangeably in this book.

2 The four points Veltz (2004) uses to characterize an "archipelago economy" can be summarized thusly: (i) The local and the global are deeply intertwined. Physical distance is no longer a relevant factor for measuring the intensity and the frequency of relations. (ii) Today, an overall horizontal network within the world economy links the major poles and nodes, and a vertical one connects these nodes. (iii) At the same time, there is a weakening of the links between poles and hinterlands, cores and peripheries. (iv) The present networks of cities differ deeply from the ancient ones in that they do not connect well-identified collective actors but instead are made from a complex addition, crossing, and entanglement of transversal business chains or social and intellectual communities.

CHAPTER 1: CANADIAN CITIES IN THE GLOBAL CONTEXT

1 According to the World Bank's WITS database (https://wits.worldbank.org/CountryProfile/en/CAN), the share of Canadian GDP accounted for by imports plus exports of goods and services increased from 52.9 percent in 1992 to 65.4 percent in 2019. While there were fluctuations over this period – a high of 82.8 percent in 2000 and a low of 58.5 percent in 2009 – the early 1990s mark a turning point leading to a structural increase in Canada's trade exposure (McBride 2005).

2 This database has been previously discussed in detail (see Elsibai et al. 2023).

3 This categorization of the types of stakeholders was created by the authors based on the governance and funding models of actors. Stakeholders participating in a funding proposal, even if part of a larger organization, are identified as separate entities. For instance, government departments and agencies are represented as distinct units, connected to their level of government. Similarly, private sector actors are presented separately from but in relation to associations and forums in which they take part (for more detail, see Elsibai et al. 2023).

CHAPTER 2: VALUE CHAINS, URBAN REGIMES, AND CITY-REGIONAL GOVERNANCE

1 This conclusion ties in with the results of studies made on the so-called second generation of FTAs whereby negotiations to further liberalize sectors (transportation, agriculture, etc.) were entrusted to nonelected bodies of representatives from both public and private sectors set up under the responsibility of ministers and their departments far from any parliamentary oversight. This procedure was criticized at the time by both parliamentarians and civil society representatives because it induced a democratic deficit (Brunelle 2014).

2 Lefebvre (1974, 89) insists on the importance of urbanization as a dominant feature of capitalist production: "The *urban* presents itself as the *significant* whose *signifieds* should be sought out."

3 Dowding (2001, 15) argues that politicians and local bureaucrats must remain central to the analysis of urban regimes, even if they are not seen as the most powerful actors.

CHAPTER 3: A HISTORY OF THE FEDERAL GOVERNMENT'S APPROACH TO GATEWAYS AND TRADE CORRIDORS

1 The commission came out with two reports. To unravel its intricate history, see Keeley (1973).

2 Among the enormities uncovered, one included the delegation of power by the city recorder to foremen who could beat up children and women, another the sixty-hour week for underaged children. But only two recommendations came out of its findings: the creation of the Bureau of Labor Statistics and a bill to make Labor Day a holiday.

3 There is an interesting forerunner worth mentioning here, which is the 1919 Royal Commission on Industrial Relations (known as the Mathers Report). Since the tabling of the Armstrong Report in 1889, overall working conditions had changed little but militancy and the number of strikes had grown significantly. Unfortunately, many of Mathers's recommendations, notably on state insurance against unemployment, minimum wage, and the eight-hour workday, fell under provincial jurisdiction. See Report of Commission appointed under Order-in-Council (P.C. 670) to enquire into industrial relations in Canada together with a minority report and supplementary report, Printed as a supplement to the LABOUR GAZETTE, July 1919.

4 The Rowell-Sirois Report had recommended, inter alia and in conformity with Keynes's theory, that an unemployment insurance scheme should be set up by the federal government. But because provinces had balked at the idea, Prime Minister Mackenzie King addressed London directly. In July 1940, the British Parliament, who could not turn down a request coming from its staunchest ally during one of the war's darkest moments, passed the corresponding amendment to the British North America Act.

5 This was known at the time as "province building" (Young et al. 1984). Prime Minister Pierre Trudeau was a staunch critic of further decentralization of powers toward provincial governments.

6 The report dedicates a subsequent chapter 6, one of its longest, to this option (RCEUDPC 1985, 297–385).

7 The notion of a paradigm shift in this context is critically addressed by some (see Van Assche 2012).
8 This also involved the further integration of the Canadian economy with that of the US – labelled by some its continentalization (Inwood 2005) – an outcome that explains the controversy raised by said recommendation.
9 It bears noting that the federal government and its provincial and territorial counterparts completed their own internal free trade negotiations and signed the Agreement on Internal Trade (AIT) in 1995, after both CUSFTA and NAFTA were signed. In turn, the AIT was replaced by the Canadian Free Trade Agreement (CFTA) on April 7, 2017. "The CFTA better aligns with Canada's commitments under international trade agreements such as the Canada-European Union Comprehensive Economic and Trade Agreement. This reduces compliance costs for Canadian firms who do business both at home and internationally" (from the CFTA website).
10 The Smart Border Accord negotiated in December 2001 was implemented intermittently over the next decade. Initial trusted trader and traveller programs were set up to facilitate integrated cross-border supply chains of large automotive suppliers and producers. They have never really been designed to facilitate "less than truckload" shipping more characteristic of smaller businesses.
11 China became the US's third major trading partner in 1986 and Canada's second in 2000 (or third, when the EU-27 is counted as one), Japan's first in 2005, Brazil's in 2008, South Africa's in 2010, and it overtook the US as the EU's major trading partner in 2020.
12 Incidentally, such a reappraisal raises an interesting question about whether the integrative trade strategy should be seen as a milestone of the same importance as its two predecessors, the export promotion strategy and the import substitution strategy, respectively, or as a mere offshoot of the export promotion strategy.
13 Both the US and Mexico also resorted to a series of bilateral negotiations to project their national interests and expand their commercial outreach.
14 This approach would prove foresighted when the US government renegotiated NAFTA and replaced it with a more exacting Canada-United States-Mexico Agreement in July 2020. Trade with non-US partners could offset inter alia the tighter rules of origin imposed by the agreement.
15 Art. 92 para. 8 of the British North America Act of 1867 states: "In each Province the Legislature may exclusively make Laws in relation to Matters coming within the Classes of Subjects next hereinafter enumerated; that is to say: ... Municipal Institutions in the Province."
16 The MSUA's mandate was "to plan, coordinate and develop new urban policies; integrate federal urban priorities with other federal policies and programs; and develop coordinating intergovernmental relationships" (Tolley and Young 2001).
17 Using "a policy community and networks framework" to study the "role of non-state actors in placing urban affairs on the public agenda," Zachary Spicer (2011) provides an illuminating sociopolitical history of the MSUA.
18 "To a significant degree, municipal governments depend on federal understanding of local needs and conditions; at the same time, the national economy is becoming more dependent on cities. Relations between local and federal governments are

difficult to develop, however, because of the provinces' exclusive jurisdiction over local government … In effect, provincial law and judicial interpretation have confined local governments to negative approaches to the control, rather than the stimulation, of urban development" (RCEUDPC 1985, vol. 3, 374–5).

19 "A number of spokespersons for local governments suggested that the federal government re-establish such a department to provide a forum for direct dealings between municipal authorities and the federal Cabinet and senior bureaucracy" (RCEUDPC Report 1985, vol. 3, 378).

20 Called "multilevel governance" by Champagne (2014, 164), the term is now widely adopted by academics.

21 According to the PACC Committee Report, the CWIP

> was remarkably successful from several perspectives. As a collaborative arrangement, the Program involved the mobilization, coordination, and co-operation of three levels of government. This level of co-operation between Canadian governments is not often achieved; that it was in this instance is a credit to all participants. It is thus hoped that from this perspective the Program will serve as a model for future efforts ... The funding formula (roughly one-third of the costs contributed by each partner) allowed the Program's partners to support projects collectively that they could not afford individually ... The Program resulted in the implementation of more than 17,000 engineering and construction projects nation-wide. (PACC 2000)

22 There are two programs managed by the department that have their own federal legislation: the Canada Strategic Infrastructure Fund (2002) and the Gas Tax Fund (2005). According to Adams and Maslove (2009), "In 2006–2007, intergovernmental transfers in Canada amounted to approximately $125 billion ... Of this, approximately $1.8 billion was allocated to Infrastructure Canada, of which $590 million represented the Gas Tax Fund (GTF) transfer." In this regard, the Gas Tax Fund was "the most significant federal fiscal intervention into urban affairs in more than a quarter of a century" (Graham and Andrew 2014).

23 For a short description of each, see Shaker (2004).

24 Created in 1976, the FCM, together with the Big City Mayors Association, "have played an important role in stimulating changes in Canadian federalism ... Since 1980, the FCM has 'sought the recognition of municipalities as a distinct level of government under the new constitution'" (Champagne 2014, 168; quoting Dewing et al. 2006, 10).

25 For the larger cities' role, notably the Big City Mayor's Caucus, in pushing this agenda, see Mau (2005, 10–12).

26 This speech led to Martin's dismissal from Cabinet. Chrétien was quite sensitive on this issue since the debacle of his mentor Trudeau's MSUA in 1979. For his part, Martin would go on making speeches on his "New Deal" once out of office, for example, at the Creative Cities Conference in May 2003 (Mau 2005, 25). Chrétien had nevertheless appointed Judy Sgro to head the Prime Minister's Caucus Task Force on Urban Issues, in May 2001, but failed to act on her report. For a résumé of the task force's report and recommendation on the development of an urban strategy and the implementation of an action plan, see Mau (2005, 12–13).

27 According to Tim Mau (2005, 27):

> Rather than create a new department, which likely would have resulted in serious opposition from the provincial governments fearing overt federal intrusion into their constitutional area of responsibility, Martin chose instead to establish a Cities Secretariat in the Privy Council Office (PCO). This new unit was established to improve the government's coordination of urban issues and to assist in both the development and implementation of the "New Deal."

28 "The Conservatives were ideologically opposed to the federal government having any direct dealings with municipalities, preferring instead to talk only to provinces" (Godfrey 2009).

29 In 1982, the FCM was "near demise," according to Chénier (2009).

30 Note that the CTC's jurisdiction on pipelines does not extend to those carrying oil and its products, which are regulated by the National Energy Board (NEB).

31 The US had previously adopted a series of measures all favouring market-based principles and practices in the transport sector, among them the Airline Deregulation Act, 1978, the Staggers Rail Act, 1980, and the Motor Carrier Act, 1980.

32 "The Canada Marine Act enacted in 1998 created a national system of ports vital to domestic and international trade. The 17 Canada Port Authorities (18 since the inclusion of the Port of Oshawa in February 2012) are authorized under their Letters Patent to manage and operate specific ports at arm's-length from the federal government on a commercial basis, and are financially self-sufficient" (Transport Canada 2012).

33 The regime in question is still inefficiently connected to local stakeholders and other levels of governments: "Airports have become powerful levers of economic growth in various regions of Canada. It would seem appropriate thus for the provinces and municipalities to play a more significant role in the development and strategy of airports in their proximity, including in facing up to the competition from American border airports" (Roy and Nadeau 2014, 58). This also applies to seaport authorities.

34 A series of brochures entitled *Freedom to Move*, published in 1985, explains the agency's role: "The powers of the new Agency are designed to ensure responsiveness to public interest, industry needs and policy direction from the government. The Agency has authority to grant transportation licenses, review public complaints and help resolve disputes between shippers and transportation firms" (Transport Canada 1985).

35 The prevalence of provincial trucking regimes, along with limited federal enforcement capacity once licences were issued, gave provinces a lead role in trucking sector deregulation.

36 The North American Forum on Integration was a civil society organization created in 2005. This quote was on its webpage. The quote was removed when the North American International Trade Corridor Partnership's website was taken down after its merger with NASCO, in 2005, but a slide presentation was recovered using the Internet Archive. The recovered slides may be viewed at: http://www.channelingreality.com/NAU/Naitpc_slides.htm.

37 As far as rail transport is concerned, the shift toward continental integration was much more advanced.

38 One such megaproject was the Trans-Texas Corridor project, a four-thousand-mile network of existing and new toll roads that would have created the largest private highway system in America. The project was dropped in 2005.

39 Statement to the Standing Committee on Foreign Affairs and International Trade on Canadian Foreign Policy Objectives, by John J. Noble, retired Canadian diplomat and director of research and communications at the Centre for Trade Policy and Law, Carleton University. March 27, 2003. www.carleton.ca/ctpl/pdf/papers/scfaitnoble.pdf.

40 The task force was cochaired by former Canadian deputy prime minister and minister of finance John P. Manley, former Mexican finance minister Pedro Aspe, and former Massachusetts governor William Weld.

41 Council on Foreign Relations, *Trinational Call for a North American Economic and Security Community by 2010*. March 2005. https://www.cfr.org/news-releases/trinational-call-north-american-economic-and-security-community-2010.

42 Sturgeon explicitly follows Peter Dicken (1992, 5) here.

43 "'Canada's prosperity and quality of life depend on our success as a trading nation,' said the Honourable Peter MacKay, Minister of the Atlantic Canada Opportunities Agency. 'An Atlantic Gateway strategy will benefit the Atlantic region and all of Canada by taking advantage of the region's geographical position and transportation assets'" (Government of Canada 2007a).

44 Under the three following programs: the Canada Health Transfer, the Canada Social Transfer, and Labour Market Agreements.

45 On federal ministries responsible for infrastructure and communities:

> From 2006 to 2013, infrastructure and communities were the responsibility of the Ministry of Transport, which was informally styled Minister of Transport, Infrastructure and Communities. From 2013 to 2015, infrastructure and communities were the responsibility of the Minister of Intergovernmental Affairs, then styled Minister of Infrastructure, Communities and Intergovernmental Affairs. (Technically, the portfolios of infrastructure and intergovernmental affairs were both the responsibility of the President of the Queen's Privy Council for Canada.) From 2015 to 2021, during the 29th Canadian Ministry, the portfolio was assigned its own ministry. (Wikipedia, "Minister of Housing, Infrastructure and Communities," last modified June 10, 2025, 01:40 [UTC], https://en.wikipedia.org/wiki/Minister_of_Housing,_Infrastructure_and_Communities)

46 The three objectives are: "Create long-term economic growth to build a stronger middle class; support the resilience of communities and transition to a clean growth economy; and build social inclusion and socio-economic outcomes for all Canadians" (Government of Canada 2016a).

47 The bill was adopted in early 2018. In his presentation, Minister of Transport Marc Garneau underlined that Bill C-49 followed on the recommendations made in the *Canadian Transportation Act Review Report*. The review was chaired by David Emerson and was set up by the Conservative government in 2014. The report *Pathways: Connecting Canada's Transportation System to the World* was submitted to the minister in 2015 (Government of Canada 2016b). This sequence illustrates the continuity between governments on these issues.

CHAPTER 5: TORONTO AND THE CONTINENTAL GATEWAY

1 One possible explanation for this neglect is that in the three elections of 2006, 2008, and 2011, the Conservative party won ten, ten, and five seats, respectively, in Quebec out of seventy-eight, none from the Montreal area.

2 In this chapter, we refer to traditional city centre/suburban dynamics to understand key trends and evolutions within the city-region of Toronto. This is used to highlight the relationships between the centre and its peripheries within the city-region. Many secondary cities of the region and neighbouring municipalities of the City of Toronto are centres of activity in themselves.

3 For instance, the regions of Peel and Durham have a similar structure in the sharing of road management responsibilities, between provincial roads, regional roads, and local (municipal) roads. While the region of Peel's jurisdiction includes a short railway line besides the activities of CN and CP on the territory, along with ViaRail and Metrolinx operations, Pearson International Airport is under direct federal authority. In contrast, the region of Durham does not operate any rail line, depending solely on the activities of CN, CP, ViaRail, and Metrolinx. However, Durham's City of Oshawa owns and operates the Oshawa Executive Airport, while the Port of Oshawa is under direct federal authority, which combines the operations of the ports of Hamilton and Oshawa.

4 In 2023, the Progressive Conservative government of Doug Ford announced its intention to dissolve Peel Region so that larger municipalities like Mississauga can be independent municipal units. Later the same year, the dissolution was abandoned due to the expected costs of such an initiative. Instead, the provincial government committed to examining and improving services to all residents of Peel Region.

5 The unevenness of local development is an additional challenge, if only to help facilitate a more coherent vision for York Region as a whole.

6 Toronto Global (2019) is a not-for-profit created to facilitate foreign direct investment and business in the region of Toronto.

CHAPTER 6: MONTREAL AND THE CONTINENTAL GATEWAY

1 Formerly known as "reconstituted cities," an expression that refers to the fifteen cities (some with a sizeable concentration of an anglophone population) that were allowed by the Liberal government of Jean Charest (2003–12) to "demerge" in 2005 and to opt out of the "one island, one city" project spearheaded by the PQ government in 2000 under Bill 170 (*Loi portant sur la réforme de l'organisation territoriale municipale des régions métropolitaines de Montréal, de Québec et de l'Outaouais* 2000, ch. 56). See Cardinal (2000).

2 Here is the breakdown of the sixty-five city council members: the city mayor, eighteen other borough mayors, who are also city councillors, and the city's own councillors. On election day, in the fifty-eight electoral districts of the nineteen boroughs, a total of 103 elective offices are filled: the office of city mayor, who is also the mayor of Ville-Marie borough, plus another eighteen boroughs mayors, who also serve as city councillors, plus forty-six other city councillors, plus thirty-eight borough councillors.

3 One representative per city with the exception of one for both Dorval and Dorval Island and two for Dollard-des-Ormeaux.

4 Greater Montreal also encompasses all or part of fourteen Regional County Municipalities (RCMs) or equivalent territories. Note, in passing, that Statistics Canada's definition of a Census Metropolitan Area (CMA) is not geographically coterminous with the territory of the municipalities making up the territory of the MMC.

5 The list includes the mayors of Montreal (plus thirteen members designated by the city council), Laval (plus two), Longueuil (plus two), as well as four mayors from the North Shore and four from the South Shore. The members of the executive are the mayors of Montreal and three boroughs on the island, the mayors of Laval and Repentigny on the North Shore, and the mayors of Longueuil and Candiac on the South Shore.

6 The creation of the MMC by the Quebec government in 2000 encroached upon some of the RCM's prerogatives because sixty-one – out of its eighty-two – municipalities belonged to RCMs. Relations between the two were quite difficult with the result that the MMC found itself in a deadlock during the first decade of its existence.

7 The Montreal Agglomeration, the Longueuil Agglomeration, and Laval are territories equivalent to an RCM according to the *Loi sur l'exercice de certaines compétences municipales dans certaines Agglomérations (RLRQ c E-20.001)*.

8 Also known under their French acronym PMDE, for Plan métropolitain de développement économique.

9 The most recent *Metropolitan Economic Development Plan 2022–2031* proposes a different approach and defines four strategic axes (energy transition, intelligent and eco-responsible organization, strengthening the ecosystem, and skills development for tomorrow) and thirteen objectives. In it there is no mention of a Montreal model while both CargoM's and Montreal International's roles have been downplayed and the Table métropolitaine de développement économique has risen in importance. Our analysis will concentrate on the MEDP 2015–20.

10 Better known by its French acronym, PMAD, or Plan métropolitain d'aménagement et de développement. Cahiers Métropolitains (Cahiers 2016, 67) has this to say about the plan:

> The PMAD is the [Montreal Metropolitan Community's] flagship plan. It acts on elements that will help structure the metropolitan area's urbanization process to make it more attractive and competitive from a sustainable development perspective. In particular, the plan underlines the importance of proper management of urbanization, focuses on integrated land-use and transportation planning, and promotes the protection and enhancement of natural areas to ensure the attractiveness and competitiveness of Greater Montréal. The PMAD proposes three major priorities related to land use, transportation and environment, which are divided into 15 objectives and 33 criteria.

11 The Land Use Planning and Development Plan (LUPDP) is better known by its French acronym SAD, for Schéma d'aménagement et de développement de l'agglomération de Montréal.

12 See *Loi sur l'aménagement et l'urbanisme* (RLRQ, chapitre A-19.1), also known under its acronym LAU.

13 The two previous plans covered the years 2010–15 and 2005–10. The first plan, *Cap sur le monde* (MMC 2003), dated February 2005, is the one that promoted and defined a cluster strategy influenced by Porter (1998). The third plan is also the outcome of a series of initiatives: the Greater Montreal Innovation Strategy, 2007; the Mission Statement for the setting up of clusters, 2007; the Greater Montreal Master Plan for FDI, 2011–15; the Plan for the reception of Strategic Talents, 2011–15; and, finally, the Strategy for the Development of Industrial Spaces, which was part of the Action Plan of the PMAD, adopted in 2013.

14 "The metropolitan cluster strategy is the core of the MMC's MEDP" (MMC 2015, 14). Mentioned 182 times, the notion of "cluster" takes the high road in the plan, over Canada (forty-seven) and Québec (fifty-one). For more on the cluster, see http://grappesmontreal.ca/metropolitan-clusters/montreals-metropolitan-clusters/?L=1.

15 "Created in 1996, Montréal International (MI) is the result of a private-public partnership. Its mission is to contribute to the economic development of Greater Montréal and enhance its international status." From its website: https://www.montreal international.com/en/.

16 In French, GEM-Mtl, Gouvernance économique métropolitaine-Montréal.

17 The observatory draws up the scorecards that provide a follow-up on the implementation of the various plans adopted by the MMC.

18 The eight challenges of the MEDP (MMC 2015) are: (i) a low productivity level, (ii) a low level of university graduation, (iii) inefficiency between labour supply and business needs, (iv) low private investment, (v) underdevelopment of new industrial spaces, (vi) deficiencies in transport infrastructures, (vii) unfocused positioning at the international level, and (viii) untapped creative industries. The low level of university graduation is quite worrisome considering that the Chamber of Commerce of Metropolitan Montreal promotes the city as the second most important university city in North America after Boston, with a total of 170,000 students, 20,000 of which are foreign students. The primary objective of the MEDP is carried over from the previous plan: to "generate prosperity through the principles of sustainable development ... and to position Greater Montréal among the top 10 North American metropolitan areas in terms of GDP per capita growth by 2030" (39). But a more realistic intermediary objective proposes "to stabilize Greater Montréal's position among the top 15 North American metropolitan areas" (40). There are also five secondary objectives and three initiatives: (i) in terms of GDP growth, (ii) unemployment rate, (iii) university graduation rate, (iv) private investment growth, and (v) sustainable development and inclusive growth, to which are added three initiatives: (a) double the amount of FDI by 2018, (b) set up meetings to attract strategic talents, both to be carried out by Montreal International, and (c) the enhancement of agricultural activities through Agricultural zone development plans or PDZAs (43).

19 The excerpt of the first strategic axis on logistics and transportation reads like a cut-down forerunner of the Quebec government's Maritime Strategy (MS) – "cut-down" because the MS uses a broader array of concepts, among them, logistics chains

(Gouvernement du Québec 2015, 9, 32); innovation chains (MMC 2015, 20, 43, 71); global supply chains (35, 71); and value-added services (71).

20 In terms of stakeholders, it should be underlined for future reference that the "Plan will broaden the scope of the agora (set up under the PMAD, D.B.) by addressing economic issues that are of particular concern to elected officials, citizens, and civil society" (MMC 2015, 58). One "inconsistency" in the results of the MEDP was the strategy put forward at one time by the city of Contrecoeur and the city of Vaudreuil, whereby the first promoted itself as an extension of Port of Montreal on the South Shore, while the second sought to position itself as a railway hub with direct access to the US. The MMC has since reached out to integrate both projects in its overall planning.

21 The first version of the plan was adopted early in 2005 by the MMC and was subsequently hotly contested and debated during public consultations held in June 2005. Following this episode, the MMC would find itself in a deadlock over the issue of division of powers with the RCMs. A new compromise between the two would be reached in 2008, which would pave the way for the adoption of the PMAD as it stands today (Arcand 2013, 40).

22 The word "centre" is italicized because it was omitted in the PMAD, thereby implying that the entirety of the CMA was concerned, although the plan itself borrowed from a study carried out on its behalf by Lambert (2010), which established quite clearly that the Island of Montreal was concerned here, not the CMA at large (26). The rest of the excerpt is explicit in this regard. This conflation probably results from the fact that the island of Montreal has no political existence and that its Agglomeration Council has a weak administrative structure.

23 As precedent, this MoU is certainly interesting, but in practical terms it served no purpose since the city was virtually bypassed by the federal government's investments in infrastructure while the Conservatives were in power in Ottawa.

24 About the agora and the observatory, the MEDP says the agora will allow the MMC "to present the PMAD's evolution, as expressed in the future PMAD scorecard," while the observatory helps disseminate information and data on Greater Montreal (MMC 2012, 206). See also Agora métropolitaine (2018).

25 This consultation mechanism is called Table Québec-Grand Montréal pour l'aménagement et le développement du territoire.

26 See Agglomeration Council (2015). The monitoring of LUPDP is assured by the Commission sur le schéma d'aménagement et de développement de Montréal, which is responsible for the follow-up on its recommendations.

27 Notably in its introduction and chapter 1.

28 The plan's chapter 4 lists some twenty-four such actions.

29 In French, "Accélérer Montréal. Stratégie de développement économique 2018–2022."

30 These action plans are quite detailed. For instance, in no. 7, on the economic development strategy ("Développement économique du territoire"), Axis 3 proposes "to improve access to employment centers and the fluidity of freight transportation," for which Strategy no. 3 provides, inter alia, the creation of an advisory committee

composed of experts and others from the business sector with experience, notably, "in sustainable urban development and real estate (or land development)."

31 See, for example, the workshop organized by the Lawrence National Centre for Policy and Management, March 9–11, 2008.

32 See TVA CIMT/CHAU 2019.

33 The MMC's report lists some twenty concrete actions and projects for Greater Montreal that should be completed to enhance Quebec's share of the continental gateway (MMC 2009).

34 The CRÉ de Montréal would be replaced by Concertation Montréal, which has nothing to do with either transport or logistics.

35 See Port of Montreal, "Neighbours of the Port," https://www.port-montreal.com/en/the-port-of-montreal/social-responsibility/community/neighbours-of-the-port.

36 CIRRELT is the Centre interuniversitaire de recherche sur les réseaux d'entreprise, la logistique et le transport (Interuniversity Research Centre on Entreprise Networks, Logistics and Transportation); KHEOPS is the Consortium international de recherche sur la gouvernance des grands projets d'infrastructure (International Research Consortium on the Governance of Large Infrastructure Projects).

37 "Obviously, we will see to it that Port de Montréal figures prominently in the government of Quebec's Maritime Strategy, as well as in the gateway and corridor strategy of the federal government" (Coderre 2015).

38 There are also at least six smaller parties, some with barely one or two elected representatives.

39 Here are two excerpts from said program: "e) Require Aéroports de Montréal, Transport Canada, Transport Québec and the Port of Montreal to provide objective and transparent data on air, road and maritime traffic and the noise generated by transportation activities in Montréal; f) Require the Port of Montreal to provide objective and transparent data on maritime traffic and noise from port and train shipment activities in Montreal," Projet Montréal (2017).

40 Previously known as Équipe Denis Coderre pour Montréal. Coderre was a Liberal member of Parliament in Ottawa (1997–2013), while Valérie Plante was a former social activist.

41 Ms. Plante would handily win a second term, beating her opponent by 14 percentage points or nearly sixty thousand votes.

42 The Office de consultation publique de Montréal (OCPM)/Montreal Public Consultation Office is an independent organization whose mission is to carry out public consultation mandates entrusted to it by Montréal's city council or the executive committee. It was created in 2002 under Bill 170, which also provided for the amalgamation of the island of Montreal's municipalities into a single city. It survived the demerger organized by the Charest Liberals in 2006.

43 Official website of the Montreal Ombudsman: https://ombudsmandemontreal.com/en/.

44 ZIP Jacques-Cartier Committee's mission is the rehabilitation of the St. Lawrence River from a sustainable perspective. It is one of twelve such ZIP committees of an umbrella NGO called Stratégies Saint-Laurent. See their website https://www.strategiessl.qc.ca/comites-zip/comite-zip-jacques-cartier.

45 Some of the most significant among these propositions would be summarily criticized by representatives from the private sector and would not make it into the twenty-seven recommendations of the report. For example, the one on access to the river would be picked up by the MMCC, which would stress that such an opening should not impair industrial and port activities (OCPM 2019, 45). The OCPM (2019, 75) would merely recommend that a view of the river should be provided.

46 The borough mayor, the Conseil régional de l'environnement (CRE), the Association québécoise des médecins pour l'environnement (AQME), and many citizens expressed their dismay at this decision. The only requirement imposed on the company was that it should limit its operations between 7 a.m. and 7 p.m., instead of the twenty-four hours planned at first. See Corriveau and Shields (2022).

47 This is done by setting up councils and/or committees composed of a small number of elected officials, as we saw in the cases of the MMC and the AC, that have little or no accountability to their own party or to their constituents. Sometimes, membership extends to other actors (as in the Montreal model, for instance), but here again, with little or no accountability.

CHAPTER 7: HALIFAX AND THE ATLANTIC GATEWAY

1 Major air exports via the airport include seafood, electronics, machinery, and industrial equipment. As indicated in the reports and as highlighted by several stakeholders, the negotiation of the Canada-European Union Comprehensive Economic and Trade Agreement played an important role in the decision to invest in air cargo services, since HIAA expected an increase in exports of sea products to Europe, especially lobster.

2 Investment in infrastructure includes several Post-Panamax cranes by the Fairview Cove Container Terminal (Ceres) and South End Container Terminal (Halterm) operators to handle super Post-Panamax vessels (HGC 2012; Interview HPA). These investments were made by the Port Authority and terminal operators.

3 As of 2016, there were 419 miles of main track operating in the province. CN owned 160 miles, Cape Breton and Central Nova Scotia Railway owned 245 miles, and Sydney Coal Railway owned 14 miles (CPCS 2016). The rail corridor that connects the Halifax Gateway to central and Western Canada and the US is operated by CN (APEC, 2006). The CN Intermodal Terminal is located near the Fairview Cove Container Terminal. The Fairview Cove Container Terminal and the South End Container Terminal both have on-dock rail (HGC 2012). CN is the only Class I freight railway serving Nova Scotia, serving Halterm and Ceres. In addition, the CN Autoport is connected to CN branch lines coming out from Windsor Junction through Dartmouth, and CN Intermodal Terminal is located across from the HPA Richmond Terminals (CPCS 2016).

4 In this trade mission, seventeen senior executives from key transportation modes related to the Atlantic Gateway and Trade Corridor transportation network joined the minister of ACOA.

5 Develop Nova Scotia owns Centre for Ocean Ventures and Entrepreneurship, but it is led by the Institute for Ocean Research Enterprise (IORE).

6 The Community Planning and Economic Development standing committee recommended that Regional Council direct staff to develop, together with the Halifax

Partnership, an action plan for years three–five of the Halifax Economic Growth Plan 2017–21, in accordance with the approach outlined in this report.

7 A Japanese company known as NYK.

8 These include Armour Transportation Group, Atlantic Canada Opportunities Agency, Clarke IT Solutions Inc., CN Rail, Destination Halifax, Gateway Facilities ULC, Greater Halifax Partnership, Halifax Chamber of Commerce, Halterm Container Terminal Limited, Halifax Harbour Bridges, Halifax International Airport Authority, Halifax Port Authority, Halifax Regional Municipality, Nova Scotia Business Inc., Nova Scotia Department of Transportation and Infrastructure Renewal, Nova Scotia Gateway Secretariat, Oceanex Inc., and Transport Canada.

References

Adams, Erika, and Allan M. Maslove. 2009. "Innovations in Transfer Payments to Local Governments: The Case of the Gas Tax Fund." Paper submitted to the Canadian Political Science Association 81st Conference, Carleton University, Ottawa, Ontario, May 27–28. https://carleton.ca/cure/wp-content/uploads/Adams-Maslove_CPSA_Paper_May15th-092.pdf.

Addie, Jean-Paul. 2013. "Metropolitics in Motion: The Dynamics of Transportation and State Reterritorialization in the Chicago and Toronto City-Regions." *Urban Geography*, 34 (2): 188–217.

Aderneck, E. 2023. "Industrial Lands Densification and Intensification: Profiling Planning Policies and Development Projects in Metro Vancouver." *PND Magazine*, January.

Agglomeration Council. 2015. *Schéma d'aménagement et de développement de l'agglomération de Montréal* (Land Use Planning and Development Plan). https://mtl.ged.montreal.ca/constellio/?collection=mtlca&portal=REPDOCVDM#!displayDocument/00000014149.

Agora métropolitaine. 2013. *Rapport: Agora Métropolitaine 2013.* https://cmm.qc.ca/wp-content/uploads/2019/04/20131022_agora_metropolitaine_rapport.pdf.

–. 2018. *Rapport de l'Agora Métropolitaine 2018.* https://cmm.qc.ca/nouvelles/rapport-de-lagora-2018-il-faut-accelerer-la-cadence-pour-atteindre-les-objectifs-du-pmad/.

Amador, João, and Sónia Cabral. 2016. "Global Value Chains: A Survey of Drivers and Measures." *Journal of Economic Surveys*, 30 (2): 278–301. https://doi.org/10.1111/joes.12097.

Andersson, Åke E. 2000. "Gateway Regions to the World – An Introduction." In *Gateways to the Global Economy,* edited by Åke E. Andersson and David E. Andersson. Edward Elgar Publishers.

Andersson, Åke E., and David E. Andersson, eds. 2000. *Gateways to the Global Economy*. Edward Elgar Publishing.

Andrew, Caroline, and Jeff Morrison. 1995. "Canada Infrastructure Works: Between 'Picks and Shovels' and the Information Highway." In *How Ottawa Spends 1995–96: Mid-Life Crises,* edited by Susan D. Phillips. Carleton University Press.

APEC (Atlantic Provinces Economic Council). 2006. *The Changing Global Economy: The Implications and Opportunities for Transportation in Atlantic Canada.*

–. 2015. *The Changing Global Market for Atlantic Manufacturing.*

–. 2016. *Trade Barriers in Atlantic Canada: Opportunities for Regulatory Reform.* https://cdn.ymaws.com/atlanticeconomiccouncil.ca/resource/collection/1E9C10E4-AEFE-4004-BF68-780000EB3733/Research_Report_-_Trade_Barriers__October_2016_.pdf.

APGST (Asia Pacific Gateway Skills Table). 2012. *Connecting Canada's Pacific Gateway Enhancing Planning Capacity in the Metro Vancouver Region.* Report commissioned by APGST.

Arcand, Ève. 2013. *Une nouvelle collaboration entre les organismes d'aménagement du territoire et des transports collectifs ? Le cas du Plan métropolitain d'aménagement et de développement de la Communauté métropolitaine de Montréal,* Mémoire, Institut National de la Recherche Scientifique.

Arteau, Richard. 2014. *L'industrie des transports de marchandises et de la logistique dans la région et dans l'agglomération de Montréal. Tendances et dynamiques actuelles.* Document préparatoire au schéma d'aménagement et de développement de l'agglomération de Montréal, Direction de l'urbanisme, Montréal. Mars.

Arter, David. 2004. "Parliamentary Democracy in Scandinavia." *Parliamentary Affairs,* 57 (3): 581–600.

August, Martine. 2020. "The Financialization of Canadian Multi-Family Rental Housing: From Trailer to Tower." *Journal of Urban Affairs,* 42 (7): 975–97.

Baldwin, Richard, and Javier Lopez-Gonzalez. 2015. "Supply-Chain Trade: A Portrait of Global Patterns and Several Testable Hypotheses." *The World Economy,* 38 (11): 1682–721. https://doi.org/https://doi.org/10.1111/twec.12189.

Bareman, Julia. 2015. "Provincial Leadership and Intergovernmental Collaboration in the Canadian Federation." Master's thesis, University of Victoria.

Bathelt, Harald, Anders Malmberg, and Peter Maskell. 2004. "Clusters and Knowledge: Local Buzz, Global Pipelines and the Process of Knowledge Creation." *Progress in Human Geography,* 28 (1): 31–56. https://doi.org/10.1191/0309132504ph469oa.

Béal, Vincent. 2011. "Urban Governance, Sustainability and Environmental Movements: Post-Democracy in French and British Cities." *European, Urban and Regional Studies,* 19 (4): 404–19.

Benito, Gabriel R. G., Bent Petersen, and Lawrence S. Welch. 2019. "The Global Value Chain and Internalization Theory." *Journal of International Business Studies,* 50 (8): 1414–23. https://doi.org/10.1057/s41267-019-00218-8.

Bird, James. 1983. "Gateways: Slow Recognition but Irresistible Rise." *Tijdschrift voor Economische en Sociale Geografie,* 74 (3): 196–202. https://doi.org/https://doi.org/10.1111/j.1467–9663.1983.tb01525.x.

Blanco, Ismael. 2015. "Between Democratic Network Governance and Neoliberalism: A Regime-Theoretical Analysis of Collaboration in Barcelona." *Cities*, 44: 123–30. https://doi.org/10.1016/j.cities.2014.10.007.

Blank, Stephen. 2008. "Trade Corridors and North American Competitiveness." *American Review of Canadian Studies*, 38 (2): 231–37. https://doi.org/10.1080/02722010809481712.

Borja, Jordi, and Manuel Castells. 1997. *Local and Global: Management of Cities in the Information Age*. Earthscan.

Boudreau, Julie-Anne. 2003. "Questioning the Use of 'Local Democracy' as a Discursive Strategy for Political Moblization in Los Angeles, Montreal and Toronto." *International Journal of Urban and Regional Research*, 27 (4): 793–810.

Boudreau, Julie-Anne, Pierre Hamel, Bernard Jouve, and Roger Keil. 2006. "Comparing Metropolitan Governance: The Cases of Montreal and Toronto." *Progress in Planning*, 66: 7–59. http://aitec.reseau-ipam.org/IMG/pdf/progress_in_planning.pdf.

–. 2007. "New State Spaces in Canada: Metropolitanization in Montreal and Toronto Compared." *Urban Geography*, 28: 30–53.

Bradford, Neil. 2018. "A National Urban Policy for Canada? The Implicit Federal Agenda." *IRPP Insight*, 24, Montreal, Institute for Research on Public Policy. https://irpp.org/wp-content/uploads/2018/11/A-National-Urban-Policy-for-Canada-The-Implicit-Federal-Agenda.pdf.

Brenner, Neil. 2004. *New State Spaces. Urban Governance and the Rescaling of Statehood*. Oxford University Press.

Brunelle, Dorval. 1997. *Droit et Exclusion. Critique de l'ordre Libéral*. L'Harmattan.

–. 2006. "The US, Its Reluctant Satellites and the Issue of Deep Integration in the Americas." *Cahier de recherche Continentalisation*, Groupe de recherche sur l'intégration continentale, Université du Québec à Montréal.

–. 2007. *From World Order to Global Disorder: States, Markets, and Dissent*. UBC Press.

–, ed. 2014. "Introduction. L'ALENA et Ses Prolongements." In *L'ALENA à 20 ans: un accord en sursis, un modèle en essor*. Éditions IEIM.

–. 2020. "Montréal: chaînes de valeur, développement économique et déficit démocratique." *Revue Interventions économiques*, 63. https://doi.org/10.4000/interventionseconomiques.9341.

Brunelle, Dorval, Claudia De Fuentes, Peter Hall, and Jean Michel Montsion. 2021. "Global Value Chains and Regimes of Urban Governance: A Comparison of Four Canadian Gateway Cities. *Canadian Journal of Urban Research*, 30 (1): 87–101.

Bula, Frances. 2012. "Industrial Land Bank Urged for Vancouver." *Globe and Mail*, December 9.

Burghardt, Andrew F. 1971. "A Hypothesis about Gateway Cities." *Annals of the Association of American Geographers*, 61 (2): 269–85. https://doi.org/10.1111/j.1467-8306.1971.tb00782.x.

Cahiers métropolitains. 2016. "Portrait du Grand Montréal. Édition 2016." Septembre. https://cmm.qc.ca/wp-content/uploads/2019/02/cahiersMetropolitains_no05.pdf.

CAI Global. 2015. Étude de positionnement économique pour le secteur de l'Assomption Sud, CargoM. https://ville.montreal.qc.ca/pls/portal/docs/page/arrond_mhm_fr/media/documents/resume_etude_cai_global.PDF.

Canadian Press. 2021. "Infrastructure Bank Chief Clashes with MPs over Private-Sector Investment." *CTV News*, March 23. https://www.ctvnews.ca/business/infrastructure-bank-chief-clashes-with-mps-over-private-sector-investment-1.5358622.

Canadian Transportation Agency. 1996. *First Annual Report.* https://publications.gc.ca/collections/collection_2012/otc-cta/TT1-1996-eng.pdf.

–. 2017. *At the Heart of Transportation: A Moving History*. https://otc-cta.gc.ca/eng/publication/at-heart-transportation-a-moving-history#sec4.

Canadian Union of Public Employees. 2020. "Infrastructure Bank-Led Privatization Project Leaves Township in Deficit." October 15. https://cupe.ca/infrastructure-bank-led-privatization-project-leaves-township-deficit.

Cano-Kollmann, Marcelo, John Cantwell, Thomas J. Hannigan, Ram Mudambi, and Jaeyong Song. 2016. "Knowledge Connectivity: An Agenda for Innovation Research in International Business." *Journal of International Business Studies*, 47 (3): 255–62. https://doi.org/10.1057/jibs.2016.8.

Cardinal, François. 2000. "Une île, une ville ... trente ans plus tard." In *Québec 2001. Annuaire politique, social, économique et culturel*, edited by Roch Côté. Fides.

CargoM. 2017. Lettre déposée par CargoM – M. Mathieu Charbonneau, Directeur général, dans le cadre de la consultation publique: *La future Cité de la logistique.* http://ville.montreal.qc.ca/pls/portal/docs/page/arrond_mhm_fr/media/documents/cargom-memoire-citelogistique-consultationpublique-2017-06-14.pdf.

Carr, Constance, and Markus Hesse. 2020. "When Alphabet Inc. Plans Toronto's Waterfront: New Post-Political Modes of Urban Governance." *Urban Planning*, 5 (1): 69–83.

Cerina, Federica, Zhen Zhu, Alessandro Chessa, and Massimo Riccaboni. 2015. "World Input-Output Network." *PloS one*, 10 (7): e0134025.

CCMM (Chamber of Commerce of Metropolitan Montreal/Chambre de commerce de Montréal métropolitain). n.d. *City Governance.* https://www.ccmm.ca/en/advocacy/metropolitan-governance/.

–. 2010. *Rapport Côté-Seguin.* https://www.ccmm.ca/fr/interventions/gouvernance-metropolitaine/rapport-cote-seguin/.

CGCC (Canadian Global Cities Council). 2018. *Planning for an Urban Future. Our Call for a National Urban Strategy for Canada*. February. https://globalcitiescouncil.ca/national-urban-strategy/.

Champagne, Éric. 2014. "Tracking the Growth of the Federal Municipal Infrastructure Program under Different political Regimes." In *Canada in Cities: The Politics and Policy of Federal-Local Governance*, edited by Katherine A. H. Graham and Caroline Andrew. McGill-Queens University Press.

Charlottetown Accord. 1992. https://www.solon.org/Constitutions/Canada/English/Proposals/CharlottetownLegalDraft.html.

Chénier, John A. 2009. "The Evolving Role of the Federation of Canadian Municipalities." *Canadian Public Administration*, 52 (3): 395–416. https://onlinelibrary.wiley.com/doi/full/10.1111/j.1754-7121.2009.00089.x.

CITM (Comité interrégional pour le transport des marchandises/Interregional Committee on the Transport of Goods). 2001. *Plan d'action stratégique 2001–2006.* https://www.cubiq.ribg.gouv.qc.ca/notice?id=p%3A%3Ausmarcdef_0000637717&locale=fr.

CITM. 2008. *Plan d'action 2008–2011.*

City of Hamilton. 2010. *City of Hamilton Truck Route Master Plan Study.* https://www.hamilton.ca/sites/default/files/2022-08/masterplan-truck-route-update.pdf.

–. 2016. *Economic Development Action Plan 2016–2020.*

–. 2018. *Transportation Master Plan Review and Update.* June. https://d3fpllf1m7bbt3.cloudfront.net/sites/default/files/media/browser/2018-06-06/draft-tmp-cityinmotion-review-update-report-1.pdf.

City of Kitchener. 2018. *You Can Make It in Kitchener.* https://www.makeitkitchener.ca/kitchener.

City of Montreal. 2013. *Montréal for Tomorrow.* April.

City of Pickering. 2017. *Understanding the Economic Opportunities for Pickering Airport.* https://www.pickering.ca/en/business/resources/economic-opportunities-pickering-airport.pdf.

–. 2018. *Airport Lands: Looking to the Future.* https://www.pickering.ca/en/business/airport.aspx.

City of Toronto. 2014. "Feeling Congested?" Recommended Official Plan Amendments for Selected Transportation Policies: Official Plan Comprehensive Review. City Council Decision. http://app.toronto.ca/tmmis/viewAgendaItemHistory.do?item=2014.PG35.2#.

–. 2016. *Congestion Management Plan.* https://www.toronto.ca/wp-content/uploads/2017/08/8e95-congestion-management-Plan-CMP-2016-2020.pdf.

–. 2017. *Port Lands Planning Framework.* https://www.waterfrontoronto.ca/sites/default/files/documents/port-lands-planning-framework-aoda---reduced.pdf.

Clark, Anthony. 2010. "Spaces of Engagement and the Politics of Scale in B.C.'s Gateway Program." Master's thesis, Simon Fraser University.

Clarkson, Stephen. 2000. *The Multicentered State. Canadian Government under Globalizing Pressures.* http://www.envireform.utoronto.ca/publications/stephen-clarkson/multi-centered-state.html.

Cobban, Timothy. 2003a. "The Political Economy of Urban Redevelopment: Downtown Revitalization in London, Ontario, 1993–2002." *Canadian Journal of Urban Research*, 12 (2): 231–48.

–. 2003b. "Timothy Cobban's Reply to Christopher Leo's Comment 'Are There Urban Regimes in Canada?'" *Canadian Journal of Urban Research*, 12 (2): 349–52.

CodeRedTO. 2019. "About Us." https://coderedto.com/about/.

Coderre, Denis. 2015. *Discours du maire Denis Coderre sur la stratégie de développement économique.* June 18. http://ville.montreal.qc.ca/portal/page?_pageid=5798,42657625&_dad=portal&_schema=PORTAL&id=25206.

–. 2021. *Retrouver Montréal.* Les Éditions La Presse.

Coe, Neil M., Martin Hess, Henry Wai-chung Yeung, Peter Dicken, and Jeffrey Henderson. 2004. "'Globalizing' Regional Development: A Global Production

Networks Perspective." *Transactions of the Institute of British Geographers*, 29 (4): 468–84. http://www.jstor.org/stable/3804369.

Cohn, Carol. 2006. "Motives and Methods: Using Multi-Sited Ethnography to Study National Security Discourses." In *Feminist Methodologies for International Relations*, edited by Brooke Ackerly, Maria Stern, and Jacqui True. Cambridge University Press.

Colliers. 2023. *Impacts of E-commerce on Industrial Lands & Transportation Systems*. Report for Metro Vancouver. Colliers Strategy and Consulting Group.

Commission for Environmental Cooperation (CEC). 2022. "North American Atlas – Political Boundaries." Statistics Canada, United States Census Bureau, Instituto Nacional de Estadística y Geografía (INEGI). Ed. 3.0, Vector digital data [1:10,000,000]. https://www.arcgis.com/home/item.html?id=92f0360e996b46febd9380e032cf57c7.

Constitutional Accord, or Meech Lake Accord. 1987. https://www.canada.ca/en/intergovernmental-affairs/services/federation/1987-constitutional-accord.html.

Corredoira, Rafael A., and Gerald A. McDermott. 2014. "Adaptation, Bridging and Firm Upgrading: How Non-Market Institutions and MNCs Facilitate Knowledge Recombination in Emerging Markets." *Journal of International Business Studies*, 45: 699–722.

Corriveau, Jeanne, and Alexandre Shields. 2022. "Feu vert au projet de Ray-Mont Logistiques." *Le Devoir*, November 5.

Côté, Marcel, and Claude Seguin. 2010. *Une métropole à la hauteur de nos aspirations*, Rapport réalisé par le groupe de travail sur les enjeux de gouvernance et de fiscalité de Montréal.

Council on Foreign Relations. 2005. *Trinational Call for a North American Economic and Security Community by 2010*. March. https://www.cfr.org/news-releases/trinational-call-north-american-economic-and-security-community-2010.

Courchene, Thomas J. 2001. "Ontario as a North American Region-State, Toronto as a Global City Region: Responding to the NAFTA Challenge." In *Global City-Regions: Trends, Theory, Policy*, edited by Allen J. Scott. Oxford University Press.

CPCS (Canadian Pacific Consulting Services). 2016. *The Nova Scotia Transportation Sector. Global Market Challenges and Opportunities*. CPCS Ref: 15534.

Cronon, William. 1991. *Nature's Metropolis: Chicago and the Great West*. W.W. Norton.

Cummins, John. 2007. *Special Report: Better Way for Gateway Project*. https://citeseerx.ist.psu.edu/document?repid=rep1&type=pdf&doi=19e1a198bad179d79ed2dd2c522b9f3a181e5fb5.

Curry, Bill. 2019. "Canada Infrastructure Bank Executive Nicholas Hann Resigns Amid Growing Industry Frustration with Pace of Project Approvals," *Globe and Mail*, July 30.

De Fuentes, Claudia, Jorge Niosi, and Jahan Ara Peerally. 2021. "Exploring Innovation and Export Interplay in Canadian Firms." *Economics of Innovation and New Technology*, 30 (8): 786–806. DOI: 10.1080/10438599.2020.1786999.

de Socio, Mark. 2010. "Marginalization of Sunset Firms in Regime Coalitions: A Social Network Analysis." *Regional Studies*, 44 (2): 167–82. https://doi.org/10.1080/00343400903095246.

Deblock, Christian, and Dorval Brunelle. 1998. "Globalization and New Normative Frameworks: The Multilateral Agreement on Investment." *Cahier de recherche 98-06*. Groupe de recherche sur l'intégration continentale, Université du Québec à Montréal.

Department of Municipal Affairs. 2019. *Strategic Public Private Partnering – A Guide for Nova Scotia Municipalities*. Nova Scotia.

DeVerteuil, Geoffrey. 2015. *Resilience in the Post–Welfare Inner City: Voluntary Sector Geographies in London, Los Angeles and Sydney*. Policy Press.

Dewing, Michael, William Young, and Erin Tolley. 2006. *Municipalities, the Constitution and the Canadian Federal System*. Background Paper, Parliamentary Information and Research Service. https://publications.gc.ca/collections/Collection-R/LoPBdP/BP-e/bp276-1e.pdf.

Dicken, Peter. 1992. *Global Shift: The Internationalization of Economic Activity*. 2nd ed. Paul Chapman.

Dijst, Martin J., and Walter Schenkel. 2002. "Urban Governance and Infrastructure: Coping with Diversity, Complexity and Uncertainty." In *Governing Cities on the Move: Functional and Management Perspectives on Transformations of European Urban Infrastructures*, edited by M. J. Dijst, Walter Schenkel, and Isabelle Thomas. Ashgate.

Ditta, Sara. 2015. *From the Ground Up: The Role of Local Governments in Building Canada's Economic Infrastructure Network*. Mowat Centre.

DOB (Department of Business). 2017. *Accountability Report 2016–2017*. Nova Scotia.

–. 2018. *Department of Business Annual Plan 2018–2019*. Nova Scotia.

Dowding, Keith. 2001. "Explaining Urban Regimes." *International Journal of Urban and Regional Research*, 25 (1): 7–19. https://doi.org/10.1111/1468-2427.00294.

Dowding, Keith, Patrick Dunleavy, Desmond King, Helen Margetts, and Yvonne Rydin. 1999. "Regime Politics in London Local Government." *Urban Affairs Review*, 34: 515–45.

Dryzek, John. 1996. *Democracy in Capitalist Times*. Oxford University Press.

Dunn, Christopher. 2016. "Harper Without Jeers, Trudeau Without Cheers. Assessing 10 Years of Intergovernmental Relations." *IRPP Insight*, 8 (September). Institute for Research on Public Policy, Montreal. https://irpp.org/wp-content/uploads/2016/09/insight-no8.pdf.

Duina, Francesco. 2006. *The Social Construction of Free Trade: The European Union, NAFTA, and MERCOSUR*. Princeton University Press.

Eckhardt, Jappe, and Arlo Poletti. 2018. "Introduction: Bringing Institutions Back in the Study of Global Value Chains." *Global Policy*, 9 (S2): 5–11. https://doi.org/10.1111/1758-5899.12613.

Elsibai, Khadeja, Jean Michel Montsion, Claudia De Fuentes, Peter V. Hall, and Dorval Brunelle. 2023. "Economic Development and Canada's Gateways: A Tale of Two Regional Development Agencies." *Canadian Journal of Regional Science*, 46 (3): 29–36.

Ernst, Dieter. 2002. "Global Production Networks and the Changing Geography of Innovation Systems. Implications for Developing Countries." *Economics of Innovation and New Technology*, 11 (6): 497–523.

Evans, Paul. 2008. "The Asia Pacific Gateway and the Reconfiguration of North America." *Canadian Political Science Review*, 2 (4): 93–98.

Evans, S.R., and M. Hutchins. 2002. "The Development of Strategic Transport Assets in Greater Manchester and Merseyside: Does Local Governance Matter?" *Regional Studies*, 36 (4): 429–38. https://doi.org/10.1080/00343400220131197.

Fagiolo, Giorgio, Javier Reyes, and Stefano Schiavo. 2010. "The Evolution of the World Trade Web: A Weighted-Network Analysis." *Journal of Evolutionary Economics*, 20 (4): 479–514.

Falk, Richard. 2000. "The Decline of Citizenship in an Era of Globalization." *Citizenship Studies*, 4 (1): 5–18.

Fellows, G. Kent, and Trevor Tombe. 2018. "Opening Canada's North: A Study of Trade Costs in the Territories." *SPP Research Paper No. 11/17*. June 18. *https://ssrn.com/abstract=3217725* http://dx.doi.org/10.2139/ssrn.3217725.

Ferguson, Mark, Hannah Maoh, and Pavlos Kanaroglou. 2012. "Simulating Sustainable Urban Gateway Development: Illustration from Hamilton, Ontario, Canada." *Transportation Research Record*, 2269 (1): 135–44.

Folco, Jonathan Durand. 2016. "Y a-t-il une démocratie participative à Montréal? Entre gouvernance métropolitaine, gestion de proximité et démocratie radicale." *Les ateliers de l'éthique*, 11 (1): 80–100.

Gauthier, Éléonore. 2019. "Spending Power, Social Policy, and the Principle of Subsidiarity." *Review of Constitutional Studies/Revue d'études constitutionnelles*. https://www.constitutionalstudies.ca/wp-content/uploads/2019/08/06_Gauthier-6.pdf.

Gereffi, Gary. 1995. "Global Production Systems and Third World Development." In *Global Change, Regional Responses*, edited by Barbara Stallings. Cambridge University Press.

–. 1999. "International Trade and Industrial Upgrading in the Apparel Commodity Chain." *Journal of International Economics*, 48 (1): 37–70. https://doi.org/10.1016/S0022-1996(98)00075-0.

Gereffi, Gary, John Humphrey, and Timothy Sturgeon. 2005. "The Governance of Global Value Chains." *Review of International Political Economy*, 12 (1): 78–104. https://doi.org/10.1080/09692290500049805.

Gereffi, Gary, and Joonkoo Lee. 2012. "Why the World Suddenly Cares About Global Supply Chains." *Journal of Supply Chain Management*, 48: 24–32. https://doi.org/10.1111/j.1745-493X.2012.03271.x.

Gereffi, Gary, Joonkoo Lee, Lukas Brun, and Mary Turnipseedl. 2012. *Nova Scotia's Ocean Technologies: A Global Value Chain Analysis of Inshore & Extreme Climate Vessels, Remotely Operated & Autonomous Underwater Vehicles, and Underwater Sensors & Instrumentation*. Center on Globalization, Governance & Competitiveness, Duke University. https://www.researchgate.net/publication/282670102_Nova_Scotia%27s_Ocean_Technologies_A_Global_Value_Chain_Analysis_of_Inshore_Extreme_Climate_Vessels_Remotely_Operated_Autonomous_Under water_Vehicles_and_Underwater_Sensors_Instrumentation.

Glückler, Johannes. 2007. "Economic Geography and the Evolution of Networks." *Journal of Economic Geography*, 7: 619–34.

Godfrey, John. 2009. "New Deal for Canada's Cities a Good Idea in Difficult Times." *Toronto Star*, January 6. https://www.thestar.com/opinion/2009/01/06/new_deal_for_canadas_cities_a_good_idea_in_difficult_times.html.

Good, Kristin. 2019. *The Fallacy of the Creatures of the Provinces Doctrine*. Institute on Municipal Finance and Governance, University of Toronto. https://tspace.library.utoronto.ca/bitstream/1807/98264/1/imfgpaper_no46_recognizingandprotectingmunicipalities_kristingood_nov_26_2019.pdf.

Goodhart, Michael. 2001. "Democracy, Globalization, and the Problem of the State." *Polity*, 33 (4): 527–46.

Goodman, Nicole, Austin Zwick, Zachary Spicer, and Nina Carlsen. 2020. "Public Engagement in Smart City Development: Lessons from Communities in Canada's Smart City Challenge." *The Canadian Geographer*, 64 (3): 416–32.

Gouvernement du Québec. 1996. *Loi sur l'aménagement et l'urbanisme* (RLRQ, chapitre A-19.1).

–. 2015. *La stratégie maritime à l'horizon 2030. Plan d'action 2015–2020* (Maritime Strategy 2030: 2015–2020 Action Plan). http://www.bv.transports.gouv.qc.ca/per/1169680/01_2015_2020.pdf.

–. 2017. *Projet de loi no 121, Loi augmentant l'autonomie et les pouvoirs de la Ville de Montréal, métropole du Québec* (Bill 121, An Act to Increase the Autonomy and Powers of Ville de Montréal, the Metropolis of Québec). Adopted September 21. https://www.publicationsduquebec.gouv.qc.ca/fileadmin/Fichiers_client/lois_et_reglements/LoisAnnuelles/fr/2017/2017C16F.PDF.

Government of Canada. n.d. *Trade Data Online*. Accessed: February 10, 2022. https://ised-isde.canada.ca/app/ixb/tdo/crtr.html?&productType=HS6&lang=eng

–. 2000. *Response to the First Report of the Standing Committee on Public Accounts*. https://www.ourcommons.ca/documentviewer/en/36-2/PACC/report-11?responseCode=8512-371-79-01.

–. 2006. *Advantage Canada. Building a Strong Economy for Canadians*. https://publications.gc.ca/collections/Collection/F2-105-2006-3E.pdf.

–. 2007a. "Canada's New Government Signs Memorandum of Understanding with Atlantic Provinces to Develop an Atlantic Gateway Strategy." News release, October 14. https://www.canada.ca/en/news/archive/2007/10/canada-new-government-signs-memorandum-understanding-atlantic-provinces-develop-atlantic-gateway-strategy.html.

–. 2007b. *The Ontario-Quebec Continental Gateway and Trade Corridor*. News Release No. H 141/07, July 30. https://www.canada.ca/en/news/archive/2007/07/ontario-quebec-continental-gateway-trade-corridor.html.

–. 2008. *Seizing Global Advantage. A Global Commerce Strategy for Securing Canada's Growth and Prosperity*. https://publications.gc.ca/site/eng/332172/publication.html.

–. 2009. *National Policy Framework for Strategic Gateways and Trade Corridors*. https://publications.gc.ca/site/eng/347485/publication.html.

–. 2012. *The Gateway and Corridor. Transportation in the Global Economy*.

–. 2016a. *Investing in Canada Plan – Building a Better Canada*. Infrastructure Canada. https://www.infrastructure.gc.ca/plan/about-invest-apropos-eng.html.

–. 2016b. *Pathways: Connecting Canada's Transportation System to the World – Volume 1.* Canada Transportation Act Review.
–. 2017. *Building a Strong Middle Class: Budget 2017.* https://budget.canada.ca/2017/docs/plan/budget-2017-en.pdf.
–. 2020. "Prime Minister Announces Infrastructure Plan to Create Jobs and Grow the Economy." News release, October 1. https://pm.gc.ca/en/news/news-releases/2020/10/01/prime-minister-announces-infrastructure-plan-create-jobs-and-grow.
–. 2021a. *Canada Community-Building Fund.* Infrastructure Canada. https://www.infrastructure.gc.ca/plan/gtf-fte-eng.html.
–. 2021b. *National Railway Network – NRWN – GeoBase Series.* https://open.canada.ca/data/en/dataset/ac26807e-a1e8-49fa-87bf-451175a859b8.
Government of Ontario. 2021. *Municipal Government.* https://www.ontario.ca/document/ontario-municipal-councillors-guide/4-municipal-government.
Governments of Canada, Ontario, and Québec. 2007. *Memorandum of Understanding for the Development of the Ontario-Quebec Continental Gateway and Trade Corridor.* July 30.
Graham, Katherine A.H., and Caroline Andrew, eds. 2014. *Canada in Cities: The Politics and Policy of Federal-Local Governance.* McGill-Queens University Press.
Graham, Stephen. 2009. *Disrupted Cities: When Infrastructure Fails.* Routledge.
Granovetter, Mark. 1985. "Economic Action and Social Structure: The Problem of Embeddedness." *American Journal of Sociology*, 91 (3): 481–510. http://www.jstor.org/stable/2780199.
GTAA (Greater Toronto Airports Authorities). 2018. *Annual Information Form for the Year Ended December 31, 2017.* https://www.torontopearson.com/ar2018/downloads/Annual_Report_2018.pdf.
GTCF (Gateway Transportation Collaboration Forum). 2014. *Presentation to Gateway Transportation Collaboration Forum.* September 9.
Gurstein, Penny, and Thomas Hutton, eds. 2019. *Planning on the Edge: Vancouver and the Challenges of Reconciliation, Social Justice, and Sustainable Development.* UBC Press.
Guy, Emmanuel. 2013. "Representations and Policy Change: Evidence from the Canadian-flag Shipping Industry." *Environment and Planning A*, 45: 1184–98.
GVRD (Greater Vancouver Regional District). 1996. *The Livable Region Strategic Plan.* January. https://metrovancouver.org/about-us/Documents/livable-region-strategic-plan.pdf.
Hall, Peter V. 2014. *A Gateway to Good Jobs? Opening Up the Conversation.* Canadian Centre for Policy Alternatives-BC. https://policyalternatives.ca/sites/default/files/uploads/publications/WorkingPaper_PeterHall_GoodJobsConf.pdf.
Hall, Peter V., and Anthony Clark. 2010. "Maritime Ports and the Politics of Reconnection." In *Transforming Urban Waterfronts: Fixity and Flow*, edited by Gene Desfor, Jennifer Laidley, Dirk Schubert, and Quentin Stevens. Routledge.
Hall, Peter V., and Markus Hesse, eds. 2013. *Cities, Regions and Flows.* Routledge.
Hall, Peter V., and Wouter Jacobs. 2012. "Why are Maritime Ports (Still) Urban, and Why Should Policy-Makers Care?" *Maritime Policy and Management*, 39 (2): 189–206.

HalTech. 2020. *Annual Report 2019–2020*. https://p6s.3cc.myftpupload.com/wp-content/uploads/2020/07/Haltech-Annual-Report_Summer-2020.pdf.

Halton Region. 2019. "Regional Official Plan Viewer." https://www.halton.ca/The-Region/Regional-Planning/Regional-Official-Plan-(ROP)/About-Regional-Official-Plan-(ROP)/Regional-Official-Plan-Viewer.

Hamel, Pierre. 2008. *Ville et débat public. Agir en démocratie*. Presses de l'Université Laval.

Hamel, Pierre, and Roger Keil. 2017. "Suburban Governance and Democracy of City-Regions." Communication presented at the American Sociological Association 112th Annual Meeting, Montreal, Canada, August 12–15.

Hamilton, Ian. 2021. "Strategic Locations: HOPA Ports Adds Third Location to Its Growing Ontario Transportation Network." Guest editorial. *Great Lakes-Seaway Review*. https://www.hopaports.ca/wp-content/uploads/2021/04/Great-Lakes-Seaway-Review_-Jan-March-2021.pdf.

Hamilton Port Authority. 2017. *Hamilton's Working Waterfront: Port of Hamilton Land Use Plan*.

Hannah, Julie. 2012. "Economic Change and the Inner City Landscape: A Case Study of Hamilton, Ontario." Master's thesis, University of Waterloo.

Harcourt, Mike, Ken Cameron, and Sean Rossiter. 2007. *City Making in Paradise: Nine Decisions that Saved Greater Vancouver*. Douglas and McIntyre.

Harding, Alan. 1996. "Is There a 'New Community Power' and Why Should We Need One?" *International Journal of Urban and Regional Research*, 20 (4): 637–55. https://doi.org/10.1111/j.1468-2427.1996.tb00340.x.

Henderson, Jeffrey, Peter Dicken, Martin Hess, Neil Coe, and Henry Yeung. 2002. "Global Production Networks and the Analysis of Economic Development." *Review of International Political Economy*, 9 (3): 436–64. https://doi.org/10.1080/09692290210150842.

HCC (Halifax Chamber of Commerce). 2009. *Transportation Committee, Action Plan*.

HGC (Halifax Gateway Council). 2010. *2010–2015 Strategic Plan: Building the Halifax Gateway*.

–. 2012. *Transportation and Logistics Sector Profile*.

HIAA (Halifax International Airport Authority). 2017. *2017 Annual Report*. https://halifaxstanfield.ca/wp-content/uploads/2022/02/HIAA-2017-Annual-Report-English.pdf.

–. 2018. *2018 Annual Report*. https://halifaxstanfield.ca/wp-content/uploads/2022/02/HIAA-2018-Annual-Report-English.pdf.

Highway H20. 2016. "About Hwy H20." http://hwyh2o.com/about-hwy-h2o/.

Hirst, Paul. 2000. "Democracy and Governance." In *Governance, Politics and the State*, edited by Jon Pierre and B. Guy Peters. Macmillan.

Hiebert, Daniel. 2000. "Immigration and the Changing Canadian City." *Canadian Geographer/Le géographe canadien*, 44 (1): 25–43.

Holm, Andrej, and Armin Kuhn. 2011. "Squatting and Urban Renewal: The Interaction of Squatter Movements and Strategies of Urban Restructuring in Berlin." *International Journal of Urban and Regional Research*, 35 (3): 644–58. https://doi.org/10.1111/j.1468-2427.2010.001009.x.

Horak, Martin, and Robert Young, eds. 2012. *Sites of Governance: Multilevel Governance and Policy Making in Canada's Big Cities*. Vol. 3. McGill-Queen's University Press.

HP (Halifax Partnership). 2017. *Annual Report*. https://halifaxpartnership.com/sites/default/uploads/pages/downloads/HP_2017_annual_report.pdf.

–. 2018. *Annual Report*. https://halifaxpartnership.com/sites/default/uploads/pages/downloads/Halifax-Partnership-Annual-Report-2018-19-WEB.pdf

HPA (Halifax Port Authority). 2017. *2015–16 Economic Impacts*. Port of Halifax. https://www.porthalifax.ca/wp-content/uploads/2016/11/Port-of-Halifax-2015-16-Economic-Impacts-Report_April-20-2017.pdf.

–. 2019. *Stakeholder Report*. Port of Halifax. https://www.porthalifax.ca/wp-content/uploads/2019/05/portofhalifax_stakeholderreport_May3_2019_.pdf.

HRM (Halifax Regional Municipality). 2007. *Atlantic Gateway. The Role of Halifax Regional Municipality*. https://www.halifax.ca/sites/default/files/documents/business/business-parks/LogisticsPark_RoleofHRM.pdf.

Hulchanski, J. David. 2010. *The Three Cities Within Toronto*. Cities Centre.

Humphrey, John, and Hubert Schmitz. 2002. "How Does Insertion in Global Value Chains Affect Upgrading in Industrial Clusters?" *Regional Studies*, 36 (9): 1017–27. https://doi.org/10.1080/0034340022000022198.

Hutton, Thomas. A. 1997. "The Innisian Core-Periphery Revisited: Vancouver's Changing Relationships with British Columbia's Staple Economy." *BC Studies: The British Columbian Quarterly*, 113: 69–100.

–. 2007. "Contours of the Post-Staples State: The Reconstruction of Political Economy and Social Identity in 21st Century Canada." *Policy and Society*, 26 (1): 9–29.

Iammarino, Simona. 2011. "Business Clusters and Industrial Districts. The Governance of the Global Value Chain." *Regional Studies*, 45 (2): 278–79. https://doi.org/10.1080/00343404.2011.553520.

Innis, Harold A. 2017. *Essays in Canadian Economic History*. University of Toronto Press.

InterVistas. 2007. *Atlantic Gateway Business Case*. Commissioned by Atlantic Canada Opportunities Agency.

Invest Durham. 2023. "Transportation and Logistics." https://www.durham.ca/en/economic-development/the-durham-advantage/transportation-and-logistics.aspx#.

Inwood, Gregory. 2005. *Continentalizing Canada. The Politics and Legacy of the Macdonald Royal Commission*. University of Toronto Press.

Ircha, Michael C. 2014. "Social License for Ports." https://ctrf.ca/wp-content/uploads/2014/07/18IrchaSOCIALLICENSEFORPORTS.pdf.

Ivany, Ray, I. d'Entremont, D. Christmas, S. Fuller, and J. Bragg. 2014. *Now or Never: An Urgent Call to Action – The Report of the Nova Scotia Commission on Building Our New Economy*. ONE Nova Scotia. https://www.onens.ca/sites/default/files/editor-uploads/now-or-never.pdf.

Jacobs, Jane. 1984. *Cities and the Wealth of Nations: Principles of Economic Life*. Random House.

Jacopo, Miro. 2011. "Visions of False Creek: Urban Development and Industrial Decline in Vancouver, 1960–1980." Master's thesis, University of Victoria.

Jessop, Bob. 1997. "The Governance of Complexity and the Complexity of Governance: Preliminary Remarks on Some Problems and Limits of Economic Guidance." In *Beyond Markets and Hierarchy: Interactive Governance and Social Complexity*, edited by Ash Amin and Jerzy Hausner. Edward Elgar Publishing.

Johnson, Heather L. 2014. *Borders, Asylum and Global Non-Citizenship*. Cambridge University Press.

Johnson, Robert. 2017. *Measuring Global Value Chains*. National Bureau of Economic Research Working Paper Series #24027.

Joy, Meghan, and Ronald Vogel. 2015. "Toronto's Governance Crisis: A Global City Under Pressure." *Cities*, 49: 35–52.

Kano, Liena. 2018. "Global Value Chain Governance: A Relational Perspective." *Journal of International Business Studies*, 49 (6): 684–705.

Keeley, Greg, ed. 1973. *Canada Investigates Industrialism*. University of Toronto Press.

Keeling, David J. 2009. "Transportation Geography: Local Challenges, Global Contexts." *Progress in Human Geography*, 33 (4): 516–26.

Keil, Roger, and Julie-Anne Boudreau. 2005a. "Arrested Metropolitanism: Limits and Contradictions of Municipal Governance Reform in Los Angeles, Montreal and Toronto." In *Metropolitan Governance: Capacity, Democracy and the Dynamics of Place*, edited by Hubert Heinelt and Daniel Kubler. Routledge.

–. 2005b. "Is There Regionalism after Municipal Amalgamation in Toronto?" *City*, 9 (1): 9–22.

Keil, Roger, Pierre J. Hamel, Julie-Anne Boudreau, Stefan Kipfer, and Ahmed Allahwala. 2016. "Regional Governance Revisited: Political Space, Collective Agency, and Identity." In *Governing Cities Through Regions. Canadian and European* Perspectives. Wilfrid Laurier University Press.

Keil, Roger, and Douglas Young. 2008. "Transportation: The Bottleneck of Regional Competitiveness in Toronto." *Environment and Planning C: Government and Policy*, 26: 488–99.

–. 2011. "In-Between Canada: The Emergence of the New Urban Middle." In *In-Between Infrastructure: Urban Connectivity in an Age of Vulnerability*, edited by Roger Keil, Patricia Burke Wood, and Douglas Young. Praxis e-Press.

Kennedy, Christopher, Eric Miller, Amer Shalaby, Heather Maclean, and Jesse Coleman. 2005. "The Four Pillars of Sustainable Urban Transportation." *Transport Reviews*, 25 (4): 393–414. https://doi.org/10.1080/01441640500115835.

Kitchin, Rob. 2014. "The Real-Time City? Big Data and Smart Urbanism." *GeoJournal*, 79 (1): 1–14.

Kooiman, Jan. 2000. "Societal Governance." In *Debating Governance*, edited by Jon Pierre. Oxford University Press.

Koza, Mitchell P., and Arie Y. Lewin. 1998. "The Co-Evolution of Strategic Alliances." *Organization Science*, 9 (3): 255–64. http://www.jstor.org/stable/2640222.

KPMG. 2012. *Transportation and Logistics Cluster: Background Material*. Toronto Board of Trade.

Kriger, David. 2016. *Regional Transportation Plan Legislative Review Backgrounder: Urban Goods Movement*. Discussion Paper for the Next Regional Transportation Plan. CPCS and Metrolinx. http://www.metrolinx.com/en/regionalplanning/rtp/technical/05_Urban_Goods_Movement_Report_EN.pdf.

Kriger, David, and Vijay Gill. 2016. "Strategic Directions and New Actions for Goods Movement in the GTHA." *Conference of the Transportation Association of Canada*. August. https://www.tac-atc.ca/en/knowledge-centre/technical-resources-search/conference-papers/strategic-directions-and-new-actions-for-goods-movement-in-the-gtha/.

Lambert, Alexandre. 2010. *Aménagement de la « plaque tournante » montréalaise. Survol du contexte d'évolution et des infrastructures logistiques stratégiques*, Étude réalisée pour la Communauté métropolitaine de Montréal.

Lambert-Racine, Michaël, Pierre Martin, and François Vaillancourt. 2010. "Une évaluation de l'impact des politiques de l'administration Bush sur les exportations canadiennes dans le contexte de l'Accord de libre-échange nord-américain." *Revue LISA/LISA e-journal*, 8 (1): 168–94.

Lasserre, Jean-Claude. 1978. "Prolégomènes pour une géographie des transports du Québec." *Cahiers de géographie du Québec*, 22 (55): 9–27.

Lawrence National Centre for Policy and Management. 2008. *Ontario-Québec Continental Gateway and Trade Corridor: Developing Competitive and Sustainable Transportation Policy*. https://www.ivey.uwo.ca/media/202749/Ontario-Quebec%20Trade%20Corridor%20Workshop%20Report.pdf.

Lefebvre, Henri. 1974. *Le Droit à la Ville Suivi de Espace et Politique*. (Anthropos, 1968), Paris, Seuil, coll. Points.

Lefèvre, Christian. 2010. "The Improbable Metropolis: Decentralization, Local Democracy and Metropolitan Areas in the Western World." *Analise Social*, 45 (197): 623–37.

Lehmann, Jean-Pierre. 2012. "China's Global Tectonic Shifts: The Dawn of a New Era." *The World Financial Review*, November 4. https://worldfinancialreview.com/1048/.

Leo, Christopher. 1997. *City Politics in an Era of Globalization*. Sage.

–. 2003. "Are There Urban Regimes in Canada? Comment on Timothy Cobban's 'The Political Economy of Urban Redevelopment: Downtown Revitalization in London, Ontario, 1993–2002.'" *Canadian Journal of Urban Research*, 12 (2): 344–48.

Leuprecht, Christian, and Robert Young. 2006. "Introduction: New Work, Background Themes, and Future Research about Municipal-Federal-Provincial Relations in Canada." In *Canada: The State of the Federation 2004. Municipal-Federal-Provincial Relations in Canada*. McGill-Queen's University Press.

Lever, Annabelle. 2010. "Compulsory Voting: A Critical Perspective." *British Journal of Political Science*, 40: 897–915.

Lévesque, Évangéline. 2010. "Ontario-Quebec Continental Gateway and Trade Corridor." *Transportation Association of Canada Annual Conference*. http://conf.tac-atc.ca/english/resourcecentre/readingroom/conference/conf2010/docs/b1/levesque-e.pdf.

Levin-Waldman, Oren M. 2005. *The Political Economy of the Living Wage: A Study of Four Cities*. Routledge.

Los, Bart, Marcel P. Timmer, and Gaaitzen J. De Vries. 2015. "How Global Are Global Value Chains? A New Approach to Measure International Fragmentation." *Journal of Regional Science*, 55 (1): 66–92. https://doi.org/10.1111/jors.12121.

LRC (Livable Region Coalition). 2004. "Livable Region Coalition Mission Statement." December.

Marcus, George E. 1986. "Contemporary Problems of Ethnography in the Modern World System." In *Writing Culture: The Poetics and Politics of Ethnography*, edited by James Clifford and George E. Marcus. University of California Press.

–. 1995. "Ethnography in/of the World System: The Emergence of Multi-Sited Ethnography." *Annual Review of Anthropology*, 24 (1): 95–118.

Martin, Roman. 2013. "Differentiated Knowledge Bases and the Nature of Innovation Networks." *European Planning Studies*, 21 (9): 1418–36.

Mau, Tim A. 2005. "Political Rhetoric or Genuine Leadership: An Assessment of the 'New Deal' for Cities." Paper presented at the Annual Meeting of the Canadian Political Science Association, University of Western Ontario, June 2–4. http://www.cpsa-acsp.ca/papers-2005/Mau.pdf.

Mayer, Margit. 2017. "Whose City? From Ray Pahl's Critique of the Keynesian City to the Contestations Around Neoliberal Urbanism." *The Sociological Review*, 65 (2): 168–83. https://doi.org/10.1111/1467-954X.12414.

Mazzucato, Mariana. 2021. *Mission Economy: A Moonshot Guide to Changing Capitalism*. HarperCollins Publishers.

McBride, Stephen. 2005. *Paradigm Shift. Globalization and the Canadian State*. 2nd ed. Fernwood Publishing.

McCalla, Robert J. 2009. "Gateways Are More Than Port: The Canadian Example of Cooperation Among Stakeholders." In *Ports in Proximity: Essays on Competition and Coordination Among Adjacent Seaports*, edited by Theo Notteboom, Peter De Langen, and Cesar Ducruet. Ashgate Publishing.

McCann, Larry D. ed., 1987. *Heartland and Hinterland: A Geography of Canada*. Prentice-Hall Canada.

MITL (McMaster Institute for Transportation and Logistics). 2011. *An Exploration of the Freight Village Concept and its Applicability to Ontario*. http://mitl.mcmaster.ca/reports/MITL_Freight_Villages_January.pdf.

Metro Vancouver. 2011. *Metro Vancouver 2040: Shaping Our Future*. Bylaw No. 1136, 2010. Adopted July 29. https://vancouver.ca/files/cov/metro-vancouver-regional-growth-strategy.pdf.

–. 2017. *2016 Census Bulletin: Population*. https://metrovancouver.org/services/regional-planning/Documents/census-bulletin-population-2016.pdf.

–. 2020. *Metro Vancouver: Regional Industrial Lands Strategy*. https://metrovancouver.org/services/regional-planning/Documents/regional-industrial-lands-strategy-report.pdf.

–. 2021. *Metro Vancouver 2020 Regional Industrial Land Inventory: Technical Report*. https://metrovancouver.org/services/regional-planning/Documents/metro-vancouver-2020-industrial-lands-inventory-technical-report.pdf.

–. 2023. *Metro 2050 Regional Growth Strategy.* Bylaw No. 1339, 2022. https://metrovancouver.org/services/regional-planning/Documents/metro-2050.pdf.

Metrolinx. 2008. *The Big Move.* http://www.metrolinx.com/en/regionalplanning/bigmove/big_move.aspx.

–. 2016. *Urban Goods Movement.* http://www.metrolinx.com/en/regionalplanning/rtp/technical/05_Urban_Goods_Movement_Report_EN.pdf.

MMC (Montreal Metropolitan Community/Communauté métropolitaine de Montréal). 2003. *Cap sur le monde: bâtir une communauté compétitive, attractive, solidaire et responsable. Rapport de consultation publique. Projet d'énoncé de vision stratégique.* https://cmm.qc.ca/wp-content/uploads/2019/04/Rapport_activites_2003.pdf.

–. 2009. *Mémoire de la Communauté métropolitaine de Montréal concernant la Porte Continentale et le Corridor de commerce Ontario-Québec.* April 23. https://cmm.qc.ca/wp-content/uploads/2019/05/20090423_memoire_porteContinentale.pdf.

–. 2012. *Plan métropolitain d'aménagement et de développement: An Attractive, Competitive and Sustainable Greater Montréal.* https://cmm.qc.ca/wp-content/uploads/2020/01/20120813_PMAD_eng.pdf.

–. 2015. *Plan métropolitain de développement économique 2015–2020* (Metropolitan Economic Development Plan 2015–2020). https://cmm.qc.ca/wp-content/uploads/2019/02/20150430_pmde-2015-2020.web_.pdf.

–. 2018. *Document de présentation de la CMM 2018.* January. https://cmm.qc.ca/wp-content/uploads/2019/04/Presentation_CMM_2018.pdf.

–. 2022. *Plan métropolitain de développement économique 2022–2031.* https://cmm.qc.ca/wp-content/uploads/2022/11/PMDE_2022-2031_Interactif.pdf.

Molle, Willem. 2002. "Globalization, Regionalism and Labour Markets: Should We Recast the Foundations of the EU Regime in Matters of Regional (Rural and Urban) Development?" *Regional Studies*, 36 (2): 161–72. https://doi.org/10.1080/00343400220121954.

Montsion, Jean Michel. 2019. "Innovation Corridors and the Golden Horseshoe: Transportation Challenges and the Emergence of a Shared Regional Vision." Paper presented at the 54th Annual Conference, Canadian Transportation Research Forum, August 24. https://ctrf.ca/wp-content/uploads/2022/08/2019172Montsion.pdf.

Moos, Markus, and Andrej Skaburskis. 2010. "The Globalization of Urban Housing Markets: Immigration and Changing Housing Demand in Vancouver." *Urban Geography*, 31 (6): 724–49.

Mossberger, Karen, and Gerry Stoker. 2001. "The Evolution of Urban Regime Theory: The Challenge of Conceptualization." *Urban Affairs Review*, 36 (6): 810–35. https://doi.org/10.1177/10780870122185109.

Mudambi, Ram, Lee Li, Xufei Ma, Shige Makino, Gongming Qian, and Ron Boschma. 2018. "Zoom in, Zoom out: Geographic Scale and Multinational Activity." *Journal of International Business Studies*, 49 (8): 929–41. https://doi.org/10.1057/s41267-018-0158-4.

Müller, Martin. 2015. "A Half-hearted Romance? A Diagnosis and Agenda for the Relationship between Economic Geography and Actor-Network Theory." *Progress in Human Geography*, 39 (1): 65–86.

Myers, Jayson. 2019. *Sparking a New Economy: Canada's Advanced Manufacturing Supercluster*. Next Generation Advanced Manufacturing. https://www.jetro.go.jp/ext_images/canada/pdf/190611_4_Ngen.pdf.

Next Generation Advanced Manufacturing. 2019. *Advanced Manufacturing Supercluster Five-Year Strategy*. https://www.ngen.ca/hubfs/Documents/NGenFive YearStrategy_EN_V1.0.pdf?hsLang=en.

Nilsen, Trond. 2019. "Global Production Networks and Strategic Coupling in Value Chains Entering Peripheral Regions." *The Extractive Industries and Society*, 6 (3): 815–22. https://doi.org/10.1016/j.exis.2019.04.004.

Norcliffe, Glen. 2001. "Canada in a Global Economy." *The Canadian Geographer*, 45: 14–30.

North American Forum on Integration. North American International Trade Corridor Partnership Slides. http://www.channelingreality.com/NAU/Naitpc_slides.htm.

O'Connor, K. 2010. "Global City Regions and the Location of Logistics Activity." *Journal of Transport Geography*, 18 (3): 354–62.

OCPM (Office de consultation publique de Montréal). 2019. *Vision du développment économique et urbain du secteur Assomption Sud–Longue Pointe*. https://ocpm.qc.ca/sites/default/files/pdf/rapports/rapport_final_assomption-sud-longue_pointe.pdf.

OECD (Organisation for Economic Co-operation and Development). 2022. *International Trade During the COVID-19 Pandemic: Big Shifts and Uncertainty*. https://www.oecd.org/coronavirus/policy-responses/international-trade-during-the-covid-19-pandemic-big-shifts-and-uncertainty-d1131663/.

Office of the Premier of Ontario. 2008. *First-Ever Joint Meeting of Ontario et Québec Cabinets*. https://news.ontario.ca/en/backgrounder/378/first-ever-joint-meeting-of-ontario-and-quebec-cabinets.

Olds, Kris. 2002. *Globalization and Urban Change: Capital, Culture, and Pacific Rim Mega-Projects*. Oxford University Press.

Ontario Ministry of Finance. 2020. *Demographic Trends and Projections*. https://www.ontario.ca/document/ontarios-long-term-report-economy/chapter-1-demographic-trends-and-projections.

Ontario Ministry of Municipal Affairs and Housing. 2021. *The Greater Golden Horseshoe Region*.

PACC (Public Accounts of Canada). 1999. *Eleventh Report of the Standing Committee on Public Accounts. Canada Infrastructure Works Program: Phase II and Follow-up of Phase I Audit*. https://www.ourcommons.ca/DocumentViewer/en/36-2/PACC/report-11/.

Pain, Kathy. 2008. "Global Cities, Gateways and Corridors: Hierarchies, Roles and Functions." Paper presented at Roundtables and International Conference of Canada's Asia-Pacific Gateway and Corridor Initiative, Vancouver.

Phillips, Carol, and Nancy Bouchier. 2014. "Building and Re-building a City Through Sport: Hamilton, Ontario and the British Empire and Commonwealth Games, 1930–2003." *Sport in History*, 34 (3): 390–410.

Pietrobelli, Carlo, and Roberta Rabellotti. 2006. *Upgrading to Compete: Global Value Chains, Clusters, and SMEs in Latin America*. Inter-American Development Bank.

Poiret, Guillaume. 2011. "La gouvernance métropolitaine écartelée entre adaptation économique et spatiale à la globalisation et respect de la démocratie locale, l'exemple de la fusion de Toronto (Canada)." *Annales de Géographie*, 681: 509–27.

–. 2017. "Une diversité accrue des suburbs, quelle conséquence politique? L'exemple du Grand Toronto." *L'information géographique*, 3 (81): 108–24.

Polèse, Mario, and Richard Shearmur. 2003. "Pourquoi Toronto a surclassé Montréal au sommet de la hiérarchie urbaine canadienne?" *Géographie, Économie, Société*, 5 (3–4): 399–420.

Policy Options. 2015. "What Will Trudeau's Agenda Look Like?" October 30. https://policyoptions.irpp.org/2015/10/30/will-trudeaus-urban-agenda-look-like/.

Port de Montréal. 2017. *Perspective de l'Administration portuaire de Montréal sur le Projet de Cité de la logistique dans l'arrondissement Mercier Hochelaga-Maisonneuve*. https://ville.montreal.qc.ca/pls/portal/docs/PAGE/ARROND_MHM_FR/MEDIA/DOCUMENTS/MEMOIRE_PORT_DE_MONTREAL.PDF.

Port of Halifax. n.d. "Cargo and Cruise Statistics." https://www.porthalifax.ca/port-operations-centre/cargo-statistics/.

–. 2018. *Cargo Statistics*. https://www.portofhalifax.ca/port-operations-centre/cargo-statistics/.

Port of Hamilton Oshawa. 2018. *Tonnage Statistics 2018*. https://www.hopaports.ca/wp-content/uploads/2019/03/Tonnage-Stats-by-Cargo-Type-2018.pdf.

Port of Montreal. 2018. *Traffic Summary*. https://www.port-montreal.com/en/detailed-statistics-history-and-summaries/historical/traffic-summary-last-10-years.

Port of Toronto. 2018. *Annual Report, 2018*. https://www.portstoronto.com/get attachment/978039b9-c550-4838-aa40-eda0ed30caa3/2018-Annual-Report.aspx.

Port of Vancouver. 2015. *Gateway Infrastructure Fee, Annual Report for the Year Ended December 31, 2015*.

–. 2018. *Financial Report, 2018*. https://www.portvancouver.com/wp-content/uploads/2019/05/2018_FinancialReport.pdf.

–. 2019. *Project to Separate Pitt Meadows Roadways from Rail Crossings Closer to Becoming a Reality*. Media release. May 31.

–. 2020a. *Financial Report 2020*. Port of Vancouver/Vancouver Fraser Port Authority. https://www.portvancouver.com/sites/default/files/2024-08/2020-Financial-Report.pdf.

–. 2020b. *Port Land Use Plan 2020*. Port of Vancouver/Vancouver Fraser Port Authority. https://www.portvancouver.com/sites/default/files/2024-08/500_POV-Land-Use-Plan_FINAL-2.pdf.

–. 2020c. *Update to Industry: Gateway Infrastructure Fee 2022 (GIF2022)*. December 9.

–. 2022. "Projects." https://www.portvancouver.com/projects/.

Porter, Michael E. 1998. "Clusters and the New Economics of Competition." *Harvard Business Review*, November–December.

Ports Toronto. 2019. "About Us." http://portstoronto.com/port-of-toronto/about-us.aspx.

Prentice, Barry E. 2006. "Gateways, Corridors and Strategic City Pairs." *Canadian Transportation Research Forum 41st Annual Meeting*.

Priemus, Hugo, and Wil Zonneveld. 2003. "What Are Corridors and What Are the Issues? Introduction to Special Issue: The Governance of Corridors." *Journal of Transport Geography*, 11 (3): 167–77.

Projet Montréal. 2017. *Program 2017*. https://d3n8a8pro7vhmx.cloudfront.net/projetmontreal/pages/1996/attachments/original/1506701286/program2017_EN.pdf?1506701286.

Provan, Keith G., and Patrick Kenis. 2008. "Modes of Network Governance: Structure, Management, and Effectiveness." *Journal of Public Administration Research and Theory*, 18 (2): 229–52. https://doi.org/10.1093/jopart/mum015.

Punter, John. 2010. *The Vancouver Achievement: Urban Planning and Design*. UBC Press.

Purcell, Mark. 2006. "Urban Democracy and the Local Trap." *Urban Studies*, 43 (11): 1921–41.

Raimbault, Nicolas. 2022. "Outer-Suburban Politics and the Financialisation of the Logistics Real Estate Industry: The Emergence of Financialised Coalitions in the Paris Region." *Urban Studies*, 59 (7): 1481–98.

Ramacieri, Constance, and Karl Dorais Kinkaid. 2017. *Rapport: Démarche de consultation publique portant sur le développement des activités industrialo-portuaires et de leur cohabitation avec les quartiers résidentiels adjacents*. Montréal.

Ray, D. Michael, Ray H. Lamarche, and Maurice Beaudin. 2012. "Economic Growth and Restructuring in Canada's Heartland and Hinterland: From Shift-Share to Multifactor Partitioning." *The Canadian Geographer/Le géographe canadien*, 56 (3): 296–317.

Regan, Wes, and Peter Hall. 2018. "Vancouver, Canada: Equitable Sustainability Planning within the Post-Industrial Urban Development Model." In *Global Planning Innovations for Urban Sustainability*, edited by Sébastien Darchen and Glen Searle. Routledge.

Region of Peel. 2016. *Official Plan*. https://www.peelregion.ca/planning/officialplan/pdfs/ROPConsolidationDec2016.pdf.

Rhodes, Roderick A. W. 1996. "The New Governance: Governing without Government." *Political Studies*, 44 (4): 652–67. https://doi.org/10.1111/j.1467-9248.1996.tb01747.x.

Robinson, Jennifer. 2013. *Ordinary Cities: Between Modernity and Development*. Routledge.

Rodrigue, Jean-Paul. 2020. *The Geography of Transport Systems*. Routledge.

–. 2021. *Constraints in the Canadian Transport Infrastructure Grid. The School of Public Policy Publications*, SPP Research Paper, 14 (6), February. https://www.policyschool.ca/wp-content/uploads/2021/02/Infrastructure-Grid-Rodrigue.pdf.

Rodrik, Dani. 2007. *The Inescapable Trilemma of the World Economy*. https://rodrik.typepad.com/dani_rodriks_weblog/2007/06/the-inescapable.html.

Roy, Jacques, and Michel Nadeau. 2014. *The Governance of Canadian Airports: Issues and Recommendations*. Institute for Governance of Private and Public Organizations, Montreal.

Royal Commission on Dominion-Provincial Relations. 1940. *Report of the Royal Commission on Dominion-Provincial Relations. Book II: Recommendations*. King's Printer. https://publications.gc.ca/site/eng/9.828175/publication.html.

Royal Commission on the Economic Union and Development Prospects for Canada. 1985. *Report of the Commission.* 3 volumes. https://publications.gc.ca/collections/collection_2014/bcp-pco/Z1-1983-1-1-1-eng.pdf.

Royal Commission on the Relations of Labor and Capital in Canada. 1889. James Armstrong and A.T. Freed, chairmen. Ottawa, Privy Council Office. https://publications.gc.ca/site/eng/472984/publication.html.

Royal Commission on Transportation. 1960. M.A. MacPherson, chairman. Ottawa, Privy Council Office.

Sagaris, Lake, Ignacio Tiznado-Aitken, and Stefan Steiniger. 2017. "Exploring the Social and Spatial Potential of an Intermodal Approach to Transport Planning." *International Journal of Sustainable Transportation*, 11 (10): 721–36.

Sahu, Vikram. 2020. "BofA Interview: Bye for Now, China? The $1 Trillion Tectonic Shift in Global Supply Chains." *Trade Finance Global*, September 10. https://www.tradefinanceglobal.com/posts/bofa-interview-bye-for-now-china-the-1-trillion-tectonic-shift-in-global-supply-chains/.

Salsberg, Lisa. 2012. "Supporting Goods Movement in the GTHA." Transport Futures Conference, Toronto May 12.

Sancton, Andrew. 2000. *Merger Mania: The Assault on Local Government.* McGill-Queen's University Press.

Sassen, Saskia. 2001. *The Global City: New York, London, Tokyo*. 2nd ed. Princeton University Press.

Schindler, Seth, and J. Miguel Kanai. 2019. "Getting the Territory Right: Infrastructure-led Development and the Re-emergence of Spatial Planning Strategies." *Regional Studies*, 55 (1): 40–51. DOI: 10.1080/00343404.2019.1661984.

Scholvin, Soeren. 2017. "The Gateway to Sub-Saharan Africa? Cape Town's Potential as a Gateway City for the Oil and Gas Sector." *The German Journal of Economic Geography*, 61 (2): 80–95. https://doi.org/10.1515/zfw-2016-0047.

Shaker, Paul. 2004. *More Than Money: The New Deal for Cities and a Federal Urban Lens*. Canadian Centre for Policy Alternatives. https://www.policyalternatives.ca/sites/default/files/uploads/publications/National_Office_Pubs/more_than_money.pdf.

Short, John Rennie, Carrie Breitbach, Steven Buckman, and Jamey Essex. 2000. "From World Cities to Gateway Cities: Extending the Boundaries of Globalization Theory." *City*, 4 (3): 317–40.

Short, John Rennie, and Yeong-Hyun Kim. 1999. *Globalization and the City.* Addison Wesley and Longman.

Smart Freight Centre. 2021. "Mission." http://www.smartfreightcentre.ca/about/mission/.

Sohi, A. 2017. "Statement of Priorities and Accountabilities – Canada Infrastructure Bank." https://www.infrastructure.gc.ca/CIB-BIC/letter-lettre-eng.html.

Spicer, Zachary. 2011. "The Rise and Fall of the Ministry of State for Urban Affairs: A Re-Evaluation." *Canadian Political Science Review*, 5 (2): 117–26.

Statistics Canada. 2012a. *Focus on Geography Series, 2011 Census: Census Metropolitan Area of Halifax, Nova Scotia*. Catalogue no. 98-310-XWE2011004. Ottawa, Ontario. Analytical products, 2011 Census. Last updated October 24, 2012. https://

www12.statcan.gc.ca/census-recensement/2011/as-sa/fogs-spg/Facts-cma-eng.cfm?LANG=Eng&GK=CMA&GC=205.

–. 2012b. *Focus on Geography Series, 2011 Census: Census Metropolitan Area of Montréal, Québec*. Catalogue no. 98-310-XWE2011004. Ottawa, Ontario. Analytical products, 2011 Census. Last updated October 24, 2012. https://www12.statcan.gc.ca/census-recensement/2011/as-sa/fogs-spg/Facts-cma-eng.cfm?LANG=Eng&GK=CMA&GC=462.

–. 2017. *Census Profile, 2016 Census*. Catalogue no. 98-316-X2016001. Released November 29. https://www12.statcan.gc.ca/census-recensement/2016/dp-pd/prof/index.cfm?Lang=E.

–. 2018. *Canadian Freight Analysis Framework*. Correction date July 7, 2021. https://www150.statcan.gc.ca/n1/pub/50-503-x/50-503-x2018001-eng.htm.

–. 2019. *Focus on Geography Series, 2011 Census: Census Metropolitan Area of Toronto, Ontario*. https://www12.statcan.gc.ca/census-recensement/2011/as-sa/fogs-spg/Facts-cma-eng.cfm?LANG=Eng&GK=CMA&GC=535.

–. 2020a. *Air Cargo Traffic at Canadian Airports, Annual*. Table 23-10-0254-01.

–. 2020b. *Air Passenger Traffic at Canadian Airports, Annual*. Table 23-10-0253-01. https://www150.statcan.gc.ca/t1/tbl1/en/tv.action?pid=2310025301.

–. 2021a. *2021 Census – Boundary Files*. https://www12.statcan.gc.ca/census-recensement/2021/geo/sip-pis/boundary-limites/index2021-eng.cfm?year=21.

–. 2021b. *2021 Census – Road Network File*. https://www12.statcan.gc.ca/census-recensement/2021/geo/sip-pis/rnf-frr/index2021-eng.cfm?year=21.

–. 2021c. *2021 Census of Population – Halifax, Census Metropolitan Area*. https://www12.statcan.gc.ca/census-recensement/2021/as-sa/fogs-spg/page.cfm?topic=1&lang=E&dguid=2021S0503205.

–. 2021d. *Employment by Industry, Annual, Census Metropolitan Areas, Inactive (x 1,000)*. Table 14-10-0098-01. https://www150.statcan.gc.ca/t1/tbl1/en/tv.action?pid=1410009801.

–. 2022a. *2021 Census of Population*. https://www12.statcan.gc.ca/census-recensement/index-eng.cfm.

–. 2022b. *Focus on Geography Series, 2021 Census of Population: Hamilton, Census Metropolitan Area*. https://www12.statcan.gc.ca/census-recensement/2021/as-sa/fogs-spg/page.cfm?dguid=2021S0503537&topic=1&lang=E.

–. 2022c. *Focus on Geography Series, 2021 Census of Population: Toronto, Census Metropolitan Area*. https://www12.statcan.gc.ca/census-recensement/2021/as-sa/fogs-spg/page.cfm?topic=1&lang=E&dguid=2021S0503535.

–. 2023. *Census Profile, 2021 Census of Population* (table). Catalogue no. 98-316-X2021001. Released November 15. https://www12.statcan.gc.ca/census-recensement/2021/dp-pd/prof/index.cfm?Lang=E.

–. 2024. *Trade in Goods by Importer Characteristics, by Industry and Related Parties*. Table 12-10-0112-01. https://www150.statcan.gc.ca/t1/tbl1/en/tv.action?pid=1210011201.

–. 2025a. *Trade in Goods by Exporter Characteristics, by Country of Destination*. Table: 12-10-0104-01. https://www150.statcan.gc.ca/t1/tbl1/en/cv.action?pid=1210010401.

–. 2025b. *Trade in Goods by Exporter Characteristics, by Industry of Establishment.* Table 12-10-0098-01. https://www150.statcan.gc.ca/t1/tbl1/en/tv.action?pid=1210009801.

Stoker, Gerry. 2004. "The Challenge of Governance." In *Transforming Local Governance. Government Beyond the Centre*. Palgrave. https://doi.org/10.1007/978-0-230-21368-5_11.

Stone, Clarence. 1989. *Regime Politics: Governing Atlanta*. University Press of Kansas.

–. 1993. "Urban Regimes and the Capacity to Govern: A Political Economy Approach." *Journal of Urban Affairs*, 15: 1–28. https://doi.org/10.1111/j.1467-9906.1993.tb00300.x.

–. 2001. "The Atlanta Experience Re-examined: The Link Between Agenda and Regime Change." *International Journal of Urban and Regional Research*, 25 (1): 20–34. https://doi.org/10.1111/1468-2427.00295.

Stone, Clarence, and Heywood Sanders. 1987. *The Politics of Urban Development.* University Press of Kansas.

Storper, Michael, and Allen J. Scott. 2016. "Current Debates in Urban Theory: A Critical Assessment." *Urban Studies*, 53 (6).

Strange, Roger, and John Humphrey. 2019. "What Lies Between Market and Hierarchy? Insights from Internalization Theory and Global Value Chain Theory." *Journal of International Business Studies*, 50 (8): 1401–13. https://doi.org/10.1057/s41267-018-0186-0.

Sturgeon, Timothy J. 2006. "Conceptualizing Integrative Trade: The Global Value Chains Framework." Paper prepared for the Integrative Trade between Canada and the United States – Policy Implications conference, organized by the Centre for Trade Policy and Law. Ottawa, December 6.

–. 2008. "From Commodity Chains to Value Chains: Interdisciplinary Theory Building in an Age of Globalization." In *Frontiers of Commodity Chain Research*, edited by Jennifer Blair. Stanford University Press.

Sutherland, John Campbell. 1922. *The Province of Quebec. Geographical and Social Studies*. Renouf Publishing Company.

Taylor, Peter J. 2004. *World City Network: A Global Urban Analysis*. Routledge.

TCSA (Toronto City Summit Alliance). 2003. *Enough Talk: An Action Plan for the Toronto Region*. https://civicaction.ca/resource/enough-talk-an-action-plan-for-the-toronto-region/

–. 2010. *Time to Get Serious: Reliable Funding for GTHA Transit and Transportation Infrastructure*. https://institute.smartprosperity.ca/sites/default/files/publications/files/Reliable%20funding%20for%20GTHA%20TransitTransportation%20Infrastructure.pdf.

Terpstra, Nicholas. 1985. "Local Politics and Local Planning: A Case Study of Hamilton, Ontario." *Urban History Review*, 14 (2): 114–28.

TIR (Nova Scotia Department of Transportation and Infrastructure Renewal). 2016. *Transportation and Infrastructure Renewal Statement of Mandate 2015–2016.*

Tolley, Erin, and William R. Young. 2001. *Municipalities, the Constitution, and the Canadian Federal System*. Revised February 2001. https://publications.gc.ca/Pilot/LoPBdP/BP/bp276-e.htm.

Tomàs, Mariona. 2012. "Exploring the Metropolitan Trap: The Case of Montreal." *International Journal of Urban and Regional Research*, 36 (3): 554–67.

Toronto Global. 2019. "About Us." https://torontoglobal.ca/about-us.

Toronto Region BOT (Board of Trade). 2016. *Annual Report: Advocacy and Action*.

–. 2017a. "Building Tech North." *On Board Magazine*, Spring, 10–15.

–. 2017b. *Toronto-Waterloo Corridor Movement of Goods Business and Consumer Impacts*. Third Report. Movement of Good Series.

–. 2019. *Infrastructure Options to Improve the Movement of Goods in Canada's Innovation Corridor*. Sixth Report. Movement of Good Series. https://bot.com/Resources/Resource-Library/Movement-of-Goods-Series-6.

TRAN (Standing Committee on Transport, Infrastructure and Communities). 2019. *Committee Report no 27*. https://www.ourcommons.ca/DocumentViewer/en/42-1/TRAN/report-27/page-66.

TransLink. 2017. *Moving the Economy: A Regional Goods Movement Strategy for Metro Vancouver. Context and Background – June 2017*. TransLink, New Westminster.

Transport Canada. 1985. *Freedom to Move: A Framework for Transportation Reform*. https://archive.org/details/39090216030136

–. 2008. *Departmental Performance Report, 2007–2008*. https://www.tbs-sct.gc.ca/dpr-rmr/2007-2008/inst/mot/mot-eng.pdf.

–. 2009. *National Policy Framework for Strategic Gateways and Trade Corridors*.

–. 2010. *Atlantic Gateway Trade Corridor Strategy. Connecting Canada with the World*.

–. 2012. *Transportation in Canada 2011: Comprehensive Review*. https://tc.canada.ca/sites/default/files/migrated/transportation_in_canada_2011.pdf.

–. 2015. *Transportation in Canada 2014 Overview Report*. https://tc.canada.ca/sites/default/files/migrated/2014_tc_annual_report_overview_en.pdf.

–. 2017a. *Evaluation of the Asia-Pacific Gateway and Corridor Initiative and the Gateways and Border Crossing Fund*. October. https://tc.canada.ca/en/evaluation-asia-pacific-gateway-corridor-initiative-gateways-borders-crossing-fund.

–. 2017b. *National Trade Corridors Fund. Call for Proposals*. https://www.canada.ca/en/transport-canada/news/2017/08/national_trade_corridorsfundntcf.html.

–. 2020. *Canadian Port Authorities*. Last modified October 7. https://tc.canada.ca/en/corporate-services/policies/canadian-port-authorities.

–. 2021. *Open Government Portal*. https://open.canada.ca/data/organization/tc.

Truffin, Barbara. 2006. "Des règles du jeu en action: l'élaboration règlementaire des droits des peuples autochtones en tension." In *Le Droit en Action*, edited by Étienne Le Roy. Karthala.

TTR (Toronto Terminals Railways). 2019. "History." http://www.ttrly.com/about/history/.

Turok, Ivan. 2009. "Limits to the Mega-City Region: Conflicting Local and Regional Needs." *Regional Studies*, 43 (6): 845–62. https://doi.org/10.1080/00343400903095261.

TVA CIMT/CHAU. 2019. "La CAQ donne un nouvel élan à la stratégie maritime." July 9. https://cimtchau.ca/nouvelles/la-caq-souhaite-donner-un-nouvel-elan-a-la-strategie-maritime/.

UNCTAD (UN Trade and Development). 2020. *Trade and Development Report. From Global Pandemic to Prosperity for All: Avoiding Another Lost Decade.*

UN-Habitat-OECD. 2017. *The State of National Urban Policy in OECD Countries: A Special Report Prepared for the United States Conference on Housing and Sustainable Urban Development (Habitat III).* Directorate for Public Governance and Territorial Development. http://www.oecd.org/cfe/region al-policy/the-state-of-national-urban-policy-in-OECD-countries.pdf.

United Nations. 2018. *World Urbanization Prospects 2018.* https://population.un.org/wup/.

US Department of Transportation. 2014. *Metropolitan Planning Organizations and Transportation Planning for Megaregions.*

Van Assche, Ari. 2012. "Global Value Chains and Canada's Trade Policy. Business as Usual or Paradigm Shift?" *IRPP*, 32. https://irpp.org/research-studies/global-value-chains-and-canadas-trade-policy/.

Veltz, Pierre. 2000. "L'économie Mondiale, une économie d'archipel." In *La mondialisation au-delà des mythes*, edited by Serge Cordellier. La Découverte.

–. 2004. "The Resurgent City." Leverhulme International Symposium, London School of Economics. Keynote Address, April 19–21. http://www.veltz.fr/pierre_veltz/articles/pierre_veltz_article_resurgent_city_london_school_of_economics.html.

Viel, Laurent, Gonzalo Lizarralde, Fella Amina Maherzi, and Isabelle Thomas-Maret. 2012. "L'influence des parties prenantes dans les grands projets urbains." *Cybergeo: European Journal of Geography.* http://journals.openedition.org/cybergeo/25310.

Ville de Montréal. 2012. *By-law 05-056-1 – Right of Initiative in Public Consultations.* https://ocpm.qc.ca/sites/default/files/pdf/P99/5-24_en_by-law_05-056-1_right_of_initiative_in_public_consultations.pdf.

–. 2013. *The Faces of Citizen Participation in Montreal.* Exhibition presented in the Hall of Honour at Montreal City Hall.

–. 2016. *Positionnement économique pour le secteur de L'Assomption Sud/A-25. Renforcer la compétitivité de l'industrie du transport des marchandises et de la logistique par la consolidation et le développement de la zone industrialo-portuaire de l'est de Montréal.* Service du développement économique. https://ville.montreal.qc.ca/pls/portal/docs/PAGE/ARROND_MHM_FR/MEDIA/DOCUMENTS/resume_etude_cai_global.PDF.

–. 2017a. *Rapport: Démarche de consultation publique portant sur le développement des activités industrialo-portuaires et de leur cohabitation avec les quartiers résidentiels adjacents.* September 12. http://ville.montreal.qc.ca/pls/portal/docs/page/arrond_mhm_fr/media/documents/20170913-rapport-cite_de_la_logistique%20.pdf.

–. 2018. Sommaire décisionnel. Consultation publique portant sur la vision de développement économique et urbain du secteur Assomption Sud - Longue-Pointe. https://ocpm.qc.ca/sites/default/files/pdf/P93/1.1_sommaire_decisionnel.pdf.

–. 2019. *Montréal Geared Up for Tomorrow: 2018 Summary Report on the 2018–2022 Economic Development Strategy.* https://ville.montreal.qc.ca/pls/portal/docs/page/affaires_fr/media/documents/accelerermtl_bilan_2018_en.pdf.

–. 2020. *Vers un Écoparc industriel de la Grande Prairie*, news release, November 6.

Ville de Montréal – Service du greffe. 2017. *Montréal Charter of Rights and Responsibilities*, 3rd ed. https://ocpm.qc.ca/sites/default/files/pdf/P99/5.2_charte_montrealaise_des_droits_et_responsabilites_eng.pdf.

Wachsmuth, David. 2017. "Infrastructure Alliances: Supply-Chain Expansion and Multi-City Growth Coalitions." *Economic Geography*, 93 (1): 44–65. https://doi.org/10.1080/00130095.2016.1199263.

Wagner, Jason. 2013. "Measuring Performance of Public Engagement in Transportation Planning." *Transportation Research Record*, 2397 (1): 38–44.

Wakefield, Stephanie. 2018. "Infrastructure of Liberal Life: From Modernity and Progress to Resilience and Ruins." *Geography Compass*, 12: 1–14.

Walks, Alan, and Brian Clifford. 2015. "The Political Economy of Mortgage Securitization and the Neoliberalization of Housing Policy in Canada." *Environment and Planning A: Economy and Space*, 47 (8): 1624–42.

Wang, James J. 2016. *Port-City Interplays in China*. Routledge.

Wang, James J., and Michael C. Cheng. 2010. "From a Hub Port City to a Global Supply Chain Management Center: A Case Study of Hong Kong." *Journal of Transport Geography*, 18 (1): 104–15. https://doi.org/10.1016/j.jtrangeo.2009.02.009.

Weiler, Joseph M. 1987. *Report of the Port of Vancouver Container Traffic Commission: An Industrial Inquiry Commission Under the Maintenance of Ports Operations Act, 1986*. Government of Canada. December 15.

Wilson, Japhy, and Eric Swyngedouw, eds. 2014. *The Post-Political and Its Discontents: Spaces of Depoliticisation, Spectres of Radical Politics*. Edinburgh University Press.

Wirth, John D. 1999. *Trade Corridors in North America*. Symposium Report, October 1–3. https://www.northamericaninstitute.org/pdf/nn24.pdf.

While, Aidan, Andrew E. G. Jonas, and David Gibbs. 2004. "The Environment and the Entrepreneurial City: Searching for the Urban 'Sustainability Fix' in Manchester and Leeds." *International Journal of Urban and Regional Research*, 28 (3): 549–69. https://doi.org/10.1111/j.0309-1317.2004.00535.x.

Working Group on the OQCGTC (Groupe de travail du Grand Montréal sur la Porte continentale et le Corridor de commerce Ontario-Québec). 2009. *Rapport du Groupe de travail du Grand Montréal sur la Porte continentale et le Corridor de commerce Ontario-Québec*. Mai.

World Bank. 2022. "Urban Development." https://www.worldbank.org/en/topic/urbandevelopment/overview.

World Economic Forum. 2016. *Competitive Cities and Their Connections to Global Value Chains*. June. WEF_2016_WhitePaper_GAC_Competitive_Cities_.pdf.

Woudsma, Clarence. 2012. "Freight, Land and Local Economic Development." In *Cities, Regions and Flows*, edited by Peter Hall and Markus Hesse. Routledge.

Yáñez, Clemente J. Navarro, Annick Magnier, and M. Antonia Ramírez. 2008. "Local Governance as Government–Business Cooperation in Western Democracies: Analysing Local and Intergovernmental Effects by Multi-Level Comparison." *International Journal of Urban and Regional Research*, 32 (3): 531–47. https://doi.org/10.1111/j.1468-2427.2008.00816.x.

Yiftachel, Oren. 2015. "Epilogue – from 'Gray Space' to Equal 'Metrozenship'? Reflections On Urban Citizenship." *International Journal of Urban and Regional Research*, 39 (4): 726–37. https://doi.org/10.1111/1468-2427.12263.

York Region. 2018. *2019 to 2023 Strategic Plan: From Vision to Results*. https://www.york.ca/media/75941/download.

–. 2019. *Economic Development Action Plan 2020–2023*. https://www.yorklink.ca/wp-content/uploads/2019/11/york-region-economic-development-action-plan-2020-2023.pdf.

–. 2022. *2022 Transportation Master Plan*. https://www.york.ca/york-region/plans-reports-and-strategies/transportation-master-plan.

Young, Robert. A., Philippe Faucher, and André Blais. 1984. "The Concept of Province-Building: A Critique." *Canadian Journal of Political Science*, 17 (4): 783–818.

Yu, Henry. 2007. "Refracting Pacific Canada: Seeing Our Uncommon Past." *BC Studies*, 156 (157): 5–10.

Zhu, Zhen, Michelangelo Puliga, Federica Cerina, Alessandro Chessa, and Massimo Riccaboni. 2015. "Global Value Trees." *PloS one*, 10 (5): e0126699.

Ziobrowski, Peter. 2018. "Shipping News: Halifax Port Expansion Needed to Ensure Ships Stop Here." *Saltwire*. October 12. https://www.saltwire.com/nova-scotia/shipping-news-halifax-port-expansion-needed-to-ensure-ships-stop-here-249711.

Zsolt, John A. 1993. "Rural Transformations: Residential Developments in the Hinterland of Toronto." *Environments*, 22 (1): 95–99.

Index

Note: "(f)" after a page number indicates a figure, and "(t)" after a page number indicates a table.

Printed and bound in Canada

Set in Zurich Condensed, Sero, and Minion
by Artegraphica Design Co.

Copyeditor: Candida Hadley

Indexer: Viktoria Cseh

Proofreader: Carmen Tiampo

Cover designer: Michel Vrana

Authorized Representative:
Easy Access System Europe –
Mustamäe tee 50, 10621 Tallinn, Estonia,
gpsr.requests@easproject.com